KRUGER
NATIONAL PARK
Questions & Answers

PF Fourie
Updated by **Chris van der Linde**

This book is dedicated to The Great Conservator.

Published by Struik Nature
(an imprint of Penguin Random House South Africa (Pty) Ltd)
Reg. No. 1953/000441/07
The Estuaries No 4, Oxbow Crescent, Century Avenue, Century City, 7441
PO Box 1144, Cape Town, 8000 South Africa

Visit **www.penguinrandomhouse.co.za** and join the Struik Nature Club
for updates, news, events and special offers

First published by SA Country Life 1978
First published by Struik Publishers in 1992
Revised edition published in 2014 by Struik Nature

10 9 8 7 6 5 4

Picture credits: Front cover: Mario Moreno/South Cape Images;
Back cover: Nigel Dennis/Images of Africa; **Peter Hayman/Penguin Random House
South Africa (Pty) Ltd:** pp 209, 212, 217; **Sally MacLarty/Penguin Random House
South Africa (Pty) Ltd:** pp 79, 85, 86, 96; **Sally MacLarty:** pp 190, 195, 197, 200

Editor: Lesley Hay-Whitton
Project manager: Colette Alves
Typesetter: Tessa Fortuin
Cover designer: Janice Evans
Cartographer: Martin Endemann
Proofreader and indexer: Thea Grobbelaar

Reproduction by Hirt & Carter Cape (Pty) Ltd
Printed and bound in China by 1010 Printing International Ltd., Hong Kong

ISBN 978 1 77584 014 5 (Print)
ISBN 978 1 77584 154 8 (ePUB)

CONTENTS

ACKNOWLEDGEMENTS

The writing of any book to be used as reference, even in a recreational sense, is a team effort and I wish to express my appreciation to the following persons who assisted in the final product.

Firstly I wish to extend my gratitude to the original author's son, Dr Dave Fourie, for entrusting me with the updating, editing and extension of his late father's book.

This publication is based entirely on factual correctness. My sincere appreciation goes to my former colleagues and other experts in their field, for reading the scripts to ensure the factual correctness of this publication. Without their input this publication would not have been possible.

I gratefully acknowledge the assistance of Dr L. E. O. Braack, Dr Andrew Deacon, Dr Sam Ferreira, Dr Salomon Joubert, Dr Johan Marais, Dr Gus Mills, Dr Danie Pienaar, Dr Freek Venter, Dr Ian Whyte, Mr Nic de Beer, Ms Navashni Govender, Mr Ken Maggs, Mr Joep Stevens and Mrs Guin Zambatis, as well as the staff of various departments, but especially staff of the Scientific Services at Skukuza.

For his time proofreading the manuscript of the book and for his advice and guidance, my sincere appreciation to Dr Salomon Joubert.

Lastly, I wish to record my appreciation to Mr David Mabunda, CEO of SANParks, for his encouragement in tackling this project.

CHRIS VAN DER LINDE
Pretoria 2013

PREFACE

Although this edition of the late P. F. Fourie's *Kruger National Park – Questions and Answers* introduces a new author/editor, it does not introduce any change in policy or intent.

When I approached the late Fritz Fourie's son, Dr Dave Fourie, with the view of updating the sixth edition and adding the new happenings in the Kruger National Park, I was pleased with his positive response.

One of the main reasons for my revision of the book was the incredible ignorance I encountered, especially among some tour guides accompanying visitors to the Kruger Park and their unbelievable lack of knowledge of the Park, its fauna and flora. I hope that, with this revised publication, the correct information will assist tour guides in making their guests' visits memorable.

The publication is, of course, also directed at the regular visitors to this wonderful conservation area, in the hope that it will bring an understanding of how nature functions and that they will be enriched by the knowledge imparted by the experts in their field who assisted in checking the publication's factual correctness.

It is also hoped that this publication will become an integral part of libraries, especially those of educational institutions, to assist students with the correct information for assignments regarding the Park and its ecological component.

Some changes have been made to the contents of the previous editions, correcting points where new information became available. New subjects have been added to inform of new management decisions and the dramatic changes that occurred since the sixth edition appeared in 1992.

Tariffs and other economic parameters are prone to regular changes. For this reason no tariffs or any monetary implications are quoted in the publication. For up-to-date tariffs it is advisable to contact SANParks Head Office in Pretoria.

The scope of this book is wide and, with its additional chapters and information, it is hoped that it will enhance any visit to the Park.

Fritz Fourie was Chief Information Officer in the Park from 1969 to 1977. During this time he met many people from all walks of life and from all over the world, who regularly asked him questions about the Park. This formed the basis of the contents of this publication. A book such as this was his dream and throughout the various editions his love and respect for nature are reflected.

The previous edition was updated by his good friend, Dr Gerrie de Graaf.

My own passion for the Kruger National Park encouraged me to revise and update the facts and to consolidate all the information in this publication. For me it was a privilege, an honour and a joy to be involved in something started by Fritz Fourie, continued by Dr De Graaf and supported by his family. My gratitude also goes to my friends, family and colleagues who assisted with the contents of this book.

It grieves me that Fritz cannot be with us to experience this edition of what he initiated, but his spirit lives on in the pages of this book.

CHRIS VAN DER LINDE
Pretoria 2013

FOREWORD

Knowledge creates awareness, appreciation and respect. These, in turn, form the cornerstones of an environmental ethic. Creating and establishing an environmental ethic is exactly what national parks are all about. In fact, in conformation with the International Union for Conservation of Nature (IUCN), our own Protected Areas Act prescribes that a national park is created to provide 'spiritual, scientific, educational, recreational and tourism opportunities which are environmentally compatible'.

The Kruger National Park is not only the flagship of our South African national parks, but also enjoys iconic status on an international scale. More than a million visitors, local and from abroad, pass through the park annually and are intrigued by its amazing diversity of landscapes, and plant and animal life. It is home to the full suite of Africa's large carnivores, 18 species of antelope in addition to African elephant, black and white rhinoceros, giraffe and hippopotamus. It also accommodates 119 species of reptiles, 35 amphibians, more than 500 birds and a myriad insects.

As more and more guidebooks on all aspects of the environment become available, people are becoming ever more aware of the wonders and intricacies of the natural world. Of all the guidebooks, *Questions and Answers* by the late Fritz Fourie has steadfastly held its place as one of the 'evergreens'. Fritz spent many years in the Kruger Park, progressing through the ranks of the Information Section and, ultimately, to head of the Section. His enthusiasm for his work, the huge base of knowledge that he acquired over the years and his relaxed and endearing interaction with literally thousands of visitors all richly contributed to the high standard and success of this publication.

The easy, laid-back fashion in which *Questions and Answers* is written has made it a highly entertaining companion in the vehicles of a growing following of Kruger Park enthusiasts. Accessible to young children and equally informative to adults, *Questions and Answers* ideally blends leisure and education and has played a major role towards the core goal of 'spiritual, scientific, educational and recreational' enrichment offered by our national parks. It is my sincere wish that this book will continue to do so for many years to come.

This is the seventh edition of *Questions and Answers*. I am particularly pleased that another of my good friends and ex-colleague, Chris van der Linde, took it upon his shoulders to update and upgrade the text. Also a colleague who served in the Information Section of the Kruger Park for many years, Chris was in an excellent position to add more facts, figures and the latest developments on the course of the Kruger National Park into the 21st century.

My very best wishes accompany the launching of this latest edition of *Questions and Answers*!

DR S. C. J. JOUBERT

KRUGER NATIONAL PARK MAP

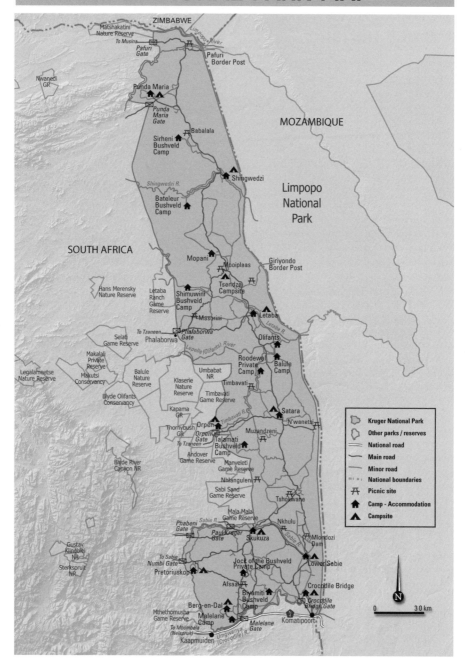

INTRODUCTION

A BRIEF HISTORY

The Kruger National Park is the largest wildlife sanctuary in the Republic of South Africa and one of the largest managed national parks/protected areas in the world. It is situated in the far northeastern corner of the country, between the Crocodile River in the south and the Limpopo River in the north. The international border with Mozambique, the eastern boundary of the Kruger National Park, follows the line of the Lebombo Mountains in the south and continues beyond them in the north to the Limpopo River. The western boundary is very irregular, separating private, communal land and privately owned conservation areas from the Kruger Park. The Park as a whole is shaped like a reversed 'L' and covers an area of 1 948 528 ha or about 20 000 km^2.

The first Europeans to set foot in the Mpumalanga Lowveld were 31 men led by Francois de Kuiper. Delagoa Bay – later Lourenço Marques and now Maputo – was a Dutch possession at the time and in 1725 the Dutch East India Company ordered an expedition to proceed from Delagoa Bay to investigate the possibility of trade with the hinterland and also to check existing trade routes to the interior. At Gomondwane, just north of today's Crocodile Bridge Rest Camp, they met a party of hostile inhabitants and, after a skirmish, beat a hasty retreat.

The next white people to pass through the territory were two parties of Voortrekkers who travelled through the central part of the Park, crossing into Mozambique via the Shilowa and Mbhatsi gorges through the Lebombo Mountains. In 1844 Chief Commandant A. H. Potgieter came to an agreement with the Portuguese and defined the boundary between the South African and Mozambican territories much as they are today. Two years later Potgieter bartered with the Swazis to acquire territory between the Crocodile and Lepelle rivers.

In 1869 gold was discovered in the Lydenburg district, and people soon flocked to the area. The Lowveld had been practically unknown before, but soon became a popular hunting area. Highveld farmers moved down the Escarpment to find winter grazing for their herds and, finding themselves in a game-rich area, proceeded to hunt. They were followed by professional hunters seeking ivory, horns and skins. Game numbers declined rapidly and in 1884 President S. J. P. Kruger proposed in the Transvaal Volksraad that a game sanctuary be established to preserve the fast-disappearing fauna of the Transvaal Republic. At that stage his was a lone voice crying in the wilderness. Public opinion was not favourable. It was some 14 years later that the area between the Crocodile and Sabie rivers was proclaimed a wildlife sanctuary in which any person found guilty of destroying, hunting or wounding game animals would be prosecuted and penalised. The proclamation was signed on 26 March 1898. The small Sabi Game Reserve and the Shingwedzi Game Reserve were the beginnings of what has grown into the world-renowned Kruger National Park. The area of the then Sabi Game Reserve was only about 4 600 km^2.

One of the first two game rangers was Paul Machiel Bester of the ZAR Police at Komatipoort. He erected the first dwelling where the present Skukuza is situated, and covered the doorway with the hide of a wildebeest. The hide was occasionally torn off by hyaenas and he had to frighten them off to retrieve it. The other ranger appointed was Izak Cornelis Holtzhausen from the ZAR Police at Nelspruit.

The Anglo-Boer War broke out in 1899 and the Sabi Game Reserve was all but forgotten. After the Peace of Vereeniging in 1902 the interim government under Lord Milner decided to reproclaim the reserve and appointed Major (later Colonel) James Stevenson-Hamilton as warden. The Scottish professional soldier obtained a two-year leave of absence from his regiment to begin the great task of saving what remained of the once-great herds of game that had been decimated by hunters and both Boer and British soldiers. He became involved in the welfare of his animal charges to such an extent that he stayed for more than 40 years, until his retirement in 1946. The continued existence and development of the Kruger National Park is largely due to his dedication and sound administration.

When Stevenson-Hamilton settled on the banks of the Sabie River, the balance of nature was seriously impaired, especially with regard to the larger mammals, and game laws virtually existed on paper only. Giraffes, hippos, buffaloes and rhinos were extremely rare, elephants occasionally wandered in from Mozambique but did not stay at first, and other species were numerically very low.

Instructions to the new warden were very vague. The only one he remembered clearly was 'to make himself as unpopular as possible' among hunters and poachers. He set to this task with fervour, earning himself the nickname 'Skukuza', which means 'the man who changes everything'. In 1904 he succeeded in getting control, and thus game protection, over approximately 10 000 km² of land north of the Sabie River that had belonged to land-owning and mining companies and private individuals. To centralise control of the area under his jurisdiction, he became Native Commissioner, Customs Official and Justice of the Peace for the territory, appointing rangers to assist him in his task.

In 1922, in the aftermath of the First World War, a demand for more agricultural land to be made available by the government and for industries to be developed, coupled to the largely unsympathetic attitude of most Lowvelders of the time, seriously jeopardised the continued existence of the Sabi Game Reserve. By this time Stevenson-Hamilton had come to the conclusion that the reserve should become a national park under central government control if its future was to be safeguarded. Fortunately he had influential friends, not least of all Senator Deneys Reitz. After a change of government, which for a time seemed to nullify all his efforts, he finally won the confidence and support of the new Minister of Lands, P. J. Grobler, a great-nephew of President Kruger.

His efforts were crowned with success when, on 31 May 1926, the National Parks Act was adopted unanimously, adding many hectares of land north of the Sabie River to the old Sabi Game Reserve. The Reserve was renamed the Kruger National Park, in honour of President S. J. P. Kruger, who had done so much for wildlife conservation in South Africa. Thus the Kruger National Park became the first national park in South Africa's system of national parks.

TOURISM

The Kruger Park got off to a slow start. In 1927 only three vehicles entered the Park. Over the years the number of visitors has gradually increased. During the 2011/12 financial year 1 411 796 guests entered the Park.

Entrance

Which are the peak seasons for visiting the Kruger Park?
The peak season for the Park falls over the mid-year winter school holiday period. Other busy times are the usual school holidays and long weekends, especially the Easter long weekend. The Park is generally busier during the winter.

Why are the numbers of day visitors restricted during busy times?

As the Kruger National Park has a limited visitor capacity in terms of vehicle numbers on the roads, parking and public facilities at picnic spots and rest camps, a quota system is used to regulate numbers of day visitors during busy times of the year. Overcrowding is avoided to maintain the serene and tranquil atmosphere of the Park.

Do day visitors to the Park have to book in advance?

Day visitors can book permits in advance, and this is advised during busy seasons, public holidays and long weekends. Entrance for day visitors is handled on a first-come-first-served basis. As the park operates a quota system, gates are closed to day visitors once the quota has been reached. A nominal fee is charged for bookings for day permits, which does not include the conservation fees payable.

How much are entrance fees?

The term 'entrance fee' has been replaced by the term 'conservation fee'. As tariffs are amended annually, enquire at the reservation facilities at Head Office, in the Park itself or on the SANParks website (www.sanparks.org).

Why do South Africans pay reduced conservation fees?

South African residents already contribute to conservation through their taxes paid to the fiscus, which funds the conservation grant received from government.

Why do Southern African Development Community nationals pay reduced conservation fees?

South Africa has treaties or agreements with all neighbouring states about transfrontier conservation. The aim is to promote the establishment and development of these as tourism destinations, and it was decided to offer reduced fees to nationals of the SADC to promote regionalism and neighbourliness.

Concessions and Wild Cards

Do senior citizens qualify for any concessions in the Park?

Yes, discounts for South African residents of 60 years and older apply in the Kruger Park and all other national parks. Please enquire when making your reservation as to the terms and conditions that apply.

Do concessions apply at all times?

No, senior citizen discount concessions are available only over fixed window periods and do not apply on Friday and Saturday nights, over long weekends and during school holidays. Certain busier camps do not offer senior citizen discount.

How is a long weekend defined?

A weekend preceded by a public holiday falling on a Thursday or Friday, or followed by a public holiday falling on a Monday or Tuesday is seen as a long weekend and thus does not qualify for concessions.

Why is no concession offered on Friday and Saturday nights?

Senior citizen discounts are not offered on these nights as they are the busiest nights of the week.

What percentage discount is applicable?

Discounts of 40% and 20% apply, depending on the rest camp and the type of accommodation. At some rest camps no discounts are offered at all. Please enquire about this when making your reservation.

Why are discounts offered only at certain rest camps?

Rest camps that are normally fully booked throughout the year do not offer discounts, as it is not necessary for these camps to attract more visitors.

When do these concessions apply?
It is not possible to fix specific dates to these concessions, but as a rule concessions apply from about mid-January to mid-March, early May to early June, mid-August to mid-September and from the first week in October to the end of November. These are the periods of lowest occupancies.

Do disabled persons also qualify for concessions?
Yes. Proof of disabilities such as blindness, deafness or being wheelchair bound, as well as receiving some sort of welfare pension, will be considered for the concession and may be applied for in advance.

Do I have to supply proof of age when applying for the concession?
Yes. Proof of age or of pensioner status must be produced on arrival.

Do concessions apply only to accommodation?
Yes. The discount is offered only on accommodation, including camping, not on conservation fees, meals, activities or purchases.

Do my guests also qualify for the concession?
No. The concession applies to the couple in whose name the reservation is made. A couple is entitled to one unit per visit. In the case of additional guests, the full bed tariff will apply, e.g. a grandchild accompanying grandparents who qualify for the concession will be charged the full bed tariff or the full unit tariff when an additional unit is required.

Is there a discount concession for groups of senior citizens?
Yes. For group discount concession please apply beforehand to:

The Managing Executive: Tourism Development and Marketing, PO Box 787, Pretoria 0001

Could these concessions alter in future?
Yes. Tariffs and concessions are subject to alteration without advance notice. Always enquire about this service when making your reservation.

I have heard a lot about a Wild Card. What is the purpose of this card?
In the past once-off entrance fees were charged at entrance gates, whether for day visits or overnight visits. The term 'entrance fees' has been replaced by 'conservation fees', which means that visitors who overnight in the Park now pay a fee for every night spent in the Park. Valid Wild Card members are usually not required to pay conservation fees.

What are the advantages of a Wild Card?
Valid Wild Card members benefit by having free or discounted access to the Park.

Does the Wild Card cover access only or is accommodation also favourably affected?
Wild Cards cover conservation fees only.

Does my Wild Card cover access to all national parks?
No. It depends on the type of Wild Card acquired.

Accommodation

How much accommodation is available in the Kruger National Park?
One of the main reasons why people visit the Park is the tranquillity it offers. Overnight facilities are restricted to prevent overcrowding, which would impact adversely on the atmosphere of the Park. There are 12 major rest camps, 14 smaller rest camps and seven concession lodges.

In total the Park can accommodate 4 356 people on SANParks-managed beds, 4 154 camping and 302 in concession camps, a total of 8 812 on any given night. This includes people participating in overnight activities such as the wilderness, backpacking, adventure or eco trails.

Where does one book accommodation?
Accommodation, including camping, can be booked in various ways.
- Central reservation office in Pretoria at 643 Leyds Street, Muckleneuk, Pretoria
  Telephone: 012 428 9111
  Email: reservations@sanparks.org
  Fax: 012 343 0905
- Online at www.sanparks.org
- Any other regional booking office

How long in advance can one make overnight bookings?
Bookings can normally be made up to 11 months in advance from the first working day of every month, e.g. July bookings open on 1 August.

What type of accommodation is available?
A large variety of overnight facilities is available. The rest camps in the Park generally cater for the middle- to lower-income market, with some higher-range products available, while the private concessions cater for the top end of the market. Overnight accommodation primarily consists of two-bed chalets in the three-star category, with bathroom and kitchen facilities. Linen (bedding and towels) is provided and in most cases air conditioning, a braai facility and a refrigerator are provided.

There are also a few budget huts and tents, which have communal kitchen and ablution facilities. Overnight hides and A-frame cabins are available for the more adventurous. Towards the higher end, there are family cottages, guest cottages and guesthouses for family or business groups. The private concession lodges provide luxury tents, cabins and suites.

Can I book donor-built accommodation?
Yes, donor-built units are available for all visitors. However, some of these units are subject to a shorter release period (three months instead of the normal 11).

Is a deposit required when reserving accommodation?
The general deposit policy is to pay 50% within 30 days of booking and the remainder 60 days before arrival. As far as possible, bookings should be fully paid before arrival in the Park.

In the event of cancellation, will the deposit be refunded?
Cancellation refunds are done on a sliding scale, with full forfeiture of deposit closer to arrival date. Application for a refund of deposit should be submitted as soon as possible, but must be within 30 days after cancellation.

Do visitors from abroad get preference when reserving accommodation?
Overseas visitors are most welcome to our country and to the Kruger National Park in particular, but they do not get preference at the expense of South African visitors. Overseas visitors make up about 10% of the total number of visitors to the Park every year and most of them travel in organised bus tours. These tour operators have block bookings and take South Africans as well as foreigners.

Is accommodation limited at certain times of the year?
No, visitors may now stay as long as they want to all year round, but it is recommended that they do not stay in one rest camp for longer than five consecutive nights in order to give others the opportunity to book the facilities.

Are all camps open throughout the year?

Prior to the mid-1970s most camps were closed during the summer months. This was primarily due to roads that were not gravelled or tarred, which made it difficult to travel during the rainy season. In the very early years malaria also played a role, as did the excessive heat and humidity during the summer. In those days there were no air conditioners and refrigerators. Since the 1980s all camps have been open throughout the year.

What are the hours of the camp receptions?

Camp receptions are open between 08h00 and half an hour after gate closing time. In case of emergency, approach the security at the camp gate or call the duty manager.

Do all the rest camps have caravan and camping sites?

All the major rest camps have these facilities, except for Olifants, where these facilities are incorporated in Balule Camp, and Mopani, where the camping facility is south of the rest camp at Tsendze. These facilities for Orpen are at the Maroela Camp, which is exclusively a camping and caravanning facility.

Facilities and activities

Are there banking and post office facilities in the Park?

Letaba and Skukuza have an Automated Teller Machine (ATM). There is a branch of First National Bank and a post office at Skukuza.

Do all camps have electricity?

Most major rest camps are linked to the national grid supplied by Eskom. However, some smaller rest camps, e.g. Sirheni, Roodewal and Shimuwini, operate with solar-powered battery systems, while Balule does not have electricity. Most major rest camps also have stand-by generators in case the supply from Eskom is interrupted.

Are there laundry facilities in the camps?

Most major camps have laundry facilities, comprising coin-operated washing machines and tumble driers. Guests should enquire at camp receptions about available laundry facilities.

Is fuel available throughout the Park?

There are filling stations at Punda Maria, Shingwedzi, Mopani, Letaba, Olifants, Satara, Orpen Gate, Lower Sabie, Crocodile Bridge, Berg-en-Dal, Pretoriuskop and Skukuza, where the mainstream fuel types are sold. Garage cards are accepted, but credit cards are not accepted for payment of fuel purchases.

Are there swimming pools in all the camps?

All the major rest camps, with the exception of Olifants, have swimming pools.

Can I prepare my own meals?

The bulk of the accommodation in the Park is self-catering, and visitors should check the description on the reservation confirmation or website, to ensure that they fully understand what is on offer. Most camps have communal kitchens where there are two-plate stoves, dishwashing facilities, with hot, cold and boiling water. There are still some camps that don't have cutlery and crockery, and visitors should ensure that they understand what they have booked. Some camps hire out chests with basic cutlery and crockery.

Why are staff at accommodation units reluctant to help visitors with the washing of dishes or grilling of meat?

It is not part of their official duties to perform these tasks. They may perform these tasks in their spare time, provided it does not interfere with their official duties.

Are there restaurants in all the camps?
There are restaurants at Punda Maria, Shingwedzi, Mopani, Letaba, Olifants, Satara, Lower Sabie, Berg-en-Dal, Pretoriuskop and Skukuza. Cafeteria-type meals can also be obtained at Nkuhlu, Afsaal and Tshokwane picnic spots during the day.

Who runs the shops, restaurants and cafeterias in the Park?
Shops, restaurants and cafeterias are now outsourced and are run by concessionaires on behalf of SANParks. A number of smaller outlets and picnic spots are still operated by SANParks.

What can I buy in the rest camp shops?
The following rest camps have shops: Punda Maria, Shingwedzi, Mopani, Letaba, Olifants, Satara, Orpen, Skukuza, Lower Sabie, Crocodile Bridge, Berg-en-Dal and Pretoriuskop. These shops are open daily and provide a selection of groceries such as meat, bread, milk, liquor and tinned foods, as well as books, maps and a good selection of curios.

Are game trophies sold in the Park?
Veterinary restrictions prevent the exportation of trophies. Treated skins, however, are sold in the shops.

What type of payment is accepted in the Park?
Payment for conservation fees and accommodation, and purchases at shops, cafeterias and restaurants can normally be made in cash or by credit card. Certain foreign currency (preferably US dollars, Euros and British pounds) is accepted as payment, but exchange rates may not be as favourable as one might obtain at a bank. It is important to note that credit cards may not be used at filling stations, and only cash and domestic garage or fuel cards are accepted.

How much waste is generated by visitors and does the Park have a recycling facility?
More than 200 000 tons of waste material such as glass, tin, cardboard, paper and plastic is collected annually. This amounts to an average of 0.5 kg per visitor per day. The waste that can be recycled is separated and the remaining waste is incinerated.

Are there film, video or DVD shows and talks in all rest camps?
Weather permitting, videos are shown in the major rest camps from Monday to Saturday. Enquire at reception about the videos to be shown.

What films, videos or DVDs are shown?
Video subjects are all nature-conservation documentaries, while slide shows and talks are also conservation orientated.

Are there any sporting facilities in the Park?
In 1999 a nine-hole golf course at Skukuza was opened to the public. Other than this facility there are no sporting facilities for visitors and they prefer it that way.

In which other activities can one participate in the Kruger National Park?
At present activities such as the Lebombo, Malopeni and Mafunyane eco trails, which are motorised overnight 4x4 eco trails, and backpacking trails such as Lepelle River, Lonely Bull and Mphongolo, morning and afternoon walks from certain rest camps and a mountain-bike trail are offered. See 'Nature Activities' on page 18.

Safety and security

What should be done in an after-hours emergency, such as serious illness?
Drive to the camp entrance gate. The gate guard will contact the duty manager who will come to your assistance. If he

is aware of a medical doctor visiting the camp, he will refer you to him/her.

Should the emergency be of a serious nature, the duty manager can arrange with the resident ranger to escort you to the nearest medical facility.

In Skukuza the gate guard will direct you to the local resident doctor.

What should I do in case of theft from my accommodation unit or vehicle?

Any theft should be reported as soon as possible to the Hospitality Service or Duty Manager of the camp where the incident occurred. Fortunately incidents of theft in the Park are very rare. Guests are advised not to leave valuables, such as cash, cameras or jewellery, unattended in the accommodation units or their vehicles. Most bungalows have been fitted with a code-operated safe. Thefts should also be reported to the nearest South African Police Service (SAPS) station. There is a SAPS station at Skukuza.

May visitors bring firearms into the Park?

Yes, visitors may bring their personal firearms into the Park. These must be declared upon entering the Park at the entrance gate, where they will be recorded, unloaded and sealed. The licensed owner is responsible for the safekeeping of the firearm/s during the stay in the Park. When the owner leaves the Park, the firearm/s will be unsealed and returned to him/her.

Occasionally one sees unarmed men working on the roadside. Is this dangerous?

These workers have a practical knowledge of nature and wild animals; they take care not to disturb animals and can usually detect danger, and take steps to avoid it. The activities of a group of people working together usually deter animals and they tend to move away from the foreign shapes, smells and sounds of the working group.

Have any workers been killed by wild animals?

A few workers have been killed but in every case they were not with the team and were in places where they should not have been. Being negligent and disobeying rules and instructions led to their deaths.

Have there been any visitor fatalities in the Park?

No animal-related fatalities have been recorded in the Park. Many visitors court serious danger by alighting from their vehicles close to dangerous animals, especially lions and elephants. A number of visitors have unfortunately died in car accidents, almost all due to speeding.

Have any visitors been injured by animals in the Park?

Incidents have been reported where visitors, while sleeping outside their accommodation units, caravans or tents, were injured by hyaenas. Fortunately these are rare incidents and underline the fact that, even in rest camps, care should be taken, as you are in the territory of wild animals. Animals such as warthogs sometimes damage the fences, which allows hyaenas access.

It has happened that visitors who fed monkeys or baboons were bitten by these animals. It is imperative not to feed any animals and it is advisable to close the vehicle's windows when stopping to observe these primates.

What should I do if I run an animal over?

Report the incident to the nearest rest camp. Do not get out of your vehicle to try to help the animal – it could be dangerous and you are unlikely to succeed.

What is the procedure when two or more vehicles are involved in a collision?

In the case of a serious accident, get a message through to the nearest traffic official, the nearest ranger, nearest rest camp or to the police at Skukuza. Wait for the official to take the necessary measurements. Do not leave your vehicle if possible. Minor accidents can be settled between vehicle owners or their insurance companies.

May a visitor report law-breakers?
Yes, but you must be prepared to return to the Park to testify against them in court should you wish to lay a charge.

Transport and vehicles

Can visitors fly into the Park?
The airstrip at Skukuza is open to private flights with prior permission to land, but will open to commercial flights in June 2014. There is also Kruger-Mpumalanga International Airport (KMIA) outside Mbombela (previously Nelspruit), and airport facilities at Phalaborwa, Hoedspruit (Eastgate) and Malelane.

How does one acquire a road map of the Park?
Road maps are for sale at gates and shops throughout the Park.

Does the Park provide transport for visitors?
No, but vehicles may be rented from Avis in Skukuza. However, the Park does offer morning, afternoon and night game-viewing drives.

Could one hold SANParks responsible for damage caused by animals to a vehicle or belongings?
No. Visitors enter the Park at their own risk and, if they observe regulations relating to behaviour on roads and in rest camps, the risk is minimal.

What happens if a visitor's vehicle breaks down in the Park?
If the breakdown is minor, for example a flat tyre, and can be repaired by someone in the vehicle, this may be done after making sure that the area is safe enough to get out of the vehicle. Only those involved in the repair are allowed to leave the vehicle.

Roadside assistance is provided from Skukuza and Letaba rest camps, where limited emergency repairs can be done. The toll-free number is 0800 030 666. There is a 24-hour Emergency Call Centre at the number 013 735 4325.

Roads and boundaries

How many entrance gates are there to the Park and what are the nearest towns and routes to follow?
There are nine entrance gates, and there are also two entrance and departure gates along the Park's eastern border with Mozambique, where the necessary customs regulations must be observed.

Gate	Nearest town/route
Crocodile Bridge	Komatipoort via Mbombela (Nelspruit) and Malelane
Malelane	Malelane via Mbombela
Numbi	White River via Mbombela, Sabie or Hazyview
Phabeni	Hazyview via Mbombela or Sabie
Kruger	Hazyview via Mbombela or Sabie
Orpen	Klaserie via Sabie or Hoedspruit
Phalaborwa	Phalaborwa via Tzaneen or Hoedspruit
Punda Maria	Thohoyandou via Makhado (previously Louis Trichardt)
Pafuri	Tshipise via Makhado or Musina

How many kilometres of roads are there in the Park?
There are currently 904 km of tarred roads and 1 747 km of gravel roads that are recognised tourist roads. There are a further 2 500 km of firebreak, patrol and

border roads, which are not accessible to tourists and are used as management roads. Many of the firebreak roads are no longer graded and are used only as patrol roads.

How many kilometres of firebreak roads are there?

There are about 2 500 km of firebreak roads, of which 450 km are along the boundaries.

What is the total length of the eastern boundary fence?

The total length of the eastern border fence is about 350 km, of which about 50 km between the Kruger National Park and the Limpopo National Park has been removed.

What is the total length of the boundaries of the Park?

The total length of the Kruger Park's boundaries is 668 km.

What is the cost per kilometre to erect a cable fence on the Park's border?

In today's terms (2013) the preparation, labour and cost of material will run to R250 000/km, which is the cost of the eastern border cable fence.

Is there a difference between the eastern boundary fence, being an international border, and the other fences demarcating the boundaries of the Park?

The eastern fence is a cable fence, while the rest of the boundary fences are not as significant. Some sections are electrified, primarily to contain elephants. The cost of erecting these fences is about R150 000/km in today's terms.

Are certain sections of the eastern border fence still electrified?

The eastern border fence is not electrified, but is a cable fence in its entirety. Only about 200 km of the western boundary

fence and 105 km of the southern fence along the Crocodile River are still electrified.

Will all the roads be tarred in the future?

Not likely.

Have the tarred roads had any effect on the distribution and movement of game?

Vegetation along the tarred roads is relatively free of dust and therefore more palatable to the animals than that along the dirt roads. Run-off water produces slightly more lush vegetation on the shoulders of tarred roads, attracting mainly small game. However, in certain areas in summer the growth is so lush that it largely impairs the visitor's view.

Lion tend to lie on tarred roads during winter, especially early morning and late afternoon, as the tarred surface warms up quickly and retains heat longer.

Generally speaking, it appears that tarred roads have more advantages than disadvantages as far as game-viewing is concerned.

Are visitors inclined to speed on tarred roads?

Apparently not. The tarred, dust-free roads enhance the possibility of sighting game (as described in the previous answer), which encourages visitors to travel slowly to enjoy the better viewing.

Are people taken out in cross-country vehicles off the beaten track?

This service is restricted to visiting scientists, VIPs and media groups.

Will more areas be created where visitors can leave their vehicles to watch game, in the open and at their leisure?

SANParks has created various picnic places, view sites and hides where visitors may alight from their vehicles to stretch their legs or enjoy a picnic. Many of these spots offer panoramic views, and the hides have been constructed at water points where visitors can enjoy bird-watching or watch animals coming to the water to drink. More areas will be created as and when the need arises.

NATURE ACTIVITIES

Are there nature activities a visitor can take part in, other than driving around the Park by oneself?

A number of nature activities have been developed that allow visitors to get closer to nature and even spend nights out in the bush. These activities are designed for the true nature lover to get closer to nature and its elements than when driving around in their vehicle or sitting in a rest camp at night.

Activities include:

- Wilderness trails
- Day walks: Morning, river, afternoon and full-day walks
- Sunset and night drives
- Morning drives
- Lebombo Overland Eco Trail
- Mafunyane Overland Eco Trail
- Malopene Overnight Eco Trail
- Adventure and backpacking trails
- Mountain-bike trail

Where can one obtain more information about these activities?

Information about all these activities may be obtained from any of the rest camp receptions in the Kruger Park and on the SANParks website (www.sanparks.org).

Wilderness trails

What is a wilderness trail?

It is essentially a spiritual encounter with nature, during which people are taken out of their everyday environment and exposed to the intricate elements that comprise the web of life. In part this

is achieved by traversing large areas of unspoiled wilderness on foot and under the guidance of qualified, armed and experienced trail rangers, whose role is an interpretive, educational, protective and disciplinary one.

It is not unusual to cover up to 15 km per day; it must be emphasised that, although the accent is not on endurance, a reasonable level of fitness is required.

The number of participants is restricted to eight for safety reasons and to enhance personal contact with participants.

To derive the maximum benefit from the trail adventure, it is recommended that friends, families, and people of similar ages, interests and levels of fitness make their bookings together.

Trailists meet at the designated rest camps by not later than 15h30 on Sundays and Wednesdays for a short briefing. They then leave for their wilderness camp by vehicle. The accommodation at wilderness trail camps is very rustic and comprises four small two-bed units – either tents or wooden units. In total, three nights and two full days are spent in the bush and the group returns to the main rest camp after breakfast on the final day.

Does one have to be very fit to do a walking trail?

Hikers need to be reasonably fit and the trails are therefore restricted to persons between the ages of 12 and 60 years. Those above 60 years wishing to participate will be required to present certificates of fitness. Children between the ages of 12 and 16 must be accompanied by a responsible adult.

Those participating undertake the trail at their own risk and need to sign an indemnity form prior to departing on the trail.

Further information about all the trails offered by SANParks may be obtained from Head Office at PO Box 787, Pretoria, 0001.

How many wilderness trails are conducted in the Park?

There are seven wilderness trails in the Park. The Wolhuter and Bushman trails are situated in the area between Pretoriuskop and Berg-en-Dal rest camps. The first leaves from Pretoriuskop and the latter from Berg-en-Dal.

The Metsi Metsi trail (in the vicinity of Tshokwane) and the Napi trail depart from Skukuza. The Olifants trail starts from Letaba, the Nyalaland trail in the far north starts from Punda Maria, while the Sweni trail starts from Satara.

What clothing, footwear and food should one take along on wilderness trails?

Clothing should be comfortable, allowing freedom of movement. It should be hard-wearing and preferably neutral in colour, e.g. khaki. White or cream or brightly coloured clothes should be avoided. T-shirts are not recommended for the walks as they do not protect the neck against the sun.

Although rucksacks, eating utensils, water bottles, beds and bedding are provided, it is suggested that the following items be taken along by the trailist:

- 3 shirts/blouses
- 3 pairs shorts
- 1 pair slacks/jeans
- 1 tracksuit
- changes of underwear and socks
- 1 pair takkies (for use in camp)
- 2 jerseys
- 2 all weather jackets or light raincoats
- 2 hats or caps (to protect the head and neck)
- 1 torch and batteries
- binoculars and camera
- sunblock
- insect repellent
- personal toiletries
- towel
- drinks (personal preferences)
- reference books (bird, animal, insect and plant books)

Footwear is probably the most important item of a trailist's equipment. Good walking shoes should provide ankle support, have reasonably thick soles and be durable and comfortable.

All other equipment, including food, is included in the tariff, although liquor and soft drinks are not provided. The food is adequate and of a type that can be expected at a rustic bush camp. Special tastes are not catered for and special items should be provided by the trailists themselves.

Each base camp is equipped with a paraffin refrigerator for perishable foodstuffs. Space permitting, arrangements can be made for soft drinks and mixers to be kept cool.

To appreciate the wilderness experience, a harmonious and co-operative approach is required. With this in mind, alcohol may be consumed only at the base camp and definitely not during walks. Inordinate consumption of liquor is likely to jeopardise the success of the entire trail.

How can I book a wilderness trail?

Bookings for a wilderness trail may be made a year in advance. Enquiries about trails may be made at any SANParks Reservation Office.

Applications for wilderness trails must clearly state the number of trailists, their ages and sex. As with reservations for accommodation, it is advisable to provide alternative dates and trail preferences.

Proof of reservation, which is issued when the booking is confirmed, must be shown on arrival at the Park.

What qualifications are required to become an honorary ranger?

To become an honorary ranger you must be a regular visitor to the Park, have a real interest in nature and environmental issues, have an above-average knowledge of nature and be fluent in English and preferably at least one other official

South African language. There are other requirements; for further information please contact the SANParks Honorary Rangers, PO Box 787, Pretoria, 0001.

Day walks: morning, afternoon and full-day walks

Where can one book to go on one of these walks?

Walks may be booked at any of the rest camps from where these activities are offered or in advance through central reservations. Please enquire at the rest camp reception for availability on these walks. Day walks are conducted from a rest camp or gate, either on foot or in a vehicle, in a suitable area identified by the local section ranger. Full-day walks can be arranged on request from certain rest camps or gates as an ad hoc activity.

This involves being in the bush for a full day, with a rest during the heat of the day, and returning at sunset.

How many visitors are allowed on such a walk?

A maximum of eight people can go on such a walk. There is no minimum.

Two armed, experienced and qualified field guides accompany the group on the walk.

How far does one walk on such an excursion?

There is no specific distance laid out for these excursions. The distance covered depends on the sightings, the terrain and the particular interest of the party, for instance birding, botany or geology. Morning walks usually take about three hours, the afternoon walks approximately two hours, while the river walks are about one to two hours, excluding travelling time. Environmental education and interpretation is the core of this experience.

Does one have to be fit for these walks?

No great distances are covered and it is not an obstacle course. The pace of the walk is adjusted to suit the participants. However, it would require some degree of fitness. Comfortable shoes and neutral-coloured clothing are recommended.

Is there an age restriction for the walks?

Generally it would be advisable for visitors over 65 years of age not to go on such walks and children under the age of 12 years are also not considered. However, with a doctor's certificate pronouncing older visitors capable of participating in such activities, exceptions may be made.

How safe is it to do these walks?

You will be accompanied by a fully qualified guide and assistant who are both professionally trained and experienced, not only in weapons skills, but also in the interpretation of what nature has to offer in the area in which you are walking.

What happens in the case of an emergency or an attack by an animal?

The secret to enjoying your walking experience is to adhere to the instructions of your guide at all times. The guide is in charge of the excursion and responsible for your safety, and it is imperative that you follow given instructions at all times. The guides are qualified in rendering first aid.

Should any injury happen during such an excursion, does one have any recourse or claim against the Park?

Before embarking on your excursion you have to complete an indemnity form and hand this to your guide. This exempts SANParks from any liability of any kind and is standard procedure when participating in any of the activities offered in the Park.

What do we need to take along on these walks?

You need to take enough water and some snacks such as energy bars, dried fruit and fruit juice. These snacks are enjoyed during a break, usually halfway through the excursion. Water bottles and backpacks are provided by the camp. Don't forget a hat and sunblock in the summer!.

What time of day do these excursions depart?

Departure and return times vary according to the time of year. Please enquire at the reception office of the rest camp to find out when your excursion departs and where to meet your guide.

Sunset and night drives

Are sunset and night drives available from all rest camps?

They are available from all major rest camps. For visitors who are booked into accommodation outside the Park, drives are available from the entrance gates to the Park.

Are the sunset and night drives conducted in open vehicles?

All drives in the Park, including sunset and night drives, are conducted in open vehicles.

How many persons are allowed on a sunset and night drive?

From the major rest camps drives are done in vehicles with a capacity of 20 seats. Larger rest camps may have more than one such vehicle. Should the demand not warrant such a vehicle, a smaller vehicle with seating for about 10 people may be used. Each vehicle is equipped with hand-held spotlights and a first-aid kit.

Will one see more animals than during the day?

Hardly likely, but you may possibly see animals that you usually do not see

during the day, such as leopards, hyaenas, porcupines, smaller members of the cat family, bushbabies, jackals and nocturnal birds such as various species of owls.

Why were sunset and night drives started?

Visitors are not allowed to drive in the Park after gate closing times. After numerous requests, organised night excursions were instituted, in order to allow visitors to see the nocturnal denizens of the bush and to share the wonders of the night.

When do these drives depart?

Visitors going on sunset and night drives should determine the times and places of departure from the respective rest camp receptions. Please note that drives take place if the weather is suitable.

What is the duration of a sunset and night drive?

After departing, the guide usually stops at a scenic spot for visitors to have a time to reflect while the sun sets. The drive returns in time for visitors who need to have a restaurant meal. This means that the duration of a night drive would be about two or three hours.

Are the vehicles equipped with spotlights?

Yes. The guide will instruct the visitors how to operate the spotlights and, by taking turns with the spotlights, visitors are invited to add to the adventure by spotlighting animals during the drive. Visitors handling the spotlights should not shine the spotlight directly into the eyes of animals as the powerful light can temporarily blind the animals.

Do I have to take warm clothing along?

Blankets are supplied on the vehicle. Winter nights can be chilly and it is advisable to take warm clothing with you, even during the warmer season.

Are the animals encountered on a sunset and night drive as dangerous as those seen during the day?

In a conservation area such as the Kruger National Park, all animals should be treated with respect. This is more true of some than others. The animals found along the routes taken by night drive vehicles have, to a certain degree, become used to visitors and vehicles. As long as visitors stay on the vehicle, there is nothing to be apprehensive about. The driver/guide is a fully qualified, responsible and experienced official, armed with a rifle to ensure the safety of the visitors.

Please note that the guide is in charge of the excursion and that his/her instructions should be followed at all times.

Will I have any recourse or claim against the Park in the event of injury or a mishap during the excursion?

Before the departure of the night drive you are required to complete and hand to the guide an indemnity form that is valid for the duration of the night drive. A visit to and participation in activities of the Park are at the visitor's own risk.

Is there an age restriction for participants on sunset and night drives?

In order to make the drive as enjoyable as possible for all participants, there is a minimum age restriction of six years.

Am I allowed to take sundowner drinks along to enjoy at the sundown stop?

Yes, you may. However, the excessive use of alcohol is not allowed during the drive and the guide is fully entitled to refuse to allow obviously intoxicated participants to board the vehicle.

Where can one book a night drive and can it be booked at the same time as booking the accommodation?

Night drives may be booked at the same time as booking your accommodation.

Rest camp receptions will, however, accept bookings at short notice, provided that seats are available.

Morning drives

Where can one book these drives?

These drives may be booked at the rest camp or entrance gate reception or in advance through central reservations.

When do the drives depart?

As departure times change according to the season, please enquire at the rest camp reception about the time and place of departure of your drive.

What is the duration of the drive?

The morning drive usually returns in time for breakfast, or for participants to vacate their accommodation should they be leaving the rest camp on the same day, which is before 09h00. The drive normally lasts about three hours.

Are open vehicles used?

Yes.

How many visitors can go on a drive at a time?

Depending on the bookings made, either a 20-seater or a smaller 10-seater vehicle may be used.

I am staying outside the Park. Is it possible for me to participate in one of these drives?

Yes. Please make the necessary reservation at the closest entrance gate to where you are staying.

Although I am staying outside the Park, is it possible for me to book an open safari vehicle drive during the day?

Yes, you may book such a drive at an entrance gate. Should this not be possible, the reception desk at your place of accommodation should be able to book you on a vehicle operated by an open safari vehicle operator in the area.

I notice many of these open safari-type vehicles in the Park. Are they operated by the Park?

No, these vehicles are operated by outside agencies under licence for their own gain.

Is it dangerous to go on such a drive?

No. As long as you stay in the vehicle and follow the instructions of your qualified, experienced guide, there is no reason to expect any danger that might spoil your experience.

Eco trails

What are eco trails?

They are outdoor adventures with 4x4 vehicles, conducted under the guidance of an experienced trail ranger.

LEBOMBO OVERLAND ECO TRAIL

The Lebombo Overland Eco Trail follows the eastern boundary of the Park, along the Lebombo hills from the extreme south to the far north of the Park.

Is this trail only for 4x4 vehicles?

Yes. Although this is not a 4x4 challenge route, road conditions on the trail vary considerably in places. Guests may be asked to engage 4x4 at places with steep inclines and muddy patches, in order not to damage the trail. Thus only 4x4 vehicles are allowed.

How many vehicles and trailists are allowed on this adventure?

Only five vehicles plus the trail leader's vehicle are allowed on the trail at a time, with a maximum of four people per vehicle. No children under 12 years are allowed, unless arrangements have been made prior to departure.

Is the trail available throughout the year?

No. The trail operates during the dry season, from the first Sunday in April to the last Sunday in October. Should there be heavy rains during this time, the route may be closed completely.

What is the duration of the trail?

The trail is a five-day (four-night) experience over a distance of more than 500 km. This trail is rated as the best of its kind, due to the diversity of fauna and flora encountered en route.

As it is such a long trail, are there camping and ablution facilities at the overnight stops?

The four overnight facilities are unfenced camping sites, each with two Enviro Loos. Each site has its own unique bush character and should therefore be left as undisturbed as possible.

There are no accommodation facilities or showers as this would spoil the unique character of each site.

As there are no showers, how would we wash?

Three rest camps (Lower Sabie, Olifants and Shingwedzi) are visited on the trail to the north to refuel the vehicles, replenish food supplies and to allow visitors to shower.

Is this a self-catering trail?

Yes. Participants are required to drive their own vehicles and cater for themselves in terms of preparing meals, providing their own food, liquor and soft drinks, carrying their own equipment on the vehicles and bringing their own firewood and water. Trailists must therefore see to it that their vehicles are fully equipped with tent, water containers, gas bottles, cooking equipment, etc.

As there are no facilities for the disposal of any waste, you are required to have suitable waste bags for this eventuality.

The waste may be disposed of on reaching one of the above-mentioned rest camps.

Where does the trail start and end?
Trailists must report promptly at 09h00 at Crocodile Bridge on a Sunday and the adventure ends at Pafuri Picnic Spot on the Thursday at 12h00.

As it is so close to the Mozambican border, what are some of the highlights?
Trailists will start off with wonderful views of the Crocodile and Komati rivers meeting at the border of South Africa and Mozambique. Some of the trail runs along the border, and along the way you will enjoy beautiful views of wide-open spaces, bushveld and magnificent trees, including huge baobabs (*Adansonia digitata*). The trail ends at the famous landmark of Crook's Corner, where three countries meet. Here the Zimbabwean border joins those of South Africa and Mozambique.

What time does the trail depart every day?
Departure times from the camping sites vary according to the season, but should normally not be later than 07h00. A stop is usually made en route for brunch.

Is it dangerous to sleep out in the bush?
As long as you stay in your tent you should be quite safe. A professional, qualified and experienced trail ranger accompanies the trail. Trailists depend on this ranger for their safety and guidance. The ranger must therefore be obeyed at all times. Failure to co-operate in this respect could lead to the immediate cancellation of the trail.

Can the Park be held responsible for any mishap that may befall me on this excursion?
All participants must complete and hand to the trail ranger an indemnity form prior to the start of the trail. This is standard procedure for anyone taking part in activities run by SANParks, and absolves the Park and its staff from any liability that may arise from any incident that results in injury or worse. For safety and ethical reasons, excessive consumption of alcohol is strongly discouraged.

What about medical assistance?
It is advisable that each vehicle should carry its own first-aid kit, and trailists should ensure that they have their own supply of general and prescription medicine. The ranger will have a first-aid kit suitable for use in the bush, but will not dispense medicine.

What about a medical emergency on the route?
There is no, or very little, cellphone reception on the route, except for the rest camps that are visited. In a medical emergency, trailists will be evacuated from the trail to medical care according to a pre-established medical emergency plan.

The trail takes place during the dry season. Is there any need to take malaria tablets?
Malaria prophylactics should be taken as a precaution whenever you visit the Park. Please consult your doctor or travel clinic.

MAFUNYANE OVERLAND ECO TRAIL

The Mafunyane Overland Eco Trail is an outdoor adventure trail, preferably undertaken by 4x4 vehicle, along the western area of the northern division of the Park. This trail is conducted under the guidance of an experienced trail ranger.

Where is it situated?
The trail starts at Phalaborwa Gate, follows various firebreak roads along the western border area through the predominantly mopane/bushwillow woodlands and ends at Punda Maria Rest Camp.

Is this trail only for 4x4 vehicles?

Although this is not a 4x4 challenge route, conditions of the terrain vary considerably. Guests may be requested to engage 4x4 at steep inclines, muddy or sandy places in order not to damage the area. Thus 4x4 vehicles are preferred.

How many vehicles and trailists are allowed on this adventure?

Only five vehicles plus the trail leader's vehicle are allowed on the trail, with a maximum of four people per vehicle. No children under 12 years are allowed, unless arrangements have been made prior to departure.

Is the trail available throughout the year?

No. The trail operates during the dry season, from the first Sunday in April to the last Sunday in October annually. Should there be heavy rains during this period, the trail may be closed completely.

What is the duration of the trail?

This overland eco trail is a five-day and four-night experience.

Is this a self-catering trail?

Yes. Participants are required to drive their own vehicles and cater for themselves in terms of providing their own food, liquor and soft drinks and preparing meals, carrying their own equipment on the vehicles and bringing their own firewood and water. Trailists must therefore see to it that their vehicles are fully equipped with tent, water containers, gas bottles, cooking equipment, etc.

As there are no facilities for waste disposal, you are required to have suitable waste bags for this eventuality.

Are there camping and ablution facilities at the overnight stops?

The four overnight facilities are unfenced camping sites, each with two Enviro Loos and rustic bush showers. Trailists have to supply their own water to shower. The unique bush character of each site should be left as undisturbed as possible. No form of accommodation is available as this will detract from the unique character of the site.

Where does the trail start and end?

The trail starts at Phalaborwa Gate every Sunday, during the trail periods, at about noon, and ends at Punda Maria Rest Camp at about 10h00 on the Thursday.

What time does the trail depart every day?

Departing times from the overnight sites will vary according to the season, but should not be later than 07h00. A stop is usually made en route for brunch.

Is it dangerous to sleep out in the bush?

As long as you stay in your tent you should be quite safe. A professional, qualified and experienced trail ranger accompanies the trail. Trailists depend on this ranger for their safety and guidance. The ranger must therefore be obeyed at all times. Failure to co-operate in this respect could lead to the immediate cancellation of the trail.

Can the Park be held responsible for any mishap that may befall me on this excursion?

All participants must complete and hand to the trail ranger an indemnity form prior to the departure of the trail. This is standard procedure for anyone taking part in any activities run by SANParks, and absolves the Park and its staff from any liability that may arise from any incident that leads to injury or worse. For safety and ethical reasons, excessive consumption of alcohol is strongly discouraged.

What about medical assistance?

It is advisable that each vehicle should carry its own first-aid kit, and trailists should ensure that they have their own supply of general and prescription medicine. The ranger will have a first-aid kit suitable for use in the bush, but will not dispense medicine.

What about a medical emergency on the route?

There is no, or very little, cellphone reception on the route, except when visiting rest camps (Mopani and Shingwedzi). In a medical emergency, trailists will be evacuated from the trail to medical care according to a pre-established medical emergency plan.

The trail takes place during the dry season. Is there any need to take malaria tablets?

Malaria prophylactics should be taken as a precaution whenever you visit the Kruger National Park. Please consult your doctor or travel clinic.

MALOPENE OVERNIGHT ECO TRAIL

What is an overnight eco trail?

This is an overnight motorised trail that allows the participants exclusive access to a remote area, which brings the adventure tourist close to the realities of the Kruger National Park wilderness.

How many overnight eco trails are there in the Park?

At the moment there is only one, but, depending on the demand for such an adventure trail, more may be considered in future.

What does the trail offer?

On this trail the emphasis is on the wilderness, remoteness and seclusion of the area through which the trail takes place. It offers a variety of experiences, such as finding and identifying animal spoor, animals and birds and their interaction, identifying trees, shrubs and other plants, as well as a variety of different landscapes.

The guide will also interpret natural phenomena such as geological structures, ecological phenomena, as well as historical and cultural information.

Is the trail area randomly selected or does it take place in a specific area?

The trail covers the area to the northeast of Phalaborwa Entrance Gate up to the Letaba River and trailists will travel along the Park's management roads, or firebreak roads, seldom used by vehicles or accessible to visitors.

Are there limitations as to the number of trailists?

A SANParks trail leader will guide a maximum of five vehicles, limited to four persons per vehicle. No children under 12 years of age are allowed, but this will be considered where one group has booked out the entire trail.

Is this a strictly 4x4 experience?

Although this is not a 4x4 challenge, road conditions can vary to the extent that guests may be requested to engage their vehicle's 4x4 traction if it has this capability. Without this capability, wheels may spin and damage the road. As a result, 4x4 vehicles are preferred on this trail, but high-clearance 2x4 vehicles are also permitted.

When and where does the trail depart from?

The trail starts at the Phalaborwa Entrance Gate on a daily basis throughout the year. Departure time is 14h00 and trailists return the following day at 12h00.

Where can I book for this trail?

Bookings can be made at Phalaborwa Entrance Gate or through central reservations on 012 428 9111.

What do I need to bring with me on the trail?

As this is a self-catering trail, all vehicles need to be fully equipped regarding own camping equipment. Guests have to provide their own water, firewood, food, gas bottles, cooking utensils and accommodation equipment.

Can weather play a part in this trail?

In case of heavy rainfall in the area, the route may be changed or the trail closed temporarily. The section ranger can also close the route at any time for management-related issues, such as fires or anti-poaching activities.

Are there camping facilities?

There is an overnight camp site on the banks of the Letaba River about 500 m upstream of the Black Heron Dam. No rubbish bins are provided at the camping site as the trail operates on a strictly 'take it in, take it out' basis, meaning that trailists have to bring all rubbish back to Phalaborwa Entrance Gate for disposal.

Ash from the fire will be collected in the ash drum transported by the trail leader.

What do trailists do as far as ablutions are concerned?

There are two Enviro Loos at the camp site. Along the way, the trail leader will stop at safe places for necessary toilet breaks, but only wilderness-accepted methods will be allowed, which also means that no toilet paper will be allowed to be left in the bush.

No shower facilities are available at the camp site, but guests are welcome to bring along their own shower equipment. Only biodegradable soaps will be allowed.

What is the possibility of getting lost on this trail?

This is hardly likely. Vehicles are not to exceed 40 km/h except in an emergency and each driver must ensure that the vehicle behind is in sight at all times. When turning off, the front vehicle must wait until the following vehicle is well in sight.

How safe is it to go on this excursion?

Trailists are dependent on the trail leader for their safety and guidance. For the safety of all, he/she must be obeyed at all times. Failing to do this could lead to the immediate cancellation of the trail.

For safety and ethical reasons the excessive consumption of alcoholic beverages is strongly discouraged.

Is malaria an issue?

Visitors to the Park should always be aware of the danger of malaria. As the overnight stop is on the Letaba River, it makes the use of malaria prophylactics essential. Please consult your doctor or travel clinic.

What happens in the case of a medical emergency?

There is cellphone reception at a few places along the route, but not at the camp site. The trail leader will, however, request that cellphones be switched off for the duration of the trail. In case of a medical emergency the trail leader will follow a pre-established emergency plan.

Do I have to complete an indemnity form for this trail?

As with all activities involving a SANParks official accompanying visitors in the bush, all participants are required to complete an indemnity form and hand it to the trail leader prior to departure on the activity.

What is the distance of the trail?

The trail is about 70 km in length.

Backpacking trails

What is a backpacking trail?

On a backpacking trail participants are expected to provide and carry their own camping equipment and food for the duration of the trail.

What is the duration of the trail?

Three of the trails stretch over four days (three nights), departing every Wednesday and Sunday. These trails are available only for part of the year. The Mangondzwana Trail's duration is three days (two nights) and is available throughout the year.

The Mphongolo Trail is run between 1 February and 30 November, the Olifants River Trail between 1 April and 31 October, and the Lonely Bull Trail between 1 February and 31 October.

How many people are allowed on the trail?

The trail will be conducted by two experienced, qualified and competent trail rangers, with a maximum of eight participants. In the case of the Olifants River Trail, the trail must be booked as a whole, i.e. you book one trail that can accommodate up to eight persons.

The other three trails must be booked for a minimum of four persons for a trail to be viable and with a maximum of eight participants.

How many backpacking trails are available and where are they operating?

At the time of going to press there are four trails.

The Olifants River Trail operates in the Lepelle (Olifants) River rugged veld and follows the Lepelle River from where it enters the Park's western boundary. This trail departs from Olifants Rest Camp where trailists meet at 08h00 on Wednesday and Sunday mornings.

Participants in the Mphongolo Trail meet at 12h00 on the same days at Shingwedzi Rest Camp. This trail operates in the large wilderness area between the Shingwedzi and Mphongolo rivers to the northwest of Shingwedzi Rest Camp.

The third trail, the Mangondzwana Trail, operates in the Kingfisherspruit

wilderness area, with the base camp situated 2 km east of Orpen Gate. Trailists check in at Orpen reception in time for the trail to depart at 15h00 on Sundays and Wednesdays.

The Lonely Bull Trail is a primitive backpacking trail. Trailists check in at Shimuwini Rest Camp on the Letaba River to depart by 14h00. The trail starts at the low-level bridge over the Letaba River downstream from Shimuwini Rest Camp, and follows the Letaba River and immediate surrounding areas.

What do I need to bring with me for these trails?

Trailists are expected to provide their own camping equipment and food for the duration of the trail. It is strongly advised that trailists not carry more than a quarter of their body weight. As trailists tend to overstock, there will be a gear check before departure on the trail. You will be weighed with and without your backpack. Should your pack exceed the required weight, the ranger may ask you to leave some items at the rest camp.

Remember that what you take along, you have to carry.

No glass items are allowed on these trails.

Are there age restrictions for trailists on this excursion?

The age limits are 12 to 65 years. Persons older than 65 years should have a doctor's note stating that they are strong and fit enough for this type of adventure.

Are there huts and ablution facilities on these trails?

There are no overnight facilities on these trails. The trails follow no predetermined routes, which allows the rangers to decide at random how far to walk and where to camp.

What do trailists do for ablutions?

Water for drinking and ablutions will be collected from natural sources or from boreholes. Guests must bring along their own water purification tablets, such as chlorine tablets, to ensure that their water is safe to drink. There are no rubbish bins or toilets, even at overnight stops. The trails operate on a strictly 'take it in, take it out' basis and adhere strictly to a 'no trace of camping' ethic.

Prior to departure from the base camp, the rangers will inform trailists about wilderness-accepted toilet ablutions.

Mangondzwana trailists will be able to use the shower facilities at Orpen Rest Camp on a daily basis.

Are there any very specific items that I have to take note of?

Trailists are advised to bring small gas stoves for cooking, lightweight and dehydrated food and to use biodegradable products – soaps and detergents – on the trail. Insect repellent will also come in handy.

Do trailists walk from the base camp?

No. Trailists will be transported by open vehicle and trailer and dropped off at a predetermined point, and collected at a predetermined point (at 10h00 in the case of the Mphongolo Trail and Lonely Bull Trail, and at 12h00 for the Olifants River Trail) on the last day and transported back to base camp. The Mangondzwana Trail is based close to Orpen Gate and Rest Camp and will depart from and return to the base camp every day.

How far do trailists walk during these trails?

On average trailists should be prepared to walk about 40 km during a trail. These trails can be physically demanding and trailists have to be reasonably fit.

What is the procedure in case of a medical emergency?

Trail rangers have first-aid kits available but, should the situation demand it, trailists will be evacuated to medical care according to a pre-established medical emergency plan.

I presume there will be no cellphone reception. What communication is used?

Communication will be established only in case of emergency. The rangers will then use a hand-held radio and/or a satellite phone for communication. Section rangers will be aware of the whereabouts of the group in the case of any emergency.

Will I have any recourse or claim against the Park in the event of injuries or worse?

Visitors enter the Park at their own risk. Participation in any nature activity will require participants to complete an indemnity form and hand it to the activity leader prior to departing on the activity. These trails are no different. Should a trailist refuse to complete and hand in such an indemnity form, he/she will be refused participation in the activity.

This indemnity form absolves SANParks from any claims.

Are fires allowed at overnight spots on these trails?

Fires are made at night, but not for cooking purposes. Fires are only for social, aesthetic and safety reasons. This means that firewood will be used sparingly. No 'bonfires' will be allowed.

What makes these trails so special?

These trails are the only ones where participants walk through the bush with their backpacks for the duration of the trail, covering up to 40 km. Trailists also spend nights sleeping in the wild, without the safety of constructed accommodation.

How safe is it to take part in such a trail?

All trailists receive a comprehensive safety briefing before the trail departs from the base camp. The trail rangers are both armed and experienced, capable and qualified officials.

Trailists depend on the rangers for their safety and guidance. The rangers must therefore be obeyed at all times.

For safety and ethical reasons, excessive consumption of alcoholic beverages is strongly discouraged.

Is malaria a problem on these trails?
Malaria prophylactics are essential whenever you visit the Park. Please consult your doctor or travel clinic.

Are more of these trails envisaged in the future?
The future could see more of these activities. When planning these trails care must be taken not to infringe on other wilderness activities in the Park.

Adventure trails

What makes adventure trails different from the other trails?
Adventure trails are non-guided trails lasting a day and are for 4x4 vehicles only. These trails afford guests the opportunity to travel in their own 4x4 vehicles off the normal tourist roads and to take a trip on designated routes leading to a real wilderness experience in the Park.

How many adventure trails are available?
At the time of writing, there were two trails available.

Where are these trails?
The Madlabantu Trail is in the vicinity of Pretoriuskop Rest Camp.

Mananga Trail is situated northeast of Satara Rest Camp in the knobthorn/ marula savanna.

How many trailists can take part in a trail such as this?
Only up to six vehicles with a maximum of four people per vehicle per trail per day are allowed.

With no guide on the trail, isn't there a danger that we might get lost?
All these trails are clearly marked and, if you adhere to the marked route, you should not get lost.

What should we do in the event of a vehicle breaking down?
It is advisable that you team up with a second vehicle to assist one another in the event of a breakdown. When on your own, try to sort out your problem yourself. If this is not possible, stay with your vehicle. You will be found, most probably by vehicles following. Do **NOT** try to walk to find help.

Are we allowed to get out of our vehicles while on the trail?
You may get out of your vehicle once you have established that it is safe to do so. It is recommended that you not move more than about 5 to 7 m away from the vehicle, so that you will be able to reach the safety of your vehicle quickly in an emergency.

As there are no ablution facilities on the trails, getting out of your vehicle is recommended only for urgent toilet breaks. Please note that only wilderness ablutions are accepted – no toilet paper is to be left in the bush.

What should be taken along on such a trail?
Trailists must carry sufficient equipment to ensure a safe journey. Sufficient drinking water is essential in the event of a mechanical breakdown. A GPS can come in handy and a standard 4x4 recovery kit is necessary. This should include a tow rope, hi-lift jack, including a base plate for sandy or muddy areas, a first-aid kit, fire extinguisher, axe, folding spade, extra spare wheel, rubbish bag, blankets, torch with spare batteries and some snacks and tinned food.

Why may only 4x4 vehicles participate in these adventure trails?

Although these adventure trails are not very challenging, a 4x4 vehicle will minimise environmental damage, as some of the trails have dongas and pass through dry river beds and clayish areas, which can be treacherous during the wet season.

Where do I book for these trails?

Trails may be booked at the following points:
Madlabantu Trail may be booked at Pretoriuskop Rest Camp.
Mananga Trail may be booked at Satara Rest Camp.

How will I know where the trail starts and ends?

When you book for the trail, permits will be issued for the day you wish to drive on the trail, and maps will also be supplied. Any uncertainties may be cleared up at the points where you book the trail.

What time do I have to report for the trail?

You may set off on the trail at any time, but no later than 11h00 in order to ensure you return before gate closure.

Mountain-bike trail

How many bike trails are there in the Park?

There is only one mountain-bike trail at present, which is offered as either a morning or afternoon trail from Olifants Rest Camp.

Are more trails envisaged in future?

Depending on how popular it is, further trails may be considered.

How many participants are allowed on the trail?

There are two armed guides and six bikers on the trail.

Where does the trail take place?

The trail takes place in the vicinity of the Olifants Rest Camp.

Where and when does the trail depart?

As departure times vary according to season, please enquire at the reception office at Olifants Rest Camp about the departure time and the meeting place of your trail.

Do trailists depart from the rest camp by bike?

No. Trailists are transported by open vehicle, and the bikes on a trailer, to a starting point away from the normal tourist roads. From the departure point, trailists venture into the bush with their guides and return after the trail to be transported back to the rest camp.

Is it a full-day trail?

No. There are morning and afternoon trails, each lasting about three to five hours.

Does the Park supply the mountain bikes or do I have to bring my own?

The mountain bikes and safety headgear are supplied by the Park.

You are welcome to bring your own mountain bike and equipment, but proof of a recent service on the bike by an accredited bicycle shop must be supplied. You would then also be responsible for your own equipment such as puncture-repair kits, tools, spares, tubes and headgear.

Are there any special items I should bring with me on this trail?

Appropriate comfortable bush clothing (in neutral colours), insect repellent, sunblock, a bush hat, comfortable footwear, binoculars and camera and, where necessary, personal medication, will make your experience more enjoyable.

Do I have to bring any food along?

Not necessarily. The trail leader will provide snacks and fruit juice, but, if you have preferences, you are welcome to bring your own refreshments and snacks.

Are there any age restrictions for this activity?

Trailists should be between 16 and 65 years of age. Strictly no persons under the age of 16. Persons older than 65 years may participate if they produce a note from a doctor stating that they are sufficiently fit.

Do I have to be fit for this trail?

The trail is a long one but should not be seen as an endurance activity. However, a fair degree of fitness and skill will make this adventure more enjoyable.

Is it safe to go through the bush on a bike?

You will be accompanied by two armed, experienced and qualified guides to ensure your safety. It is imperative that you follow their instructions to ensure a safe and enjoyable experience.

What distance is covered on this trail?

The distance is about 21 km.

Will we be biking all the time?

No. There will be opportunities to leave the bikes and do short walks to viewpoints along the route. It is advisable to have comfortable walking shoes for the walks.

Are we likely to see much game during the walks?

Being in close proximity to the Lepelle River, you can expect to see a good variety of game as well as many bird species.

What happens in an emergency?

You are accompanied by skilled and trained guides who will be responsible for your safety. It is most important that you follow their instructions implicitly.

Prior to the trail, all safety drills and aspects regarding the trail will be communicated to you.

What about a medical emergency?

The guides carry a first-aid kit and a hand-held radio for communication with Olifants Rest Camp. Should it be necessary, trailists will be evacuated from the trail according to a pre-established medical emergency plan.

Do I have to sign an indemnity form for this trail?

As with all activities taking place in the bush of the Kruger National Park, you will be required to sign an indemnity form and hand it to your guide prior to departing on the trail.

How and where can I book for this trail?

Bookings may be made at Central Reservations 012 428 9111 or at Olifants Rest Camp 013 735 6606/7.

ANIMAL BEHAVIOURAL TRAITS

The following discussion and comments regarding behavioural traits common to most land mammals, especially most antelope, and to some extent other herbivores and carnivores, may serve to clarify some terminology used to describe animal behaviour that causes considerable speculation amongst wildlife enthusiasts and visitors to conservation areas.

Territories

Several animal species, at all levels of the taxonomic scale, exhibit territorial behaviour. This implies that a fixed area is claimed by a dominant animal (usually males, but occasionally also females) from which intraspecific contenders are barred. Territories are established to ensure territorial proprietors' access to females for reproductive purposes. This ensures that the prime males sire the offspring.

Territorial demarcation is achieved through scent-marking, dung deposits, urine, patrolling and posturing. Secretions from a number of glands are deposited on various objects, such as grass stalks, twigs and branches of shrubs and trees, and rocks, or transferred along footpaths as the animals walk. Important glands include the preorbital (in front of the eyes and obvious in many species) and interdigital (between the hooves) glands. Often the secretions may be seen as sticky and smelly blobs on the objects.

Many species, including rhino, augment scent-marking with strategically placed dung middens and urine spraying along regularly used patrol routes. In some species, notably roan and sable antelope and tsessebe, territorial males deposit small piles of droppings at regular intervals when they cross or walk on open ground, such as a road. Territorial males frequently undertake patrols along the borders of their territories and/or seek some high ground from where they make themselves visible to would-be contenders. This latter form of territorial advertising is referred to as 'static-optic marking'.

The ability of the territorial male to maintain his dominance is regularly tested by other males. These interactions take place in a highly ritualised fashion. This is to minimise injury and the possibility of death. Low-intensity interactions may be limited to posturing, during which dominant males make themselves as intimidating as possible. This is achieved by lifting the head, cocking the ears, holding the tail in different positions away from the body and raising the hair of the mane and/ or back, as is done by the nyala. Should the intensity of the contact increase, the two males will usually engage in a pushing duel, until the submissive animal finally gives way. The exit of the submissive animal may be accompanied by swipes of the horns by the dominant male, seldom with the intention of causing serious harm.

Home ranges

Home ranges are the areas frequented by herd members, i.e. the females and their offspring. In some species where the male establishes a territory, the home range of the breeding component of the species may be limited to the male's territory. However, in many species the home ranges of the females may overlap a number of territories. In such cases the territorial male will go to great lengths in trying to herd the breeding group back into his territory when they approach its boundary. The attempts by the male are often accompanied by displays and posturing, often to little avail.

Home ranges are the areas frequented by the breeding group and include the selection of optimal habitat, and the vital resources of reliable water and grazing. Home ranges are not defended, as is the case in territories, and freely overlap between adjoining breeding groups. They may also vary seasonally, depending on the availability of grazing and water. Where territories serve the function of genetic fitness, home ranges serve to ensure the best possible conditions to meet the needs of the herds. The most senior female usually takes the leadership role in guiding the herd to the most favourable areas, even on a daily basis.

Though home ranges are not rigidly fixed or defended they are remarkably constant, with herds occupying the areas of their range for several years. Even in the case of migratory species, i.e. those species that leave their winter and summer ranges in rhythmical fashion and over long distances, the concentrations habitually occupy the same areas according to the dictates of the season year after year. In the Park wildebeest and zebra are known to migrate over large distances, as do elands and elephants.

Unfortunately, these spectacular migrations have been severely disrupted by boundary fences, which sever established migration routes. Fortunately, however, the world-renowned migrations of the wildebeest and zebra populations of the Serengeti Plains in East Africa are still intact.

Social organisation and reproduction

SEPARATION OF SEXES AND SOCIAL INTERACTIONS

With very few exceptions, the breeding herds of the different species are comprised of a dominant herd male and a varying number of females and their offspring. Young are generally born with a sex ratio close to 1:1. This implies that at some stage young males are separated from the herds. This is usually achieved when the dominant herd male actively drives young males approaching sexual maturity from the herds. In most cases this is accompanied by ritualised displays between the herd male and the youngsters. Breaking the family ties does not come easily and can involve fierce chasing until the young male gets the message. This process may take several days.

When the young males are severed from the breeding herds they form all-male alliances, often referred to as 'bachelor' groups or herds. Within these bachelor groups a definite dominance hierarchy exists, from an alpha male to the most submissive member. The dominance hierarchy is established through the same ritualised displays and posturing as those displayed in territorial encounters, only at a lower intensity. Though dominance is primarily established on the basis of age, all members of the bachelor group contend for higher status, with a great deal of interaction taking place amongst the members of such a group.

The dominant member of the bachelor group will usually challenge established territorial males with the aim of ousting the incumbent from his territory. If successful, the challenger will take over the territory and the breeding herd while the evicted male will live a solitary existence. This will ensure that the best possible genetic material is perpetuated in the population.

COURTSHIP AND MATING

From the aforesaid it is clear that the interactions between individuals of a herd are governed by an array of rituals. Courtship behaviour is no exception. However, it is not just ritual displays that are involved, but also important signals that are transmitted through chemical compounds, in particular, compounds called pheromones. Pheromones are species-specific, i.e. signals that are conveyed are specific to a particular species, each species having its own signal.

Snakes constantly flick their tongues. This serves the function of smell. When the tongue flicks out it collects small particles, i.e. molecules, and when it is withdrawn, the tips of the forked tongue are inserted into two holes in the palate known as the Jacobson's Organ. From there the molecules are transferred to the brain, which translates the information for the snake. Through time this Jacobson's Organ evolved into the vomeronasal cavities of mammals. It is believed that this organ transfers the signals received from pheromones to the brain, which in turn, dictates the male's response as explained below.

As the female starts entering her oestrus cycle, the male will approach her from the rear and sniff her genital area. This stimulates the female to urinate, into which the male inserts his nose. He then lifts his head at an angle, pulls back his lips to expose his teeth, inhales deeply and appears as if he is grimacing. In this process, called *flehmen*, it is believed that the pheromones from the female's urine pass through the vomeronasal organ and send a signal informing the male at which stage of the oestrus cycle the female is.

Should the male get positive signals from *flehmen* he will approach the female and attempt to raise one of his front legs between the hind legs of the female in an action known as *laufschlag*.

As the female progresses further into her cycle, *flehmen* and *laufschlag* are repeated more frequently, with *laufschlag* becoming more intense. If the female is not ready to receive the male, she will move away. Once she is ready to mate she will stand firm and allow the male to mount.

RAISING THE YOUNG

There are two acknowledged ways in which the young are raised, i.e. *ablieger* and *nachfolge*. *Ablieger* calves are raised by concealing the calves for a period of time after birth. This period varies from one species to the next, which may be up to six weeks in the case of the roan antelope.

Young that are concealed after birth are normally weak and incapable of following their dams. During the period of concealment they lie up in some cover, such as clumps of tall grass, shrubs or something similar. Especially during the early stages they will not flee from danger but rather rely on 'freezing' to evade it. Nursing of the young is very sparing during the daytime, asually confined to early morning. For the rest of the day the mother joins the herd and does not actively protect her calf.

During the period of concealment the female stimulates the young to urinate and defecate by sniffing and licking the genitals. The mother then ingests the excretions. This behaviour is believed to minimise any telltale smells. All external glands are non-functional while the young are concealed, to achieve the same result.

Mothers do not actually conceal their young. Instead they lead the young close to shelter and then stand and watch as the calf walks away and suddenly drops into the cover. The mother then rejoins the herd in its normal activities.

Young of the '*Ablieger*'-type are seldom born in rigidly defined calving/lambing seasons, with births dispersed throughout most of the year. This also minimises the opportunities for predators to locate the young.

In the '*Nachfolge*'-type the precocious young are strong and agile within a few hours of birth. They are usually born in a well-defined season and follow their mothers almost from birth, for example impalas and wildebeest. Irrespective of how strong they may be, they are nevertheless vulnerable to predation at an early age, and the confined birth season aids survival by 'flooding the market' for a short while, after which the young become strong enough to avoid predators effectively.

CARNIVORES
In the aforementioned discussion the focus has been largely on herbivores, particularly antelope. However, these behavioural traits do not only apply to antelope, but, in slightly varying and disguised fashion, also to carnivores and the smaller species of mammals, e.g. mongooses, rodents, etc.

CHACMA BABOON *Papio ursinus orientalis* (Kerr 1792)

What is the distribution of baboons?

They are widely distributed in suitable areas throughout all the ecozones of the Kruger National Park. Savanna areas with tall trees and rocky outcrops are the preferred habitat. High densities are generally found along the major rivers, in particular, on the Luvuvhu and Limpopo flood plains.

How many baboons are there in the Park?

Although it is impossible to count these animals, it is estimated that there could be as many as about 300 troops. The number of individuals in a troop can vary between 10 and 100, with the average size of a troop in the Park ranging between 30 and 50. This means that the number of baboons in the Park may be in excess of 10 000.

What type of habitat do they prefer and what do they eat?

Baboons prefer open savanna with some large trees, ranging from sub-desert to light woodland, as well as riverine forests, rocky outcrops and montane country. They are seldom found in rainforests or open grasslands.

They are omnivorous and their diet includes a wide variety of roots, tubers, fruit and berries, and a large variety of invertebrates, eggs and small birds. Occasionally they will attack and kill newborn lambs of smaller antelope. This predation of young antelope, which may be due to a protein deficiency, usually occurs during droughts or towards the end of winter, when food is scarce. In spite of this, antelope generally show no fear of baboons.

What are their major physical features?

Baboons are medium-sized members of the order Primates. The males can attain a mass of 27 to 35 kg, which makes them twice the size of the females, which reach a mass of 15 to 20 kg. The colour varies from brownish-grey to dark brown or almost black. Adult males have a dark mane on the neck and shoulders. The hair is long and coarse, the ears are pointed and the muzzle long and broad. The tail is about equal to the body in length. The proximal section, or top third, of the tail is held upright, with the rest hanging down. In the males the canine teeth are considerably longer and sharper than in the females. There are callosities of thickened skin on the rump. In the males the callosities meet in the middle below the anus, while in the females they are widely separated. Should the male genitalia not be visible, males may be distinguished by their larger size, larger canine teeth and longer muzzles.

Why do some baboons show bright pink, swollen behinds?

When a female is sexually receptive the skin on her rump swells and turns bright pink. Maximum swelling occurs about five or six days after ovulation when she is ready for mating, and there is an increased chance of conceiving. At the start of the oestrus cycle the female will allow any male to mate with her, but at the time of actual ovulation she will mate only with a dominant male.

Do baboons always live in troops or do some of them live a solitary life?

Baboons are gregarious animals with strong social ties. They are very dependent on the protection afforded by numbers. Solitary animals are seldom encountered and could indicate sickness, injury or old age.

Do baboons have a specific leader and how is dominance established?

In a large troop there is more than one dominant male, but there is always a supreme leader. Smaller troops usually have a single dominant individual. Strict hierarchical order is maintained. Occasionally fierce fights for dominance or leadership occur, and maintaining or achieving dominance depends largely on bluff and intimidation, something at which baboons excel.

Often a dominant male will intimidate others by a show of bravado, which may include gaining higher ground, making his hair stand on end to make him appear bigger and stronger, and chasing lesser members of the troop around. This behaviour is usually accompanied by grunts and barks meant to frighten lesser members of the troop and potential rivals. Acts of intimidation also include running around barking and breaking branches off trees and shrubs.

All males outrank females.

Do males often kill each other in fights?

Mortalities would be extremely high if every confrontation led to a serious fight. Even in the event of a serious fight the loser can still save his skin by adopting a submissive posture. This he does by presenting his hindquarters to his victor, a gesture that is usually accepted. Threats from a superior can also be warded off in this manner, thus avoiding a physical encounter.

In baboons, as in most other animals, serious physical harm and mortalities are minimised through open, elaborate, ritualised posturing and displays. Although conflict may be diffused in this way, males do occasionally kill each other, in which case serious injuries may also be sustained by the victor.

Is there a dominance hierarchy amongst other members of the troop?

Dominance exists among other members of the troop. A female, accompanied by a dominant male during the few days that she is on heat, could dominate a more dominant rival female. Her male escort will intimidate other females that normally dominate her. A dominant female's offspring will try to intimidate another grown-up female as long as its mother is nearby.

A mother's dominance is based on her physical strength and self-confidence, and it will rub off on her offspring. The mother's confidence will encourage her young to act in a self-assured way. If she mates with a dominant male, her offspring could inherit dominating features. A mother low in the hierarchical order is usually more nervous and, because she often yields to others in the troop, her young may very well adopt the same submissive attitude.

Do baboons have sentries?

Large troops are usually widely scattered when feeding and moving through their area. During this activity individuals can be found on high perches. Baboons are naturally inquisitive and from time to time use these perches to survey the surrounding area. There is no indisputable proof of an organised system of sentries. Individuals are believed to act as sentries of their own accord. Communication through sounds and 'body language' is highly developed among baboons, and signs of possible danger are very effectively transmitted to the troop.

Are baboons territorial animals?

Each troop has its area and intruders are actively driven away. Troops often threaten each other on the boundaries between territories, but they seldom exchange blows. They hold their ground in extensive rituals of bluff or even chasing one another to and fro across territorial borders.

For instance, troop A crosses the boundary and chases troop B for some distance into troop B's territory. The deeper A penetrates into the opposition territory the more they lose confidence, while troop B gains in confidence and then reverses the chase. Territorial animals become bolder the nearer they get to the core of their territory.

Where do baboons sleep?
Baboons sleep at night in big trees, on rock ledges or, where available, in caves that are generally inaccessible to most other animals. This makes it difficult for their enemies to reach or surprise them in their sleeping places. Baboons are diurnal and normally do not move around at night.

Will baboons defend their young against predators or humans?
Given enough time and room to escape, they usually do so. They do not always take refuge in trees but often scamper along the ground screaming and barking in alarm or discontent. When cornered, or if a young baboon screams in alarm, the adult males will fiercely attack the cause of the alarm. Under these circumstances they are so dangerous that even predators are intimidated and will keep clear.

How strong is the connection between mother and child?
Baboon females are excellent mothers. During the initial few weeks a mother will not allow any other member of the troop even to touch her baby. Later she will allow other females to attend to her baby and other juveniles to play with it. Mothers are extremely devoted and will defend their young fiercely.

If an infant dies, the mother often carries the tiny corpse with her, sometimes for a week or more, despite its advanced state of decomposition.

Do baboons migrate?
Baboons do not migrate seasonally but according to the availability of food and water. They are very dependent on water, and normally live near permanent water where food is usually abundant, even in winter.

Are their senses well developed?
They have very keen binocular eyesight, good hearing and a fair sense of smell.

Do they have a specific breeding time?
There is no fixed breeding season but there appears to be a peak in births during the summer months, as with most animal species. This ensures that there will be sufficient food. A single baby is born after a gestation period of just more than six months. Twins are rare.

What is the life span of baboons and what are their major enemies?
Their life span in the wild is about 18 to 20 years. In captivity, ages of 40 years have been recorded.

Leopards are considered their major enemy but lions also kill a number of baboons. The sight of any of these big cats causes hysterical cries and barks. On retreating to safety, they will keep the enemy in sight for as long as possible until they pose no further threat to the troop.

Lesser enemies include larger eagles, pythons, poisonous snakes, crocodiles and occasionally caracals.

To what diseases are baboons susceptible?

Schistosoma or bilharzia has been recorded among the baboon populations of the Park.

There is also a high incidence of pleuritis and a pulmonary disease that is caused by mites entering the air passages and lungs.

In 40% of the adult population indications of arteriosclerosis of the aorta and the coronary arteries have been found.

A mild form of nephritis occurs and a number of baboons show minor kidney lesions caused by this disease. Tapeworms are found in a quarter of the baboon population, while other endoparasites including *Oesophagostomum* are found in more than 80% of the baboons in the Park.

A number of parasitic and probably also some viral diseases can be transmitted from baboons to humans – one of a few good reasons why these primates should be left alone.

What other members of the order Primates can be found in the Park?

Apart from chacma baboon the following primates are regularly recorded in the Park: vervet monkeys (*Chlorocebus pygerythrus*) are widely distributed throughout the Park, while samango monkeys (*Cercopithecus albogularis*) are occasionally found in the extreme northern section of the Park.

There are also two smaller primates. These are the nocturnal thick-tailed bushbaby (*Otolemur crassicaudatus*) and the small lesser bushbaby (*Galago moholi*).

Primates are not well represented in South Africa – probably due to the scarcity of rainforests. This is why the great apes, such as the gorilla (*Gorilla gorilla*) and the chimpanzee (*Pan troglodytes*), are altogether absent from this region.

VERVET MONKEY   *Chlorocebus pygerythrus* (F. Cuvier 1821)

What are the distribution and habitat of the vervet monkey?

It is distributed in suitable habitat in southern Africa and well represented in all the ecozones of the Park. Vervet monkeys are found in wooded or savanna country close to water, but riverine vegetation is their preferred habitat. They are more arboreal than baboons but are equally at home on the ground.

What are their major physical features?

Vervet monkeys are much smaller in build than baboons – males have a mass of about 5 kg and females slightly less. They are light grey in colour with relatively long tails, which are not prehensile like those of many of the New World monkeys.

Their faces are black and framed by an almost white line of fur, which makes them look like old men.

The exhibiting of a vivid blue scrotum and red penis is an important sexual manifestation in the male. He also displays his scrotum by parading around with the tail held high. A female on heat will display her swollen genitalia.

What is their general behaviour?

As in the case of baboons, they are sociable and gregarious, and with a similar dominance hierarchy. Troop sizes are smaller, consisting of 15 to 25 individuals. It is believed that old males are chased from the troop and live the rest of their lives alone.

Vervet monkeys are very cunning. In the Kruger Park they are commonly seen at picnic spots where they quickly make off with visitors' food. They have learnt to associate humans with food because visitors feed them; unfortunately they may become aggressive and attack people to get at their food, and from time to time the monkeys have to be shot at these picnic spots.

Vervet monkeys show territorial behaviour and are not inclined to vacate their territories. Depending on the availability of food, territories vary in size between 0.1 and 1 km².

How do they communicate and are they aggressive?

Mutual grooming forms a very important part of the social structure of a troop. Many vocalisations have been recorded, with contact calls including chirps, grunts, chatters and barks. Alarm calls include low, loud barks and screams. Different threats result in different calls, such as a high-pitched chatter when encountering a snake, a short, tonal call for a leopard and staccato grunts when observing raptors.

Aggression is shown by looping the tail over the body, threat is displayed with a direct stare and a greater threat is shown by raising the eyebrows to reveal the contrasting pink of the eyelids. Other threatening displays include an open-mouthed gape, shaking of branches, jumping up and down, slapping the ground or bobbing the head up and down.

Dominant males sometimes intimidate subordinates by holding the tail erect to display the blue scrotum, red perianal region and white fur between the scrotum and perianal region, a display known as the 'red, white and blue' display.

What do they eat?

They have an omnivorous diet consisting of seeds, berries, fruit and other vegetable matter, eggs, nestling birds and invertebrates. When fed in the vicinity

of picnic spots or rest camps, they can become a nuisance and aggressive and a danger to humans.

Are they intelligent?

They are very intelligent and cunning, but highly strung and quite nervous by nature. They are easy to tame but this is a dangerous practice because they become treacherous and aggressive when mature. They should not be kept as pets. A special permit, which is not readily issued, is needed to keep them in captivity, a practice that is not recommended at all.

What is the gestation period and life span?

After a gestation period of about seven months a single baby, very seldom twins, is born. Babies are born throughout the year, with a peak in summer. In nature the life span is about 15 years, but in captivity an age of 24 has been recorded.

What are their enemies?

Leopards and smaller members of the feline family are the main predators of Vervet Monkeys. Eagles, particularly the Crowned Eagle (*Stephanoaetus coronatus*), and pythons also take their toll.

Vervet Monkeys are often alerted to the presence of leopards by baboons, who become almost hysterical when they have spotted one and will follow the prowling leopard, screeching and barking at it from the trees. Leopards probably kill quite a number of monkeys as they sleep huddled together in large trees.

When an eagle is spotted, its presence is signalled from the tops of trees by screeching and barking.

Are there any samango monkeys in the Park?

Samango monkeys (*Cercopithecus albogularis*) are not permanent residents in the Kruger Park although they do occasionally enter the Pafuri area in the far northern part of the Park during exceptionally wet years. They are found in groups of up to 30 individuals along the banks of the Luvuvhu River.

How do they differ from vervet monkeys?

Samango monkeys (males about 9 kg, females about 4.5 kg) are slightly larger than vervet monkeys, with longer, darker hair cover, brown-black limbs and tail, and a darker face compared with the vervet monkey's white-fringed facial features. Samangos and vervets seldom share the same habitat, with samangos being less destructive in their feeding habits – they feed more selectively, without destroying the vegetation.

Samangos are omnivorous and feed on wild fruits, leaves, sprouts and buds, flowers, gum, insects, small birds and bird eggs. They are very water dependent.

THICK-TAILED BUSHBABY   *Otolemur crassicaudatus*
(Geoffroy 1812)

What is the distribution of the thick-tailed bushbaby?

It occurs sparsely in densely forested areas of ecozones B, C, D, F, M and N of the Kruger Park. It favours trees with very sparse grass around them. It is well represented in the extreme northern part of the Park and also found in the Skukuza, Pretoriuskop and forested areas of the Malelane Mountain Bushveld.

What are its major physical features?

The body and bushy tail are covered in a woolly coat of long, thick, soft hair. The upper parts are grey-brown to brown with paler underparts. There are dark rings around the eyes and the dark grey ears are naked. Flattened discs of soft, thickened skin cover the tips of all the digits and hand palms. Each digit has a nail, except the second digits on the feet, which are equipped with a claw.

Male and female animals have the same head-and-body length: 27–47 cm. The bushy tail is longer than the body and in both sexes ranges from 35 to 45 cm. Males have a mass of 0.9 to 1.6 kg and females 0.9–1.45 kg.

The head can be rotated almost 180 degrees.

What is their general behaviour?

They are nocturnal animals, with an activity peak in the first two hours after sunset. These little animals are very agile, jumping from branch to branch with the greatest of ease. They can leap as far as 2.5 m and as high as 2 m in a single jump. When on the ground they move along on all fours, with the tail held high, or they jump about on their hind legs.

Thick-tailed bushbabies sleep in dense vegetation in broad-leaved nests, forks of trees, hollows in trees and also in abandoned birds' nests. Much time is spent on mutual grooming prior to setting off to forage.

They are arboreal and vulnerable to predation when on the ground.

Thick-tailed bushbabies are semi-gregarious and form stable groups of two to six individuals, both male and female. They rest together during the day and usually forage alone at night along reasonably fixed routes.

Are they territorial and do they actively defend their territory?

Both sexes are territorial and usually forage alone. Males hold territories of about 0.2 km² and females about 0.07 km². The range of a male's territory may cross those of several females. Territories of neighbouring males do not overlap, but during the non-breeding season subordinate and juvenile males will be tolerated in the dominant male's territory. Female home ranges generally overlap, with females tending to remain within their home range. Males are likely to move annually.

It has been observed that thick-tailed bushbabies, both male and female, will actively defend their territory by tackling each other with their fists and vicious bites. Their fights often end in death to one of the animals.

They show aggression towards any intruder or any form of danger by cocking their ears, staring with wide eyes, open-mouthed baring of the teeth and growling and spitting. They may also rear up on their hind legs with raised hands, ready to grab and bite.

Do they demarcate their territory?

Both sexes mark their territories by leaning their bodies to one side and urinating over their feet, leaning to the other side and repeating the process. This process is known as urine washing. A urine scent trail is thus left by the dominant male as he moves through his territory.

In addition, territories are also marked by secretions from cheek, lip and perianal glands, and also a yellowish, oily secretion from the chest glands.

How do they communicate?

Usually quiet little animals, they vocalise by making various sounds, depending on a specific situation. Long, hard and mournful screams, similar to the cries of a baby, are uttered, hence the common name. These calls could possibly be connected with territorial communication.

Contact calls consist of squeaks, clicks, croaks and barks. Alarm calls could include squeaks, shrill whistles, chatters, chirps, yaps and yells. Alarm signals include a grating sound produced by scraping the horny combs on the outer edges of the feet against surfaces.

What is their gestation period and life span?

Breeding takes place during the summer months, i.e. the rainy season. After a gestation period of about 18 weeks, between one and three babies are born.

The babies are weaned and fully able to take care of themselves after about three months. The life span of thick-tailed bushbabies is approximately four years.

What do they eat?

They are omnivorous and feed mainly on fruits, flowers, seeds, gum, insects, small birds, small reptiles and eggs. They are not dependent on water as they obtain enough moisture from their food intake.

What are their enemies?

Thick-tailed bushbabies' main predators include large owls, snakes (especially Southern African python), genets, civets and African wild cats.

LESSER BUSHBABY *Galago moholi* (A. Smith 1836)

What is the distribution of the lesser bushbaby?

It is widely distributed throughout the Park in ecozones A, D, E, G, H, J, K, L, N and O, especially in woodland and woodland savanna areas, and in particular knobthorn acacia (*Acacia nigrescens*) communities. It is found in abundance in the area west of Tshokwane, in the Skukuza area, along the Sabie River and towards Crocodile Bridge Rest Camp.

What are its main physical features?

Lesser bushbabies are covered in a thick, soft, long furry coat. The upper parts are grey to grey-brown and the underparts much paler. The tail, which is bushy and darker than the general body colour, is about twice the body length (about 37 cm) in both sexes. Dark rings around the eyes and a white nose stripe are very characteristic. The hands and feet are similar to those of the thick-tailed bushbaby. Lesser bushbabies are excellent jumpers and can attain distances of 5 to 7 m in a single leap.

Body mass for the male ranges between 150 and 230 g and for the female between 150 and 180 g. The head can be rotated almost 180 degrees.

What is their general behaviour?

In all aspects, their behaviour is similar to that of the thick-tailed bushbaby.

Their territorial behaviour and demarcation of territory is similar to that of the thick-tailed bushbaby. The territories of the lesser bushbaby are, however, slightly smaller.

Even their communication is similar, except that they do not utter the long, hard, mournful scream, and may mob attack when threatened.

What is their gestation period and life span?

Lesser bushbabies breed twice a year – at the beginning and end of the summer rainy season. After a gestation period of four months, two infants are usually born. They are weaned after two to three months and will then follow the mother around and start to eat solid food. Their life span is about two years.

What do they eat?

They are omnivorous but are very partial to the gum of trees, especially *Acacia* trees. They also eat insects, fruits, seeds, flowers and eggs. They are known to eat only the heads of small birds. Because they obtain sufficient moisture from their food, they are considered water independent.

LION
Panthera leo (Linnaeus 1758)

What is the distribution of lions in the Park?

They are found in all the ecozones of the Park, but more commonly seen in the southern half of the Park. They are particularly common in the eastern parts of the central and southern districts in the Satara, Tshokwane, Lower Sabie and Crocodile Bridge areas.

As lions are carnivores, the density is determined by the density of their prey species.

Are they well distributed throughout Africa?

Lions are becoming less common throughout the savanna areas of Africa, and are mostly confined to conservation areas. In South Africa, outside of the Kruger National Park, they are found in a number of private game reserves on the western boundary of the Park and in the Kgalagadi Transfrontier Park. They have been introduced to various other national parks and provincial game reserves, conservancies and private game farms and lodges.

How large is the average pride?

The size and composition of prides and even groups can change from day to day. A lion pride is not a cohesive unit in the sense that members are together all the time. Members, or even small sub-groups of the pride, may be widely scattered.

Pride sizes are normally measured by the number of females in the pride, as males are nomadic and do not form permanent members of the pride. The ratio of adult females to males is usually two to one, but a pride studied in the Sweni area, southeast of Satara Rest Camp, achieved a size of 42 animals for a while, which consisted of two adult males, 10 adult females, one sub-adult male and 29 cubs.

Females usually remain in the natal pride, while males leave the pride at between two and four years of age, with litter mates tending to form lifelong coalitions.

What are their main physical features?

The lion is a massive cat, the biggest of the African carnivores. Its coat is short and pale tawny to sandy-brown in colour with paler underparts. The ears are black on the outside, as is the tasselled tip of the long tail. Cubs are faintly spotted. So-called 'white' lions are very pale buff genetic variants.

The manes of adult males vary in colour from tawny to black, and in size from a slight ruff around the neck to a luxuriant growth framing the face, covering the head between the ears and neck, shoulders and chest and extending as a fringe below the belly. The mane darkens and becomes black as the male ages.

The head is large with a strong, heavy muzzle. The pattern of spots at the roots of the whiskers is unique and can be used for identifying individuals.

Shoulder height of males is up to 1.2 m and in females about 90 cm, with males having a mass between 190 and 225 kg and females 130 to 150 kg.

Were lions ever found on continents other than Africa?

At one time lions occurred in Europe and the Middle East. They became extinct in Israel in the 13th century, in Pakistan in the early 1840s, in Iraq in about 1914 and in Iran in 1941. They were once widespread in India, but the last remaining lions are the endangered group of less than 200 animals found in the Gir Forest National Park and Wildlife Sanctuary in the state of Gujarat.

When is the best time for spotting lion?
During the summer months it is advisable to do early-morning and late-afternoon drives as lions prefer to spend the hot parts of the day in shade or dense vegetation, making it difficult to spot them. They are seen more readily during the day in the cooler winter months. Being mainly nocturnal, they are often seen on night drives.

Do lions move around during the day?
Although lions are inactive when not on the hunt, they can nevertheless walk up to 20 km a day when necessary.

Do lions hide during rainy weather?
They tend to hide in thickets, often sitting in a hunched position with their backs in the direction from which the rain is coming.

Which habitat do they prefer?
They favour open woodland, open grassland savanna and thick bush and scrub. They tend to avoid true desert and rainforest. In the Park they occur mainly in the central plains where there is an abundance of prey species.

What are the preferred prey species of lion?
Lions generally favour medium to large prey such as zebras, wildebeest, African buffalo and giraffe. They prey on at least 37 species of large and small mammal, ranging in size from hippos, young elephants and giraffes, down to impalas, warthogs, ostrich, small crocodiles and even mice and tortoises. They sometimes kill other carnivores but rarely eat them.

In the Park they tend to prey more upon zebras and wildebeest in wet spells and upon buffalo and waterbuck during dry spells.

A kill does not necessarily signify a lion's preference, but may rather be as a result of the availability and vulnerability of the prey. Preference ratings differ from one area to another and even within the same area at different times. The rating is calculated by dividing the kill frequency by the relative abundance of the prey. On this basis it was found that waterbuck appear to be the preferred prey of lions. In proportion to the numbers of waterbuck in the Park, therefore, lions kill more waterbuck than any other prey. On the other hand, if the actual numbers of animals killed are considered, wildebeest, zebras and impalas actually feature more prominently than waterbuck.

Considering the biomass of prey killed, larger animals would provide the largest biomass, especially African buffalo and giraffes, followed by wildebeest, zebras, impalas, kudu and waterbuck.

Lions frequently scavenge.

Do lions prefer large prey to smaller animals?
They show a definite preference for larger prey.

Do lions kill only when they are hungry?
Lions are opportunistic predators and will attempt to kill whenever the opportunity presents itself. Although they kill only to sustain themselves, they do occasionally kill much more than they can consume. This usually happens when the prey animals are in a weak and emaciated condition and unable to escape or offer resistance.

On some occasions during droughts, when prey animals concentrate in large numbers around the last remaining water holes, lions, particularly young individuals, have been seen to kill several head of prey in a herd.

During the severe drought of 1996, a pride of lions killed five adult and 10 young African buffalo from a starving herd in one locality near Punda Maria. Similarly, near Lower Sabie a pride of lions killed six buffalo from a herd.

Is it true that herbivores know whether a lion is hungry or not?

It is highly improbable. Herbivores are not concerned about lions when they are visible and at a safe distance. They show concern only when they smell or hear a lion without being able to locate it, or when a lion is obviously trying to stalk them.

Do lions eat carrion?

Lions normally kill to eat, but when prey is scarce or conditions for hunting are unfavourable they will not hesitate to eat putrid meat.

Do lions scavenge?

In addition to killing their own prey, lions will readily scavenge food from other predators such as leopards, cheetahs, African wild dog and hyaenas.

How often do lions kill?

This depends on the size of their last prey, the size of the pride and on the availability of suitable prey. They feed about every three to four days, but can go without food for up to a week.

A study conducted in the Lower Sabie area showed that the study pride killed only a zebra foal during the full period of observation, which lasted 24 hours a day for 14 days.

How much meat can a lion consume at one meal?

Average daily consumption for a male is about 7 kg and for a female about 4.5 kg. Lions can consume about 15 to 20% of their body weight when emaciated, which in the case of a large male could be as much as 35 to 40 kg.

How many animals does a lion kill per year?

It depends on the size of available prey and the size, age and physical condition of the lion. The killing rate of an individual lion in the Park is about 15 animals per year. Estimates by different authors in different areas vary between 10 and 70 animals killed by one adult lion per year.

What are the biggest animals attacked by lion?

Normally giraffes will be the largest prey attacked by lions. Cases have been reported of lions successfully attacking weakened and old hippos on dry land as well as diseased and disabled rhinos.

Healthy, adult hippos or rhinos are more than a match for a lion, or even a pride of lions, and are therefore seldom attacked.

Do lions attack elephants?

Elephant calves have occasionally been attacked by lions when no adults were present. However, a fully grown elephant is more than a match for any pride of lions.

It has been reported from Botswana that elephants up to 15 years old have been killed by lions. The possibility of elephants of this age being handicapped in one way or another should not be excluded.

Are lions sometimes injured by their prey?

There are records of lions that have been killed by sable antelope, kudu, African buffalo, giraffes, snakes and even porcupines. When a lion attempts to kill a porcupine, quills may become lodged in its mouth or paws, causing eventual death from infection or starvation.

Can a single lion kill a large animal such as a giraffe or African buffalo?

Although solitary lions are occasionally successful in attacking adult giraffes or buffaloes, these large species are normally hunted by a number of lions at a time.

How do lions kill their prey?

The method of killing varies with the species and size of the prey. Small animals are usually swatted down and then grabbed with both paws. The killing bite is directed at the back of the neck, throat, head or even the chest.

Animals such as wildebeest, zebras and African buffalo are often killed by suffocation, the lion clamping its jaws over the mouth and nostrils of the prey. Frequently, prey is held down by the pride, which starts feeding before the prey is dead. This quickly leads to the death of the prey animal.

Many authors have indicated that prey animals are killed by breaking the neck. However, it is interesting to note that in several hundred kills examined by George Schaller, an authority on lions, he could not find a single instance in which the prey's neck was broken.

A lion is generally unable to run as fast as its prey, but when it charges unexpectedly, and the prey is still accelerating, it can come up from behind or even run alongside before attacking.

Do lions attack their prey from the front?

Prey is seldom attacked from the front because many prey species carry very effective horns and also because an animal is usually in flight when the lions attack.

Do lions kill their prey quickly?

Small prey probably succumbs quickly, but larger prey often dies from strangulation, suffocation or loss of blood, processes which can last some time.

A buffalo bull can sometimes ward off a lion attack for an hour or longer before the lions manage to get hold of a vulnerable part of its body. As one lion attacks the throat, the others usually start to tear the animal apart resulting in death through loss of blood rather than through strangulation or suffocation.

Where is one most likely to see a kill?

Most kills are made near a water hole, especially during times of drought.

When do lions hunt?

Although they tend to hunt during the night, a great deal of hunting also takes place during the cooler part of the day.

Do the females do most of the hunting?

In prides where both sexes are present, females kill proportionally more than the males. However, single males and male groups do kill their own prey.

When a large animal is attacked by a pride of both sexes, the greater mass and superior strength of the males gives them superiority over the females.

Do lions use a specific strategy when they hunt?

Lions hunt as a group and, according to various authors, they use a variety of strategies to catch their prey.

Some people believe that the males take up a position from where they can induce the intended prey to run in the direction of the hiding females, who stalk downwind to get into position. The males move upwind in a semicircle into a position where the prey will get their scent, causing the prey to flee downwind in the direction of the waiting females.

If one is lucky enough to observe the hunt from start to finish, the above strategy appears to be used most often. However, some authors doubt the existence of co-operative hunting and assume that each member of the pride goes its own way to catch and kill a victim. One should be careful not to apply human reasoning to the actions of animals.

Schaller points out that, when several lions spot potential prey, they usually fan out and stalk them over a broad front. This fanning action may be well co-ordinated in that those on the flanks will move rapidly while those in the centre will stop or advance slowly. They are thus encircling their intended prey, enhancing their chances of a kill. On spotting the predators, the prey scatter in all directions and in the process some could head in the direction of the hidden members of the pride.

Do lions normally hunt in groups?
One lion or even the whole pride may attack the intended prey. Single lions, however, account for about half of all the kills in the Park.

How far can a lion chase its prey?
When stalking, a lion will approach to within about 30 m of its prey before charging. A lion has little stamina and is exhausted after running more than 200 m. Almost 90% of hunts consist of stalks followed by a short run. In the remaining 10% the prey is ambushed.

Do lions often become man-eaters?
Although people have been attacked and killed and often devoured by lions, man-eating has never posed a serious problem in the Park. A number of people fleeing the civil war in Mozambique during the 1970s and 1980s, and crossing through the Park, were killed by lions, but these were not normal circumstances. It is considered that, once a lion kills a human, the lion loses its instinctive fear of humans and may kill a human again should the opportunity arise.

Does a lion necessarily become a man-eater after only one attack on a human?
Not necessarily so, although it may (refer to the previous answer).

What causes a lion to become a man-eater?
It is often claimed that the main culprits are old or incapacitated lions. This, however, is not always the case. Many a man-eater has proved to be a healthy animal in its prime.

Most man-eaters probably started including human flesh in their diet after an accidental encounter with a human, losing their fear of humans and finding it easier to kill in future encounters.

Do lions kill other predators?
They seldom kill other predators for food, but hyaenas or jackals that approach too close to a feeding pride risk being killed by the lion. African wild dogs, cheetahs and leopards are killed by lions in the Park but are seldom consumed.

Could vultures lead lions to a dead animal?
Lions are vulture watchers: vultures find carcasses from the air. Hyaenas and even jackals also follow them to the potential food source.

Are lions cannibalistic?

Lions are confirmed cannibals and the urge is not necessarily caused by hunger. Reproduction – the need to sire their own offspring – leads them to commit infanticide to get the lionesses into a state of oestrus quickly. Although cases of cannibalism have been recorded, they make up a minute percentage of lion kills.

Males frequently kill cubs when they take over a pride, and have been known to eat them.

Why do male lions kill cubs that are not their own?

If the new males kill the cubs the female comes into oestrus very soon, which allows the male to sire and raise his own cubs in the pride.

Does a lion necessarily become a habitual cannibal after one such act?

No, not necessarily, and if it should happen it would be a rare phenomenon.

Do all males possess a mane?

Maneless lions are exceptional, but the sizes of manes do differ. The mane starts growing when the lion is about six months old.

Why do some males have black manes?

The mane usually becomes darker with age, but inherited pigmentation also plays a role.

What speed can a lion reach when charging?

A lion is deceptively fast over a short distance. Claims of up to 80 km/h have been made but not yet proven – this seems rather fast for an animal the size of a lion with its relatively short legs and bulky body. Shorter sprints of 40 to 60 km/h would be more realistic.

Can lions climb trees?

Yes, but this does not happen very often. They are surprisingly agile in this respect, especially females. Lions can climb trees far better than humans.

Are their senses well developed?

Their sense of smell is good and their senses of hearing and sight, especially their night vision, are excellent.

Can the females roar?

Males and females roar very similarly, but the male roar is somewhat deeper in tone and louder than that of the female. It is nevertheless difficult to judge the sex of a lion roaring in the distance.

How far can a lion's roar be heard?

In studies in the Kruger Park roars could be heard up to 4.5 km away, but the actual distance depends on the individual roaring as well as factors such as denseness of vegetation, wind force and direction and even the air humidity.

At what age do lions start to roar?

Cubs start to imitate the sounds their parents make at the age of about one month, but a full roar is achieved only once they reach adulthood at 5–6 years.

Do lions have a repertoire of different calls?

Lions are capable of an impressive variety of sounds, such as moans, grunts, snarls, growls and roars, as well as purring. Cubs can make mewing sounds and can also purr. Lionesses usually grunt when calling their cubs.

What is the purpose of roaring and when do lions roar?

Apart from communicating with other members of the pride, which may be spread over a large area, roaring is a way to advertise a lion's presence and location, and to warn other lions that the area is occupied.

Lions roar in different situations. They often appear to roar spontaneously, but they may in fact be replying to a distant call. Lions tend to roar more often during the night than during the day.

Roaring is more common on still, quiet nights, seldom occurring during windy or rainy conditions.

Do lions communicate well?

They use an impressive array of facial expressions, body movements and sounds to communicate, expressing affection, aggression, irritation, contentment, etc.

Is there a way that one lion or lioness could avoid aggression from another?

Rubbing or 'greeting' serves as a safety measure to avoid fights. A lion can avoid aggression from a stronger opponent by showing submission in rolling onto his back, exposing the throat.

What are the signs of aggression?

Aggression is shown by staring at the intruder, crouching with the head held low, forelegs set wide apart and ears pinned back and twisted to show the black at the back of the ears. A great display of aggression is an open-mouthed gape with teeth bared. The tail whips from side to side, and growls or coughs indicate that an attack is imminent.

Can lions swim?

Although they do not readily take to water, they can swim and it is not uncommon for them to cross a river. Tourists have reported watching two females swim across the Sabie River to join a male on the other side.

Are lions territorial?

Lions vigorously defend their territories against intruders. Females established in a pride will usually spend their entire lives in such territories. Males come and go as they gain tenure of the pride or are evicted by a superior coalition of males.

Each pride confines itself to a definite area, the main prerequisites for which are water and sufficient prey throughout the year.

Nomadic lions wander widely, in small prides of about three, but also single males, often following the movements of game. Resident lions remain in an area for a year or longer, or even their entire life. The latter show a high degree of territorial marking.

Do lions' home ranges overlap?

Home ranges often overlap, but activity zones or focuses of activity seldom do. Very often two prides in an area will deliberately avoid each other to prevent a confrontation, and direct confrontation is remarkably infrequent, as are actual fights between members of different prides.

What is the size of a home range?

Home ranges depend on the size of the pride and the availability of prey and water. They can be as small as 20 to 30 km^2 or as large as a few hundred square kilometres. Pride movements are more frequent during the wet season. In winter, when it is dry, they are compelled to concentrate near the permanent watercourses.

How do male lions mark their territories?

Spraying of urine is a common way of marking but they also scrape the soil with their paws and scratch tree trunks.

How big is the territory?

Again it depends on the size of the pride or group and the density of prey species, as well as the population density of lions in the area in general. In winter it could be a few hundred metres around a water hole. After the rains, when the game is spread out, the territory could cover many square kilometres.

Do females become solitary?

Yes, they do, but not as often as males. Old females are sometimes driven from the pride.

Do lions have a social hierarchy?

While males tend to be dominant over females at kills, there is no dominance hierarchy among males or females.

After a kill, males take the food they want from the females, and cubs get what the adults leave. In times of food shortage, starvation is the major cause of cub mortalities.

Are males the leaders of the pride?

There appears to be no consistent leader in a lion pride and either a male or a female can take the lead. Pride females often act independently of males.

Is the lack of a constant leader not detrimental to the pride?

A rigid leadership system would probably be of little advantage to a lion pride because it could prohibit the pride from adjusting to various prey conditions. It could even lead to a lack of initiative during hunting. A large male coalition usually leads to a longer tenure, reducing the number of cubs lost to infanticide at take-overs. Females have little choice when it comes to which males hold the pride tenure.

Are young adults expelled from the pride?

There is no hard-and-fast rule. One or more of the dominant males may drive off a young male, but young females are tolerated provided the pride is not too numerous for the available prey. Young males and females may leave the pride of their own accord. When a pride becomes too large, one or more female groups with one or more males may break away to form a new pride that in turn will have to establish its own home range. Female groups may also be taken over by nomadic males.

Another interesting phenomenon is that one or more males may hold tenure over two distinct prides of females.

When do young lions become independent?

The majority of young lions become independent at 2.5 to 3.5 years of age. In general, when the cubs are 17 to 18 months old the mother ceases to lead them to kills or to care for them in any way.

Does a pride of lions accept a stranger?

Pride males will readily accept a strange female when she is on heat. A pride of females will also tolerate strange males when a female is in oestrus. These male outsiders are seldom accepted as permanent members of the pride.

Do males often fight over females or in territorial disputes?

High-intensity fights are not as common as one would imagine. Males do not dispute the possession of a female. Many of the encounters that do take place consist of a few slaps accompanied by much vocalisation and baring of teeth. Determined biting and fights in which one of the combatants is killed are very rare.

Lions also have great recuperative powers and even large wounds tend to heal well. Each lion in a group or in a pride usually knows and responds to the fighting potential of every other member. Even when a stranger is driven out of the pride's area, the pursuer usually maintains a certain distance and adjusts his speed to that of the intruder.

Are males more aggressive than females?

Aggression between pride members is very rare except when competing for food at a kill. A female could in fact be more dangerous than a male, as females with cubs are extremely dangerous and intolerant of anything that could endanger the cubs.

Do males and females sometimes fight each other?

Usually not, because males are dominant over females. However, two or more females will attack a male if he harasses them or endangers their cubs and may even put him to flight. A female with cubs may also attack a male and although he could resist her attack he usually refrains.

Do males sometimes intimidate females?

Males often deprive females of a kill. Irrespective of who made the kill, the strongest male usually secures the best for himself. If the prey carcass is small he may take it over entirely, but if the prey is big and he is not too hungry he will allow other members of the pride to feed with him.

Do the females secure food for their cubs?

Apparently not. During the first three to four weeks the cubs suckle, which is gradually supplemented with meat. As soon as the cubs can walk properly the mother leads them to kills. When a lioness is very hungry, however, she will prevent the cubs from feeding until she has had her fill, and it is not uncommon for a female to take food from her cubs.

What are their breeding habits?

Cubs are born all year round, with females in the same pride often synchronising births. In the Park the breeding peak seems to be from March to July.

After a gestation period of about 3.5 months, an average of two to four cubs weighing about 1.5 kg each are born and concealed in dense cover.

Cubs are born blind but their eyes open after three to 10 days. They walk within two weeks and are introduced to the pride at six to eight weeks, or later if there are older cubs in the pride. Weaning starts at 10 weeks and is completed within six months.

How often do females produce cubs?

Lions have a high reproductive potential. Females are polyoestrus and are cyclic throughout the year. Should a female lose her litter in some way, she will mate again within a few days to a few weeks. She can then give birth to another litter within three months.

Under normal circumstances the birth interval is usually 24 months.

What is the size of the average litter?

The number can range from one to six, but two to four cubs seem to be the average.

At what age are lions sexually mature?

Females become sexually mature at about three years of age and can therefore give birth to their first litter at about 3.5 years of age. Males take a few months longer to reach sexual maturity, but breed only once they become pride males at about five years old.

Do lionesses breed throughout their adult life?

Lionesses probably reach the limit of their breeding capability at about 11 or 12 years of age. It is not impossible for females to conceive into old age.

What is the normal life span of a lion?

In captivity ages around 20 years have been recorded. In the wild they probably reach an age of 13 to 15 years.

Is cub mortality high?

Cubs are subjected to a variety of mortality factors, and only about half of all cubs grow to adulthood. Of those that die before adulthood, about a quarter are killed by adult lions or other predators. Cubs must compete with the rest of the pride members for food at a kill. In times of food scarcity, many cubs die of starvation. Lionesses sometimes abandon their cubs for unknown reasons, and starving cubs too weak to walk are usually left to their fate. Cubs that become separated from their mother usually either starve to death or fall prey to other predators.

Diseases and parasites take their toll, and bush fires, snakes and even ants attacking newborn cubs can account for a number of mortalities.

Will a lioness allow cubs other than her own to suckle?
Lactating females permit small cubs of any litter to suckle from them with no discrimination. Cubs of different ages may be seen suckling together from the same female.

How long do cubs suckle?
Cubs suckle from any lactating female in the pride. Weaning starts at 10 weeks and is typically completed within six months. Females can lactate for up to eight months after giving birth, but cubs of up to 12 months old have been seen suckling.

Does the lioness conceal her cubs when she goes hunting?
She does, in dense vegetation, under logs, in holes in the ground, and the cubs are so well concealed that the chance of detection by other predators is limited. They even crawl into crevices and keep quiet to remain undetected.

Do lions have 'babysitters'?
In a study in East Africa, little evidence was found to support claims that 'babysitters' guard the cubs of a hunting lioness. However, it is quite normal for any female near cubs to function as a guard. The cubs themselves will seek and get protection from another female in the absence of their own mother.

Is it true that lions usually mate over a two- to three-day period?
A mating pair usually leaves the pride for between one and three days. They often go without food during this period, but may join the pride temporarily when a kill is made.

At the beginning of the mating period, intervals between copulations could be about every 20 minutes but may become longer towards the end of the period. The lion's virility is amazing. A case has been reported of a mating pair that copulated 157 times in 55 hours, or once every 21 minutes. This male did not eat for three days and it is not known whether lack of appetite or lack of time, or both, was the reason!

Are mating lions dangerous?
They are aggressive during this time and should be given a wide berth.

Does the male or the female initiate copulation?
Although either the male or the female can initiate copulation, it is by far more often the female that does.

Do lions have enemies?
Apart from man and other lions, adult lions do not have natural enemies that would attack them. It has been reported that hyaenas and occasionally African wild dogs have killed old and severely incapacitated lions. Quite a number of cubs that are concealed while adult females are hunting are probably killed by hyaenas, African wild dogs and jackals. elephants and buffalo have been known to kill lions in confrontations that are usually initiated by the lion.

Can a crocodile kill a lion?
Large crocodiles can and do kill lions occasionally, but small crocodiles in turn are sometimes killed by lions.

What are the normal causes of death in lions?
Most lions die from diseases, starvation or old age, or as a result of violent attacks from their own species. Old lions are sometimes killed by groups of hyaenas.

Lions host a number of endoparasites such as *Babesia*, a blood parasite that causes anaemia in cubs, tapeworms such as *Taenia gonyamai*, and trypanosomes. Mange, caused by a mite, *Sarcoptes scabiei*, also accounts for some deaths.

Although parasites could kill them, healthy animals are usually capable of living with quite a heavy infestation. After all, parasites would become extinct if they killed all their hosts by overtaxing them.

Although bovine tuberculosis has been present in the Park since about the 1950s, it became a real problem during the 1990s, as lions killed and consumed tuberculosis-infected prey, such as African buffalo. Tuberculosis may be responsible for severe loss of condition and may eventually lead to the death of the lion.

Outbreaks of the bacterial disease anthrax are also a mortality factor.

Is there more than one subspecies of lion?

Some taxonomists regard the extinct Cape lion, the Kalahari lion and the Kruger Park lion as three different subspecies. In fact, as many as 21 subspecies have been described. Other authorities, however, regard all lions as members of one species.

The Cape lion apparently had a more prolific mane than those from the Kalahari and the Lowveld, while those from the Kalahari tend to be lighter in colour than their counterparts from the Kruger Park. It is a well-known fact that animals of the same species or subspecies can, for instance, develop more fur when translocated to a colder climate, while their colour could become lighter when they move to drier and hotter areas. One should therefore be careful not to use these changed features to describe a new subspecies.

The Kalahari lion usually has a larger mane than the Kruger lion. This may be due to the fact that the manes of the Kruger lions are combed out, as it were, by the bushes through which they move.

LEOPARD   *Panthera pardus* (Linnaeus 1758)

How widely are leopards distributed in the Park?
They are found in all the ecozones of the Park, but are more commonly found in ecozone H, the riverine habitats along the Sabie, Shingwedzi, N'waswitsontso and Luvuvhu rivers.

What is their preferred habitat?
They are found in most habitats with an annual rainfall of more than 50 mm, and along river courses with less rainfall. They have a wide habitat tolerance and prefer areas of broken country with heavy cover for shelter and hunting, such as rocky outcrops and mountains.

Where can they be seen in the Park?
Leopards may be seen throughout the Kruger Park. They are usually spotted along rivers, lying on a branch of a tree, in thickets and on rocky outcrops.

What are their main physical features?
The leopard is one of nature's most beautiful creatures. This graceful and strongly built cat has a comparatively long body with a thick neck, short, powerful legs and a long tail. It is stockier in build than the cheetah and serval, the only other spotted cats of comparable size.

The base colour is pale buff to golden-yellow, with black spots forming rosettes on the flanks, hips and shoulders and spots on the face and legs. The underparts are whitish. There are two black bars across the throat. The tail is long and spotted for about half its length, with black bands towards the tip, and is white underneath. The ears are small and rounded.

Leopards found in arid areas are paler than those found in denser, forested areas.

Males can attain a mass of up to 70 kg and females up to 40 kg. Both sexes attain a shoulder height of about 70 to 80 cm.

Are there black leopards in the Park?
The gene for melanism – the opposite of albinism – is actually recessive and, to produce a black leopard, extensive inbreeding would be necessary. Seen at an oblique angle, black specimens still show faint spots and rosettes. None have been observed in the Park.

Are there albino leopards in the Park?
Albinos have been recorded in Africa but these cases are very rare. None have been recorded in the Kruger Park.

Why are leopards so seldom seen?
Although they are both diurnal and nocturnal, they are more active during the night and are very covert by nature. This, coupled with their excellent camouflage and the type of habitat they prefer, makes them quite difficult to spot.

What does their diet consist of?
Leopards take a wide range of vertebrate prey, ranging from mice to wildebeest, and including baby giraffes, a wide variety of antelope, hares, primates, small carnivores, porcupines, ground roosting birds, reptiles and even fish. They also eat fruit and readily scavenge.

In the Park impalas are taken more than any other antelope.

How do leopards hunt?
Leopards are very efficient hunters. They may either lie in ambush or stalk their prey and then pounce on it.

How do they locate their prey?
Leopards rely on their excellent sight and hearing to locate their prey. Their sense of smell is also very well developed.

Why do they hang their prey in trees?
Leopards do this to safeguard their prey from other predators such as lions, African wild dog and hyaenas. These predators have been known to drive a leopard off its kill in order to obtain the food.

How do they manage to get very heavy prey into a tree?
Leopards kill their prey with a bite to the back of the skull, the nape of the neck or the throat. Larger prey is disembowelled; the guts are pulled out and discarded and sometimes covered with soil. This makes the prey animal lighter and allows the leopard to haul it into the tree. The carcass is grabbed by the throat and, with sheer muscular strength, hauled up into the tree and cached on a suitable branch.

Leopards will also feed on the ground when the prey animal cannot be hoisted into a tree, such as young giraffes.

Do they return to the prey they left in a tree?
Yes, it is very common for leopards to return to their prey, especially if they are not disturbed.

Do leopards eat carrion?
Although they usually kill their own prey, they will readily eat carrion.

How much does a leopard eat per day?
Leopards can consume anything from 8 to 17 kg of meat in 12 hours. Normal daily consumption would be in the region of 1.5 to 2 kg. The average interval between kills is about seven days.

How many prey animals are killed annually by a leopard?
A leopard probably needs about 400 kg of meat per year and, as it usually consumes only about a third of a carcass, it has to kill 1 000 to 1 200 kg of prey every year. The number of prey animals killed will depend on their size. If a leopard kills only

average-sized impala with a body mass of about 50 kg, it will have to kill about 24 to 28 of these antelope per annum.

Is it possible to identify a leopard kill?
Experts can easily identify a leopard kill. It starts to feed either on the viscera or on the meat of the thighs or the chest.

It is said that baboons could kill a leopard. Is this true?
A leopard that is hunting baboons usually stalks up to a troop where they are roosting for the night, grabs a victim and hastily retreats with it.

Occasionally, however, hunger drives a leopard rashly to attempt to snatch a baboon from a troop in broad daylight. When this happens, a number of big baboon males usually go to the aid of the shrieking victim and attack the leopard, which in turn could be severely injured or even killed.

Are leopards dependent on water?
Leopards are independent of water, obtaining enough moisture from the blood of their prey, but will readily drink water when it is available. They can live in arid areas but do not like true deserts.

What is the difference between a leopard and a cheetah?
The cheetah has a slender build with long legs to run down its prey. It has a small head with distinctive 'tear streaks' from the inner corner of the eyes to the lips. The cheetah has small single spots, not the rosette pattern of the leopard.

In contrast the leopard has a more powerful appearance with a bigger head, thick neck, very muscular body and short limbs.

Do leopards roar?
No, not like a lion. They utter coarse grunting, rasping sounds and also emit snarls and growls. Cubs mew.

Is the leopard a solitary animal?
It is solitary by habit, and the only groups of leopards likely to be seen will probably consist of the mother and her cubs.

Mating pairs may be seen together for a few days and share kills, but males play no part in raising the cubs.

Are leopards territorial?
Both sexes are solitary and territorial and defend a territory. Territorial males have priority of access to females, while territorial females have priority of access to food.

Male territories may overlap female territories. Border confrontations are usually avoided but, should a leopard wander too far into a neighbouring territory, it will probably become involved in a territorial fight.

Do they mark their territories?
Both sexes spray urine, and dung and tree scratching are also used to demarcate territories. Males also scrape the ground with their hind feet.

Where do they hide during the day?
Being less active during the heat of the day, they spend the major part of the day in thickets, dense undergrowth, among rocks and in shady trees. Despite their nocturnal habits, they are often seen during the day, especially on cool days and during winter.

Can the leopard be a danger to humans?
Although the leopard is elusive where man is concerned, it is very bold and courageous. Should a leopard consider itself to be in danger or cornered, it will not hesitate to attack viciously.

Do leopards attack humans?
It is said that this large cat will attack more readily than a lion when encountered in

the bush. Due to its elusiveness and low density, however, close contact between leopards and humans seldom occurs.

Have any humans been killed by leopards in the Park?

Glen Leary, father-in-law of ranger Harold Trollope, was fatally attacked by a leopard near the old Voortrekker road between Pretoriuskop and Malelane in 1926. In addition, a number of fatal attacks have been recorded through the years.

Since 1992, a gate guard was killed by a leopard at Shingwedzi Rest Camp and the wife of a senior staff member was killed by a leopard in broad daylight in the staff village at Skukuza in 2001. A schoolboy, on his way home from school, was killed by a leopard in Skukuza staff village and a student doing a night drive was fatally attacked by a leopard on the bridge over the Matjulu River near Berg-en-Dal Rest Camp.

Do leopards ever become man-eaters?

Leopards can become man-eaters, but the incidence is much lower than with lions. Males are usually the culprits. Peter Turnbull-Kemp, an authority on leopards, reported that out of 152 man-eating leopards, only nine were females. No cases of man-eating leopards have been reported for the Kruger National Park.

Are leopards cannibalistic?

Cannibalism among leopards is very rare. Their solitary disposition may explain this phenomenon.

What are their breeding habits?

Breeding takes place throughout the year. After a gestation period of 106 days, between one and six cubs (in the Park usually two), weighing about 600 g each, are born in dense cover or hollows in trees.

Birth intervals are 17 months.

Cubs are born blind and their eyes open after six to 10 days. They remain hidden in dense vegetation for about six weeks, after which time they start taking solid food. They are frequently moved to new hiding spots.

Does the male help with the protection and rearing of the cubs?

No. After mating the male takes no further interest in the female or in the cubs after they are born.

When do the cubs become independent?

Young leopards can become independent at the young age of a year, but often stay with the mother until they are about two years old in order to learn all the skills required for their survival. Full maturity is reached at about three years.

Is cub mortality high?

Cub mortality is fairly high: in the Park it is estimated at about 50%. Cubs left alone by the mother are sometimes killed by lions, hyaenas, jackals and even African wild dogs. Pythons could also be a factor.

What is the potential life span of a leopard?

In the wild they would live for about 12 to 15 years.

Do other predators prey upon leopard?

Poisonous snakes, crocodiles and pythons have been known to kill leopards. Old and disabled leopards can fall prey to hyaenas and African wild dogs.

Are leopards very susceptible to disease?

Leopards suffer from a number of diseases such as cat flu, pneumonia, stomach blockages, mange, parasites and deficiency diseases, but in general these diseases are not life-threatening.

Are their numbers increasing?

It is not known. Their numbers likely tend to fluctuate depending on environmental conditions and the availability of prey.

CHEETAH

Acinonyx jubatus (Schreber 1776)

What are the main physical features of the cheetah?

The cheetah has a small head, long legs and a thin waist. The head, body and legs and two thirds of the long tail are covered in black spots; the last part of the tail is banded, ending in a white tip. The base colour of the upper parts is buff to tawny, while the underparts, chin and throat are white. The anterior belly is faintly spotted.

There is a short ruff on the neck and a very short mane from the back of the neck to the shoulders. Up to the age of 12 weeks, cubs have a mantle of long grey hair extending along their backs to the base of the tail.

The head and ears are small and rounded. The eyes are large and yellowish-brown. A conspicuous brown line, known as the 'tear stripe' or 'tear streak', runs from the inside of the eyes to the corners of the mouth.

The legs are long and the claws of the adult are non-retractile and blunt, except for the dewclaw on the front paws, which ends in a sharp hook.

Shoulder height in both sexes is between 0.8 m and 1 m, with the males attaining a mass of about 60 kg and the females around 50 kg.

The anatomy of the cheetah is adapted for speed. Apart from its long legs, slender body and small head, the nasal passages and lungs are large, the heart is large and strong and the adrenal glands are well developed.

Are cheetahs widely distributed throughout Africa?

South of the Sahara they are found sparsely from Chad and the Sudan through parts of East Africa, Zimbabwe, Angola, Namibia, Botswana and in South Africa. They were once found throughout most of southern Africa.

What is their distribution in the Park?

They occur in all the ecozones of the Park but are more common in the southern and central districts, particularly in ecozones A and D between Skukuza and Pretoriuskop and in ecozones F and G in the Satara, Kingfisherspruit, N'wanetsi, Tshokwane, Lower Sabie and Crocodile Bridge areas.

What type of habitat do cheetahs prefer?

They favour open grasslands, light woodland, bush, scrub and desert fringes. They prefer open areas as they have to run down their prey, and densely wooded terrain would make this difficult. In the Park this would include the southeastern parts of the mixed bushwillow woodland and thorn thicket habitats. They are also found in the Delagoa thorn thickets and the thornveld/marula/knobthorn savanna habitats. They avoid forest and woodland with thick undergrowth.

How many are there in the Park?

Cheetahs have never been plentiful in the Park and, given their limited habitat preference, it is estimated that there are not more than 200 in the Park.

What do they eat?

Cheetahs prey mainly on smaller and medium-sized antelope such as steenbok, duikers and impalas and also the young of larger antelope. Warthogs, hares and ground-roosting birds and even ostriches feature prominently in their diet. In the Park impalas make up 45% of cheetah kills.

Do they eat carrion?

They normally hunt their own prey, but will occasionally eat carrion.

Do they kill other predators?

Very seldom, if ever.

How did the cheetah get its name?

It probably comes from an Indian word *chita* meaning 'spotted one'.

What kind of sounds do cheetahs make?

They snarl, growl and spit like a cat and can also purr. They utter a peculiar whistle similar to the chirping of a bird, especially when the mother communicates with, and calls to, her cubs. They cannot roar at all.

It is sometimes claimed that cheetahs are not true cats. Is this so?

No. Cheetahs are true cats. The non-retractile claws of the adult cheetah and the method of hunting led to the popular misconception.

Can cheetahs climb trees?

Cheetahs sometimes climb trees with a slanted trunk or jump onto low branches, but their blunt claws do not allow them to climb trees properly.

How fast can cheetahs run?

Cheetahs are definitely the fastest land animals and many exaggerated claims about cheetah speeds have been made. One authority timed a cheetah with a stopwatch and recorded a speed of 114 km/h. A number of other claims of speeds in excess of 100 km/h have been made, although most of these claims are guesstimates.

One could probably accept that the average cheetah in its prime could reach 90 to 100 km/h, or slightly more.

How far can a cheetah run at top speed?

Although the cheetah's anatomy is adapted for speed, it has little stamina. Charges and chases are seldom over a distance exceeding 250 to 300 m. Even when the prey is quickly overtaken, brought to ground and killed, the hunter usually appears to be exhausted.

How close does a cheetah come to its prey before it charges?

The distance varies according to the type of prey and the vegetation cover in the area, but it is usually 10 to 30 m if it is to have any chance of success.

What is the success ratio for kills?

Hunting success is related to the distance between the cheetah and the prey when the charge commences, and whether the cheetah or the prey had a flying start.

When the prey spots the cheetah in good time, killing success could be one in 10 attempts, or even lower, whereas the success where the prey was unaware of the cheetah starting its charge could be as high as one in two attempts.

Do cheetahs always hunt alone or do they sometimes hunt in a group?

Hunting in a group is common and the success rate of a group is usually significantly higher on bright moonlit nights.

How is the prey caught and killed?

The classic cheetah hunting technique is a high-speed chase, during which the prey is tripped up by knocking it off balance. In the process the dewclaw is dug into the flank and pulled backwards. The cheetah may also slap the hind legs of the prey to bring it down. Once the prey is down the cheetah grabs it by the throat and it is strangled by a sustained grip of the throat. Death of the prey is in almost all cases due to strangulation.

The teeth of cheetahs are too short for the stabbing killing bite used by other cats.

If possible, the prey is dragged into shade or cover in order to avoid the attention of other carnivores and vultures.

Cheetahs are very messy eaters, as they have to eat quickly before they are robbed of their kills.

Are cheetahs often robbed of their kill?
Their slight build, small teeth and timid disposition make cheetahs very vulnerable to attacks by other predators, and they are often robbed of their kills by lions, hyaenas and leopards. In the Park cheetahs lose 14% of their kills to spotted hyaenas. This may be one of the reasons why the majority of their hunting is done during the day when other predators are mostly inactive. Jackals usually avoid cheetahs because cheetahs are fast enough to catch them.

Do cheetahs kill their prey quickly?
Cheetahs can take between five and 25 minutes to kill their victim. Their relatively small canines, small mouths and claws cannot effectively hold their prey down, which contributes to their inability to kill quickly. Once the prey is grabbed by the throat, the cheetah usually positions itself behind the animal and away from the hooves and horns.

Is it possible to identify a cheetah kill?
Carcasses of animals killed by a cheetah can be recognised by the manner in which the jugular vein is severed and the trachea, or windpipe, is crushed. Deep claw marks are absent, the rib cartilages are usually chewed up, the heart, liver and kidneys are eaten and the intestines are dragged out. Meat on the hindquarters, spine, forequarters and the base of the neck is consumed. When a single cheetah feeds on a carcass it may not even get further than the hindquarters. The haphazard way in which a carcass is butchered is typical of a cheetah kill.

Do they return to a kill?
Cheetahs very seldom return to a kill. The kill cannot be secured, and if the cheetah returns it may be confronted by another predator or scavenger at the carcass.

How many animals does a cheetah kill per year?
The cheetah is often deprived of its prey by other predators before making a sufficient meal of it, which means it would have to kill again. Should it kill animals the size of impala, it could very well kill about 30 or more per year.

On the other hand, a cheetah very often kills considerably smaller prey and may make a kill every two or three days, or about 150 smaller animals a year.

How much food does it consume per day?
Like most predators, cheetahs can consume a large meal at one sitting. Normal consumption would be between 1 and 3 kg per day but, depending on the energy expended in securing its prey, up to about 12 kg can be consumed during a single session.

Are cheetahs cannibalistic?
Cannibalism seems to be very rare.

Do cheetahs drink water regularly?
They are water independent, but will drink when water is readily available.

Are they solitary animals?
About 50% of cheetahs are solitary. Females are solitary or are accompanied by cubs of up to 18 months of age. Males are usually solitary but some males form coalitions of up to four animals, usually brothers.

Are they diurnal in habit?
They are mostly diurnal and least active during the heat of the day. Nocturnal hunting has also been recorded.

Are they territorial?
Females live in overlapping home ranges, but will avoid contact with other females. Home ranges vary in size according to the food supply. In the Park with its available food supply, ranges can be 100 to 200 km².

Males hold territories in which they monopolise access to females, and which they defend savagely: male cheetah intruders may even be killed. Territorial males scent-mark traditional sites on rocks and trees by the spraying of urine and with cheek and chin glands.

Females on heat attract males by the smell of their urine.

Are cheetahs dangerous to man?
They are among the timidest of predators. Only when cornered will a cheetah turn to attacking its pursuer. As far as wild animals go, it is very trustworthy when tamed.

No report of a cheetah killing a human being could be found in available literature.

Is there a specific breeding season, and how long is gestation?
Cheetahs breed at any time of the year. After a gestation period of about three months, two to five cubs, each with a mass of about 250 to 300 g, are born. Cubs are hidden in dense cover. They are blind at birth, and their eyes open at two to 11 days.

How long is the birth interval?
About 15 to 18 months.

How long do the cubs stay hidden and when are they weaned?
Cubs are moved frequently and remain hidden for up to six weeks. Solid food is taken after a month and the cubs are weaned at about three to six months but will stay with the mother for 15 to 24 months. The mother brings live prey for them to practise their hunting skills on when they are four to five months old.

Is cub mortality high?
About half the cubs die within the first few months of life. On the Serengeti Plains of East Africa, 5% of cubs reach maturity while 67% are killed by lions, but in the Kruger Park predation on cubs is probably lower because the thicker bush provides better protection for cubs. All the causes of cub death are not known, but small cubs are vulnerable to eagles and mammalian predators such as hyaenas, leopards and lions. Diseases such as cat flu, mange and rickets may also play a role.

What is the life span of a cheetah?
It is said to be between 15 and 20 years in captivity, but one can assume that it would be in the vicinity of 12 years in nature.

Is it difficult to breed cheetahs in captivity?
With the current knowledge and refined techniques, many problems of the past have been overcome and the success rate is high.

Is it feasible to breed cheetahs in pens and then to release them into a natural environment?
This is a possibility but it should first be established whether the areas of intended release have suitable habitats.

What is the sex ratio in nature?

There are about three males to two females.

Do males often fight over females?

Apparently not. Fights, if they occur, seldom lead to severe injury or death.

Cheetahs of both sexes occasionally fight at a kill, but usually a carcass is shared without antagonism.

At what age are they sexually mature?

Sexual maturity is reached at about 21 to 24 months although the young usually stay with their mother up to the age of 15 to 24 months.

What are their major enemies?

Hunters and poachers are enemies of cheetahs, but these beautiful cats may also be killed as cubs by hyaenas, lions and leopards. The effect of injuries is vital for an animal with such a specialised way of hunting; a crippled cheetah has little chance of survival. Man has the biggest impact on cheetah populations through habitat modification and eradication.

How can other predators kill fleet-footed cheetahs?

Leopards and lions do not go out of their way to kill cheetahs, except the cubs, but they can stalk and surprise them. Hyaenas and African wild dogs have far more stamina and therefore can tire out a cheetah, but they probably wouldn't bother.

Does competition with other predators affect cheetahs?

Competition for food with other predators and predation on cubs are limiting factors in the survival of cheetahs. They seldom take food from another predator, but are often robbed of their kill by lions, leopards, hyaenas and African wild dogs.

Can one keep cheetahs as pets?

In South Africa, it is against the law to keep cheetahs as pets.

Are cheetahs still being hunted?

Although protected in conservation areas, they are still being hunted when they wander beyond the boundaries of conservation areas. They do kill domestic stock in farming areas and therefore come into conflict with organised agriculture, although attempts are being made to mitigate this through monetary compensation when they are hunted legally. Their skins are coveted trophies, like those of leopards, fetching high prices on illegal markets. It is not sure how successful the fur trade in these animals is at present.

Is it easy to hunt them?

Cheetahs are not as covert and cunning as leopards. Their diurnal way of life makes them easy targets for hunters and poachers; this leads to their rapid disappearance from areas where they are not protected.

They are actually not that easy to hunt with a rifle and most killings are through trapping them in cage traps.

What other mortality factors affect the cheetah?

Cheetahs are susceptible to a number of diseases such as pneumonia, cat flu, mange, rickets, feline distemper, liver diseases and tuberculosis, but none of these are population limiting. Parasites also play a lesser role in cheetah mortality.

Are cheetahs in danger of becoming extinct?

Not at this stage, but it would be better if their numbers could be increased by controlled breeding and release.

Is it not possible to boost their numbers in some way?

Some years ago more than 50 of these cats were introduced into the Park, mainly from Namibia.

The population increased to about 200, but in the long run such introductions proved unsuccessful, as release was usually into the existing territory of another dominant male, leading to fights.

Eliminating threats such as habitat fragmentation and retribution killing by farmers and stockowners could be the best way to increase their numbers.

Is the king cheetah a separate species?

The so-called 'king cheetah' is not a different species or even a subspecies. It is a colour variation carried on a recessive gene, a mutant form, similar to the white lion. It was first reported in Zimbabwe in the 19th century. The main difference between the king cheetah and the regular cheetah is that in the king cheetah the spots, especially on the back, appear to be fused together in a stripe pattern.

Reports of this form of melanism being seen in the Park are received from time to time.

SPOTTED HYAENA *Crocuta crocuta* (Erxleben 1777)

Where can spotted hyaenas be seen in the Park?

They are found in all the ecozones of the Park, occurring in high densities in the central areas, including in the vicinity of Kingfisherspruit, Satara, N'wanetsi and Tshokwane. They are also commonly found around Crocodile Bridge and Lower Sabie.

What type of habitat do they prefer?

They have a wide habitat range but prefer open grassland and open savanna.

What are their main physical features?

The spotted hyaena is built somewhat like a heavy, large, powerful dog.

The head and body are covered in short, wiry and coarse hair. The coat has a yellow-grey to reddish-brown base colour, which is covered with irregular dark spots that tend to fade with age. The head is massive, the neck very strong and well developed, and the muzzle heavy and black. The ears are rounded.

The front legs are longer than the hind legs and the forequarters more heavily built than the hindquarters, which gives a sloping outline to the back. The tail is bushy with a black tip. Unlike the domestic dog, which has five toes on the front foot, the hyaena has four toes.

It is difficult to distinguish females from males as they both have prominent genitals, those of the female mimicking those of the male. Females have a fat-filled scrotum and an erectile clitoris almost the same size and shape as the male's penis. Careful scrutiny is needed to tell the sexes apart.

Contrary to popular belief, they are not hermaphrodites (carrying both male and female sexual organs).

Females are larger than males, with a mass of up to 80 kg, compared with that of the male of up to 75 kg. Females are about 90 cm at the shoulder and males about 85 cm.

What are their habits?

They are mainly nocturnal, but are quite regularly seen during the day, especially early morning.

They form clans numbering up to about 30 individuals, always led by a dominant female. There are separate dominances between males and females, but females dominate all males. High-ranking females have priority of access to food and resting sites, and rear more cubs than lower-ranking females. High-ranking males have priority of access to females.

Clan companions greet each other by standing alongside each other, nose to tail. Each lifts the hind leg nearest its partner, and erects the penis or clitoris, and the two then sniff and lick each other's genitals.

Hyaenas are territorial and pitched battles take place to defend territories. Territories are patrolled by resident clan members and demarcated by depositing anal-gland secretions on grass stalks, called pasting, ground-pawing to release digital secretions, and middens containing large accumulations of white faeces. Most pastings are found close to middens, and males scent-mark more than females.

Carrion is detected by smell, apparently from as far away as 4 km downwind. Live prey is detected by sight and sound. The sound of other predators feeding attracts hyaenas from as far away as 10 km.

Lions usually cannot be displaced from a carcass when an adult male lion is present, but lionesses and sub-adults can if they are outnumbered 4:1 by hyaenas. Lions, however, quite easily steal carcasses from hyaenas.

What is the size of a territory?

It varies from a few to many square kilometres, depending on the density of the hyaena population, the available prey and the number of other predators that supply carrion.

It is well known that hyaenas are scavengers, but do they ever kill their own prey?

When carrion is freely available they usually make use of it, but if the need arises they do kill their own prey. They are more resourceful and formidable predators than their reputation would suggest.

Whether hyaenas scavenge or kill their own prey depends very much on the conditions in which they find themselves. They are great opportunists and will not overexert themselves by hunting their own prey if there is a

chance of obtaining sufficient carrion left by other predators, or of robbing a lesser predator of its kill.

Where predators and their prey are plentiful, hyaenas may live largely as scavengers, but in the absence of other large predators, and thus an insufficient supply of carrion, they revert to hunting.

Hungry hyaenas will take great risks in snatching meat from feeding lions, and many of them are mauled and even killed in the process.

Hyaenas regularly hunt baby impalas when they are born in the early summer, as they are plentiful, easy to separate from their mothers and make easy prey.

How do they hunt?

Their usual method of hunting is either singly or in packs, running down their prey, in very much the same way as African wild dogs. A chase can go on for up to 3 km in order to tire out the intended prey. On average it takes them two or three attempts to make a kill in this way.

They often pounce on animals floundering in mud at receding water holes, as would any predator. They kill by disembowelling the prey and severing major blood vessels.

How fast can they run?

Although they have tremendous stamina and can maintain their lope for extremely long distances, they are not very fast and probably cannot exceed 50 km/h. They can maintain this speed for up to 2 to 3 km.

Do hyaenas run in packs?

The basic social unit is called a clan, which in the Park can number up to 30 individuals of both sexes and all ages. Clans, or packs, usually remain stable in composition. All males must leave their natal clan as sub-adults and join another clan. Females usually remain within the natal clan. The clan is very loose and members are often scattered singly and in small packs. Solitary individuals are common, but they belong to a clan.

What is the biggest animal killed by hyaenas?

Adult wildebeest, zebras, waterbuck and kudu may be pulled down and devoured by packs of hyaenas. These predators demonstrate an uncanny ability to select vulnerable prey such as sick, old or disabled animals and through natural selection remove inadequate animals. In the Park there have been several cases recorded of sick or crippled African buffalo being killed by hyaenas.

What other prey do they kill?

They are carnivorous, scavengers and team hunters, taking almost anything. In the Park their main prey species are impalas, wildebeest, waterbuck, kudu and zebras. Prey is disembowelled and about 25 kg can be consumed during one meal. Undigested parts of the carcass, such as hooves, horns and hair, are regurgitated.

Excess food is often cached and stored in shallow water, very often in drinking troughs. They are independent of water but will drink when it is readily available.

When do they hunt?

Usually they hunt their larger mammalian prey at night, but hunting can also take place at dawn or dusk.

Do they really have the strongest jaws of the mammalian predators?

Yes. They have tremendously powerful jaw muscles and very strong premolar teeth. Even the thick thighbones of buffalo are crushed and eaten, allowing hyaenas to access the highly nutritious marrow.

Do they attack other predators?

Not often, but old, weakened lions occasionally fall prey to hyaenas, and even young and healthy cheetahs and leopards could be attacked. Being great opportunists, they will readily attack and kill the young of many predators that are left hidden while the mother is out hunting.

Will hyaenas attack humans?

As a rule hyaenas will run away from humans, but when hungry or cornered they can become extremely dangerous. When driven by hunger they will attempt to enter rest camps to scavenge from rubbish bins, and will even enter human dwellings in search of food.

They are bolder at night and many a person sleeping out in the open has been attacked. In this respect they can be more dangerous than lions.

Are they cannibalistic?

Cannibalism of very young members does occur but seems to be rare.

Do hyaenas eat strange objects?

They have been known to chew on vehicle and aircraft tyres, and staff vehicles have had bumpers damaged and steering wheels and seats chewed off vehicles left open.

When it was still fairly easy for hyaenas to enter rest camps, they would chew on articles left outside, such as shoes, kitchen utensils and clothing.

There are records of hyaenas scooping fish out of pools that were drying up.

What are their breeding habits?

All the females in the clan breed. Although the pups den together, each female suckles her own. They breed all year round but births tend to peak in the rainy summer season.

After a gestation period of about three months, an average of two pups, with a mass of 1.5 kg each, are born in the communal den. Twins are usually of different sexes, occasionally both males but rarely both females.

Pups are born with their eyes open and teeth well developed and they fight savagely to establish dominance, especially if they are both females.

There is an average interval of about 1.5 years between births. For about the first nine months of their lives, mother's milk is the main source of nutrition for the pups. Adults bring very little food to the den.

What is their average life expectancy?
They have a life span of about 15 to 20 years.

Pups are born a very dark brown, almost black, colour and adult coloration is attained at about four months. Weaning starts at nine months and is complete at 12 to 16 months. Pups accompany adults at about six to nine months. Permanent teeth erupt at 15 months. Males are fully grown at 30 months and females at 36 months, and they are sexually mature at three years.

Are the hyaena's senses well developed?
The large eyes, ears and nostrils indicate well-developed senses.

What sounds do they make?
The most distinctive call is a drawn-out 'whooo-oop', probably one of the most typical night sounds of the African bush. Contact calls include grunts, groans, squeals, whines and chatters. The characteristic giggling is uttered when they are excited or being chased, and submissive animals scream and yell when they flee.

Hearing their hysterical cacophony at a kill is an unforgettable experience.

Their different sounds serve as a very effective form of communication. The drawn-out whooping sound is a long-range contact call and assembly signal.

Is the hyaena really a coward?
Hyaenas have often been labelled cowards, but they are no more cowardly than any other carnivore. When hungry or cornered, they can put up a terrific fight. A case has been recorded where two cornered hyaenas killed a fully grown, healthy lioness.

Are they clever animals?
They are cunning and are undoubtedly the most intelligent large carnivore, with the most sophisticated social system. They could be more intelligent than the domestic dog. Hyaenas often watch vultures and their movements that could lead them to a possible meal. They also engage in opportunistic, organised attacks on lions to remove them from a kill.

Can hyaenas change sex?

The widespread belief that hyaenas can change sex probably arose from the fact that the external labial swellings of the female are so prominent that they superficially resemble the scrotum of the male. Although hyaenas are difficult to sex, especially when they are young, they are definitely not hermaphrodites and do not change sex.

What are their major enemies?

Hungry hyaenas often take incredible risks in an effort to snatch meat at a kill. Male lions are known to kill spotted hyaenas but rarely eat them. Pups are occasionally killed by other hyaenas, either by a dominant female or hyaenas from other clans.

Are they susceptible to diseases?

Although susceptible to diseases and parasites like all other animals, they do not seem to be very vulnerable in this respect and are rarely affected by epizootics.

Spotted hyaenas do contract mange and suffer from infestations of the dangerous intra-muscular nematode *Trichinella spiralis*, which may cause severe emaciation and paralysis, and eventual death.

Are hyaenas related to dogs?

Members of the family Hyaenidae are most closely related to the Viverridae, the mongooses and African civets, and are more closely related to cats than dogs.

Do hyaenas feature in witchcraft?

There are many superstitions about the hyaena and in tribal medicines the nose, tail, ears, whiskers, lips and genitals are used in certain potions.

> Because the status of the brown Hyaena (*Hyaena brunnea*) and the aardwolf (*Proteles cristata*) in the Park is questionable, uncertain and unknown, these two animals have not been included in this publication. During research on lions and cheetahs in the Lower Sabie–Crocodile Bridge area in the 1980s, aardwolf were regularly seen. However, indications at the time of writing are that neither of these species had been recorded in the Park during the past 12 years.

AFRICAN WILD DOG   *Lycaon pictus* (Temminck 1820)

What is the distribution of African wild dogs in the Park?

This endangered carnivore, numbering about 350 animals in the Park, occurs in suitable habitat in all the ecozones of the Park. They are more commonly seen in the southern parts in the areas of Skukuza, Pretoriuskop, Stolsnek and Malelane, in the central districts of the Park between the Sabie River and Tshokwane, and along the western boundary of the Park in the Kingfisherspruit area. They are also scattered throughout the northern regions.

What type of habitat do they prefer?

They prefer open savanna, woodland, bushveld and broken hilly areas. In the Park competition with lions tends to keep African wild dogs out of areas of suitable habitat with abundant prey.

What do they eat?

Wild dogs kill a much narrower spectrum of prey species than lions or leopards. They are the most carnivorous of the canids, with the main prey being antelope in the 15 to 45 kg range. Impalas make up 75% of their kills and other smaller antelope about 15%. Other prey includes the young of wildebeest, zebras, tsessebe, kudu and even African buffalo.

In contrast to lions and leopards, African wild dogs prey much more heavily on animals in poor condition and newborn young during the calving and lambing seasons of their prey species. Predation by African wild dogs may therefore have a smaller impact on the prey population than a comparative toll by lions or leopards.

Wild dogs do not readily hunt adult wildebeest and zebras. These two species tend to stand their ground, and instances have been recorded where zebra stallions have attacked African wild dogs that ventured too close to mares with foals.

They are water independent, obtaining enough moisture from their diet, but will drink when water is readily available.

What are their main physical features?
A lean, long-legged dog with a large head, a heavy muzzle and powerful jaws. The coat is mottled with richly coloured black, brown, yellow, yellow-brown and white blotches, giving rise to its other popular name of 'painted wolf'. Each dog has a unique colour pattern through which it may be individually identified.

The ears are large, upright and rounded. There is a black line running from the muzzle up the forehead to between the ears. The tail is not blotched, is bushy and ends in a white tip.

There are no dewclaws on the front legs and four toes on each foot.

Male and female both stand about 75 cm high at the shoulder and both have a mass of up to 35 kg.

Is their hunting method cruel?
African wild dogs lack the strong jaws and teeth and the sharp, powerful claws that are needed to catch and hold down a prey animal, so they kill their prey by tearing it apart. When African wild dogs close in for the kill, they waste no time in pulling the prey animal down and killing it. The prey of lions and other cats can die a slower death, especially when it is suffocated and mauled, as is often the case when African buffaloes or giraffes are killed.

It should be kept in mind that the prey of African wild dogs is probably in such a state of shock that it feels little pain.

How do they hunt?
When the pack encounters prey, such as a herd of impalas, individuals in the pack break away and chase after an animal that is acting differently from the rest in the prey herd, such as limping or not keeping up with the fleeing herd, or old or sick individuals. Usually only one or two dogs then bring down the selected prey animal, while the others immediately converge on it as soon as it has been secured.

How far do they chase their prey?
Most pursuits end after a short chase, but the distances can vary from a few hundred metres to 3 km and more.

Are their senses well developed?
They have very well-developed senses of smell and hearing and their sight is also keen.

How successful are they in capturing prey?
The success rate differs from area to area and is higher during the lambing and calving seasons of their prey. A success rate of about 50% is experienced when pursuing adult prey. This rate increases to just about 100% when they attack lambs, calves or disabled prey.

In denser vegetation their success rate may be considerably lower. The belief that once they have selected their quarry they will not give up the pursuit is not substantiated. In fact it has been proven that they usually give up if they do not run down their prey within the first 3 km.

When setting out to hunt they usually move in single file but soon tend to spread out into a formation more suitable for locating prey.

How fast do they run?
Prey is chased at speeds of up to 55 km/h over distances of up to 3 km. When not hunting they either rest or trot along at about 8 km/h, covering considerable distances in a day.

When do they hunt?
Peak hunting times are in the early morning and late in the afternoon.

What sounds do they make?
Contact calls include chatters, chirps, twitters and yelps. A musical but surprisingly quiet 'hooo' is used as a long-range contact call and can carry as far as 3 km. They twitter during intense social interactions such as pre-hunt rallies and greetings. The alarm call is a short, deep growl or bark. Pups whine in distress.

Do they tend to attack sick animals?
When attacking large prey they do tend to select old, sick or injured animals. This makes the hunt that much easier.

What is the killing rate of a dog?
In the wild these carnivores are very active and need up to 3 to 4 kg of meat per day to meet their energy requirements for hunting and moving around. Comparatively speaking, a wild dog consumes more food per body mass than a lion. If only impalas were preyed upon, a single African wild dog might kill up to 50 per year because only about 60% of any prey animal can be consumed.

Can African wild dogs go without food for a long time?
This is unlikely for an animal as active as a wild dog. It may be assumed that they probably need to kill almost every day.

Will they eat carrion?
Wild dogs prefer fresh meat from their own kills but will scavenge when the opportunity arises.

Do they attack other predators?
Their normal prey does not include other predators.

Are they cannibalistic?
Up to now, no case of cannibalism has been recorded in the Kruger Park. If it does occur, it must be considered an extremely rare event.

What is the sex ratio?
Latest studies in the Park have confirmed a 50:50 male to female ratio as the norm, although a preponderance of males has been recorded in other parks in Africa.

Is this sex ratio not unfavourable?
It has been speculated that a larger proportion of males is actually of benefit to the pack.

Females with young cannot hunt for the first few weeks after birth and are fed by other members of the pack. A larger number of males, which are not as tied down as females with pups, therefore can help to secure the survival of the offspring. As only the alpha female normally breeds, all other pack members, male and female, feed her and the pups.

What are their habits and behaviour?
Wild dogs are predominantly diurnal but will occasionally hunt by moonlight. They form nomadic packs of up to 30 individuals, consisting of six to eight adult dogs and up to 18 pups. The largest recorded pack in the Kruger Park in recent years was 51, and it consisted of 22 adults and 29 pups from two females. Packs stay at the same den site for up to 13 weeks while pups mature. After a kill they feed very quickly to avoid having their kill stolen.

All pack members care for the pups by regurgitating meat, or allowing them to feed first at a kill. Subordinate adults of both sexes may stay at the den as guards while the pack hunts. A dog begs for meat by grinning, forequarters lowered, tail lowered and giving a penetrating wail.

If a subordinate female gives birth the alpha female may kill the pups, adopt them and raise them with her own, or allow the mother to raise them herself.

Packs bond by intense social interactions, mostly involving mutual sniffing and muzzle licking.

An alpha pair dominates the pack and only they perform a linked urine-marking ritual to display their dominance. Territories are also marked by faeces. Young, sexually mature adults disperse and regroup in single-sex packs of up to five animals, and new packs form when dispersing groups of opposite sexes meet.

Do they have a social hierarchy?

They do have a social hierarchy, with the alpha male and female clearly dominant during breeding. However, the amity that exists between members of the pack is very noticeable, and there is little strife, even when the whole pack is crowded around a kill where the pups are given priority of access.

There is hardly any growling and snapping, as is the case with lions.

The 'greeting' ritual of the African wild dog most probably serves to strengthen social ties. In this procedure two dogs will walk parallel to each other, bodies touching, ears back and lips drawn to expose the teeth, while at the same time they nibble and lick each other's mouths. Partners are frequently changed, and the ritual is accompanied by twittering and wailing sounds.

Do males often fight?

Fights appear to be very rare, except during the mating season when males may fight for dominance.

Is there a definite pack leader?

There appears to be some kind of dominance, but both males and females share most tasks equally, including hunting and the feeding of the pups. While some dogs hunt, others guard the den if there are pups.

Are African wild dogs territorial?

Even though they range over hundreds of square kilometres, territorial behaviour is noticeable. They mark territories and are aggressive to intruding packs. However, they do have activity zones that shift frequently. During the denning period their movements are restricted to the vicinity of the den. When the pups are old enough to follow the pack, the den is abandoned.

What are their breeding habits?

A bitch on heat urinates more frequently than other members of the pack. Immediately after she has urinated, her mate urinates on the same spot. Copulation is brief. Typically only the alpha pair in the pack will breed, and they will intervene to prevent any other pack members from mating. In the Kruger Park they are strictly seasonal breeders, producing litters during May and June, but occasionally late litters are born in July, August and September.

After a gestation period of about 70 days an average of six to 10 pups (litters of up to 21 pups have been recorded), with a mass of about 300 g each, are born in a den or burrow. Pups are born blind and naked and are black in colour. The eyes open after about 10 to 14 days and pups take regurgitated meat from about three weeks and are weaned at five to 10 weeks. Adult coloration is attained at six to eight weeks and pups leave the den to join the pack at about three months.

Is pup mortality high?

Mortality is very high among pups and few actually survive to adulthood. Causes of death in young pups are lions, hyaenas, other African wild dogs (usually the alpha pair), desertion and disease. When pups accompany the pack after leaving the den, many of them succumb to the hard life of roaming over a large and difficult terrain.

When prey is vulnerable and abundant, dog populations can increase dramatically. During the drought of 1991/1992 when the prey animals were weakened, the southern population of African wild dogs increased from 67 in 1990 to 139 in 1993.

Are African wild dogs good parents?
Wild dogs actually care better for their young than many other predators.

Both males and females regurgitate food for the pups.

What are their major enemies?
Their main enemies are lions and hyaenas, which kill about 60% of pups. Other predators include leopards, and some very young may be taken by large raptors.

Are they susceptible to disease?
Distemper and especially rabies (leading to death) may affect small African wild dog populations.

Is the African wild dog related to the domestic dog?
Both belong to the family Canidae but not to the same genus. The domestic dog (*Canis familiaris*) and some jackal and wolf species are members of the genus *Canis*, whereas the African wild dog belongs to the genus *Lycaon*, of which *Lycaon pictus* is the only species.

Domestic dogs have four toes and a dewclaw on the forefeet and four toes on the hind feet. The African wild dog lacks a dewclaw, having four toes on both the fore and hind feet.

Do they attack human beings?
When desperately hungry African wild dogs may attack a human being, but normally they try to avoid confrontation.

BLACK-BACKED JACKAL

Canis mesomelas

(Schreber 1775)

What is their distribution in the Park?

A large number of black-backed jackals occur in the Park and are often seen by visitors. They are found in ecozones A, B, D, E, F, G, I, J, K, L, O and P, but are common only in the central savanna districts.

What is their preferred habitat?

Black-backed jackals occur throughout the Park, which implies that they are found in a wide range of habitats. They are, however, particularly partial to trampled, short grass areas created by high densities of herbivores.

What do they eat?

They are omnivorous, feeding on rodents, hares, small antelope and the young of larger species, small carnivores, ground-roosting birds and their eggs, reptiles, amphibians, berries, fruit, insects and other invertebrates. They also scavenge and eat carrion. They often eat grass, presumably to aid digestion.

They are water independent but will readily drink when water is available.

What are their main physical features?

The top of the neck and back are black, flecked with white. The black 'saddle' is broadest at the neck and narrows towards the base of the tail, making it easy to distinguish this species from other jackals. The face, flanks and legs are reddish-brown, separated from the mottled baack by a black line. The underparts are almost white.

The ears are large, triangular and with rounded tips, reddish on the back. The tail is bushy and the same colour as the flanks at the base, becoming darker towards the black tip. The muzzle is narrow and pointed.

The jackal is a true 'dog', with five toes on the front and hind feet. Some authors are of the opinion that the jackal and the wolf are the ancestors of the domestic dog.

Jackals stand about 40 to 45 cm at the shoulder, with males having a mass of about 12 to 14 kg and females 8 to 10 kg.

What sounds do they make?

The long-range contact call is the characteristic 'nyaaa-a-a-a' wailing howl ending in three or four short yaps. Pups whine. A sharp bark or rumbling growl is an alarm signal given by adults to pups. Alarm calls include snarls, growls, yelps and sharp yaps. When distressed they utter a shrill chattering sound.

Are they solitary animals?

They are nearly always solitary, but live in pairs or in family groups of up to six. Large numbers of jackals seen around kills are temporary aggregations.

Are they nocturnal?

Although predominantly nocturnal, they are active throughout the day and night, and most active at dawn and dusk. During the day they spend their time lying under bushes or in underground burrows and tall grass.

Do they hunt in packs?

No, they usually hunt alone or in pairs. It is common for one of the pair to attempt to lure a female antelope away from her newly born young so that the other can snatch the lamb.

What are their habits and behaviour?

They have very keen senses of smell, sight and hearing. Carrion is detected by smell and carcasses can be found from as far as 1 km downwind. The sound of large

carnivores on a kill also attracts jackals, and they follow large carnivores and even vultures in anticipation of a meal.

Rodents are captured with a high-arching pounce, pinning them down with the forefeet and then biting them across the back and neck. Tougher prey is shaken vigorously and larger prey animals like lambs are killed by a sustained bite to the throat, causing death by suffocation.

When large carnivores are on a kill, jackals may wait their turn or dash in and snatch scraps.

Mating pairs form at about three years and remain together for life. Only when one partner dies will the other find a new mate. Pairs occupy a home range that both animals scent-mark with urine.

Their shelters include self-dug burrows or abandoned burrows that they modify, dens, termite mounds and dense underbrush.

Are they territorial?

They appear to have home ranges that are marked but not defended. The fact that large numbers of jackals gather at a lion kill indicates that they are opportunistic feeders, ignoring territorial boundaries when food becomes available.

What are their breeding habits and life expectancy?

After a gestation period of about 60 days, two to eight (average five) pups with a mass of about 200 g each are born in dens, burrows or dense vegetation. Only one or two survive past 14 weeks. Peaks of births occur during the dry winter months of July to October. Pups are born blind, and their eyes open after about 10 days. Young feed on regurgitated food up to the age of two months and are weaned at about eight to 10 weeks. Pups begin foraging at about 3.5 months and their permanent teeth erupt at six months.

They reach sexual maturity at 11 months but do not breed until they have paired up and a home range has been established. They are fully grown at one year. Pups will leave the parental den at about six to eight months or will remain with their parents to help raise later litters. Potential life span is eight to 10 years.

What are their major enemies?

Their main enemies are lions, leopards and cheetahs. Young also fall prey to lions, hyaenas, eagles and disease.

SIDE-STRIPED JACKAL   *Canis adustus* (Sundeval 1846)

What is the distribution of the side-striped jackal in the Park?

Rarer than the black-backed jackal, but widespread within the Park. They occur in ecozones A, B, D, E, F, G, I, J, L, N, O and P.

What type of habitat do they prefer?

As in the case of black-backed jackal, they are widely distributed throughout the Park, but side-striped jackals prefer habitats with denser ground cover.

They are mostly associated with the grassland flats of the far northern regions, the *Combretum* woodlands of the southern regions and the tall grasslands of the Pretoriuskop area.

What do they eat?

They are omnivorous scavengers, feeding on almost anything they find dead. Apart from carrion they forage for insects, small rodents, reptiles, invertebrates, snakes, small antelope, birds as big as guineafowl, fruit and seeds.

They are water independent, obtaining enough moisture from their diet, but will readily drink when water is available.

What are their main physical features?

The base colour is grey to greyish-buff, with an indistinct pale stripe, outlined with darker grey, along the flanks and across the back just behind the shoulders. The underparts are paler. The legs are brownish-grey and the tail is bushy, black on top and almost always ends in a white tip.

The ears are large and triangular with rounded tips and dark grey on the back. The muzzle is small, short and pointed.

There are five toes on the forefeet and four on the hind feet.

Both sexes have a shoulder height of about 40 cm and a mass of 10 to 12 kg.

What are their habits and behaviour?

They are predominantly nocturnal but occasionally seen at dawn and dusk. They live in pairs but tend to forage alone. Both parents bring food to the pups, either in their mouths or regurgitated.

They shelter in rock crevices, dense cover, abandoned burrows that they modify, holes in the ground, dens and termite mounds.

Home ranges and core area territories are scent-marked by males with urine, anal glands and dung.

What sounds do they make?

Contact calls include 'kow-kow' barks, repetitive 'nya-a' barks, hoots, yelps, howls and cackles. Pups whine. Alarm calls include growls, snarls, screams and persistent sharp yaps.

What are their breeding habits and expected life span?

After a gestation period of about two months, four to six pups, with a mass of about 200 g, are born towards the end of the drier winter months, usually August to October. Pups are born in breeding chambers in dens, abandoned burrows or dense thickets. They are born blind, and their eyes open at the age of about 10 days. Pups feed on regurgitated food for about two months and are weaned at about two months, at which time they start foraging. They become sexually mature at 10 months and disperse from the family at about 11 months. Life span is about 10 to 12 years.

What are their major enemies?

Major enemies include lions, leopards and hyaenas, and young may fall prey to raptors.

SERVAL
Felis serval (Schreber 1776)

Are they widely distributed throughout the Park?
They occur in suitable habitats in all ecozones of the Park but are more commonly found in the Pretoriuskop area and on the northern Lebombo plains.

What kind of habitat do they prefer?
They prefer tall, dense, well-watered grasslands. They are particularly associated with reed beds and marshes and are always found near water. They are absent from desert or rainforest habitats.

What do they eat?
They are carnivorous and ground-roosting birds and rodents feature prominently in their diet. Small antelope such as steenbok, duikers and klipspringers have been recorded as prey animals. They also prey upon reptiles, frogs, snakes and fish.

Prey is sometimes disembowelled and excess food may be cached. Up to 15 attempts at capturing prey may be made daily, with a 50% success rate.

What are their main physical features?
An elegant, lightly built cat with long legs and neck, and a small head. The base colour varies from white to light golden-yellow with distinct black bands over and around the neck and back, with most of the rest of the body covered in spots of varying sizes. The medium-length black-banded tail has a black tip.

The large and rounded ears are black on the back, with a yellowish patch in the centre, and white on the front surface.

A distinct 'tear mark' runs from the inside of the eyes to the corners of the mouth.

Both sexes attain a shoulder height of between 45 and 65 cm, with males having a mass of up to 18 kg and females 13 kg.

Are they solitary animals?
They are usually solitary; when seen in pairs it is either a mating pair or a mother with her young.

When can they be seen?
They are both diurnal and nocturnal but more active during the late afternoon, during the night and in the early morning.

They are seldom seen during the hotter part of the day, which they spend in dense cover. At night they are active and noisy.

What sounds do they make?
The characteristic call is a high-pitched 'how! how! how!'. Kittens mew, and alarm calls include hisses, snarls and growls.

Are they aggressive?
Servals are quite mild-natured animals and, unless provoked, will never harm humans.

How do they hunt?
Prey is located by sight or hearing and caught with the slap of a paw or a high, arching pounce. Birds may be snatched from the air. Their long legs suggest that they may also run their prey down. Playing with their prey before killing and devouring it is quite common.

Are they territorial?
Home ranges cover about 10 km², but only core areas are defended as territories. Both males and females scent-mark their territories with urine, and by rubbing chin and cheek glands on grass or soil. Raking the ground with their hind feet also releases digital secretions. Faeces are left exposed.

Why are they so rare outside nature reserves?
Servals have a bad reputation as notorious poultry thieves on farms, and as a result are usually destroyed on sight. They are also not as cunning as leopards or their other field relative, the caracal.

What are their breeding habits?
Births occur throughout the year, with a peak during the rainy summer season. Male and female will stay together for a few days while the female is in oestrus. After a gestation period of about 2.5 months, litters of up to three kittens, each with a mass of about 250 g, are born in dense grass or under bushes. Kittens are blind at birth, and their eyes open after about 10 days. Solid food is taken at one month and they are weaned at about four or five months.

What is their life span?
In nature they probably live up to 12 years.

What are their major enemies?
Although adults are not generally preyed upon by other predators, they may be killed by leopards and some may succumb in territorial fights.

Eagles, hyaenas, African wild dogs, jackals and other predators could kill the young serval kittens.

CARACAL   *Felis caracal* (Schreber 1776)

Are caracals widely distributed throughout the Park?
Caracals are found in suitable habitat in all the ecozones of the Kruger Park, but are more commonly seen in woodland areas near rocky outcrops.

What type of habitat do they prefer?
Caracals occur in a variety of habitats, from fairly dense bush to open and drier savanna and woodland regions. They often frequent rocky outcrops but avoid true deserts and rainforest habitats.

What are their main physical features?
Caracals are the largest of the African small cats, very robustly built, especially adult males. Tawny to reddish-brown upper parts, interlaced with silvery-grey hair, faintly spotted whitish underparts.

There are distinctive black markings on the face at the base of the whiskers, from the inside corners of the eyes to the nose and above the eyes. The chin is white. The hind legs are slightly longer than the front legs. The backs of the ears are black with a heavy sprinkling of silvery white. The long tassels of black hair on the tips of the ears are unique among African cats. The tail is short, reaching only to the hocks.

Males reach a shoulder height of about 50 cm and females about 45 cm. Males can attain a mass of up to 18 kg and females about 13 kg.

What do caracals eat?

Caracals are carnivorous and in the Park feed mainly on impala lambs and smaller antelope such as steenbok, duikers and grysbok. Hares and hyraxes as well as a variety of birds up to the size of francolins and guineafowl are regularly taken. Also included in their diet are small reptiles, rodents, amphibians and arthropods.

They are capable of leaping into the air to catch birds. They usually stalk their prey and then pounce on it or knock it down with a sideways swipe.

Do caracals scavenge?

Caracals rarely scavenge but will cache excess food, to which they will later return if they are not disturbed.

What are their daily food intake requirements?

Males require about 500 g of meat per day and females about 350 g.

Are they dependent on water?

Caracals are water independent and obtain sufficient moisture from the blood and other body fluids of their victims. They will readily drink where water is available.

What sounds do they make?

Contact calls include barks, chirrups and meows. Alarm calls include snarls and growls.

Are their senses well developed?

Their senses of smell, sight and hearing are very well developed.

Do they climb trees?

Caracals are excellent climbers and jumpers, capable of leaping 3 to 4 m into the air.

Are they solitary animals?

A female with her young and a courting couple are often seen, but generally they are solitary animals.

What are their social habits?

They are predominantly nocturnal but may be seen at dawn and dusk. Their hunting behaviour is classically feline. They detect their prey by sight or sound, the prey is stalked and rushed at from close range, pounced upon and grabbed with the claws, and killed with a bite to the throat or the nape of the neck.

Fur and feathers may be plucked from the prey. With smaller antelope, feeding begins at the soft skin inside the thighs, with the hindquarters eaten first, then the shoulder. The intestines are not removed from the prey.

Are caracals territorial?

Both sexes defend a territory. Male and female territories may overlap but same-sex territories do not overlap. Territories are marked with urine, and scratching on trees and the ground also releases digital secretions used for territorial marking.

What is their mating behaviour and life history?

Caracals breed all year, with a peak of births during the summer. Males detect that a female is in oestrus from the smell of her urine. Mating is repeated over a period of about three days.

After a gestation period of 80 days litters of up to four, but on average two, kittens, with a mass of about 300 g each, are born in abandoned dens of other animals, rock crevices or dense vegetation. Kittens are blind at birth, and their eyes open after about six to 10 days. Kittens first eat solid food at four weeks and are weaned at four to six months.

The young are fully grown at 10 months, when the family splits up.

Are they dangerous to humans?

Caracals are dangerous and savage opponents and can attack fearlessly and with great determination when cornered. They can put up a terrific fight and are more than a match for dogs. When not disturbed or threatened they will seldom, if ever, attack humans and would rather avoid conflict.

Can they be domesticated?

They can be tamed but it is doubtful whether they can be trusted.

What are their major enemies?

Kittens fall prey to eagles, hyaenas, jackals and other predators. Adults do not have many enemies but, as they have become serious pests in sheep- and goat-farming areas, they are usually exterminated on sight.

AFRICAN WILD CAT *Felis silvestris lybica* (Forster 1780)

What is the distribution in the Park?

African wild cats are found in all the ecozones of the Park, but less common in the area south of the Sabie River. The subspecies *F. s. cafra* (Desmarest 1822) is well represented in the Kruger National Park.

What type of habitat do African wild cats prefer?

They are found in a variety of habitats with sufficient cover, such as thickets, stands of tall grass or rocky hillsides, and where there are holes in the ground or

in trees, caves, rock crevices and burrows dug by other animals where they can hide during the day.

What are their main physical features?
The African wild cat is similar to, but slightly larger than, an ordinary domestic tabby cat. The upper parts of the body are grey, the lower parts lighter and the stripes rather indistinct. The base colour is tawny-brown to grey but the colour varies according to the habitat. It is paler in drier habitats and darker in the moister habitats.

A dark stripe runs along the midline of the neck and back, two distinct stripes circle the neck and there are six or seven faint stripes on the flanks. The upper legs are banded and the chin, chest and throat are white.

The tail is long, darkly banded and black tipped. The undersides of the feet are black and the backs of the ears are rufous-brown, chestnut to orange.

Both sexes are about 35 cm at the shoulder and have a mass of about 5 to 6.5 kg.

What are their social behavioural patterns?
They are predominantly nocturnal, but are sometimes seen during the day in the early morning or when it is overcast and cool. They are occasionally seen basking in the sun outside their burrows. Shelters include abandoned aardvark burrows, termite mounds, cavities under the roots of large trees or thick undergrowth. Usually solitary, they spend most of the time on the ground, but are agile climbers and readily flee into trees if pursued.

They detect their prey by sight and sound, stalk in a crouched posture with head low, using cover, rushing forward and pouncing on prey. They grapple the prey with the claws of their front feet. Birds are ambushed at water holes and snatched from the air. Precise killing bites are used, depending on the type and size of prey.

Are they harmful creatures?
They are not aggressive towards humans but can become poultry thieves. Apparently they are difficult to tame and remain fierce and untrustworthy.

What do they eat?
Their diet changes seasonally according to the availability of food. Mammals up to the size of hares, dassies and the young of small antelope, birds as large as guineafowl, invertebrates and reptiles are included in their diet. As they are

carnivorous and able to catch only small prey, their intake requires that they hunt 10 to 20 times a day.

Mice and rats are their preferred prey but when these are scarce African wild cats will readily switch to arthropods and birds.

Are they territorial?
Male and female territories may overlap but same-sex territories do not overlap. African wild cats mark territories with urine, tree scratching to release digital secretions, and with cheek- and chin-gland secretions.

How do they show aggression?
Spitting with the ears flattened is a defensive threat, arching the back and tail and fluffing up the hair is a neutral threat. Tail twitching and approaching stiff-legged with the head held low, ears pinned back and teeth bared, while spitting, hissing and growling is the more aggressive threat.

What sounds do they make?
They make very similar sounds to those of a domestic cat, but deeper in tone and harsher. Contact calls include meows and alarm calls are hisses, spitting and growls. The screeching and caterwauling during mating is similar to that of domestic cats.

What are their breeding habits?
Mating takes place July to January and most births are between September and March when summer rains improve food supplies. After a gestation period of just more than two months, between two and five (average three) kittens, weighing about 80 to 135 g, are born in holes, hollows in trees, crevices in rocks or dense vegetation.

The mother may move them to a new refuge every few days to avoid predation. Their eyes open after 10 to 14 days and they take solid food after about a month. Kittens are weaned after some two or three months and the family disperses after about five months.

Hybridisation with domestic cats may lead to the extinction of their currently pure genetic form. This is one of the main reasons why Kruger Park staff are not allowed to have domestic cats as pets.

Are they dependent on water?
They obtain enough moisture from the blood and other body fluids of their prey but will drink when water is readily available.

What are their major enemies?
Predators include virtually all other carnivores their size or larger, as well as large raptors.

AFRICAN CIVET
Civettictis civetta (Schreber 1776)

What is their distribution in the Park?
Civets occur commonly in all ecozones of the Kruger Park.

What type of habitat do they prefer?
They give preference to woodland with dense undergrowth, usually where there is surface water, maybe because this is where the vegetation is thicker and more productive. They are also found in marshy areas but not in semi- and true deserts. They are found in all the habitats of the Park, favouring warm, bush-covered areas near permanent water.

What are the main physical features of the civet?
Civets are stockily built. The coat is greyish or grey-brown, with coarse, wiry hair; it is irregularly and heavily marked with black

stripes, blotches and spots. The head is dog-like and it has black nostrils outlined by white patches on the sides of the muzzle; a black mask around the eyes extends down to the cheeks and the forehead is paler.

A conspicuous black dorsal crest runs from the neck to the tail. When the civet is angered or alarmed this crest stands erect, making it look even more impressive.

There are broad black bands on the sides of the neck, running down onto the throat and chest. The ears are small with round tips. The limbs are short, usually black, and the small feet have five sharp non-retractile claws. The tail is bushy, with black bands and a black tip.

Males can attain a shoulder height of about 40 cm and females about 32 cm. The mass is up to 20 kg. Length from nose to tip of the tail is about 1.4 m.

What do they eat?
Civets are omnivorous and have a wide dietary range. The young of small antelope, insects, rodents, birds, reptiles, eggs, amphibians, fish, invertebrates, fruit, roots and vegetable matter, and carrion all form part of their diet. There have been recent observations of extensive middens in the southern part of the Park containing the remains of large quantities of millipedes, which most animals avoid. They frequently eat grass, probably to help digestion.

They are water independent, obtaining enough moisture from their prey and food, but will drink water when it is readily available.

What sounds do they make?
The normal call, which is seldom uttered, is a series of low-pitched grating coughs, hisses, growls and spitting coughs. Contact calls also include meows.

What are their social habits?
They are predominantly nocturnal but sometimes seen in the late afternoon. Most active from after sunset until about midnight, during the day they shelter in holes, rock crevices and dense cover.

Food is probably located by scent and sound. Prey is killed by multiple bites, often with fierce shaking. The teeth are adapted to crushing rather than cutting, and vertebrate prey is held down with the forepaws and torn apart with the canines and incisors.

They are solitary animals but occur in family groups of a mother with her young.

When disturbed, an African civet either slinks away quietly or freezes and dashes off suddenly with quick changes in direction. In defensive threat it stands sideways on and erects the crest of long mane hair along its back, in order to make itself look bigger and more formidable.

Are they territorial animals?
Well-defined paths and roads are followed within the home range. Whether they defend home ranges as territories is not known. They return regularly to chosen middens for their excretions, which suggests that they could be territorial.

Rocks, stumps and trees along paths and roads within the home range are marked with a thick, yellowish perineal-gland secretion. The tail is characteristically held upright when marking.

They also frequently scent-mark by wiping the everted anal gland onto smooth objects. These marks have a rank odour that lasts for up to three months. This form of marking is a further indication of territorial behaviour. (The anal-gland secretion used to be used as a base in perfumes.)

They defecate in middens near paths. Middens have the same odour as scent marks and may be used by more than one African civet. Adult males also spray urine.

Are African civets plentiful in the Park?
Civets are plentiful but due to their nocturnal lifestyle are very seldom seen.

What are their breeding habits?
Civets breed during the wetter summer months. After a gestation period of just more than two months, litters of up to four young (average two) weighing about 600 g each are born between August and January. They are born fully furred but blind. They are born in rock crevices, holes in termite mounds and dense cover and remain hidden for a week. The eyes open within 10 days, they take solid food after a month and are weaned at about five months.

What are their major enemies?
Their nocturnal way of life probably protects them from a wide variety of enemies. Diseases and fights could be their major mortality factors. Their main predator enemy seems to be the spotted hyaena.

GENETS
Genetta spp.

What is the distribution of genets in the Park?
In the Park the genets are represented by two species. More predominant in the northern regions of the Park is the large-spotted genet (*Genetta tigrina*, Schreber 1776), with the small-spotted genet (*Genetta genetta*, Schreber 1776) more conspicuous in the southern regions.

What type of habitat do they prefer?
The large-spotted genet prefers mopane/bushwillow woodlands, thorn thickets, thornveld, tree mopane savanna, stunted knobthorn savanna, knobthorn/marula savanna, Lebombo Mountain bushveld, alluvial plains and sandveld communities. This species is dependent on water.

The small-spotted genet is found in dry scrubland savanna, open savanna woodland, forest fringes and particularly in rocky terrain with cover. Usually associated with drier areas, it is water independent but will drink when water is available.

What do they eat?
Both species are carnivorous, feeding on small rodents, insects, lizards and small reptiles, bats, snakes, a variety of invertebrates, birds, frogs, eggs and fruit.

What are their main physical features?
The genets are long-bodied, cat-like creatures with short legs, narrow, pointed faces, large conical ears and ringed bushy tails. Their greyish bodies are richly marked with dark reddish-brown to black spots that tend to fuse to form longitudinal stripes along the back and shoulders. The tails are ringed in black; the large-spotted genet's tail ending in a black tip and the small-spotted genet has a white-tipped tail.

In both species there are white patches below the eyes; the small-spotted genet has a black chin and the large-spotted genet's chin is white. The legs of the small-spotted genet are black and those of the large-spotted genet are white or pale buff. The feet in both species have retractile claws, which make them excellent climbers.

Male large-spotted genets have a mass of up to 3.2 kg and females 2.5 kg. Head and body length are the same for both sexes: 50 to 55 cm. Both male and female small-spotted genet can attain a mass of up to 3 kg, with the males having a body length of about 57 cm and females about 50 cm.

What is their social behaviour?
The habits of both genet species seem to be very similar. They are strictly nocturnal and seldom seen during the day. Activities start soon after sunset and continue until about 01h00. Solitary animals, they shelter during the day in hollows in trees, rock crevices, holes, boulder piles, abandoned burrows and dense undergrowth.

They forage mainly on the ground, but they also climb trees to rob birds' nests or to kill roosting or nesting birds. They hunt by stalking, rushing and pouncing like a cat, killing the prey with several bites.

Are they territorial?
Home ranges may overlap with the ranges of neighbouring same-sex or opposite-sex individuals. They are not necessarily territorial, but home ranges are marked with urine, communal dung middens and anal and perineal-gland secretions that have a strong musky odour.

What sounds do they make?
Contact calls include coughs, meows and purrs. Alarm sounds include hisses, spits, growls, whines and screams.

What are their breeding habits?
After a gestation period of about 70 days, litters of up to five (average three) kittens, with a mass of about 100 g each, are born during the rainy summer season of August to March. Kittens are born in isolated spots such as termite mounds, hollows in trees, rock crevices, abandoned burrows or very dense undergrowth.

Kittens are born fully furred but blind. Their eyes open at 10 days, solid food is taken after about six weeks and they are weaned at about two months. They are independent at six months.

Are they related to the domestic cat?

Genets are not true cats, although their behaviour and physical features are similar. They are more closely related to the African civet than to domestic cats.

What are their major enemies?

Genets are a minor item in the diet of larger carnivores and are sometimes killed by larger owl species.

Mongooses are well represented in the Kruger Park but some species are more regularly seen. The most commonly seen are the banded, slender and the dwarf mongooses. For the purpose of this publication only these three mongoose species will be discussed.

BANDED MONGOOSE   *Mungos mungo* (Gmelin 1788)

Is the banded mongoose widely distributed in the Park?

This mongoose is distributed in suitable habitats in all the ecozones of the Park.

What type of habitat do they prefer?

They are found in all the habitats of the Park, favouring savannas, thickets and scrub thickets with termite mounds. They are usually not far from water and overnight in rock crevices, abandoned burrows and old termitaria.

What do they eat?

They are carnivorous, and insects and their grubs make up the major part of their diet. They also take rodents, lizards, snakes, frogs, birds and their eggs, as well as berries and fruits. In rest camps they search through garbage cans for scraps of food.

What are their main physical features?

This medium-sized mongoose has a coarse, brownish-grey coat, conspicuously marked with transverse dark brown stripes alternating with lighter-coloured bands of about the same width. The bands extend from beyond the shoulders to the base of the tail. The banding is less pronounced towards the underparts.

The feet are black, ending in five toes, all with nails. The nails on the front feet are longer, as they are used for digging.

The medium-length tail is bushy at the base, tapering to a thin, darker tip. The length from nose to tail is about 75 cm and mass is about 2 kg.

What are their social habits?

The banded mongoose is diurnal, emerging from the den after sunrise and returning before sunset. They prefer sheltering in old termitaria where there are several exits that can be used as bolt holes to escape danger.

They are very gregarious, moving around in groups of more than 20. The largest pack recorded in the Kruger Park was 75. Packs sleep together and forage in loose groups, with each mongoose obtaining its own food. When foraging, the pack moves in the same general direction and keeps contact by a continual high-pitched twitter.

The alarm call is a sharp chittering that causes pack members to freeze, stand up and scan the surroundings, and slip quietly away. Sudden alarms send them diving into nearby cover. If there are young in the pack, adults bunch around them and the pack moves off together. Smaller predators such as jackals are driven off by group attacks. Snakes are tackled in the same way.

Food is mainly detected by smell and sight, and obtained by digging in the soil and rooting in dung. Prey with distasteful secretions, such as frogs and millipedes, is rolled and rubbed in the soil to clean it.

These active little animals move about with much rustling of the grass, as they actively search for food under dead leaves, debris and stones. When alarmed, they disappear in a flash, but the patient visitor will see them reappear after a few minutes, nervously and warily scanning the surrounds for the source of the alarm.

Are they territorial?

Packs live in home ranges that may be territories, as meetings between packs are very aggressive. Each home range contains several dens that are used in rotation for a few days at a time. Pack members groom and anal-mark each other. Scent-marking takes place with anal and cheek secretions and urine.

What are their breeding habits and life span?

Reproduction is triggered by day length. Courtship is lively, with much chasing and rubbing. Male and female anal-mark each other. The male's anal gland enlarges in the breeding season.

Females in a pack tend to synchronise breeding. After a gestation period of 60 days, litters of up to five young, having a mass of 20 g each, are born between October and February. Females can have two litters during this time. Females suckle each other's offspring indiscriminately and, until the young are about five weeks old, babysitters, usually adult males, stay at the den while the rest of the pack forages. Adults catch prey and give it to juveniles.

Young are born in maternity chambers in burrows, in abandoned termite mounds, rock crevices, hollow trees and logs. They are blind at birth and sparsely furred with darkly pigmented skin. Eyes open after 10 days, they take solid food after three or four weeks and accompany adults at about five weeks. They attain adult coloration at about six weeks and reach sexual maturity at about 10 months. Life span is estimated to be about 12 years.

Are they aggressive?

The hair on their back and neck bristles when they feel threatened, making them appear larger. They approach the element of danger with a stiff-legged walk. They usually mob-attack, the members of the pack bunched together, with those in the front rising onto their hind legs while snapping, biting, spitting, growling, screeching and screaming.

What are their major enemies?

Their main predators are birds of prey and large snakes, leopards, hyaenas, jackals and lesser felids.

SLENDER MONGOOSE

Galerella sanguinea
(Rüppell 1836)

What is the distribution of the slender mongoose in the Park?

A common mongoose species in the Park, it occurs widely in suitable habitats in all ecozones of the Park.

What type of habitat does the slender mongoose prefer?

The slender mongoose has a wide habitat tolerance, occurring in savanna, woodland, forest, thickets, brush and scrub, preferring dense cover close to water.

What do they eat?

They are mostly insectivorous but also take reptiles, small rodents and birds, a variety of invertebrates and fruit. During winter they feed more on vertebrates than insects. They will scavenge roadkills. They are water independent, obtaining enough moisture from their food, but will drink when water is readily available.

What are the main physical features of the slender mongoose?

This is a small mongoose, with short legs and a long, low-slung, sinuous body. The long tail is covered in short hair, with a characteristically black tip. The base colour is variable but in the Kruger Park it tends to be grizzled greyish to reddish-brown.

The underparts are paler. The ears are small and set low on the sides of the head.

The eyes are red in adults, and green in the young up to six months of age. The lower legs and feet are dark. The digits of the feet splay readily and the nails are short and sharply curved, which makes this mongoose a very agile climber.

Males have a mass of up to 800 g and a full length of about 64 cm, and females have a mass of up to 550 g and a total length of about 60 cm.

What are their habits?

The slender mongoose is predominantly diurnal, but most active in the early morning and late afternoon. They tend to bask in the morning sun before beginning their daily activities. They sometimes forage at night when flying termites are around.

The tail is characteristically arched over the back when they are darting across open terrain. The slender mongoose usually walks with the nose close to the ground, back arched and the tail trailing with the tip turned up.

They shelter in hollow logs, termite mounds, rock crevices and holes in the ground, and are predominantly solitary. The male territories may overlap those of females, but territories of same-sex

individuals do not overlap. Regularly used paths within territories are marked with cheek- and anal-gland secretions and with urine and dung middens.

Almost all foraging is done on the ground. If alarmed they dive for cover, with the tail held low, flicking it upwards as they reach cover.

What sounds do they make?
Contact calls include 'whoos', chirps and whistles. Alarm calls include screams.

Do they show aggression?
Aggression is demonstrated by bristling the hair on the back and tail to make it appear larger. Other forms of aggression include staring, crouching with teeth bared, rushing, snapping, biting, snarling, growling and spitting. A foul-smelling liquid is discharged from the anal glands to deter predators.

What are their breeding habits?
Young are born during the wetter summer months, between October and March. After a gestation period of 60 days, up to four cubs may be born in burrows, hollow trees, rock crevices or termite mounds. Pups are blind but fully furred at birth; the eyes open at about three weeks. They take solid food after a month and are weaned at two to three months.

What are their major enemies?
Main predators are birds of prey.

DWARF MONGOOSE   *Helogale parvula* (Sundeval 1846)

What is the distribution of the dwarf mongoose in the Park?
These small animals are commonly found in all the ecozones of the Park, except ecozone C, the Malelane Mountain Bushveld. They are commonly found on the granitic soils in the western parts of the Park.

What is their habitat preference?
They prefer open grassland and wooded savanna, scrub, brush and thickets, favouring areas with numerous termite mounds that they utilise as den sites.

What do they eat?
Considered to be carnivorous, they feed mainly on insects such as beetles, grubs, crickets, grasshoppers and termites. They also eat rodents, lizards, snakes, scorpions, birds, eggs, berries and fruit. They are water independent, obtaining sufficient moisture from their food, but will drink water readily when it is available.

What are their main physical features?
The dwarf mongoose is the smallest of the mongoose family and Africa's smallest carnivore. The base colour of the wiry coat is brown to dark brown all over, with white or grey grizzling visible only at close quarters. The medium-length tail tends to be darker than the body. The soles of the feet are naked.

Males and females are of the same size and mass; the total length is about 45 to 47 cm and the mass up to 340 g.

What are dwarf mongoose's habits?
Strictly diurnal, they sleep in secure refuges such as termite mounds that are safe and warm, as well as rock crevices, hollow trees, logs and burrows.

They are highly gregarious, living in groups of up to 35 individuals. Groups consist of a breeding pair with successive litters of their offspring. The breeding pair is dominant and maintains this status for life. Older animals dominate younger ones, but juveniles have priority of access to food, and females dominate males. Foraging routes and sleeping sites are determined by the dominant female.

Territories are passed down through the generations and are defended by the group. Anal and cheek glands are used to mark upright objects close to the sleeping site. Anal-gland secretions used for marking last for about three weeks. Marking is especially heavy after border disputes. Fights with bordering groups are usually won by the larger pack, but rarely lead to serious injury and are hardly ever fatal.

Sick and injured adults are cared for by huddling, grooming and feeding, until they recover or die.

Young are carried from den to den by their babysitters.

Group members forage together with a number acting as sentries. Adults do not share food with each other, but babysitters will give food to juveniles.

They have a symbiotic relationship with hornbills (*Tockus* spp.). The mongoose exposes insects during foraging activities, while the hornbills warn the mongoose against predatory birds, their main danger.

What are their breeding habits and life span?

Each group has a dominant pair, from which most members of the group are bred. Should a subordinate female give birth, the dominant female will kill the pups. Births are recorded from the beginning of the rainy season and, after a gestation period of about 50 days, an average of four young are born in burrows, hollow trees, rock crevices and termitaria.

They are born blind and fully furred; the eyes open after about 10 days. They leave the nest at about four weeks and are weaned at six to seven weeks. Life span can be between 10 and 18 years.

What sounds do they make?

Contact calls include chirps, chirrups and twitters. The young emit peeps. Alarm calls include churrs ('tchrr') and shrieks. They also respond to the warning calls of hornbills.

What are their major enemies?

Birds of prey, snakes, jackals, honey badgers and the large grey mongoose. Dwarf Mongoose that are less than four months old are heavily taken.

STRIPED POLECAT

Ictonyx striatus (Perry 1810)

What is the distribution of the striped polecat in the Park?

Striped polecats are rarely seen in the Kruger Park. They occur marginally in ecozones A, C, D, I, L, N and P. Sightings are more common in the southern Lebombo Mountain area, in the area between the Letaba and Lepelle rivers and in the north in the Punda Maria and Pafuri areas.

What type of habitat do they prefer?

They prefer open short grasslands, savanna woodland and areas of rocky cover.

What do they eat?

They are carnivorous, with insects such as scorpions, beetles, grubs, larvae, grasshoppers and crickets making up about 60% of their diet. They may also take small rodents, birds and their eggs, frogs and small reptiles.

They are water independent, obtaining enough moisture from their food, but will drink water when it is readily available.

What are their main physical features?

This animal is strikingly patterned in black and white. There is a white patch on the forehead, with white between the eyes and ears, and four white stripes down the back. The ears are round and have white tips. The bushy tail is white flecked with black, and the underparts and legs are black. The coat is long and silky.

The toes on the front feet have long claws for digging. Males have a nose-to-tail length of about 73 cm and a mass of up to 1.5 kg, and females measure about 63 cm and have a mass of about 900 g. Shoulder height is only about 10 to 12 cm.

What are their habits?

Polecats are strictly nocturnal animals and are seldom seen. They are solitary or sometimes observed in pairs. They

move around with a characteristic trot with the back arched and the tail held horizontally.

During the day they rest in rock crevices, abandoned burrows, rock piles, self-dug holes in soft soil or dense vegetation.

Anal-gland secretions are used to mark home ranges and only the core area of the home range is defended as a territory.

Prey is detected by scent and sound. Underground insects are dug up with the front claws, and smaller rodents are bitten anywhere on the body until they are helpless and then killed with a bite to the neck.

When they are angered or excited, the long dorsal hairs become erect and the fluffy tails is raised and curled forwards over the back. This action allows them to use the vile-smelling secretion from their anal glands as defence, should it be necessary.

What sounds do they make?

Contact calls include a high-pitched yapping. Alarm calls include growls and screams.

What are their breeding habits and life span?

After a gestation period of 36 days, litters of up to three young are born in the rainy season between October and March. Young with a mass of 10 to 15 g each are born helpless and blind. They crawl after two weeks, their eyes open after four to six weeks and they are weaned at about two or three months.

Only one litter per year is produced, unless the young die early, when the female may breed again.

They have an estimated life span of six to eight years.

What are their main enemies?

Because of the foul-smelling anal secretions they use in defence, striped polecats are rarely killed by any of the carnivores. They are sometimes preyed upon by owls, and their young by smaller felids.

CAPE CLAWLESS OTTER *Aonyx capensis* (Schinz 1821)

What is the distribution of this otter in the Park?

Cape clawless otters are found in ecozone H of the Kruger Park, being common in the adjoining areas and found in all perennial and some of the seasonal rivers. They are also found in vleis and dams throughout the Park.

What is their preferred habitat?

They prefer running water and areas near permanent water where dense vegetation cover, holes or rocks are available. They cannot live in polluted water.

What do they eat?

They are carnivorous, favouring crustaceans such as crabs. They also eat shellfish, frogs, fish, snails, insects, small mammals and birds.

They go through an extensive cleaning routine of their food before eating it, and a similar routine of washing themselves after meals.

Being semi-aquatic, they are very water dependent, requiring perennial water bodies for their livelihood.

What are their main physical features?

The fur of the otter is short and dense and varies in colour from light to very dark brown, appearing darker when wet. The underside, throat and chest are white, and the face has whitish marking. The head is broad, with small eyes and ears. The legs are short, with five toes on each foot. The forefeet have no nails (hence the common name) and barely noticeable webbing. The hind feet have nails only on the third and fourth digits and are webbed about halfway.

The tail is thick at the base, tapering sharply to a thin tip. The underside of the tail is flattened, which allows the otter to change direction in the water. The ears and nose can be closed under water.

They can reach a total length of 1.60 to 1.75 m; males can attain a mass of about 20 kg and females about 14 to 16 kg.

What are their habits?

Otters are predominantly nocturnal, but are active during the late afternoon and early evening, and are sometimes observed at dawn or in the early morning.

Usually solitary, they are sometimes found in pairs and family clans.

They shelter in holts (dens) in dense vegetation, under rocks or burrows dug by themselves, and dense reed beds.

Otters are more at home in water than on land. They swim by using their webbed hind feet for propulsion and the tail as a rudder; they can dive underwater for up to 30 seconds. They walk with an arched back.

Fish are hunted by sight, while crabs and molluscs are felt for and captured with the dexterous forefeet and then bitten to death. Fish are usually eaten from the head backwards, except for the bony-headed barbel. Crabs are crushed and eaten with the shell.

After swimming they dry themselves by rubbing against vegetation, rocks or the ground.

Home ranges along rivers can be up to 14 km long and are marked by urine, spraints (faecal deposits) and anal secretions.

Do they make any sounds?

A wide range of contact calls include chirps, growls, squeals, whistles, mews, moans and screaming wails. When alarmed, they utter a loud snort and run to the water for refuge.

What are their breeding habits and life span?

Breeding season in the Park occurs during March and April. After a gestation period of two months up to two young are born, with a mass of about 200 g each. Young are hidden in nests in dense vegetation, mainly in holts. They are born blind; their eyes open at about one month when they leave the nest. They are weaned at three or four months, but remain with their mother for about a year. The life span is about 10 years.

What are their major enemies?

Crocodiles pose the biggest threat to otters. Young fall victim to large birds of prey and large snakes. Other medium-sized predators usually have an unpleasant time catching otters, as they have a tough, loose skin that allows them to 'turn in their skin', like the honey badger, and bite their attacker viciously; they grip tightly, growling and snarling.

HONEY BADGER   *Mellivora capensis* (Schreber 1776)

What is their distribution in the Park?

Found in all the ecozones of the Park.

What type of habitat do they prefer?

They occur in all the habitats in the Park, but are uncommon in the forested areas.

What do they eat?

Being omnivorous, honey badgers have a wide dietary range that includes a variety of insects, grubs, rodents, snakes, lizards, birds and their eggs, roots, bulbs, fruits, berries and, of course, honey. They favour honey and have a symbiotic relationship with the Greater Honeyguide (*Indicator*

indicator), which guides them to beehives. Because of their thick skin, honey badgers are impervious to bee stings when digging out a beehive, and the Greater Honeyguide gains by getting honey, wax and grubs from the raided hive.

What are their main physical features?

This stoutly built, tough-looking little creature has tremendous attitude and fears nothing and nobody. It stands about 30 cm high at the shoulder, and has a mass of about 13 to 14 kg and an overall length of up to a metre. There is a pale grey mantle on the top of the head, down the back and on top of the tail, and the remainder of the body is black with a white line separating the two colours of fur. The eyes and ears are small and the legs are short and powerful. The ears can be closed during a raid on a beehive or digging.

The skin is very thick and quite loose around the neck, giving honey badgers great resistance to bites and enabling them to turn around in their skin to bite their attacker. This tough, loose skin plays an important role in their defence. They are good climbers and diggers, with sharp-edged, long claws of up to 35 mm on the forefeet. The tail is short and bushy and usually held upright as the animal moves about.

What are their habits?
In the Park they are found to be mainly active from dusk and through the night.

They are solitary or found in monogamous pairs. Territoriality in the wild is as yet uncertain but home ranges are marked with dung middens and anal-gland secretions. Home ranges of males and females may overlap, but those of same-sex individuals do not overlap.

Honey badgers are powerful diggers and can dig themselves into sandy ground in about two minutes. Prey animals, such as small rodents, are dug out of their burrows, and they demolish rotten logs to uncover insect larvae and grubs. They are nomadic and dig a new den almost every day.

Self-dug or abandoned holes in the ground, burrows, hollow trees and hollow tree trunks or logs are used as shelters.

Honey badgers have a well-founded reputation for ferocity when disturbed. They have been observed killing a python almost 3 m long, and a honey badger has been spotted attacking an older lion and severely biting it around the mouth. The black-and-white pattern serves as a warning to other animals to stay away. Under extreme duress they release a foul-smelling secretion from their anal glands.

Hunting honey badgers may be shadowed by a Pale Chanting Goshawk (*Melierax canorus*) or by a black-backed jackal, hoping to grab any prey that escapes the honey badger.

What are their breeding habits?
Births peak during the summer rainy season, when an average of two pups, with a mass of about 115 g each, are born after a gestation period of six months. The pups are born in secluded spots, such as burrows or hollow tree trunks. They are born blind with a naked, pink skin that turns a mottled pattern after about a week. The eyes open after about three weeks and the mantle shows its distinctive pattern at about this time. Adult coloration is attained at about six weeks and they emerge from the shelter at two to three months.

What are their main enemies?
Honey badgers probably do not have many enemies, except maybe the African rock python. Disease and fighting could be responsible for most mortalities.

HERBIVORES

ANTELOPE

How many different species of antelope are found in the Park?
Eighteen different species of antelope are found in the Park. They are: suni (*Neotragus moschatus*), steenbok (*Raphicerus campestris*), klipspringer (*Oreotragus oreotragus*), Sharpe's grysbok (*Raphicerus sharpei*), red or Natal duiker (*Cephalophus natalensis*), common or grey duiker (*Sylvicapra grimmia*), mountain reedbuck (*Redunca fulvorufula*), common or southern reedbuck (*Redunca arundinum*), impala (*Aepyceros melampus*), greater kudu (*Tragelaphus strepsiceros*), nyala (*Tragelaphus angasii*), bushbuck (*Tragelaphus scriptus*), eland (*Taurotragus oryx*), waterbuck (*Kobus ellipsiprymnus*), tsessebe (*Damaliscus lunatus*), blue wildebeest (*Connochaetes taurinus*), roan antelope (*Hippotragus equinus*) and sable antelope (*Hippotragus niger*).

Are they well adapted for survival in their specific habitats?
The antelope of southern Africa are mostly adapted to savanna and open types of habitat, as are predominantly found in the Park. They possess sharp vision with a wide angle of view and a keen sense of smell and hearing. They are very fleet-footed, which allows them to flee from predators, and some are big and powerful as adults, having few natural enemies apart from lions.

If their vision is so sharp, why do they not recognise humans in a motor vehicle?
Antelope do not distinguish colour and can see only in shades of monochrome. They, like most other animals, recognise human beings by their upright stance. Lack of binocular vision might further hamper their ability to recognise a person in a vehicle when no part of the body is outside of the vehicle.

When the accepted outline of a vehicle is broken, such as when a person is leaning out of the vehicle, animals will react by moving away from the vehicle.

Animals react to a large extent on movement to detect the object. Most predators make use of this phenomenon by freezing during the stalk to get close enough for an attack.

Are antelope very dependent on water?
Some antelope, such as waterbuck, are very dependent on water, the impala less so. The steenbok and klipspringer can possibly exist without water for considerable periods. Most antelope, however, will drink readily where water is available.

In general, antelope are adapted to survive in conditions of drought. Water is very efficiently extracted from their food, they do not sweat much and their faeces are usually deposited as dry pellets.

Are antelope territorial in habit?
All antelope show territorial behaviour to some extent. Some may actively defend a territory, e.g. klipspringer, while others live in home ranges. Most antelope use scent glands, usually situated below their eyes and between their hooves, to mark their territories or home ranges.

Do males often kill rivals in territorial fights?
Fighting behaviour is highly ritualised, with displays of aggression, and many a fight terminates by out-bluffing the opponent. In 'low-intensity' encounters

opponents usually use elaborate displays in which posturing with the head, ears and tail plays an important part. 'High-intensity' sparring usually takes the form of a pushing duel, ending when the subordinate animal turns and flees. Even in real and serious encounters, relatively few combatants are killed.

Do antelope and other herbivores know when lions are not hungry?

Herbivores maintain certain flight or escape distances from their enemies. This distance varies from species to species, or even among members of the same species. Larger animals usually have a shorter flight distance than smaller species.

It is difficult to determine whether herbivores actually know when lions are hungry or not. When herbivores have an enemy in sight they are not unduly alarmed because they can maintain a safe flight distance. They tend to become very nervous when they can hear or smell a predator without being able to see it.

What is the general life span of an antelope?

Estimates of longevity vary considerably. Some authors base their claims on life span in captivity, while others attempt to estimate what it could be in the wild. To establish an average life span is very difficult. Factors such as the influence of different habitats, number and density of enemies, incidence of diseases and climatic conditions all play a part in an animal's survival.

In general, small antelope live five to 10 years, medium-sized antelope 10 to 15 years and the bigger antelope up to 20 years or slightly more. They also live longer in captivity than in the wild. In captivity they are not subjected to predation and food shortages, and veterinary assistance is readily available to attend to injuries and diseases, while the opposite is the case for animals in the wild.

Are there springbok and gemsbok in the Kruger Park?

No, they prefer the drier, more open areas of South Africa. Springbok and gemsbok are more suited to arid and semi-arid habitats and the associated feeding material and forbs. There are no records that these antelope ever occurred in the Kruger Park. As it is SANParks' policy to maintain the Park in as natural a state as possible, introduction of new species to the Park is not an option, but the reintroduction of species, where there is positive proof that they previously occurred naturally in the Park, will always be considered.

Have any antelope been introduced into the Park?

No antelope were introduced into the Park. Some species, of which the numbers were very low, were supplemented by translocating them from other areas where they still existed in fair numbers. This included antelope like oribi, suni, red duiker, mountain reedbuck, roan antelope, eland and Lichtenstein's hartebeest.

Were these antelope extinct in the Park?

No, only oribi and Lichtenstein's hartebeest were not found in the Park at this stage. The last oribi had been seen in the Park in about 1943 and Lichtenstein's hartebeest had last been recorded in the area that is now the Kruger Park towards the end of the 1800s. It has since been established that Lichtenstein's hartebeest actually did not occur naturally in the Kruger National Park, as had been believed. Most of these animals that had been reintroduced from Malawi were captured and relocated to the new Limpopo National Park in Mozambique. Those that could not be captured were left to live out their natural lives in the Park.

Suni were thought to exist in small numbers in the Nyandu bush in the remote northeastern border area of the Park. To supplement their small numbers, suni were translocated from northern KwaZulu-Natal to the Kruger Park during 1979, 1981 and again in 1992.

The others were translocated to the Park to strengthen the numbers of existing populations.

All antelope species previously recorded in the Park are now represented here.

Will more antelope be translocated to the Park?

Should the need arise to augment the numbers of rare species, it may be considered. It is, however, also accepted that there will always be numerical differences between species due to differences in social organisation, habitat preferences and other ecological traits.

Which is the biggest antelope?

The eland, with a mass of 700 to 900 kg and a shoulder height of 1.4 to 1.8 m, is the biggest and heaviest antelope in the Park.

Which is the smallest?

The suni is the smallest antelope found in the Park. It has a shoulder height of about 35 cm and a mass of about 5 kg.

Which antelope is considered to be the fastest?

The speed of animals is something of a controversial topic, and exaggerations are rather the rule than the exception. How does one measure a wild animal's speed accurately? Are the speeds claimed for different animals a record, or just a rough estimate? Has any species of animal been tested thoroughly? Was a representative sample of the population tested by a foolproof method? The common method of chasing an animal with a vehicle gives only a rough estimate of the speed of that particular animal.

It is commonly believed that the hartebeest family, of which the tsessebe is represented in the Park, is the fastest, and speeds of up to 80 km/h have been claimed.

Which antelope is the best jumper?

Of the antelope in the Park, the impala is probably the best long jumper, with reputed leaps of approximately 10 m. Kudu and eland are reputedly the best high jumpers.

Are there any gazelles in the Park?

No. The only member of the gazelle family found in South Africa is the springbok (*Antidorcas marsupialis*), which is not found in the Park.

What is the difference between a gazelle and an antelope?

Gazelles belong to a sub-group of the antelope family and are mostly confined to the more open savannas and grasslands. They are very fleet-footed and usually have lyre-shaped horns.

Is the deer family represented in the Park?

No. Deer are not found in Africa south of the Sahara.

How do deer and antelope differ from each other?

Antelope have horns, which are bony structures consisting of an inner core of porous bone covered by an impervious bony sheath. They are unbranched, never shed, and if broken are never replaced. Deer have antlers, which are branched structures of solid bone and are shed annually.

Can antelope be dangerous to man?

Like roan, sable antelope are courageous and high-spirited, very dangerous and apt to charge when wounded or held at bay. Gemsbok and bushbuck are also dangerous when wounded. A few hunters have been killed and some seriously injured by bushbuck. Wounded sable or gemsbok should not be approached even if they are incapable of getting up as they can inflict severe injuries with their horns, and even use their horns to repel stones thrown at them.

Which antelope is considered the most beautiful in the Park?
Most people regard the sable antelope as the most magnificent of all antelope. The kudu, however, also has tremendous support in this respect.

Do antelope migrate in the Park?
Although wildebeest and Burchell's zebra (*Equus quagga*) undertake seasonal migrations, large-scale migrations, such as those that take place in the Serengeti, do not occur in the Kruger Park. The major migratory routes of the wildebeest and zebra were severed by the western boundary fence of the Park, erected in the mid 1960s.

Movements in search of suitable grazing occur during periods of drought, but this is on a very small scale.

SMALLER EVEN-TOED UNGULATES

SUNI   *Neotragus moschatus* (Von Dueben 1846)

Are these animals rare and where are they most likely to be found?
The suni, also known as Livingstone's antelope, are extremely rare in the Kruger Park and are classified in the *Red Data Book* as Vulnerable.

Their distribution is limited to the extreme northern parts of ecozones M and N and to some extent into the western parts of ecozone N of the Park, occurring marginally in suitable habitat of the dense thickets of the sandveld communities and the alluvial plains in the Punda Maria vicinity.

They are also found in dense vegetation along rivers.

To supplement existing dwindling numbers, a number of suni were translocated and released in suitable habitats in 1979, 1981 and 1992. All these animals originated from KwaZulu-Natal.

Because of their habitat preference and their distribution, visitors do not often see these small antelope.

What do they eat?
They are mainly browsers, feeding on shoots, flowers, fruit, mushrooms and other fungi. They often follow monkeys, feeding on the fallen fruit, leaves and shoots dropped during their foraging. They are water independent, obtaining sufficient moisture from their food.

What are their main physical features?
This is the smallest of the mini antelope found in the Park, with a shoulder height of only about 35 cm and a body mass of about 5 kg.

The upper reddish-brown body parts are flecked with whitish hairs, with the underparts whitish. The hairs around the snout are dark. The tail is edged in white and is white underneath.

Only the rams have horns, which are straight and point backwards, heavily ridged and 7 to 13 cm long.

They have interdigital glands, well-developed preorbital glands and keen senses of sight, hearing and smell.

What are their habits?

Suni are active at any time, but mainly in the early morning and late afternoon, tending to rest up in thickets during the hottest part of the day.

They are usually single, but also found in pairs or a pair with a lamb.

Territories are scent-marked with a musky secretion from the preorbital glands that is deposited on stems and twigs in the feeding area. As the animal walks, the interdigital glands between the hooves mark pathways. Mutual grooming occurs between pairs and herd members.

Characteristically the tail is flicked from side to side.

What are their breeding habits?

They breed throughout the year, with a peak in the rainy summer season. A single lamb is born after a gestation period of six months, with about seven months between births. The lamb, which has a mass of less than 1 kg, is born in dense cover and hidden for a week.

What is their average life span?

They have a life span of about eight years.

What are their major enemies?

Predators include leopards, lions, hyaenas, Nile crocodile and Southern African python. Young suni are also taken by large raptors and jackals.

Habitat changes play a role in the decline of their numbers, especially the clearance of bush for development. In addition, the increase in the number of nyala places grazing pressure on the suni's habitat.

Deaths caused by domestic and feral dogs in areas outside of conservation areas are a problem, and their habit of using regular trails makes them extremely vulnerable to poachers' snares.

SHARPE'S GRYSBOK *Raphicerus sharpei* (Thomas 1897)

Are they well distributed in the Park?

Sparsely distributed in the Park in ecozones A, E, F, I, J, L, M, N, O and P, with the major populations found along the Lebombo mountain range south of the Lepelle River, along the central and northwestern border north of the Lepelle River and in reasonably high density north of Punda Maria and in the Pafuri area.

What type of habitat do they prefer and what do they eat?

In the Park they prefer low scrub and brush with medium grasses, open woodland savanna and thickets including rocky outcrops and adjacent grasslands. They avoid thick, tall grassland and prefer mixed woodlands, mopane shrubveld, mopane/*Combretum* woodlands, tree mopane savanna, knobthorn/marula savanna, rugged veld and the Lebombo Mountain Bushveld.

Sharpe's grysbok are mainly browsers of broad-leaved shrubs, but also fruits and berries. They occasionally graze on grass and herbs.

They are water independent, but will drink when water is available.

What are their main physical features?

The reddish-brown upper parts are speckled with white hair, giving the animal a grizzled appearance. The underparts and inner legs are whitish, and there is a dark band from the nose to between the eyes. The ears are large with light-coloured hair on the inside.

They stand and move with a hunched posture, the hindquarters higher than the shoulder.

Only the rams have horns, which are short, straight, smooth and lightly ridged at the base, with a length of up to 5 cm.

They have a shoulder height of about 55 cm and a mass of about 10 to 13 kg.

They have preorbital scent glands as well as interdigital glands. Rams also have preputial glands.

What are Sharpe's grysbok's habits?

They are predominantly nocturnal, but are sometimes seen at dawn and dusk. Shy and secretive, they lie concealed in thick cover. They are solitary, but pairs or females with lambs are seen. It is believed that pairs share a territory that is defended by the ram. Territorial demarcation is done with preorbital secretions and interdigital glands.

When disturbed, they move off in a slinking run, not stopping to look back until they feel safe to squat down and hide again.

What are their breeding habits?

Breeding takes place all year ,with a peak during October and November. After a gestation period of seven months a single lamb with a mass of about 1 kg is born in dense cover. It stays hidden for a month and is weaned after about three months.

What are their major enemies?

Predation by leopards, cheetahs, caracals, jackals, African wild dog and hyaenas. The young also fall prey to eagles and pythons.

What is their average life span?

About 10 years.

RED DUIKER   *Cephalophus natalensis* (A. Smith 1834)

This seems to be a very rare antelope. What is its distribution in the Park?

This rarely seen little antelope seems to be confined to the Pretoriuskop and Skukuza areas and along the Sabie River between Skukuza and the Nkuhlu picnic site. In the southern Kruger Park a small population is found as a breakaway from the main distribution area.

Also known as the Natal duiker, it is predominantly distributed along the eastern seaboard of KwaZulu-Natal and northwards along the Mozambican seaboard and interior.

Most of the areas with natural red duiker populations were cut from the Park by boundary adjustments in the past. Red duikers captured on Mariepskop were reintroduced, but the success of the reintroductions is doubtful.

What is their preferred habitat and what do they eat?

They frequent dense areas of woody vegetation along rivers and wooded ravines. A browser, also eating fallen leaves and fruit, berries, buds and shoots. They follow monkeys around to feed on items dropped or knocked down by these primates. They are independent of water, obtaining sufficient moisture from their diet.

What are their main physical features?

The upper body parts are rusty, reddish-brown with slightly lighter underparts, and it is whitish under the throat. Both sexes have horns, with those of the male being slightly longer, reaching 7–10 cm. In some populations females may not have horns. The horns are heavily ridged at the base, with a grooved middle section and a smooth tip. The tail has a black-and-white tip and the ears are edged in black.

Both sexes reach a shoulder height of about 50 cm and a mass of about 14 kg.

The red duiker has keen senses of smell, hearing and sight.

Typical of the duiker species, it carries a dark, tufted crest between the horns.

Are they territorial and what are their habits?

Because of their shy nature, secluded habitat and low density, little is known about these mini antelope. Diurnal, with activity peaks at dawn and dusk, they are believed to be inactive at night. They are predominantly single, but found in monogamous pairs or a pair with their offspring.

Territories may overlap and are marked by rubbing the prominent preorbital-gland secretions against bushes and grass stalks, augmented with interdigital-gland secretions and communal dung middens. Social relations are maintained through mutual grooming.

Home ranges always include favourite resting sites. When disturbed or alarmed, these wary antelope will freeze at first. If the threat persists, they will flee at the last moment, expertly threading their way through thickets.

What are their breeding habits?

After a gestation period of seven months a single lamb is born. It weighs about 1 kg and is much darker than the adults. The average interval between births is about nine months.

Lambs are born throughout the year, with a peak during the summer months.

What is their average life span?

Longevity is about eight or nine years.

What are their major enemies?

Outside of conservation areas, habitat destruction and consequent fragmentation of populations poses a major threat to red duikers.

They are heavily poached by snaring and hunted with dogs.

In nature their main predators include leopards, lions, jackals, lesser felines and larger eagles.

The status of this small antelope is uncertain as no sightings have been reported for many years. A female was sighted at the Game Capture Unit offices in Skukuza in July 2008, indicating that these very shy antelope are still in the area.

GREY DUIKER *Sylvicapra grimmia* (Linnaeus 1758)

Where are grey duikers found in the Kruger Park?

Grey duikers are the widest distributed of the smaller antelope in the Kruger Park, and in South Africa generally. They belong to the antelope genus that probably has the widest range of

distribution and the largest number of species and subspecies in Africa.

Grey duikers are found in suitable habitat throughout the Kruger Park, preferring woodland savanna, scrub and brush. They occur commonly in riparian vegetation along rivers and watercourses.

What are their main physical features?

The upper parts vary from a grizzled grey to reddish-yellow and the underparts are usually whitish to grey. The front of the forelegs is dark brown to black.

A black band on top of the muzzle runs to the upper forehead. The inside of the ears is whitish.

Usually only the rams have horns but some horned females have been observed. The horns are up to 18 cm long, straight, heavily ridged at the base and smooth at the tip.

There is a characteristic tuft of hair between the horns of the ram. The ewe also has this tuft of hair, which at a distance resembles a single horn. The tail is dark on top and white underneath.

Grey duikers have a shoulder height of about 60 cm and a body mass of 20 to 25 kg.

What do they eat?

They are almost exclusively browsers, preferring the leaves from a variety of broad-leaved trees and shrubs. They also eat twigs, seeds, fruit, roots, tubers, fungi and flowers. They have been recorded as feeding on birds and insects.

Independent of water, they obtain sufficient moisture from their diet, and rarely drink water even if it is readily available.

What are their habits?

Like other duiker species they are mostly nocturnal, especially in areas where they are regularly disturbed or hunted. They are most active at dawn and dusk and may be active all day when it is cloudy or cool. They rest in the cover of thickets and long grass.

They are usually solitary, but sometimes a female is seen with a lamb. They frequent game paths, making them vulnerable to poachers' snares.

They avoid predators by lying quietly or freezing motionless, dashing away at the last moment when the perceived danger is too close. When fleeing, they run with a distinctive diving, zigzag motion from which the name (Afrikaans for 'diver') is derived.

Their senses of smell, sight and hearing are very well developed.

Are they territorial?

Yes. They fight to defend their territories. In the Park their territories are about 0.2 km^2 and are marked with secretions from preorbital glands rubbed onto shrubs and grass stalks and with interdigital glands. Territories of neighbouring same-sex individuals do not overlap.

What are their breeding habits?

Breeding seems to occur throughout the year. After a gestation period of about seven months, a single lamb is born in dense cover, where it remains hidden for up to three months, with the ewe returning at regular intervals to suckle and clean the lamb.

What is their average life span?

Their life span is about 10 years.

What are their major enemies?

Predators include lions, leopards, wild dogs, cheetahs, jackals and hyaenas. Young also fall prey to caracals, pythons and eagles.

STEENBOK

Raphicerus campestris (Thunberg 1811)

Is the steenbok well distributed throughout the Kruger Park?

This small antelope is found in all the ecozones of the Park, with higher densities in the open plains of the eastern regions and lower densities in the western parts of the Park.

What type of habitat do they prefer?

Fairly dry and open plains are preferred, as well as lightly wooded areas with stands of medium to short grass and brush cover. They are not found in desert-type habitats, rocky areas and densely wooded forest areas. In the Park they prefer the *Acacia tortilis* (umbrella thorn) savanna areas.

What are their main physical features?

This small, graceful little antelope has a glossy coat, rufous-brown on the back and sides with white underparts and a short brown tail that is white underneath. The ears are large with a distinct leaf-like pattern of dark blood vessels.

Only the males have horns, which rise from the top of the head, straight and smooth, except at the base where they are lightly ridged. Horns can reach a length of up to about 18 cm. Shoulder height is about 50 to 55 cm and the body mass around 12 kg.

Scent glands are situated between the hooves and on either side of the lower jaw, and distinctive preorbital glands are visible in front of the eyes. Their senses of sight, smell and hearing are very well developed.

What are their behavioural patterns?

Steenbok are considered to be both diurnal and nocturnal. Diurnal activities are usually early morning and late afternoon. They tend to become more nocturnal under conditions of environmental pressure, such as droughts. Can be active all day during cool weather.

They avoid predators by lying up in thick cover. They freeze when danger approaches and leap up at the last moment, dashing off in a zigzag pattern with intermittent bounds, stopping from time to time to check the pursuing danger. Lambs will lie flat with ears pinned back on their necks to avoid detection until the danger has passed.

In South Africa this beautiful antelope is the symbol of cleanliness, as it scrapes a depression in which it deposits its dung, which it covers with sand. In this process the dung and urine are mixed with soil and deposited in the scrapes. During the scraping process digital secretions are also released that could assist in territorial demarcation.

Do they defend a territory?

Yes, territories are demarcated through interdigital and preorbital glandular secretions. Territories are defended by various displays such as horn threats, pawing the ground, horning of

vegetation, mock charges and chasing of the intruder. When threatened, they will readily stab at the contender for the territory with their horns.

What do they eat?
Steenbok browse and graze according to the local or seasonal availability of their preferred food. In the Park only 0.02% of feeding time is spent on eating grass. Feeding is by selective browsing of tree and shrub leaves, while forbs are the main food items. They also take tubers, bulbs, roots, berries and fruits.

Steenbok obtain enough moisture from their diet to make them water independent, but will drink readily when water is available.

Is it true that they mate for life?
Not enough research has been done to provide a conclusive answer to this question. Steenbok are usually solitary animals, but it is thought that monogamous pairs may share territories.

What are their breeding habits?
After a gestation period of about 5.5 months a single lamb, with a mass of about 1 kg, is born. Lambing occurs throughout the year, with a peak during the summer months. The lamb is hidden away in clumps of dense, tall grass and thickets for up to a month. Females become sexually mature after about six months.

What is their average life span?
Their life span can be eight to 10 years.

What are their major enemies?
Their main natural enemies include lions, leopards, cheetahs, caracals, hyaenas, wild dogs, jackals, pythons and large eagles.

KLIPSPRINGER   *Oreotragus oreotragus* (Zimmerman 1783)

Are these small antelope restricted to rocky areas of the Kruger Park?
Klipspringers have patchy distribution, being mostly confined to hills with large boulders. They are particularly common in the Lebombo Mountain, north of the Letaba River, the hilly areas north of Punda Maria and in the Pafuri area, and in the Malelane mountains in the southwest.

What are their main physical features?
This small, stoutly built antelope has a grizzled coat, which is yellow speckled with brown. Its underparts are whitish and it has greyish legs. It has a brittle, hollow-haired coat that affords excellent protection against contact with sharp rocks.

The muzzle is short and sharply tapered. Prominent black patches in front of the eyes mark the openings of the preorbital glands. The ears are white inside with a black border.

Its short, stocky legs have small hooves with rubbery centres and hard rims to provide grip and help with agility on rocks.

The shoulder height is about 50–60 cm and the body mass 10.5–13.5 kg.

Only the males have horns, which are straight and mainly smooth, except for the bottom third, which is ridged. The horns reach a length of 12 to 15 cm.

Their senses of smell, sight and hearing are very well developed.

Apart from the distinctive preorbital glands, the males also have preputial glands, situated in the foreskin of the penis.

What are their behavioural patterns?
Klipspringers are predominantly diurnal, with activity peaks in the late afternoon.

They live in pairs with sub-adult lambs. Single animals are usually unmated rams. Larger groups of two or three pairs are more common in drier seasons, and tend to separate into pairs when breeding commences in the spring. They shelter between rocks and in clumps of bushes.

They are very agile and can jump from one rock to another or even run up gradients that appear inaccessible to any other animal but a baboon.

They often stand in a tiptoe pose with their backs arched and hooves bunched together on prominent boulders.

Are they territorial?

They are strictly territorial and faithful to the territory. Both sexes mark their territory by depositing a sticky secretion with a sharp, tarry smell through the preorbital glands on twigs and grass stems. Males usually over-mark female scent deposits.

It is thought that their habit of standing on prominent boulders and outcrops is to advertise their presence in the area and also to keep a lookout for predators.

Threat displays include horn threats, horning of vegetation, pawing the ground, mock attacks, and stabbing and chasing intruders.

Can they be aggressive?

When threatened, they tend to freeze and then flee to higher ground, often turning around to determine whether they are still being pursued. This also indicates to predators that they have been spotted. They can outrun any land animal over rocky terrain.

What do they eat?

Klipspringers are strictly browsers, eating leaves, shoots, fruits and flowers of a wide range of evergreen shrubs, trees, bushes and forbs, berries, seed pods and sometimes fresh grass shoots.

They also chew soil and bones to satisfy certain mineral requirements.

They are water independent, obtaining moisture from their diet, but will drink when water is available.

What are their breeding habits?

Lambs are born throughout the year, but with a peak during the summer months when browse is abundant. A single lamb, with a mass of about 1 kg, is born after a gestation period of about seven months. The lamb is hidden in rocky recesses or in thick vegetation in rocky habitats for two to three weeks and is weaned after four to five months. The young male's horns become visible after six months.

Lambs stay close to their parents once they become mobile, and learn what to eat by watching the parents. They are weaned at four to five months.

When danger threatens, lambs react to warning whistles from the adults by lying flat and motionless with their ears pinned back.

What is their average life span?

Life span is about eight years.

What are their main enemies?

Main predators include leopards, caracals, jackals, serval and hyaenas. They are sometimes also taken by large eagles, baboons and large snakes.

COMMON (SOUTHERN) REEDBUCK

Redunca arundinum (Boddaert 1785)

How widely are they distributed in the Park?

As they have specific habitat requirements, common reedbucks are very patchily distributed in ecozones B and C of the Park and marginally in ecozone L.

In the Park they are predominantly found in the Malelane Mountain Bushveld between Pretoriuskop and Malelane, the grassland areas north of Mlondozi in the Lower Sabie area, the marginal vleiland areas of the mopane shrubveld north of Letaba and the vlei areas of the northern plains.

What habitat would they be expected to frequent?

The main habitat requirements of reedbucks are tall grass areas with scrub, reed beds and vlei areas close to perennial watercourses.

What are their main physical features?

Reedbucks have a greyish-brown to buffy yellow coat, darker on the back with white underparts. They are white under the neck, with a distinctive white crescent-shaped pattern under the throat that is more obvious in the males. The chin and lips are white.

Dark bands are visible down the front of the forelegs, and are less distinct down the lower hind legs.

The ears have triangular-shaped tips and there is a bare glandular patch on the side of the neck below the ear. The tail is bushy and white underneath.

Only the males have horns, which rise from the top of the head and sweep forward with an even curve. The bottom two-thirds are ridged and the tips are smooth. At the base of the horns is a distinctive band of pale, soft, rubbery tissue. Horns can reach a length of 40 cm.

They have scent glands beneath the ears and inguinal glands in the groin.

Shoulder height in rams can be up to 1 m and in the ewes up to 90 cm. The mass of the rams is about 90 kg and the ewes about 80 kg.

What are their behavioural characteristics?

Reedbucks are mostly nocturnal, although feeding extends into daylight in winter or during droughts, when grazing declines.

Monogamous pairs share a territory that is defended by the dominant ram. Territorial occupation is advertised by proud posturing with the neck erect and the head held high, showing the white throat band, running with an exaggerated rocking-horse motion, ritual urination and defecation, and loud whistling.

Intruders are confronted with the same displays and fighting is highly ritualised, with horns clashing, escalating to forward and downward jabs. Submission is shown by the lowering of the head.

Occasionally groups of 10 or more congregate on good grazing.

How do reedbucks show aggression?

Territorial display is shown by means of mock and real charging, threats, head tossing, symbolic head butting by tossing the head, horn threats, butting, rushing and chasing.

The alarm call is a loud, high-pitched nasal whistle and snorts, which may also tell the predator that it has lost the element of surprise. Alarm displays also include an alert posture and stamping. They freeze to avoid detection and then slink away if not detected. They flee at a gallop with occasional long leaps. When fleeing, they employ trotting and stotting, with the jerking of the hind legs backwards and outwards producing a 'pop' sound from the sudden opening of the inguinal glands in the groin, and jumping with the hind legs tucked up, hindquarters high and the head back, snorting at each jump.

What are their breeding habits?

A male courts by approaching the female with the head low and stretched forward, nuzzling and sniffing the female's genitals.

After a gestation period of about seven months, a single lamb, with a mass of about 5 kg, is born. Lambing occurs throughout the year, with a peak during the rainy summer months. The lamb is born in thick cover and remains hidden for about two months. Mothers visit once a day and more at night to suckle and clean the lamb.

What is their average life span?

Their life span is about 10 years.

What does their diet consist of?

This reedbuck is mainly a grazer, feeding on grasses and forbs, with a preference for freshly sprouted grass, especially after fires. It will turn to browsing if the nutritional quality of grazing falls too low.

The major component of their diet is 'unpalatable grasses' that are avoided by other grazers. During winter grassy plants and herbaceous material, largely avoided by other grazers, supplement the diet.

Reedbucks are very water dependent, needing to drink several times a day during the dry season.

What are the main threats to their existence?

Their conservation status is threatened by habitat loss from the destruction of wetlands, badly managed burning of grasslands and vleis, and overgrazing.

Reedbucks are vulnerable to predation mainly by lions, leopards, African wild dogs, hyaenas and cheetahs. The young are preyed upon by large snakes, servals, jackals and large eagles.

MOUNTAIN REEDBUCK

Redunca fulvorufula
(Afzelius 1815)

How widely are they distributed in the Kruger Park?

This is a very uncommon antelope in the Park, found in low density only in the southwestern corner in suitable habitat in the Berg-en-Dal and Stolsnek areas. Refer to ecozone C on the map inside the cover.

What are their main physical features?

Mountain reedbucks can be confused with the common reedbuck, except that in the mountain reedbuck there is a distinctive dark line running down the front of the forelegs and a less prominent line runs down the front of the hind legs.

They have a thick, woolly coat. The upper parts are greyish, and it is yellowish to reddish-brown on the neck, with white underparts. The ears are narrow with rounded tips. There are dark glandular patches on the sides of the neck below the ears. The neck is noticeably thinner in the female and the muzzle is pointed.

Only the males have horns, which rise from the top of the head almost straight back, with the tips hooked sharply forward, ridged to the hook. Horns, which start growing at about 15 months, can reach a length of up to 35 cm. The bushy tail is grey on top and white underneath. Inguinal glands are situated in the groin and scent glands behind the ears.

They have very keen senses of smell, sight and hearing. Males and females attain a mass of up to 35 kg and a shoulder height of around 75 cm.

What is their preferred habitat?

They prefer the dry, grass-covered, stony slopes, with scattered bushes and trees, of the hills and mountains in the Berg-en-Dal and Malelane areas. Proximity of water is also important.

What do they eat?

They are almost exclusively grazers, preferring grass that has been burned within the past year, and also forbs.

They very occasionally browse on leaves. They are dependent on water in the dry season, but can go without water for a few days when the moisture content in their diet is sufficient.

What are their behavioural patterns?

They are both diurnal and nocturnal, but more active in the early morning, late afternoon and during the night. They tend to rest up during the day in the cover of bushes and trees, with herd members lying close together. Group sizes are small, with two or three individuals, but in summer aggregations of up to 15 animals have been seen.

What are their breeding habits?

Males court by approaching females with the head stretched forward. After a gestation period of about 7.5 months a single lamb, with a mass of about 3 kg, is born in dense cover. The lamb lies hidden for two to three months, with the ewe visiting once or twice a day to suckle and clean the lamb.

Births occur all year round but tend to peak during the summer.

What is their average life span?

The life span is about 12 years.

How do they react to danger?

Their alarm signal is a shrill, loud, nasal whistle. They freeze to avoid detection and if not detected will slink away. Exaggerated trotting and stotting causes the inguinal glands to open with a popping sound. They flee with a rocking-horse motion and frequent leaps to higher ground, stopping infrequently to determine if they are still being pursued. The bushy tail is raised to expose the white underside.

Do they actively defend their territory?

A territorial ram will chase young rams of nine to 15 months out of his territory, after which they join the bachelor groups that are always found on the periphery of dominant ram territories.

Territorial aggression is shown with horn threats and horn tossing. Horning the ground, nodding of the head, mock and real charges and chasing all form part of this ritual.

What are their major enemies?

Lions, leopards, the lesser felines as well as large snakes and eagles, jackals and serval are the main danger to these antelope.

Mature rams usually hold a territory, while rams without territories are alone or found in bachelor groups. Female herds have unstable membership and home ranges that overlap several male territories.

IMPALA *Aepyceros melampus* (Lichtenstein 1812)

How widely are they distributed throughout the Kruger Park?

The preferred habitats of impalas are open savanna bushveld, especially those associated with *Acacia* trees and shrubs. They are widely distributed throughout the Park, but are almost absent from the mopane Shrubveld of the plains north of Letaba and are found in low densities in the tall-grassed landscape of the Pretoriuskop area. They avoid tall grass habitat.

What are their main physical features?

The glossy coat is chestnut brown in colour, with a darker, more reddish upper back. They are paler on the flanks and legs, with white underparts, throat, lips and patches around the eyes. They have large ears with black tips. There is a black patch in the middle of the top of the head, a variably darker brown muzzle, a black stripe down the top of the tail and a black stripe down each buttock. A very distinctive feature is the two tufts of black hair above the ankle of the hind legs.

Only the males have horns, which are lyre-shaped and heavily ridged on the lower two-thirds, with smooth, sharp tips. The horns measure between 50 and 75 cm. Shoulder height ranges between 75 and 90 cm; the males reach a mass of about 65 kg and females about 50 kg.

Are their senses well developed?

They have very keen senses of smell, hearing and sight.

Herd vigilance is very important for detecting predators. Within each herd there is usually one individual not feeding or drinking at any particular time that can be regarded as the sentinel on watch.

What are their behavioural patterns?

Impalas are mainly diurnal and very gregarious. They move around in small herds of usually about 15 individuals, but groups of 50 or more are often seen. Aggregations of 100 and more are sometimes found in winter or during droughts when food and water become restricted. Females and young live in breeding herds, which often include a few adult males.

They often associate with other animals such as zebras, blue wildebeest, giraffes and baboons. This could also be because there are then more eyes, ears and nostrils to help detect danger.

Reciprocal grooming is important in the social structure of herds and helps to get rid of ectoparasites from areas that each animal cannot groom for itself. The incisor teeth are loose in their sockets, allowing them to comb ticks out of their coats. Impalas spend more time grooming than any other antelope.

Territorial rams seldom have time to groom, and as a result have a higher tick load than herd members.

With such large herds of impala around, does inbreeding occur?

Inbreeding cannot be discounted but, during the rutting season, an intensive mating season from April to June, certain events take place that limit the possibilities of inbreeding.

Between July and February some adult males live together in bachelor groups. From February onwards these bachelor groups fragment as the testosterone levels in the males respond to the shorter days. Fighting becomes more frequent and more intense, with a lot of bush-horning taking place.

By the beginning of April prime males begin leaving the bachelor herds to establish territories and drive other males out. They then advertise their presence by 'roaring', a sound that is a mixture between a cough and a grunt, with the neck stretched forward, the chin lifted upwards, the tail held out and fluffed out, and the penis extended.

They urinate and defecate on large middens, scent-mark grass and twigs with the glands on their foreheads and deter competitors by snorting, chasing and horn threats.

Persistent intruders are attacked with fights involving charges and wrestling with locked horns. Fights are usually short, and often fierce, but highly ritualised, thereby minimising serious injury, although serious injuries and deaths have been recorded. Losers are pursued until they are out of the territory.

All this territorial activity occupies so much time that the dominant male has very little time to feed, losing body condition rapidly and doing very little mating, until he is replaced by a fresher challenger, when the whole procedure is repeated. At the peak of the rut a territory is held for only about a week. This ritual allows for the spreading of genetic material in such a way that inbreeding very rarely occurs.

Breeding herds move through male territories and the resident male will then check the females' reproductive condition by smelling their urine and genitals. They will then try to prevent females in oestrus from leaving the territory, by herding them with horn threats and 'roaring'.

Mounting for about 10 seconds is repeated until mating has been achieved.

A female that has been successfully mated is no longer herded.

What do they eat?

They are very selective grazers and browsers. Their diet includes a variety of grasses, with a preference for green grass. They turn to browsing during the winter months or according to the availability of the different food types and the season. Food items include flowers, pods, bark and fallen leaves, herbs, succulents and fruit.

They are water dependent and will drink readily, sometimes twice a day, when water is available.

Do they show aggression?

When alarmed they will jerk the head and flick the tail, and sometimes kick up and backward with the hind feet releasing in the process a scent from the glands situated in the tufts of hair in the hind feet.

When threatened they display horn threats, head tossing and bobbing, and vegetation horning. There are also real or mock charges and chasing, and horn stabbing.

What are their breeding habits?

The shorter day length from April stimulates breeding and in the Park mating peaks during May. The mating and lambing seasons are short, and lambing peaks during December in the Kruger Park. A single lamb, seldom twins, of about 5 kg is born after a gestation period of about 6.5 months. After birth lambs are hidden for about two days and then join the nursery crèche.

What is their average life span?
The life span is about 12 years.

Is there really such a thing as a nursery crèche for impala lambs?
When the lambs are still very young, they are often seen herded together into a shady area. There are a few ewes in the direct vicinity of the young ones while the rest of the herd feeds nearby.

Every now and then a ewe will come in from feeding and take over the nursing responsibility of a ewe that then leaves to join the rest of the herd.

This has come to be called a nursery or crèche.

Why is the lambing season so short and not spread over the year as with many other animals?
As there is a very specific mating season, as previously described, it follows that there should also be a very defined lambing season.

The short lambing season in actual fact is the key to the survival of the impala, as all the young ones arrive in a very short period of time. This means that there are too many for the predators to take out of the system, and as a result it is guaranteed that some will reach maturity, to breed and thus ensure their survival.

Since the impala is the most prolific antelope in the Park, with numbers in excess of 130 000, it can be expected that they are also the most available prey species of the predators.

In most years only about 15 to 20% of the year's lamb crop has actually reached maturity.

It is true that ewes can delay the birth of their lambs?
There has been speculation that ewes can delay the birth, should the availability of grazing not be optimal. Some have speculated that this could be for up to three weeks.

There is no proof that ewes can hold back on the lamb being born and this theory should be accepted as just that, a theory.

One must bear in mind that, if the foetus has reached full term and is about to be born, if it were held back for three weeks, it would not stop growing. In those three weeks the foetus would probably more than double in size, which would make it physiologically impossible for the ewe to give birth.

It is possible that under certain circumstances the rutting may start later than usual, which would then result in the lambing season also being later. The late lambing in such cases could give rise to this theory.

What are their major enemies?
The main predators are lions, leopards, cheetahs, African wild dogs, hyaenas and crocodiles. Lambs are preyed upon by jackals, caracal and large eagles.

BUSHBUCK

Tragelaphus scriptus (Pallas 1766)

How widely are they distributed in the Park?

They are distributed throughout the Park, but mainly found along watercourses and riverine habitat, especially along the Sabie, Letaba, Luvuvhu and Limpopo rivers. They are also present in the densely wooded areas around Pretoriuskop and Punda Maria.

What are their habitat preferences?

Bushbuck prefer dense cover in the underbrush of woodland and forest and the riparian vegetation along watercourses. Since they are water dependent, their habitat should always be close to permanent water. They may move seasonally when temporary surface water is available.

What are their main physical features?

The general colour varies from yellowish to brown, with distinct white stripes and spots on the flanks and thighs and spots on the cheeks. The general colour varies according to sex and distribution in the Park. In the southern part of the Park, they are lighter in colour, with fewer, less prominent spots and stripes than the bushbuck found in the north and west of the Park. Within a distribution area, females are lighter in colour than the males.

In all forms there is a white patch high up on the throat and a conspicuous white band at the base of the neck. The inner parts of the thighs and forelegs and the inside of the lower limbs are lighter to whitish in colour. The very bushy tail is white underneath.

The muzzle has a dark brown to black stripe from the nose to between the eyes.

Only the males have horns, which rise above the eyes. The horns are twisted, shallowly corkscrewed and triangular in cross section, with a prominent ridge. Horns normally reach a length of 35 to 45 cm.

They have excellent senses of smell, hearing and sight. They have inguinal scent glands.

The shoulder height in males is about 80 to 95 cm and in females about 70 to 85 cm. The weight of males ranges between 50 and 75 kg and the females 35 to 55 kg.

What is included in their diet?

They are predominantly browsers, preferring leaves, shoots, buds, fruit and flowers, though newly sprouted grass is taken seasonally. Being water dependent, they will drink daily.

What are their habits?

They are mainly nocturnal, but also active during early morning and late afternoon. Their social organisation probably varies according to locality and habitat. They are mainly single, but found in pairs or pairs with their young.

Home ranges vary in size and may overlap with those of neighbours. Males demarcate territories by horning bushes and soil, and rubbing the neck against bushes and trees. This is the reason why the hair low on the neck is often worn off.

Two males compete for dominance by circling each other with the crest along the back erect, the tail erect and the heads turned towards each other. Horn clashing and chasing may follow, ending in the engaging of horns as they try to push and twist each other off balance. In exceptional cases, fights may be fatal.

Bushbuck avoid predators by hiding, freezing to avoid detection and even taking to water when threatened. The alarm call is a loud, dog-like bark.

Rams can be very pugnacious and have been known to kill predators, dogs and even humans.

Bushbuck associate with baboons and vervet monkeys, as they drop seed pods, berries and fruit during their foraging. This becomes a handy food source for the antelope.

Bushbuck are very good swimmers and have been recorded covering distances of 3 km in the water.

What are their breeding habits?
Males determine when a female is on heat by smelling her urine and genitals. Females in oestrus are monopolised by dominant males.

After a gestation period of six months a single lamb, with a mass of about 4 kg, is born in dense cover. Lambs are born throughout the year, but peak in summer.

Lambs remain hidden for up to four months and the social bond between ewe and lamb is maintained by mutual licking.

What is their average life span?
The life span of the bushbuck is about 12 years.

What are their major enemies?
The are largely preyed upon by lions, leopards, African wild dogs, hyaenas and crocodiles. Young bushbuck are taken by jackals, caracal and possibly pythons.

NYALA   *Tragelaphus angasii* (Angas 1849)

What is the distribution of nyalas in the Park?
Nyalas are patchily distributed, predominantly in the far northern section of the Park. They are common in the Pafuri area along the Luvuvhu and Limpopo rivers and along the Shingwedzi River. They can also be found along the Sabie River close to Skukuza, where a number of them were released in 1980.

They occur in lower densities in the mountainous area north of Punda Maria and the Nyandu sandveld area south of Pafuri. Refer to ecozones H, I, L, M, N and O on the ecozone map of the Kruger Park.

What type of habitat do they prefer?

They are generally found in thick riverine bush communities along watercourses and in low-lying woodland savanna, and normally not far from water.

What are their main physical features?

This is a medium-sized antelope, with the male much bigger than the female. It is halfway between the kudu and bushbuck in size, all of them belonging to the same family. Males attain a shoulder height of up to 1.2 m and the females about 97 cm.

Mass is about 120 kg in the males and about 65 kg in the females.

Adult males and females look completely different. Males attain their adult colouring at about 15 months; they have a slate grey to almost black coat, with between eight and 14 distinct transverse white stripes on the sides and flanks, and white spots on the belly and thighs. There are three white spots on the cheeks.

A conspicuous mane of long hair runs from the top of the head to the root of the tail. The hair is white at the tips, with a white stripe evident down the middle of the back when the mane lies flat. The mane is raised when the animal is alarmed, frightened or disputing dominance. From under the jaw along the neck, under the belly and the backs of the hind legs is a long, shaggy fringe of dark hair. This is unlike any other antelope found in Africa.

The tail is dark and bushy and the ears large, with a rusty tinge on the back. A distinct white chevron is visible between the eyes, but it is very faint in the female. The bottom half of the legs is almost yellow in colour, with a dark brown to black band separating this from the body colour. This helps to distinguish a young nyala male from a bushbuck ram.

Females and young nyalas are chestnut brown in colour, with up to 18 stripes down the sides and on the flanks, and a few spots on the thighs. The mane is very short and dark.

Only the males have horns, which rise in a beautiful lyre shape, with shallow corkscrews. They are ridged up the outside of the curve, ending in whitish tips. Horn length can reach about 70 to 75 cm.

Are they territorial?

There appear to be no indications of territorial behaviour, although inter-male dominance displays are often observed when males are in close proximity to females. This could be when a female is in her oestrus cycle, which lasts for about 19 days. Home ranges, rather than territories, may overlap those of neighbouring herds.

Displays by males include the raising of the mane and strutting past the opponent with slow, high steps, the head down and the horns pointed forward with the tail curled upward to show the white underside.

Sparring includes head pushing and horn clashing. Posturing is shown by vegetation horning, ground pawing and ground horning, rushing and chasing.

Serious fights are rare but when they do occur they are fierce.

What are their behavioural patterns?

Nyalas are both diurnal and nocturnal, feeding mainly at night and resting up during the heat of the day.

They are not really gregarious, but herds of more than 15 are sometimes observed on suitable feeding sites especially during dry winter months and droughts. They are usually solitary, with no permanent social bonds beyond the mother and her two youngest offspring. Males usually become solitary or roam in pairs as they become old.

In the Park individuals, pairs or pairs with their young are commonly seen. When disturbed or alarmed they tend to freeze to avoid detection, will revert to stamping or flee into dense vegetation. They also react to the alarm calls of kudu, impalas and baboons.

What do they eat?

Nyalas browse and graze according to the seasonal and local availability of vegetation. They eat both fresh and fallen leaves, fruit, shoots, flowers, grasses and herbs.

They often associate with baboons and monkeys that drop fruit and leaves during their foraging, which is then utilised by the nyala. They are water independent, obtaining sufficient moisture from their diet, but will drink when water is readily available.

What are their mating and reproduction patterns?

Young are born throughout the year, with a peak during the wetter summer months.

Males test the oestrus cycle of females by sniffing the base of the tails and inserting their noses in their urine. A male courts by approaching with the head outstretched and butting the female between the hind legs with his foreleg. When the female is receptive the male puts his neck across hers, pushing her head down; he then places his head on her rump and mounts.

After a gestation period of about seven months a single lamb, of about 5 kg, is born in thick vegetation. The lamb remains hidden for two to three weeks.

What is the average life span?

Life expectancy is about 13 to 15 years.

What are their main enemies?

Mainly lions, leopards, African wild dogs and hyaenas. Young are preyed upon by jackals and large eagles. Like the bushbuck, the nyala is a formidable and dangerous quarry.

It is with the nyala where the different naming of the male and female becomes apparent. The male is called a bull and the female a ewe.

GREATER KUDU *Tragelaphus strepsiceros* (Pallas 1766)

What is their distribution in the Park?

Kudu are widely distributed in the Kruger National Park and found in all the ecozones. How-ever, they are found in low densities in the mopane shrubveld of the northern region.

What is their preferred habitat?

They prefer woodland savanna, lowland valley bushveld and hills with dense bush and thickets. They are not found in arid areas or in open grassland.

What are their main physical features?

This tall, very elegant and majestic antelope stands about 1.4 m tall at the shoulder in males and about 1.25 m in females. Males on average have a mass of 230 kg and females 180 kg.

Males are fawn-grey in colour and females a more rufous-brown. Older bulls are darker. Both sexes have a short mane from the top of the head to the shoulders, from where it continues as a white stripe down the middle of the back. Up to 10 narrow, transverse white stripes run across the back and down the flanks.

Adult bulls have a distinct long, beardlike fringe under the throat and a belly fringe.

The ears are very large, and as a result it has an excellent sense of hearing.

Both sexes have a distinct white chevron between the eyes, which is paler in the female. There are usually three white spots on the cheek, and white on the top lip and chin. The tail is bushy and white underneath.

Only bulls have horns, which rise from the top of the head in long, smooth and magnificent spirals, with a distinctive ridge along their length. The horn tips are usually far apart. Young males begin to show horn growth at about five months. Horns vary in length between 1.1 and 1.5 m.

What do they eat?

Kudu browse on a wide variety of plants. In the Park they feed on 148 different plant species, including aloes and euphorbias, showing a preference for *Acacia* and *Combretum* species.

They browse on leaves, shoots, vines, seed pods, tubers, succulents, flowers, fruits, berries and forbs. For most of the year in Kruger Park forbs make up 65% of their diet but, when new growth sprouts, this drops to about 20%. They also eat newly sprouted green grass and herbs.

They are water independent, but will drink regularly when water is available.

What are their habits?

Kudu are diurnal and nocturnal but most active during the morning and late afternoon. They browse for only a short while on each tree or bush. Males will break down lesser branches with their horns should leaves be out of reach.

Males do not seem to be territorial. They wander widely but tend to return to a fixed core area. Cows, sub-adults and calves form small family herds of up to 10 animals but temporary aggregations at water holes and suitable feeding areas in the dry season can result in groups of up to 30 individuals.

Bulls tend to join female herds between May and August when females usually come into oestrus.

It is during this time that dominance displays between bulls are seen. Dominance is based on size and displays of fighting ability. During the mating season bulls thrash bushes and do ground horning. There is a great deal of horn clashing, lunging and wrestling with horns locked, but fights are rare. Fatalities sometimes occur from stab wounds or the horns getting inextricably entwined (see the sculpture at Skukuza).

Do the horns not get entangled in bushes?

When dashing through thick bush, bulls tilt their heads upward to allow the horns to lie almost level with their backs. This makes it less likely for them to get entangled in the vegetation. When fleeing they tend to run in a zigzag fashion, breaking through thickets with amazing ease.

How do they react to danger?

As in the case of most animals, kudu tend to freeze to avoid detection, skulking away if not detected. They are alert and nervous on open ground. The alarm call is a loud bark.

When fleeing, they run off in a bounding, zigzag pattern with the tail curled up, showing the white underside as an alarm signal. They stop intermittently to check whether they are still being pursued.

They are excellent jumpers and can clear heights of 2 to 3 m with comparative ease.

Are kudu dangerous animals?

Despite their size and formidable horns, kudu are normally inoffensive and rarely charge or attack, even in self-defence. However, like almost all wild animals, they cannot be trusted, even in captivity.

What are their mating and reproduction habits?

A dominant male checks the reproductive condition of a female by the sniffing of her urine and genitals. After inserting his nose in the urine of the cow, the bull pulls his head back, pulls his lips apart and bares his teeth in an activity referred to as *flehmen*. This behaviour is common to most antelope. If the cow is receptive, the bull then approaches with the head stretched forward, putting his neck on the female's and pressing down. There may be mutual licking at this point. Before mounting her he will rest his chin on her rump.

A single calf with a mass of about 15 kg is born in dense cover after a gestation period of between seven and eight months. Cows leave the herd to give birth and the calf may remain hidden for a month or more.

Although calves are born throughout the year, there is a definite peak towards the latter part of the summer.

What is their average life expectancy?

Life expectancy can be up to 15 years.

What are their major enemies?

Adult bulls are seldom attacked by predators other than lions, African wild dog and sometimes hyaenas. Cows and calves are attacked by leopards, cheetahs, African wild dogs, jackals and caracals.

WATERBUCK

Kobus ellipsiprymnus (Ogilby 1833)

What is their distribution in the Kruger Park?

Waterbuck are found throughout the Park near water. They are especially abundant along the Letaba and Lepelle rivers during the dry winter months. They are often also found in hilly country.

What would be considered as suitable habitat?

Flood plains, reed beds, grassland, woodland and thickets close to cover and near permanent water are the most suitable habitats. In the Park waterbuck are found predominantly in rocky areas near permanent water, rivers and streams.

Describe their main physical features?

Waterbuck are stockily built, with short legs and a coarse, shaggy coat that is greyish-brown in colour. The lower legs are dark brown and a white band is visible immediately above the hooves.

Ears are ridged in black with black tips.

A white band stretches from just below the ears to the throat where it ends in a white collar on the upper throat. Facial markings include white eyebrow stripes, white around the muzzle, white chin and lips. The most conspicuous marking is the white circle on the rump.

Only bulls have horns, which are long and lyre-shaped, spreading sideways then slightly inwards and forwards with a smooth curve. Horns are heavily ridged until close to the tips and are about 70 to 85 cm in length.

Calves resemble cows and are lighter in colour. As bulls age they become darker in colour.

Bulls have a mass of about 270 kg and stand about 1.4 m at the shoulder. Females are about 1.1 m at the shoulder, with a mass of about 180 kg.

Waterbuck have interdigital glands, and a very oily coat. The bulls have a distinctive musky, goaty odour.

What do they eat?

Waterbuck are mainly grazers with a preference for tall grass. They turn to browsing when the protein in the grass is of low quality, and have been seen to eat marula fruit, forbs and leaves. Their favoured grass species varies according to locality. In the Kruger Park they seem to prefer *Cynodon dactylon* and will also include reeds and rushes in their diet. They are very water dependent and require water daily.

Do they migrate?

If water is available they seldom move to another area. They do not undertake seasonal migrations.

Are waterbuck territorial?

They are territorial and a bull will not tolerate intruders.

Occupation and status are advertised with a proud posture, head and neck erect, displaying the white throat band. Shaking the head and lowering the horns in the direction of the adversary is a strong threat. Subordinate bulls are tolerated in the territory and will be allowed to move through the territory as long as they show submission by lowering the head with the horns held back against the neck.

What are their behavioural patterns?

They are crepuscular: most active during the early morning and late afternoon but also feeding at night.

Herds consisting of only cows or only bulls are quite common. They usually associate in herds of up to 10 animals, but in summer, with optimal grazing available, aggregations of up to 30 individuals have been recorded.

Females and young form nursery herds, bulls are territorial and males without territories form bachelor herds.

What are their mating and reproduction habits?
Nursery herds have home ranges that overlap male territories. A female in oestrus is herded into the male's territory after the bull has tested her reproductive condition by sniffing her urine and genitals by means of *flehmen*.

Courting is by way of rubbing his face and the base of his horns against her flanks and rump. Should the cow be receptive, he will rest his chin on her back and tap between her hind legs with his foreleg before mounting.

After a gestation period of almost nine months a single calf with a mass of about 13 kg is born in thickets, where it will stay hidden for three to four weeks. Calves are born throughout the year, with a peak during the summer months.

Males start growing horns at about nine months, when they are evicted from the herd to join bachelor groups. Female calves stay within the herd in which they are born.

What is their average life expectancy?
Longevity is estimated to be about 13 to 15 years.

Is it true that waterbuck meat is inedible?
Although not inedible, it is seldom eaten by humans. Bulls specifically have a strong musky, goaty odour, due to an oily secretion of the skin. When the skin or hands of the person skinning the dead animal come into contact with the meat, the meat becomes tainted, taking on a strange taste.

Is it true that crocodiles do not kill waterbuck?
With their dependence on and their habitat proximity to water, waterbuck can and do fall prey to crocodiles. Crocodiles are very opportunistic predators and will certainly kill waterbuck should they have the opportunity to do so.

Is a waterbuck bull dangerous?
A wounded or cornered waterbuck bull will defend himself and will not hesitate to charge. It is a very dangerous adversary.

How do they react when under pressure?
They show aggression by horn threats, ground horning, real and mock charging, rushing and chasing. When alarmed, they freeze to avoid detection, then skulk or run away in a trotting gait. They show an alert posture with stamping of the forefeet. They will readily take to water when threatened, sometimes submerging their bodies, with only the nostrils protruding.

Which predators prey on waterbuck?
Lions, hyaenas and Nile crocodiles are their main predators. Young fall prey to African wild dog, leopards and cheetahs.

LICHTENSTEIN'S HARTEBEEST

Sigmoceros lichtensteinii (Peters 1849)

After some Lichtestein's hartebeest had been 'reintroduced' to the Kruger National Park from Malawi during the late 1980s, it was established that they did not naturally occur in the Kruger National Park, as had originally been accepted.

All of these animals, which were kept in the breeding camp at N'waswitshumbe, were translocated to the Limpopo National Park in Mozambique.

The few remaining loners outside the breeding camp were left to live out their lives as naturally as possible. It is estimated that they would have died out by the end of 2010.

TSESSEBE

Damaliscus lunatus (Burchell 1823)

How widely are tsessebe distributed in the Park?

They are patchily distributed in the Kruger Park and found primarily in the mopane shrubveld and mopane/bushwillow habitats north of Letaba. They have also been seen in the sourveld areas around Pretoriuskop and the Lebombo Mountain Bushveld along the eastern border of the Park.

Refer to ecozones A, B, E, F, I, L, N, O and P on the ecozone map of the Park.

What type of habitat do tsessebe prefer?

They prefer open woodland and grass-land bordering on woodland. They frequent areas of short to medium-height grass, where visibility is good, and consequently avoid tall grass, dense scrub or bush habitat.

What vegetation is included in their diet?

Tsessebe are almost exclusively grazers that prefer short to medium-length grasses such as *Panicum coloratum, Cenchrus ciliaris* and *Themeda triandra*. They are fond of freshly sprouting grasses, especially after fires.

What are the tsessebe's main physical features?

The tsessebe is a fairly large and awkward-looking animal with a long face with a black muzzle. The eyes are set high up on the face to allow for good vision when the animal is feeding. The coat is glossy reddish-brown with a purplish sheen. The lower parts of the shoulders, upper parts of the legs and the outer thighs are dark brown to black. There is a distinct hump on the shoulders and the back slopes down to the rump. The underparts are paler and the area around the base of the tail is very light to whitish. A black tassel ends off the tail.

Both sexes have horns that sweep outward and then backwards and up towards the tips. Horns are ridged almost to the tips and reach a length of up to 50 cm.

Males have a shoulder height of about 1.2 m and a mass of approximately 145 kg. Females are slightly smaller, at about 1.1 m, with a mass of about 125 kg. They have preorbital and interdigital glands.

What are their behavioural patterns?
They are both diurnal and nocturnal. Breeding herds can consist of up to 10 cows and calves and a territorial bull. Males without territories form bachelor groups. Dominance hierarchy among the cows is maintained, with the alpha female leading the herd.

Young males of about a year old, who are evicted from the herd by the territorial bull, join bachelor groups on the periphery of territorial areas.

Tsessebe freeze when predators approach, snort in alarm, do some foot stamping and flee at great speed, stopping to assess the source of danger.

Aggression is shown with horn threats, head tossing and nodding, horn clashing in a kneeling position, ground horning and pawing, chasing and mock or real charges.

Are they territorial?
Territories are patrolled by the territorial bull, which marks the area with dung and a sticky, clear preorbital secretion; this is rubbed off on grass stems that are sometimes manoeuvred into the opening of the gland just in front of the eye. They also rub their faces on the ground, on termite mounds, dig up the soil with their horns, smear themselves with mud and paw the ground to release interdigital-gland secretions.

Bulls show territorial dominance by standing prominently on raised ground such as termite mounds. Adversaries are challenged by head shaking and rearing up.

What is their mating and reproductive behaviour?
Territorial bulls herd females together and parade in front of them with the head up, the nose forward and the ears drooped against the side of the neck. They take exaggerated high steps with the forelegs.

Mating usually takes place during March and April and calving peaks during November.

After a gestation period of about eight months, a single calf with a mass of about 10 to 12 kg is born. Calves are gathered in nursery crèches with one or two adults acting as sentinels.

What is their average life span?
Longevity is about 12 to 15 years.

Why are they so rare in the Park?
Apart from predation, the scarcity of suitable habitat is the most probable reason.

Are there any plans to try to increase the number of tsessebe in the Kruger Park?

In the past, intensive research and breeding programmes were carried out in breeding camps. The idea was to build up breeding herds to release them into suitable habitat. It was hoped that the Park's annual controlled burning programme would eventually establish suitable conditions for this antelope in different areas of the Park.

This operation was not entirely successful and predation took a higher toll than was envisaged.

What are their major enemies?

Their main predators include leopards, lions, African wild dog and hyaenas, while the calves are preyed upon by jackals, caracal and cheetahs.

Tsessebe are considered to be the fastest antelope species in the Park, attaining speeds in excess of 70 km/h.

ROAN ANTELOPE   *Hippotragus equinus* (Desmarest 1804)

What is the distribution of the roan antelope in the Park?

These animals, which are considered rare, are found mainly north of the Letaba River in the mopane bushveld and the mopane/bushwillow woodlands of the northern plains. The major concentrations, though in low densities, are found on the northeastern plains between Letaba and Punda Maria and there is a small relict population south of Pretoriuskop. Due primarily to the fencing of the Park, small pockets of roan antelope have disappeared from other scattered localities.

Refer to ecozones A, C, L and P on the ecozone map of the Kruger Park on the inside of the cover.

What habitat do they prefer?

The roan antelope has very strict requirements for lightly wooded savanna with large areas of medium-height to tall grass and access to water. These antelopes do well in vlei areas and are seldom found more than 3 km from water. Bush encroachment and overgrazing of their grass areas degrade roan antelope habitat and lead to the suppression of the population.

What is their diet?

They are grazers that prefer medium-height to tall grass species such as *Themeda triandra*; they graze the top stratum of the grass, selecting the leafy parts above the stems. They will browse if the grazing is poor and will also crop new growth up to 2 cm. They chew bones and soil to obtain certain mineral elements.

What are their main physical features?

Roan antelope are the second-largest antelope, with the males standing about 1.4 m at the shoulder and the females around 1.3 m. Males have a mass of up to 275 kg and females about 230 kg.

They have a predominantly greyish to brown coat with dark brown legs; calves are a much lighter rufous-brown colour. The underparts are paler. A characteristic feature is the very distinct black-and-white facial mask. The ears, which are very long and thin, up to 30 cm long, with tassels of dark brown hair at the tips, are also characteristic. The tail ends in a black tassel. A short, black-tipped mane extends from the back of the neck to just beyond the shoulders.

Both sexes carry horns, with the bull's more robust than the cow's. They rise from the top of the head, sweeping gracefully backwards in an even curve for about 75 cm. The horns are heavily ridged almost to the tips and look like mini versions of the horns of the sable antelope.

Roan antelope have preorbital and interdigital glands.

Are they gregarious?

Herds normally number between six and 12, consisting of a herd bull, a number of cows and their offspring. Larger aggregations may be found at good grazing areas or near water.

What are their general behaviour patterns?

They are diurnal and nocturnal, being most active in the morning and late afternoon, spending the hottest part of the day in shade.

Females and calves live in nursery herds of 10 to 12 animals. A dominant hierarchy exists among the cows, with the dominant cow taking the lead in determining the movements of the herd within their home range. The other cows act as sentinels at the periphery of the herd.

Young bulls form bachelor groups and adult bulls not associated with a herd live as solitary animals. Breeding bulls associated with nursery herds maintain an exclusion zone of 300 to 500 m around the herd. They challenge adversaries by adopting a dominant pose with an arched neck, the chin tucked in and the ears out sideways. Submissive behaviour includes the lowering of the head, upright ears and the tail being swished or tucked between the legs.

Non-submissive intruders are met with horn clashing and head pushing. Serious altercations can extend over lengthy bouts of horn hooking and wrestling from a kneeling position.

Both bulls and cows mark their home ranges by using dung and urine, thrashing vegetation, ground pawing to release interdigital-gland secretions and ground horning.

What is their mating and reproductive behaviour?

A herd bull checks the reproductive condition of a cow by sniffing her genital area. This stimulates the cow to urinate, upon which the bull inserts his nose into the urine, pulls back his lips in a display called flehmen, by which he determines the reproductive status of the cow. He courts a cow on heat by following her closely and tapping between her hind legs with his foreleg. This behaviour is called *laufschlag*. *Flehmen* and *laufschlag* are common in virtually all antelope species. (See description in 'Courtship and Mating' on pages 34 and 35 of the Introduction.)

After a gestation period of about nine months a single calf, with a mass of about 17 kg, is born and hidden in tall grass for six weeks. Cows leave the herd to give birth in isolation. Calves are born throughout the year, with a peak during the summer months. Calves attain adult coloration at about four months. Calves rely on concealment for survival and will not flee even when closely approached. Cows visit about twice a day to suckle and clean the calf.

What is their average life expectancy?

Life span is 12 to 15 years.

The *Red Data Book* describes the roan antelope as endangered. Why is this?

A number of injudicious water holes created in the preferred habitats of roan antelope resulted in the rapid increase of the wildebeest and zebras. Both these species are short-grass grazers and soon depleted the tall grass favoured by the roan antelope. Subsequent drought and sub-optimal habitat conditions soon took their toll on the roan population. Mortality of calves in this sub-optimal habitat in the Kruger Park was up to 80% before the age of six weeks.

The water holes that had played a part in the demise of the roan antelope population were closed in 1994, and small breeding nuclei of roan were placed where they are breeding well and from where they will gradually be released into their rehabilitated habitats.

The numbers of roan antelope decreased dramatically, because of the mentioned reasons, from more than 500 animals in the late 1970s to fewer than 50 during the mid 1990s.

What are their main enemies?

Lions are the major natural enemy of the roan. Calf mortality is high owing to the mother's habit of hiding the calf; this was especially the case after the overgrazing of their habitat. The calves were easy prey to a variety of predators that included lions, leopards, hyaenas, cheetahs, jackals and some of the lesser felines.

Roan antelope are also very susceptible to anthrax. An annual vaccination programme against anthrax, conducted by helicopter, was stopped in 1992 at the time that the population was severely reduced. This was done to prevent the possibility of further losses due to stress as a result of the vaccination operation.

SABLE ANTELOPE *Hippotragus niger* (Harris 1838)

How widely are they distributed in the Kruger Park?

Sable antelope have a wide but patchy distribution throughout the Park. Their favoured habitats are moderately wooded savannas with tall grass. Their highest densities are in the sourveld areas of Pretoriuskop and the sandy soils woodlands, characterised by prominent white termite mounds, to the east of Phalaborwa. However, scattered herds may be found in most habitats, particularly in the western half of the Park.

Refer to ecozones A, B, C, D, E, F, J, K, L, N, O and P on the ecozone map of the Park. Highest densities are found in the Pretoriuskop, Phalaborwa entrance gate and Nhlanguleni picnic site areas.

What type of habitat do they prefer?

They prefer open savanna woodland, avoiding short grass and dense woodland. Rarely found far from water.

What do they eat?

Sable feed on grass of up to about 1.5 m and will turn to light browsing towards the end of winter when the quality of available grazing is poor. To obtain sufficient minerals they will chew on bones and eat soil. They are very water dependent and drink daily.

What are their main physical features?

Sable are generally considered to be the most beautiful and most graceful of all African antelope.

Adult bulls are very dark brown to black over most of the body, while females and young bulls are more reddish-brown. The belly, inner thighs and the rump patch are white. The backs of the ears are bright russet, with russet on the forehead just below the horns. The face has contrasting

bands of black and white, with a dark band running down the top of the muzzle. A black stripe runs from each eye to just above the mouth.

An upright black mane runs from the top of the head to the shoulders. The tail ends in a black tassel.

Both sexes have horns, the bulls' being heavier and thicker. The horns rise from above the eyes and sweep backwards in a very elegant curve. Horns are heavily ridged but smooth at the tips and can attain a length of up to 1.65 m.

Males are larger and more robustly built than females, reaching a shoulder height of about 1.5 m and a mass of up to 250 kg, and the females stand about 1.3 m at the shoulder, with a mass of up to 210 kg.

Are they gregarious?

Yes. Sable antelope are commonly found in herds ranging from eight to 20 animals or even more. The herds consist of a herd bull, cows and their offspring.

What is their general behaviour?

Sable are both diurnal and nocturnal, being most active during the morning, late afternoon and the early evening up to midnight. They rest in shade during the heat of the day. They drink daily, often from a kneeling position.

Breeding herds have a dominance hierarchy among the cows, with an alpha, or leader, cow that determines movements throughout their home range. Young bulls that have not been evicted from the breeding herds are submissive to the adult cows.

A herd traditionally consists of a dominant bull, for breeding purposes only, and a few cows and sub-adults. Young males are evicted from the herd by territorial bulls during their third year and then form bachelor herds. Older females act as sentinels, staying on the periphery of the herd while the others are feeding or resting.

Sable defend themselves by backing into a bush and warding off potential danger with aggressive sideways slashing of the horns.

Do they migrate?

Being selective grazers and water dependent, sable will occupy different parts of their habitat during different seasons but do not migrate over long distances.

Do sable associate with other game?

They rarely associate with other game. At water holes they will usually temporarily mingle with other game, but move away as soon as they have finished drinking. It has been recorded, at water holes, that sable are able to displace other antelope, zebras and even African buffalo cows.

Are they territorial?

Mature bulls are territorial and patrol along roads and paths. They scent-mark with faeces, ground pawing to release interdigital-gland secretions and, through bush thrashing, breaking off leaves, branches and bark.

Preorbital and interdigital glands are present and secretions from the glands are deposited on vegetation or the ground as they walk about. Status is advertised by lateral display with arched neck, the chin tucked in and tail lifted. Submission is indicated by lowering the head and tail.

Territorial fights between bulls are characterised by horn clashing, horn wrestling in a kneeling position and sideways slashing with the horns.

What are their breeding habits?

There is a birth peak during the wetter summer months of February and March. A territorial bull will test a cow's reproductive condition by sniffing her genitalia, thereby stimulating her to urinate. The bull inserts his nose into the stream of urine and performs *flehmen* (pulling back his lips and inhaling deeply); if he receives a signal that the cow is in oestrus, he will follow the cow and kick up between her hind legs with his foreleg, a ritual referred to as *laufschlag*. If the cow is ready to receive the bull she will stand and allow him to perform *laufschlag*, after which copulation takes place (see the description of courtship behaviour on pages 34 and 35 of the Introduction).

After a gestation period of eight to nine months, a single calf with a mass of about 15 kg is born in dense cover. The calf remains hidden for up to three weeks, during which time the mother visits twice a day to suckle and clean the calf.

What is their average life span?
They have a life span of about 10 to 15 years.

How do they demonstrate alarm and aggression?
Alarm signals include loud snorts and adopting an alert posture, stamping and fleeing, with the herd in a loose but cohesive formation.

Aggression includes displays of horn threats, head tossing, horn clashing usually from a kneeling position, ground horning and pawing, mock and real charges as well as sideways slashing with the horns. Sable can be very dangerous when wounded or when at bay, and will charge with little provocation.

What are their main enemies?
Lions are the main enemy. Calves and sub-adults are preyed upon by leopards, hyaenas, cheetahs and African wild dogs. Predators are very wary of adult sable bulls because of their dangerous horns.

Sable antelope translocate well and they are very popular game-ranch animals. Demand by hunters drives up prices, resulting in regular translocation of sable to game ranches and hunting farms, where they are sought-after for hunting, resulting in perilously low stocks. They are classified in the *Red Data Book* as Vulnerable.

ELAND
Taurotragus oryx (Pallas 1766)

How widely are they distributed in the Park?
Eland are predominantly found north of the Lepelle River. There is a small herd in the Pretoriuskop area. They are found in the mopane shrubveld, the mopane/bushwillow woodland areas along the western border of the Park, the alluvial plains west of Shingwedzi and north of the Luvuvhu River, the sandveld areas of the north, and the tree mopane savanna east of Punda Maria.

Refer to ecozones B, L, M, N, O and P on the Kruger Park ecozone map.

What type of habitat do they prefer?
They prefer scrubland and open plains, grassland and woodland savanna, avoiding forested, desert, swampy and extensive open grassy plains areas. In the Park they prefer the areas as described above.

What do they eat?
Eland are predominantly browsers, eating leaves and twigs, but also berries, flowers, forbs and seeds, and they dig for roots, tubers and bulbs. They will graze on green grass, especially the fresh growth after a fire. They also eat dry fallen leaves.

Describe their main physical features?
The eland is the biggest African antelope. It is very large and bulky, with ox-like features. Males can attain a shoulder height of up to 1.7 m and a mass of about 900 kg, while cows reach a shoulder height of about 1.5 m and a mass of up to 500 kg.

The coat is a dull fawn colour with five to 10 very faint vertical white stripes down the flanks. In some populations the stripes are absent. Older bulls become blue-grey in colour, especially around the neck. There is a distinctive brown patch on the back of the forelegs just above the knee. Males have a very distinctive patch of dark bristly hair on the forehead overlying glandular skin. This hair is often caked in mud. The ears are smallish and both sexes have a dewlap, which is more developed and pronounced in the bulls.

Both sexes have horns rising from the top of the head, nearly straight with smooth spirals and a spiral ridge. The horns of the bulls are longer, heavier and more prominently ridged than those of the cows and can reach a length of up to 0.65 m.

What are their behavioural habits?

Eland are both nocturnal and diurnal. They prefer feeding at night when the moisture content of the vegetation is higher. They pull vegetation into the mouth with their lips, not the tongue. They break down branches with their horns to get to the twigs and leaves.

They are gregarious, with herd sizes varying seasonally from two to five animals during the rainy season, to more than 100 in the northern regions of the Park during the winter months.

Eland are not territorial, but they are very nomadic and move over vast distances in search of suitable habitat and feeding areas. They are not water dependent, obtaining sufficient moisture from their diet, but will drink readily when water is available.

Bulls and cows have separate dominance hierarchies, with the older and larger animals more senior in rank, but bulls dominating cows. Threat is displayed by head shaking with the head held high, horn jabbing, charging and blows with the horns when subordinates do not move away quickly enough. Submission is shown by moving away with a lowered, shaking head.

Bulls fight with horns clashing and locking, pushing and twisting. The loser breaks away and runs off. Aggressive behaviour is ritualised but occasional injuries and near fatalities have been recorded.

Bulls rub the hair on their forehead in the soil where they or an oestrus female have just urinated, caking it with mud. As they walk, eland, especially the large bulls, make a clicking sound, the origin of which has not been finally determined.

Although slow runners, eland are good jumpers, with adults clearing up to 2 m.

When threatened by predators, eland herds bunch together with calves in the centre, and will counterattack with hooves and horns.

What are their breeding habits?
Breeding takes place throughout the year, with a calving peak during the rainy summer season.

Bulls and cows test each other's urine by sniffing and *flehmen*. Oestrus cows are shadowed by dominant bulls, who drive lesser bulls away. The bull then courts the cow by rubbing his head on her flanks, licking her, resting his head on her back, sniffing and licking her genitalia and pawing and horning the ground.

After a gestation period of nine months, a single calf weighing about 30 to 35 kg is born. The calf remains hidden for two weeks. The calf can stand very soon after birth and can follow its mother after three or four hours. Calves will follow any adult and try to suckle from any female. Calves bond more closely with other calves than with their mothers and form crèche groups within the herd.

What is their average life expectancy?
Eland have a life span of 15 to 20 years.

Could the eland be used for meat production?
Eland have the important potential for sustainable meat production and could possibly produce more meat than cattle under drought conditions. If eland ever became a viable source of meat production, it would probably be in the arid areas of the country.

Are eland dangerous animals?
The eland is one of the most timid wild animals and will seldom charge, except when wounded or cornered. It must always be remembered that wild animals are just that: that they never lose the wild streak and cannot be trusted.

What are their major enemies?
Lions and hyaenas are the principal enemies of adult eland, while calves fall prey to lions, leopards, cheetahs and African wild dogs.

BUSHPIG   *Potamochoerus porcus* (Linnaeus 1758)

What is the distribution and preferred habitat in the Park?
They occur predominantly in ecozone M, the extreme northern parts of ecozone N and in parts of ecozone H. The highest-density populations are found north of the Luvuvhu River and the riverine forests of the Limpopo Mountains. Small populations have been reported along the Lepelle, Sabie and Crocodile rivers. They prefer dense bush and forest, particularly along rivers.

What are their main physical features?
Bushpigs closely resemble their domestic counterparts, but their coats are coarse, and much more hairy and shaggy. The dorsal mane is yellowish against the rusty to brownish-black coat; there are yellowish-white tufts on the ear tips. The bushpig has a tufted tail but, unlike the warthog, it does not hold it erect when running.

Piglets are brown with faint stripes that fade after about four months. The colour of the coat is largely determined by the soil in which they dig for roots and tubers and in which they take their regular mud baths. The mud baths probably serve to lower body temperature and offer protection against parasites and the sun.

Scent glands are situated in the hooves, neck, lip and chin. Bushpig boars also have preputial glands.

Their tusks are not as prominent as those of the warthog. Sometimes protruding from the upper jaw, some tusks have been measured at 16 cm.

In a life spanning about 15 years, boars can reach a mass of up to 110 kg and sows about 60 kg, Shoulder heights range from 55 to 88 cm; .

Are they solitary animals and what do they eat?

Bushpigs are gregarious and are found in sounders numbering between five and 15 individuals. They are omnivorous, eating grass, roots, tubers, bulbs, corms and fruit. They will also take carrion, larvae, eggs, worms, small birds, rodents and snakes. They are not water dependent, but will drink when water is available.

Do they have a social hierarchy and are they territorial?

It is accepted that a sounder has a dominant boar and that a dominance order should therefore exist. The mixed sounders usually consist of a dominant boar and sow and subordinate sows and their piglets. The territory, aggressively defended against intruders, is marked with digital- and neck-gland secretions, dung middens and urine. Territorial boundaries shift to some extent, depending on the availability of food. Well-worn rubbing posts are found throughout the territory and the dominant boar also gouges trees to mark his territory.

What are their reproduction habits?

Breeding takes place during the summer rainy season. After a gestation period of four months an average of three or four piglets are born in a large grass nest. Piglets are weaned at about three to six months, after which they are cared for by the dominant boar.

Do they cause crop damage?

Being predominantly nocturnal, but sometimes foraging during early morning or late afternoon, they have ample opportunity to visit cultivated crops. They are very destructive feeders, devouring large quantities and trampling even more underfoot.

Where are they most likely to be found in the Park?

They are rare in the Park and, because of their nocturnal habits and habitat preference, are seldom seen by visitors or staff. During the day they hide in dense undergrowth; the most likely places to see bushpigs in the Park are in the Pafuri area in the north and along the Crocodile River in the Malelane area in the south.

What are their major enemies and are they dangerous to man?

Leopards and lions are their most important natural enemies, although bushpigs as a rule are not very plentiful in typical lion habitat. Leopards usually pounce and retire to a tree as quickly as possible to escape the wrath of these pigs.

Normally bushpigs will flee from humans but will not hesitate to charge when cornered or wounded. Boars are particularly courageous and will charge the source of danger on sight, especially when there are piglets in the sounder. Their short tusks are very sharp and can inflict serious slashing wounds.

WARTHOG   *Phacochoerus aethiopicus* (Pallas 1776)

What is the distribution in the Kruger Park?

Warthogs are widely distributed in suitable habitat in all the ecozones throughout the Park. They prefer open savanna and are found in high densities in the areas between Lower Sabie and Crocodile Bridge; in the areas of Orpen, Tshokwane, N'wanetsi and Phalaborwa, as well as between the Luvuvhu and Limpopo rivers.

What do they eat and are they destructive to crops?

Warthogs are omnivores. They are essentially selective grazers, preferring short grasses and newly sprouted grasses after fires. They also favour roots, bulbs and tubers that are dug out with the shovel-like snout. They have a distinct preference for seasonal fruit such as berries and the marulas that are abundant during February.

Warthogs customarily go on their knees when feeding. Also included in their diet is carrion, as well as rodents and small reptiles. They sometimes chew on bones, rocks and soil to extract the required mineral content of their diet.

Are they dependent on water?

Warthogs are water independent, obtaining sufficient moisture from their diet. They will, however, drink regularly when water is available.

What are the main physical features?

Depending on the type of soil in which the last mud bath was taken, the skin appears predominantly grey and almost devoid of hair. A black to yellowish-brown mane runs down the back of the neck and shoulders down to the back, with whitish whiskers along the jaw line. Enormous wart-like protuberances, two pairs on the boar and a single pair on the sow, project from the flattened face, from which the animal's

name is derived. The warts are not true warts and are not pathological in origin.

The eyes are set high up on the face. The long, thin tail, with a tuft of dark hairs at the tip, is held upright when the animal runs.

Scent glands underlie the facial warts, the lips and chin, and the boars also have preputial glands. Warthogs have poor sight but an acute sense of smell and hearing.

Body mass in boars is about 100 to 150 kg, in sows around 65 kg. Shoulder heights vary from about 70 cm in the case of boars and about 60 cm in the sows. Boars have larger tusks than sows. In boars tusks of up to 60 cm have been measured, and up to 30 cm in sows.

What is the purpose of such large tusks and are warthogs dangerous to man?

Tusk size obviously has survival value for the warthog. Roots, bulbs and tubers are dug up with the upper tusks, while the very sharp but shorter lower tusks are used in combat. The upper, larger tusks curve upward and then inward, while the shorter tusks protruding from the lower jaw are straight and pointed.

When chewing, the upper and lower tusks grind against each other, honing the lower tusks into very sharp and dangerous instruments.

Warthogs will usually flee from man but, when wounded or at bay, they may become dangerous defending themselves. They often become vary tame and approachable but are potentially dangerous, especially when a sow is in oestrus.

What are the social structures and behaviour of warthogs?

Old boars are usually loners, but a family generally consists of up to five or more individuals, usually a boar, a sow and piglets of one or successive litters.

Warthogs are diurnal, but less active during the hotter hours of the day, when they tend to lie down in old aardvark holes or shady, secluded spots. Sows often form nursery sounders comprising one or two sows and their offspring. Young boars form bachelor sounders with siblings remaining within the natal home range.

In the Park home ranges of up to 4.5 km² are demarcated by wiping their mouths against vegetation and other objects, with the secretions from the glands enclosing the warts, and scent-marking with urine. Home ranges of neighbouring individuals and sounders often overlap, with only the core area around the burrow being seriously defended. Home ranges include several burrows used communally by several sounders at different times.

Through mutual grooming family ties are maintained. Foraging can lead to meandering of more than 7 km per day within their home range. Warthogs shelter mainly in old aardvark burrows, which they modify to suit their requirements and line with grass. Young warthogs enter the burrow headfirst and adults backside first. In this position they can defend themselves against enemies, as their backs are covered and the predator has to reckon with the dangerous tusks.

Because warthogs have very little body hair and they have very small fat reserves, they have a low tolerance to low temperatures. They conserve heat by insulating their burrows with grass, basking in the sun and huddling together.

How do they communicate?
Contact calls include snorts and grunts. The alarm call is a single loud grunt and they squeal loudly when distressed. They also respond to alarm calls of birds, especially the Oxpecker and Grey Touraco. Piglets squeal to attract parental attention when they are in distress.

The upright tail when they run is probably a visual communication signal by which individual members of a sounder keep contact.

Does their wallowing in the mud serve a specific purpose?
Warthogs are fond of taking mud baths as they aid in lowering body temperature and protect them against the sun. The dry mud on the skin serves to get rid of ectoparasites,

such as ticks, and affords protection against biting and stinging insects.

What are their breeding habits?

A boar detects when a female is on heat from the smell of her urine. He champs his jaws, salivates profusely, grunts rhythmically and rests his head on her rump. If she is receptive, copulation, which is very brief, follows.

Breeding takes place during the summer rainy season and an average of four piglets are born after a gestation period of four months. Sows leave the sounder to give birth. Piglets are born in grass-lined burrows and are moved to raised recesses in the burrow to protect them from drowning during heavy rains that may flood the burrow. Each piglet suckles from its allocated teat and is not allowed to suckle from another. Piglets remain in the burrow for up to seven weeks but will leave it for short periods when they are around one to three weeks of age to feed on grass. Piglets are weaned at about six months, but remain with the mother for up to a year. They follow behind their mother in a fixed order.

What are their major enemies?

Young warthogs are eaten by carnivores from the size of jackals upwards and are heavily preyed upon by lions, leopards and cheetahs. They are also taken by large raptors and pythons. Adult animals mainly fall prey to lions and spotted hyaenas as well as African wild dog, although fully grown boars are rather difficult customers for any of these predators.

Warthog meat is supposed to be delicious. Is this true?

Warthog meat is said to be tasty, but it is doubtful whether it could really compare with meat from domestic stock.

LARGER EVEN-TOED UNGULATES

AFRICAN (CAPE) BUFFALO   *Syncerus caffer*

(Sparrman 1779)

What is the distribution of African buffaloes in the Park?

African buffaloes are found in suitable habitat in all ecozones of the Kruger National Park, with the highest density occurring on the grasslands of the eastern half of the Park.

What type of habitat do African buffaloes prefer?

African buffaloes prefer open woodland savanna with patches of dense cover such as thickets, reeds or forest. They are associated with rivers, swampy areas and grassy plains. Although they have adapted to a wide range of habitats, they are very seldom found in areas where the annual rainfall is less than 250 mm.

What do they eat?

African buffaloes are primarily nonselective grazers and browse very little. These herbivores prefer leaves to stems, and grass species five to 80 cm tall, high in crude protein. Buffaloes will consume between 15 and 18 kg of dry vegetation per day. They graze for eight to 10 hours a day and are more able than other animals to push in amongst bushes to reach grass.

What are their main physical features?

Buffaloes look much like heavily built cattle except for their prominent, heavy horns. Adult bulls are dark brown to black, and cows and calves more reddish-brown. Calves are covered in longish hair, and adults have short, coarse hair that becomes sparse with age. They have large heads, thick necks, massive bodies and short limbs.

Very old bulls have a pale, white appearance around the face and horns.

Horns grow from thick, heavily ridged bosses on the forehead, flare sideways, then downwards and then curve upwards at the tips. Viewed from the front, the two horns form a shallow W-shape. Bulls carry heavier bosses and horns than cows, and in old bulls the bosses join across the head. The horns are very rugose for a third of their length and then smooth to the tips.

Apart from the horns, the large, frayed, droopy ears are also conspicuous.

Bulls stand about 1.5 m tall at the shoulder and have a mass of 550 to 650 kg. Cows are a little smaller, about 1.4 m at the shoulder, with a mass of about 530 kg.

How can one distinguish between African buffaloes and wildebeest?

From a distance they are similar in colour, with ox-like features, but there are some marked differences. Wildebeest are slenderly built in contrast to the massive, stout appearance of African buffaloes. The wildebeest's horns are much smaller, and its back has a distinct slope in profile.

Are African buffaloes gregarious?

Yes they are. Living in herds offers protection against predators. They often form large herds of more than 100 animals, and herds of over 1 000 animals are often recorded in the Park. Large herds form during summer, but tend to split up in the winter, and especially during periods of drought.

Old bulls become solitary or roam around in small groups of between two and 40 animals.

Is the dominant bull the leader of the herd?

Fierce fights during the rutting season determine the dominance hierarchy amongst the bulls. However, as in the case of other bovids, it is a dominant cow that leads the herd.

Are they diurnal or nocturnal animals?

Buffaloes tend to be more diurnal than nocturnal. Most of the grazing activities take place during the early morning or late afternoon, but it also happens during the night. They are water dependent and need to drink water at least once a day.

Their habit of spending the hot hours of the day in dense vegetation, ruminating, often makes it difficult to spot them. They rest and ruminate close together, even touching. On cold winter nights they sleep in a tightly packed group for warmth.

What are their social habits?

Herds consist of small clans, comprising one or several dominant bulls, cows and calves. The basic social units are family groups of related cows with their calves. There are separate dominance hierarchies among bulls and cows. Bigger, older animals tend to be high ranking, but cows rise in status when they have a calf at foot. High-ranking animals tend to be at the front centre of the herd when predation risks are smaller and food is more plentiful.

Some adult bulls form small bachelor groups. Bachelor bulls return to the herd for mating; while in the herd they lose body condition and dominance rank, which they build up again when they return to their bachelor group status.

Dominance is displayed with the head held high, while standing sideways on to the opponent. Other displays include head tossing and horn hooking. Submission is indicated by lowering the head, approaching the opponent and putting the nose under the opponent's belly. Fights are most commonly over access to cows in oestrus.

Herds travel in column formation when not feeding and in a broad front when grazing and moving.

The current author observed a herd of more than 3 000 African buffaloes walking in single file along the Mlondozi Spruit north of Lower Sabie Rest Camp. The formation stretched for more than 3 km.

Are their senses well developed?
Their senses of sight and hearing are not acute, but their sense of smell seems to be well developed.

Are they territorial in habit?
Although not territorial in habit, they will frequent a specific home range for many years.

What sounds do they make?
Buffaloes make very similar sounds to cattle. During the mating season, they grunt and bellow hoarsely. When stampeding, they utter snorts of alarm. Buffalo calves bleat like the calves of cattle.

Are African buffaloes nomadic?
They frequent well-watered areas where there is sufficient food, and probably move away only under extreme conditions. They are not migratory, but move in response to seasonal changes in the availability of grazing. Individuals may travel considerable distances. An adult bull fitted with a radio collar in the Satara area 'disappeared' and was eventually located in the far north of the Park, about 30 km south of the Luvuvhu River.

Are they dangerous to man?
They are extremely dangerous when wounded or cornered, but if left in peace they seldom pose a threat. While in a herd, African buffaloes seldom show aggression to humans, but old bulls on their own are very unpredictable and may charge for no apparent reason. They investigate disturbances by raising the head with the nose held high, and they may walk towards the source.

Hunters generally regard a wounded African buffalo as one of the most dangerous animals. Once a buffalo charges its adversary, only a well-placed bullet fired from a high calibre rifle can stop it. During the charge the head is held high to keep the adversary in sight and only at the last moment is the buffalo's head lowered for the physical attack.

It is said that a wounded buffalo tends to ambush its pursuer. Is this strictly true?
Many hunters have made this claim, but it is doubtful whether it could really be proven. What probably happens is that the hunter tracks the wounded animal for some distance until the latter, exhausted and feeling cornered, charges its pursuer.

Is the buffalo as tough as it is made out to be?
Yes, indeed, as a number of hunters have found out too late! A charging buffalo presents a very difficult target for a brain shot, and the massive horn bosses often deflect the bullet. Ask any ranger, hunter or person working in the bush which animal they consider most dangerous, and the answer will invariably be the buffalo.

Can an African buffalo run fast?
It is claimed that a buffalo can attain a speed in excess of 50 km/h.

A herd of buffalo looks frightening. Will it charge a vehicle?
Buffaloes are very inquisitive and will often stare, nose raised high, at a vehicle or other object. At the same time they may take a few steps forward, while snorting and making

a defiant sweeping motion of the massive head and horns. When not threatened, they are almost as harmless as cattle.

On the other hand, their tendency to stampede when alarmed could be dangerous if one happens to be in their way. When threatened, herds bunch more closely, with adults on the outside and cows and calves in the centre. Predator attacks are sometimes driven off by the victims' companions and predators may be attacked on sight.

What are their breeding habits?

Buffaloes breed all year round and after a gestation period of about 11 months a single calf with a mass of about 30 to 45 kg is born. Births peak during the summer, usually between January and April. Calves associate with their mothers for about two years. Cows calve every two or three years.

What are the African buffalo's major enemies?

Lions are their only significant natural enemies, although adults as well as immature animals sometimes fall prey to crocodiles. Old or solitary bulls are often killed by lions, usually in a team effort.

Young animals may fall prey to African wild dogs and hyaenas, and figures indicate that only 30 to 45% of calves reach maturity.

A single lion facing a buffalo has a formidable task. It has often been observed that a bull, or a small party of bulls, charges and frightens off lions. If attacked, a bull will go down fighting fiercely. Many a lion has been injured in such battles, a number of them fatally.

Do African buffaloes suffer from cattle diseases?

They are susceptible to most of the cattle diseases, among which are foot-and-mouth disease, anthrax, brucellosis and bovine tuberculosis.

Foot-and-mouth disease is at times quite common among African buffaloes. Despite being a highly fatal disease, anthrax has up till now not been a significant factor in mortality.

African buffaloes are also susceptible to bovine tuberculosis, which is now spreading through the Park.

During the latter part of the 19th century, buffalo populations in many parts of Africa, including the Kruger National Park, were decimated in a rinderpest pandemic.

GIRAFFE   *Giraffa camelopardalis* (Linnaeus 1758)

What is the distribution of giraffe in the Park?
They occur in all the ecozones of the Kruger National Park, except L, with the highest density in the area from north of the Olifants Rest Camp to the Crocodile River in the south.

The Satara and Crocodile Bridge areas have the bulk of the population, with approximately one giraffe every 2 km². North of the Lepelle River they are quite rare (one giraffe per 6.2 km²).

North of the Letaba River there is only one giraffe to about 50 to 100 km², and they are almost absent in the Punda Maria and sandveld areas of the north.

Why are they so rare in the northern part of the Park?
Giraffes show a particular preference for *Acacia* trees, especially the knobthorn acacia, which is rather scarce in the far northern section of the Park.

How many giraffes are in the Park?
According to the last aerial census there are about 7 100 giraffes in the Park.

Are giraffes well represented in South Africa outside the Park?
Large populations exist in the private game reserves west of the Park, and smaller populations are found in many of the smaller provincial and private game reserves. They were also reintroduced into the Willem Pretorius Game Reserve in the Free State, the Hluhluwe section of the Hluhluwe-iMfolozi Park in KwaZulu-Natal and also into the Kgalagadi Transfrontier Park in 1990.

What type of habitat do they prefer?
They prefer savanna and open woodland, especially where *Acacia* species (thorn trees), *Combretum* (bushwillows) and

Terminalia (cluster-leaves) dominate. Bulls are sometimes encountered in light forest, but they usually stay there only temporarily. Cows and calves show a definite preference for more open country.

Is there any specific reason why giraffes prefer more open areas?
Dense forest impairs their vision and, because of their long necks, makes it difficult to flee, thus making them more vulnerable to predators.

Are they able to negotiate uneven terrain?
They are sometimes found in the foothills of the Lebombo Mountain, where they graze on the fresh spring growth on the *Combretum* trees, but uneven terrain impairs movement.

What do giraffes eat?
They are almost exclusively browsers, grazing only in very exceptional circumstances. Even at times when they appeared to be eating grass, close investigation proved that the plant eaten was a small creeper of the genus *Cucumis*. Their favourite food is the foliage of the *Acacia* trees and in the Park about 30% of their intake is made up of knobthorn (*Acacia nigrescens*), while about 20% comprises other *Acacia* trees, nearly 20% *Combretum* species, and 7% is made up of buffalo thorn (*Ziziphus mucronata*).

Giraffes browse more than 100 species of trees and shrubs in the Park. Fruit of the monkey orange (*Strychnos madagascariensis*) and the sausage tree (*Kigelia africana*) are well utilised. They also eat the flowers of the *Acacia* when in bloom and a variety of flowers, fruit and seed pods.

Why do they show such a marked preference for certain plant species?

Taste and/or smell could play a role, but the exact reason is unknown.

Does the composition of their food vary during the different seasons?

Their favourite food trees are deciduous and so they have to compensate by feeding on less palatable evergreen trees during the winter.

Do they get enough food in winter when many trees are bare?

The amount of food available in winter is a limiting factor in their survival. They are naturally forced to feed on evergreen substitutes such as *Euclea* species, but even this source of food is limited. Many of the deciduous trees, however, are bare for only a short time of the year.

Does heavy browsing by giraffes have an influence on their food trees?

In many parts of Africa it has been found that heavy browsing by giraffes has led to the stunting of certain trees. The 'pruning' of their favourite food trees into various shapes, such as dome, pyramid, hourglass or even cigar forms, is quite conspicuous in many areas in the Park. Twigs are pulled into the mouth by the lips and the 45-cm-long prehensile tongue, and the leaves are shredded off into the mouth. Giraffes consume up to 80 kg a day, and between 10 and 12 hours each day may be spent browsing.

Where can these tree shapes be seen?

They are quite conspicuous where *Acacia* species are dominant or sub-dominant trees in the veld type. Many examples can be seen along the H1-3 tar road between Satara and Tshokwane, the S37 Trichardt road, the S90 old main road, and the Gudzane road, the S41 dirt road east of Satara where the stunted knobthorn trees show various shapes trimmed by giraffes.

Is it not strange that giraffes prefer thorny food plants?

The evolution of some African plants, especially the genus *Acacia*, appears to have been influenced by the giraffe and other large browsers that are now extinct. The development of thorns and spines was probably to protect these plants from the browsers. It is interesting to note that Australia, where there is the largest variety of thornless *Acacia* species, has no large browsing herbivores.

Are *Acacia* species the only trees that are 'pruned'?

Yes, with a few exceptions. A very small number of *Combretums* show signs of giraffe browsing. The basic form of more than one stem does not lend itself to 'pruning' in different shapes. In about 90% of cases, an obviously 'pruned' tree will be a knobthorn (*Acacia nigrescens*), and in a few cases probably Delagoa thorn, *Acacia welwitschii* ssp. *delagoensis*.

At what height do giraffes feed?

This depends on the type and amount of food available. In winter, when they are forced to feed on some evergreen shrubs, they come down to almost ground level and thus compete with browsers of a lesser height. A comfortable feeding height would probably be 2 to 5 m, depending on the individual's size.

Do they compete with other herbivores during times of abundant browse?

Their feeding overlaps to some extent with browsers such as kudu and eland, and even more so with elephants when grass becomes scarce and the latter reverts to browsing. The elephant has, with the aid of its trunk, about the same reach as a giraffe. To determine the exact amount of competition between giraffes and elephants is very difficult, owing to differences in food preferences and the fact that elephants often consume more grass than leaves.

Are there any peculiar plants that giraffes feed on?

They sometimes feed on the tamboti tree (*Spirostachys africana*), which is poisonous to human beings. *Combretum* seeds, which are also poisonous, but less so than tamboti, are also frequently browsed.

Do giraffes ruminate?

Yes. They have four-chambered stomachs like other ruminants.

Are they very dependent on water?

They are water dependent and drink regularly when water is available, but can apparently go without water for up to a month, obtaining enough moisture from their food.

How much water can a giraffe drink at a time?

A big bull may drink up to 25 litres or more per day.

Can they store water to see them through periods when no water is available?

They cannot conserve water, but they probably get additional moisture from their food and, to a lesser extent, from dew on the plants they eat.

What are the main physical features?

The main physical features of this unique animal are so obvious that they hardly need be given in detail. They have a distinctive patchwork body patterning, large brown eyes with long eyelashes, a long neck and legs, a relatively short body and a long tail. The sloping nature of the back is mostly due to the long dorsal spines of the thoracic vertebrae, to which the strong neck muscles are attached. The forelegs are longer than the hind legs.

How did the giraffe get its name?

Its common name is derived from its Arab name *xirapha*, which means 'one who walks fast'. In early times people thought the giraffe was a cross between a camel, because of the way it walked, and a leopard, because of the blotches. This led to the word *camelopardalis*. The gait of the giraffe is similar to that of a camel: it walks with the left legs together and then the right legs, not cross-legged like other four-legged creatures.

Is the giraffe related to any animal?

The only animal it is related to is the okapi (*Okapia johnstoni*), which occurs in the central African rainforest. Although this animal's neck is longish, it is not nearly as long as that of the giraffe. The okapi is very dark brown in colour, with a few vertical stripes and a few small spots. It looks very different from the giraffe, but the layman could still see the relationship between the two animals.

How many cervical or neck vertebrae does the giraffe have?

Seven, like most other mammals.

What is the purpose of the relatively small horns?

This is not known. They are useless as protection against predators and, although bulls use them in fights, they appear to do little harm.

Are the horns of the bull different from those of the cow?

The cow's horns are shorter and more slender than the bull's and have a tuft of hair at the tip; the tip of the bull's horn is bare and the horns are thicker. Thus it is possible to identify the sex of a giraffe even if only the head of the animal is visible.

Why are the tips of the bulls' horns bald?

This is probably because the bulls become involved in many fights and mock fights in which the horn tips frequently come into contact with the opponent's body. It has also been suggested that keratin deposits could be a contributory factor.

Are the calves born with horns?
Yes. At birth the horns are cartilaginous and about 25 mm long. They ossify as they grow, and their bases fuse completely with the parietal bones of the skull.

Is it true that some giraffes have more than two horns?
Some subspecies of giraffe show a tendency to develop more knobs, or so-called horns, on the skull. Besides the two parietal or main horns, a frontal horn and occipital horns can develop. The frontal horn of the subspecies *G.c. giraffa* is poorly developed and usually not much more than a slight knob.

There are authors who claim that giraffes have seven horns. This is due to bony structures that sometimes develop on the zygomatic arch of the skulls of old bulls. It is not a constant feature and should therefore be disregarded. Extra bony outgrowths on the face commonly occur in the bulls and are probably caused by head hitting during fights.

How many subspecies of giraffe are there in the world?
There is only one species, but this is divided into a number of subspecies based on minor differences. Some taxonomists describe 11 or more subspecies, but others recognise only nine subspecies. The giraffes in the Park belong to the subspecies *G.c. capensis*.

Why are some individuals darker than others?
They usually become darker with age and this is more pronounced in the bulls than in the cows. A very dark giraffe is usually an old male.

Is the blotch pattern of giraffes in the Park more or less the same?
Yes, but no two individuals have exactly the same pattern. It is, however, interesting to note that a small percentage have a star-like configuration on the buttocks, while a few have blotches that bear a strong resemblance to the star-like patterning of the Kenyan giraffe *G.c. tippelskirchi*.

Are there albino giraffes in the Park?
Yes, but such individuals are fairly rare. About 10 cases are mentioned in the literature, and some of them have been documented photographically.

How tall can a giraffe grow?
Bulls grow to a height of about 5 m to the top of the head, and cows to about 4.4 m.

What is their mass?
Bulls have a mass of up to 1 200 kg or more, and cows up to about 900 kg.

How fast can giraffes run?
They are reputed to reach speeds in excess of 45 km/h.

How far can they run?
This has probably not been tested scientifically. According to hunters in the 19th century who ran them down with horses, giraffes could maintain a brisk pace for a distance of about 7 km. It was said that a horse had to be very fit to outdistance a giraffe.

Do giraffes have very strong hearts to pump blood up their long necks?
In relation to other mammals, their hearts are not exceptionally large but are very strong. The blood pressure at the heart is about 260/160, compared with the 120/80 in a healthy human being. The neck arteries also have valves like the veins to prevent a back-flow of blood.

Why do giraffes not become dizzy when they lift their heads after drinking?
A network of blood vessels at the base of the brain, called the *rete mirabile*, serves as a mechanism to prevent too great a back-flow of blood. When the giraffe

bends down, this mechanism reduces the pressure of the blood at the base of the brain to about 120/80.

How fast does the heart beat?
About 60 beats per minute.

Why is it so difficult for a giraffe to bend its neck?
The neck muscles connected to the dorsal spines of the thoracic vertebrae make it difficult for the giraffe to lower its head and neck to ground level.

Do giraffes migrate?
Giraffes do not migrate, but move from one area to another for food and water. During spring they move around to feed on the flowers and young leaves of their preferred food sources.

They will remain in the same area for a number of years if food and water are always available.

What is the average size of a giraffe herd?
Giraffes form very loose aggregations of individuals, both male and female, with the number of animals in a 'herd' varying from day to day and even in a single day. The largest group recorded in the Kruger Park numbered 46 animals.

A concentration of giraffes is often spread over such a large area that it is difficult to decide whether it is one large herd or merely a loose aggregation of smaller groups. 'Herds' in the Kruger Park usually consist of fewer than 20 animals.

Why are bulls often alone?

Males of many animal species tend to be solitary when they cannot compete successfully for females, and this is to a certain extent also true for giraffes. Solitary bulls often move from one giraffe herd to another in search of cows on heat.

Do old bulls have a pungent smell?

It is said that old bulls do have a peculiar smell, and hunters of the 19th century called them by the evocative name of 'stink bulls'.

What are their social behaviour patterns?

Giraffes are both diurnal and nocturnal, being most active in the early morning and late afternoon, but also feeding at night in bright moonlight. During the heat of the day they tend to stand in the shade and ruminate.

They tend to be solitary, but also occur in loosely associated same-sex or mixed herds. High-ranking bulls stand with their heads held high to exaggerate their height and bulk; subordinates show submission by bowing their heads and dropping their ears.

Young bulls may form bachelor groups while mature bulls are almost always alone, except when they join a female herd for mating. Young bulls engage in neck wrestling and neck twining to establish rank; neck twining also occurs in courtship or preliminary to serious fights. Mature bulls fight for dominance by striking at the opponent's neck, rump and flanks with the back of their heads, i.e. the horns.

Does a herd have a dominant bull?

Bulls move around so much that a herd can have a different dominant bull at different times.

Who is the actual leader of the herd?

When both bulls and cows are present in a herd, it is difficult to say. Sometimes a cow and sometimes a bull will lead the way to a new feeding area or a water hole.

Does the composition of a giraffe herd vary a lot?

Yes. Within their home range members of different herds mix freely. Family groups are more stable.

Are they territorial in habit?

They do not defend a territory, but usually have a home range of anything between 20 and 70 km^2, in which they may remain for years.

Do bulls often fight?

They frequently indulge in fights ranging from low-intensity sparring to serious fights for dominance.

How do the bulls fight?

They usually stand side by side facing in the same direction or in opposite directions, and then hit each other with sweeping blows of the neck and head. These fights are seldom fatal and usually end when one or both animals become too exhausted to continue.

One often sees a few young giraffes with an adult. Do they have 'babysitters'?

As the young have to fend for themselves from a very early age, they feel more secure in the presence of adults. This type of 'babysitting' is therefore fairly frequent. An adult male with a number of calves accompanying him is not a rare occurrence. The young continually change their 'babysitters'.

Are giraffes very inquisitive?

They are probably among the most inquisitive animals in the Park and will stare at strange objects for a long time.

Do they have 'sentinels'?

No, but every member of the herd is constantly on the lookout for enemies. If one sees something suspicious, it will stare at it or even move to a position where it will have a better view of the object of concern. When other members of the herd notice this behaviour, they also try to locate the cause of the suspicion.

Because of their good vision and lofty view, giraffes often locate danger before most other ungulates become aware of it. If game-watchers are looking for predators, it is worthwhile watching giraffes: when members of a herd stand motionless and erect facing in the same direction, it is often an indication of the presence of one or more predators.

Are their senses well developed?

Their sense of sight is very well developed. Their hearing seems to be adequate, but is probably not as well developed as their sight. There is still controversy about their sense of smell; some authors claim that it is well developed, while others refute this. The nostrils can be closed voluntarily, but the reason for this is not known.

Are giraffes mute?

For many years it was believed that giraffes were mute. Normally they are quiet animals, but they do possess rudimentary vocal cords, which allow them to utter grunting or bellowing sounds, usually under stress.

Can giraffes swim?

Giraffes are among the few species of mammals that apparently cannot swim. It has been observed in the Park and elsewhere that they occasionally wade through fairly deep water, but rivers often serve as an efficient barrier to their movements.

How do giraffes sleep?

They usually sleep standing up, but also lying down. They probably do not sleep more than about 20 minutes in 24 hours. Most of their rest is attained through many short doses of light sleep, called a polyphase sleep pattern. This contrasts with the monophase sleeping pattern of carnivores, whereby the animals sleep for a long period and then become active for another long period.

What is the mating procedure?

They mate throughout the year. Bulls move from herd to herd searching for cows on heat. Cows urinate when a bull approaches, and he tests the urine by *flehmen* and sniffing. If a cow is coming into oestrus, the bull will stay with her until displaced by a higher-ranking challenger. Courtship involves sniffing and licking, nudging with the head and resting the head on the female's back. Copulation itself is very brief.

How does the mother give birth?

Standing up, so the calf drops more than 1.5 m to the ground. Parturition can take between one and two hours; it usually takes the calf another hour to stand up.

How big is the calf at birth?

After a gestation period of 15 months (the giraffe is the only ruminant with a gestation period of longer than a year), a single calf, with a mass of about 100 kg and a height of about 1.5 m, is born.

How long does the calf suckle?

For eight to 10 months, sometimes longer. From the age of about one month the calf starts to supplement its milk diet with leaves.

Does the mother defend her calf against predators?

During the first few weeks after the birth of the calf the mother will try to manoeuvre it between her front legs when confronting an attacker. Cases have been recorded of a cow beating off a lion attack.

When does the calf become independent?

The mother–calf relationship is very loose. When the calf is about six weeks old the mother no longer defends it and it has to watch and follow her when she moves on or flees from danger. The young grow fast – females can reach a height of 4.3 m in five years.

How long does the calf stay with the mother?

Usually for more than a year and even up to maturity. A mother and one or more daughters with their own offspring is not an uncommon social grouping. Calves can stray from their mothers and survive in a strange herd with other adults.

How long is the interval between calvings and for how long do the females reproduce?

The calving interval is about 20 months. A female can probably reproduce up to the age of 20 years or even longer, giving birth to 10 calves in her lifetime.

What is the life span of a giraffe?

The record is 28 years (attained in a zoo), and in the wild longevity is probably not more than 25 years. A Park ranger observed two giraffes with distinct markings over a period of 19 years. When he first saw them they were fully grown, and when they were last seen they must have been in their mid-20s. Giraffes are sexually mature at about three and a half to five years, and fully grown at about seven years of age.

Are giraffes susceptible to diseases?

They are vulnerable to sudden spells of cold weather, especially if their condition is poor due to scarcity of food at the end of the winter or early spring. There are indications that many of them died during the rinderpest pandemic towards the end of the 19th century. A few cases of death caused by anthrax have been recorded. In general, however, high mortality due to disease has not been experienced in the Park.

Giraffes harbour quite a number of endo- and ectoparasites and, according to surveys, eggs of Schistosoma matheei, the bilharzia parasite, were found in the faeces of 19% of giraffes in the Park.

Why do giraffes sometimes chew bones?

Like many other wild herbivores, and cattle, giraffes sometimes chew or eat strange objects such as soil, faeces and bones. This behaviour is called pica; the chewing of bones in particular is called osteophagia. This usually happens at the end of winter when the giraffe's diet is deficient in calcium, phosphorus or trace elements.

Chewing bones can be dangerous because they sometimes harbour the bacterium Clostridium botulinum, which secretes a most potent toxin. This causes botulism, a fatal disease.

Are they vulnerable when drinking?

They are vulnerable and they fully realise it. On approaching a water hole, a giraffe will stop frequently to scan the surroundings. It usually drinks for 10 seconds and then lifts its head and neck to check for potential danger. When satisfied that it is still safe, it will proceed to drink again.

The slightest sound or movement will make it jerk up its head and move off.

Some giraffes appear to suffer from a skin disease. What is it?

These are wart-like growths caused by a virus. They are very unsightly, but not fatal unless secondary infection sets in.

Were giraffes heavily hunted in southern Africa in the past?

Yes. They were killed mostly for their meat and for their skin, which was used for sandals and whips.

Is giraffe meat tasty?

The meat of cows and young animals is quite tasty, but no better than that of beef or mutton.

How were they hunted in the past?
They were often shot from horseback after they had been run down. The hunter had to have a strong horse with good stamina.

Are giraffes aggressive towards human beings?
They are very docile creatures and will rarely try to attack humans. There are records of cars being damaged by bull giraffes kicking at the vehicles. This behaviour is highly exceptional, however, and visitors need not be alarmed. However, if a giraffe is cornered it will defend itself like any other threatened beast.

What are their major enemies?
Young animals occasionally fall prey to leopards, cheetahs and crocodiles, while hyaenas and African wild dogs pose a minor threat. lions are practically the only natural enemy of adult giraffe.

How do lions kill a giraffe?
The method most often recorded is when lions chase the giraffe without really attempting to attack it. This usually takes place at night. The giraffe, under stress and anxious, stumbles through gullies, over rough terrain, over a log or puts a foot in a hole, which causes it to fall down. Once the giraffe is down, it is difficult to get up and it is then that the chasing lions swarm all over the hapless animal and seize it by the throat to suffocate it.

Lions will also encircle a giraffe, making mock charges at it, enticing it to chop at the attackers with its front legs or kick out with the hind legs. Eventually this wears the animal down, to the extent that it falls down and the lions then attack in their natural method. There are few recorded instances of lions jumping onto the back of the giraffe in order to kill it, except in the case of a smaller giraffe or a sick or very old animal, where the sheer mass of the lion could cause it to be brought down easily.

Can lions easily kill giraffes when they sleep?
Giraffes sleep very lightly and normally only for a few minutes at a time. It seldom, if ever, happens that all the individuals in a herd sleep at the same time. Solitary giraffes lying down to sleep are particularly vulnerable as it takes them quite some time to get up in order to defend themselves or to flee.

Can a giraffe defend itself when attacked by lion?
When cornered by lions, it will chop or kick at the predators. Should a lion manage to leap onto the back of a giraffe, the giraffe will run underneath branches in an effort to dislodge its assailant.

Do lions kill many giraffes?
While they often fall prey to lions, the actual number of giraffes killed is not known. In fact, as far as biomass is concerned, the lion's most important food is giraffe.

Are cows more vulnerable to lion attacks than bulls?
Lions kill twice as many bull giraffes in the Kruger Park as cows. Although a bull, by virtue of his greater size and strength, can put up a more efficient fight than a cow, he follows certain behavioural patterns that render him more vulnerable.

There are twice as many solitary bulls than there are solitary cows. Animals in a herd are safer than loners, simply because there are more eyes, ears and noses to detect possible danger. Bulls show a tendency to move into thickets at times, while cows and calves usually keep to the more open areas where predators can be spotted more easily, and there is less chance of being cornered.

Like the males of many other herbivores, bulls have a shorter flight distance than cows and allow a lion to come closer than a cow would. In flight the males usually run at the rear of the herd, where they are more vulnerable to attack than the cows and calves.

Is calf mortality high?
Yes, higher than that of adults of either sex. In the Park the calf mortality can be as high as 48%. The loose mother–calf relationship definitely plays a role in this respect.

Can a giraffe outdistance a lion?
The lion may be faster over a very short distance, but the giraffe has much more stamina and is a strong runner. It is almost impossible for a lion to get hold of a running giraffe.

Are giraffes killed by poachers?
Giraffes with broken snares around their legs are found from time to time, but this is relatively rare. Before the Park was fenced, giraffes that moved outside the area sometimes got entangled in snares set at their normal feeding level.

HIPPOPOTAMUS   *Hippopotamus amphibius* (Linnaeus 1758)

What is the distribution of hippos?
Hippos once inhabited just about every river in Africa from the north to the south. Hippos are still present in many rivers in the Afrotropical region. In South Africa they are more or less confined to game reserves in the Lowveld and KwaZulu-Natal. The hippopotamus is distributed throughout the Kruger National Park, especially in and along the perennial rivers and larger dams.

What habitat do they prefer?
They prefer streams, rivers, swamps, deltas and marshes near grassland for grazing. They prefer quiet waters at least 1.5 m deep in which they can submerge themselves, by standing or kneeling on the bed of the water source.

Are hippos very dependent on their water habitat?
They spend most of the day in the water, although on cool, overcast days and during winter, when the sun is not so hot, they sometimes leave the water for considerable periods to rest on sandbanks. They are, however, dependent on the water to keep their skins moist.

Do they have any special adaptation for an aquatic life?
Their elongated bodies with rounded contours help them to move easily in the water. The eyes, ears and nostrils are positioned so that they are above the surface when the rest of the hippo's body is submerged in water.

Do they graze during the day?
Their habitat extends quite a distance from water. At night they come out to feed on land, usually staying within 2 to 3 km of water, but during times of drought they have been seen up to 30 km away from their water refuge as they search for grazing. On cool, overcast days they may leave the water to graze nearby.

How long can a hippo live on land?
This depends on weather conditions, but would probably be for no longer than a few days. Prolonged exposure to the hot sun causes severe blistering of the skin, which in turn causes festering sores.

Do they eat fish?
No. They are grazers, feeding mostly on grass, but to some extent also on the

young shoots of reeds. Strangely, for such large creatures, hippos graze short grass, preferably not more than 10 to 15 cm in height. Grazing is done by with their broad, fat lips.

It has been observed that hippos are sometimes surrounded by black fish. What is the reason for this?
The fish belong to the genus *Labeo* and feed on vegetable matter stirred up by the hippo.

How much does a hippo eat per night?
An adult can eat about 60 kg of grass per night.

Do they destroy cultivated crops?
They are destructive and where farms border on game reserves they compete severely with man for his crops.

As a herbivore, why does a hippo need such large and impressive teeth?
When a feature is as extraordinarily well developed as the hippo's teeth, it is an indication that it has survival value. The canines, and to a lesser extent the incisors, are used in fights with rivals, often with deadly effect. In most of these fights the victor is the contestant with the larger canines. He is usually also the one who mates successfully and passes his genes on to the offspring.

How do hippos graze with teeth that seem to be in their way?
Grass is plucked with the strong lips and not the teeth. The molars masticate the food.

What is the mass of a fully grown hippopotamus?
Bulls attain a mass of approximately 1 500 to 1 800 kg and cows about 1 300 kg. The highest recorded mass for a bull hippopotamus in the Kruger National Park stands at 2 005 kg.

How thick is the hide?
The hide, with its fatty tissue, is about 50 mm thick and is said to make up about 16% of the animal's body mass.

Do hippos have any hair?
The skin is virtually naked apart from a scattering of bristles around the lips, the ears and the tip of the tail.

What is their shoulder height?
Shoulder height is about 1.5 m for bulls and 1.4 m for the cows.

What is their body colour?
Brownish-grey to nearly black, with a pinkish tinge around the muzzle, eyes and throat.

What are their social habits?
Hippos live in pods of up to 30 animals, consisting of cows and their offspring, young bulls and a single dominant bull that defends the pod's stretch of water as a territory in order to monopolise access to the cows.

If suitable water is restricted, several pods may occur close together. Neighbouring bulls meeting at territorial boundaries usually stare at each other, turn and spray dung and urine. A bull may hold a territory for as long as 12 years.

Fights over territory and cows are fierce, the teeth being used to stab and slash at the opponent. Battle injuries are often fatal and losers are driven out of the territory. Young bulls are tolerated in the pod until they reach the age of about six years, when they are driven out by the dominant bull. Dominant bulls sometimes kill youngsters, but mothers and babysitters defend their offspring against these infanticidal attacks.

Hippos scatter dung by wagging their tails as they defecate. Scattered dung usually builds up as communal dung heaps where hippo trails leave the water. When a bull approaches another hippo, the latter defecates and urinates in the water. With his vomeronasal organ the bull tests the water for signs of cows in oestrus. Should he find a cow ready to mate, a brief courtship that involves yawning and sparring precedes mating, which takes place in the water. The hippopotamus is the only southern African land mammal that mates in the water.

Yawning displays the tusk-like teeth and is a dominance signal and a sign to intruders of their own species, other species and humans to keep away.

Do hippos sweat blood?
No. Sub-dermal glands produce a reddish-pink secretion (sometimes referred to as 'blood sweat'), which protects the skin against the sun and dehydration, and enables the hippo to stay in the water for long periods.

How many toes do they have?
Four toes are encased in each rounded hoof on the end of each of their short legs.

What is the record length of their canine teeth?
According to records, the longest normal canine measured was 105.4 cm. A malformed canine, 121.9 cm long, is also on record. The length of a tooth is measured on the outside curve and nearly half of it is inside the jawbone. Average upper canines are around 22 cm in bulls and 14 cm in cows. Lower canines can grow to about 60 cm and can weigh about 3 kg.

At what age do the canine teeth reach their maximum length?
This is difficult to determine. The teeth continue to grow throughout the hippo's life and are subjected to considerable wear. It is interesting to note that, with the movement of the jaws, the smaller, upper canines move over their lower counterparts, honing them and thus keeping them sharp.

Are these teeth ivory?

Yes, and it is claimed to be finer and of better quality than that of the elephant.

Can a human being outrun a hippo?

Most probably not. The hippo is deceptively fast for an animal of its size and mass and could probably reach 30 km/h.

Some hippos have terrible scars. How did they get them?

When bulls fight they often seriously injure one another. Many a victor of such a fight subsequently dies from the wounds inflicted by his opponent.

Do they make any sound?

Hippos are particularly noisy animals, frequently making loud, snarling roars, accompanied by rumbling snorts. When surfacing, they snort and make blowing noises.

Are hippos strictly gregarious?

Hippos normally live in herds of 10 to 30 individuals, but much larger herds have been reported from different parts of their range. Old bulls evicted from a herd usually become solitary, although such individuals are rare.

Are they nomadic?

Seasonal movements do not occur, but when water holes and rivers dry up during droughts they move to more permanent water resources.

Overcrowding can also lead to movement in search of new habitats, and distances of 20 km per night can be covered under these circumstances.

It has been noticed that hippos are found in man-made dams. Were they introduced there?

No, not necessarily. 'Dethroned' lone bulls often move fairly long distances overland, usually during the night, to dams and even temporary pools, where they can find refuge. When the latter dry up they return to permanent water.

Are hippos territorial in habit?

The aquatic part of their habitat is defended as a territory while the land part where they graze is their home range. The latter is pear-shaped with the narrow end at the water, and is usually 3 to 8 km long.

Bulls defend their territories fiercely against male intruders. These fights are among the most vicious in the animal world, and are accompanied by loud grunts and raucous cries. The neck, with its large blood vessels, and the forelegs and flanks are prime targets during these fights.

Do they follow certain routes to their grazing ground?

Hippos like to follow well-beaten paths to and from feeding grounds. These paths consist of a very characteristic double trail – each one made by the feet on one side of the body.

Why do hippos yawn so much?

Besides the physiological reasons responsible for yawning in other animals and also humans, hippos use their yawning to intimidate others. The extent to which they can open their mouths is amazing, which serves to display their huge teeth to any possible contestant.

Hippos appear to dive and surface continuously. Why do they do this?

They do it for the cooling effect and also to prevent skin damage from the sun's rays.

How long can a hippo stay submerged?

The current author has timed hippos staying submerged for more than 10 minutes, but it is doubtful whether they regularly submerge for more than five or six minutes. The hippopotamus normally submerges for no more than a minute or two.

Can they walk on the river bed?
They are capable of walking on the river bed and do so frequently.

Why do hippos swish their tails when defecating?
It probably has some territorial implication, but the reason for this behaviour is not clear.

Hippo faeces scattered in the water serve as a fertilising agent. Rich in nitrogen, they encourage the growth of a wide variety of water plants, especially algae, which forms a nutritive base for many aquatic organisms on which fish feed.

What type of hierarchy exists in a hippo pod?
Mature hippo bulls jealously guard and defend their territories and a pod of hippos usually has one single dominant bull.

It is said that cows will tolerate a bull's attention only when they are on heat. Young bulls are driven out of the pod before they can compete with the dominant bull.

Is a hippo dangerous to man?
An enraged hippo is capable of launching an attack without warning and they should therefore be treated with the utmost caution.

It is justifiably claimed that the hippo is one of the most dangerous of wild animals. Hippos are especially dangerous when they return from their grazing grounds and find a human between them and their aquatic territory. Many women and children fetching water in rivers where hippos abound have been killed or maimed by a returning hippo.

During April 2009, two women on a walking safari along the Crocodile River were attacked by a hippo and severely injured. Hippos are extremely dangerous and can attack without any provocation.

Is a camp fire a deterrent to hippos?
It was once believed that a camp fire would scare hippos off, but a camp and/or fire close to a water body often receives hostile attention from a resident hippo, especially if it is a solitary bull.

Would a crocodile attack a hippo?
The large size, thick hide and death-dealing canines and incisors of the hippo make it far superior to a crocodile, which would seldom if ever take a chance with an adult hippo.

What are a hippo's major enemies?
Apart from lions and crocodiles, which occasionally attack young stray hippos or weakened adults, the hippo has hardly any other enemies, except for man.

How are hippo numbers regulated in a natural ecosystem?
Lack of food, disease and to some extent fights among bulls keep their numbers under control. During the severe drought of 1969 to 1970, more than 140 carcasses of hippos that had died from starvation were found in the Letaba–Olifants area of the Park.

Why were these animals hunted so frequently in the past?
They were hunted for their meat, fat and hides, and also to stop their raids on farm crops. The thick parts of the hides were used for sjamboks, while the rest of the hides made good leather when tanned.

Is hippo meat tasty?
Many people regard it as tasty, but beef and mutton have more flavour.

Do hippos have to be culled?
The culling of hippos in the Kruger Park was last undertaken in the 1980s. Culling is considered only when rivers become overcrowded, causing considerable trampling of the vegetation on and near the river banks. Conservation of this nature is based solely on the desiccated condition of the Park's perennial rivers.

How long is the gestation period?

After a short gestation period of eight months, a single calf weighing about 30 kg is born in shallow water, reed beds or in dense cover. The birth process is fast, which enables calves born in water to surface immediately for the vital first breath of air.

Can hippos have twins?

Twins are rare. The cows usually give birth to a single calf.

Can calves suckle under water?

Yes, but they have to surface frequently to breathe. They also suckle on land.

At what time of year are the young born?

In the Park they are born at any time of the year, but most births occur in the summer months.

Do hippos mate in water or on land?

They mate either in water or on land.

What is the potential life span?

Approximately 30 to 40 years. The record was set by 'Peter the Great', a hippo bull that lived in a New York zoo from 1903 to 1953 and died at the age of 49.

How many hippos are there in the Park?

According to the 2009 census, they number approximately 3 100 but their numbers fluctuate.

How are hippos counted?

From a helicopter.

What are their closest relatives?

Hippos belong to the order Artiodactyla, or even-toed mammals, having four toes on each foot. They are further classified under the suborder Suiformes, which includes pigs. There are only two genera, each with one species, namely the ordinary hippo (*Hippopotamus amphibius*) and the pygmy or dwarf hippo (*Choeropsis liberiensis*) from Liberia. Had it not been for the sterling work done by zoological gardens, *Choeropsis liberiensis* would probably have been extinct by now.

What are their major enemies?

Their main predator is man. Newborn and very young hippos are sometimes killed by lions and hyaenas, but mostly they fall prey to crocodiles.

BLUE WILDEBEEST   *Connochaetes taurinus* (Burchell 1823)

What is their distribution?

They are widely distributed throughout the Park and are found in ecozones A, B, D, E, F, G, I, J, K, L, N, O and P. They seem to concentrate mainly in three major areas south of the Lepelle River namely:
(i) the area northeast of Satara, the Mavumbye/Gudzani and Bangu areas;
(ii) the area between the Sweni River and the Mlondozi Dam, especially ecozone F, north of Lower Sabie; and
(iii) the open plains between Lower Sabie and Crocodile Bridge, especially ecozone F.

What type of habitat do they prefer?

They prefer open plains or lightly wooded savanna as long as there is short grass.

What do they eat?

Wildebeest are selective grazers, particularly attracted to the short, freshly sprouting grasses after a burn.
They are water dependent, usually found within 10 km of water. They will drink daily, in mid-morning or the afternoon, if water is readily available, but can go without water for a few days.

What are their main physical features?

This boisterous, robust-looking animal is about 1.4 to 1.5 m high at the shoulder and can attain a mass of 260 to 290 kg. Both sexes carry horns, with those of the bull heavier than the cow's. The horns grow from bosses on the forehead, hooking upwards and inward.

The bulls are dark grey to dark brown with a silver sheen, black on top of the muzzle with a russet tinge to the forehead, especially in younger animals, and a number of darker stripes visible on the neck, shoulders and body. This gave rise to the alternative name of 'brindled gnu'.

There is a mane of long black hair on the back of the neck and a fringe along the throat. The tail has a long whisk of black hair almost reaching to the ground.

The back slopes toward the hindquarters and the legs are thin compared with the size of the body.

The broad, flattened muzzle and large nostrils are conspicuous.

What are their habits and general behaviour?

They are diurnal and nocturnal but more active during the day, with grazing peaks in the early morning and late afternoon. During the heat of the day they stand resting in the shade. If no shade is available, they will stand facing the breeze, cooling the blood that flows through the horn bosses. Half of the time spent grazing is during the night.

Wildebeest are highly gregarious, forming herds of up to 30 individuals and often associating with zebras, impalas and giraffes. With food and water available, cows and calves live in herds with fixed home ranges. As food and water become depleted, herds tend to leave their home ranges and amalgamate into larger herds.

Mature bulls hold small mating territories and only bulls with territories can mate. Territories are fixed in sedentary populations, but move with the herds in migratory populations. Neighbours interact on their boundaries and during serious confrontations combatants go down on their knees and horn wrestle. Territorial bulls are often seen alone.

Wildebeest appear to be very restless. Is this so?

They are very inquisitive by nature and, when they run away from an enemy or even suspected danger, they will not go very far before halting and turning around to try to locate the cause of concern. This of course made them easy targets for hunters. Their continuous snorting and blowing through the nostrils, while running in circles, creates the impression that they are nervous. Because of their disjointed appearance and their restless attitude, they have been described as 'an animal that was designed by a committee and put together with spare parts'.

They certainly are very nervous at a water hole, and when approaching the water will stampede away at the slightest hint of danger. Drinking usually commences only after a number of trials.

Are they dangerous to human beings?

They are very tenacious and tough, and can be dangerous when injured, wounded or cornered, although in the wild they are normally timid and inoffensive.

Do they migrate?

Wildebeest are well known for their very strong migratory instinct. On the Serengeti Plains of central Africa they migrate in their tens of thousands over hundreds of kilometres. Because of fences, long-distance migrations are not possible in the Kruger National Park, but seasonal movements in search of grazing and water do occur in the Park. Whereas the traditional migration used to take on a west–east–west route, it is now more a south–north–south movement.

They will move to distant rainfall, possibly in response to the sound of thunder, the sight of lightning or even the smell of rain.

Are wildebeest territorial by nature?

During the breeding season bulls will establish a small territory to which they lure females. Territories are marked with preorbital-gland secretions (which have a sharp, tarry smell) on trees, shrubs, rocks, the ground and other wildebeest, by pawing the ground to release digital secretions from the glands between their front hooves, and with dung and urine middens.

Why are wildebeest less common in the Pretoriuskop area than in the past?

Bush encroachment was responsible for this state of affairs and, as pointed out in the section on controlled burning, action is being taken to restore the habitat to a condition as close as possible to the original situation.

What sounds do they make?

Contact calls include deep grunts and a 'ge-nu' snort, from which the common name 'gnu' is derived. The alarm call is a loud snort.

What are their breeding habits and expected life span?

Territorial bulls herd cows and check their reproductive condition by sniffing and *flehmen*. Cows coming into oestrus are courted by persistent mounting attempts and by the bulls' rearing up onto their hind legs. Unreceptive females avoid this attention by running away or merely lying down. Mating and copulation take place as soon as the cow stands for the bull, and may take place repeatedly at short intervals. Cows may mate with other bulls in quick succession.

Mating usually takes place from late April to early June, and calves are born from December to January.

After a gestation period of between eight and eight and a half months, a single calf, with a mass of about 20 kg, is born within the herd. Births are synchronised, with a sharp peak to saturate predators. The calf can stand within minutes of being born and can run with its mother very soon afterwards.

It will take solid food after about two weeks and is weaned at about eight months.

Horns grow straight up until about eight months and then start growing sideways.

The expected life span of a wildebeest is about 15 years.

What are their major enemies?
Their main predators are lions, African wild dog, hyaenas and crocodiles. Calves fall prey to wild dogs, leopards and cheetahs.

Why are wildebeest and zebras so often seen in each other's company?
This is because of their grazing preferences. Wildebeest favour the bottom section of the grass as their preferred grazing stratum, while zebras prefer the middle stratum. The wildebeest therefore follow zebras around because zebras open up the preferred grazing stratum for them.

ODD-TOED UNGULATES

BURCHELL'S ZEBRA   *Equus quagga* (Gray 1824)

Are zebras widely distributed throughout the Park?
They occur widely and commonly in suitable habitat in all ecozones of the Park. Highest densities are found on the open plains of the central regions and in the eastern parts of the Park.

What types of habitat do Burchell's zebra prefer?
Zebras prefer open woodland, scrub and grassland, but avoid areas with dense shrub, tree thickets and riparian vegetation.

What do they eat?
Essentially grazers, they will occasionally browse when under grazing pressure.

They prefer short, green grass but will readily take tall, coarse growth and will eat the fire-scorched leaves and twigs of mopane and round-leaved teak.

Zebras are non-selective bulk feeders and are less sensitive to food quality than other large herbivores, and can maintain body condition on very poor forage.

Are they dependent on water?
They are very water dependent and are seldom found further than 12 km away from water. They drink at least once daily,

mostly during the morning, with an average intake of about 14 litres a day. Zebras have a distinct preference for clean water.

How do they manage to keep in good condition, even when food is scarce?
The fact that zebras are always fat and look well nourished stems from their adaptability. Most other grazers use their tongues to crop the grass and feed it into their mouths, but zebras use their front teeth. They can therefore graze down to soil level and at times even dig up corms and rhizomes, particularly during times of drought.

What are their main physical features?
This stockily built member of the horse family can attain a shoulder height of up to 1.4 m and a mass of about 340 kg for stallions and about 300 kg for mares. The maximum shoulder height is attained at about three years and the maximum mass at about five years.

The most striking feature is the pattern of black stripes on a white to buff background. The stripes are broad and run obliquely across the hindquarters, with a brownish shadow stripe in between the black stripes on the rump and sometimes the shoulders. The stripe pattern extends to the underside and the stripes fade out on the lower legs.

The ears are short and an upright mane of stiff hairs reaches along the neck to the shoulders. The tail has a whisk of long black hair on the end.

The coat is short and sleek.

Is there much variation in the stripe patterns of individual zebra?

Zebras are easily recognisable by their characteristic stripes. Just as no two humans have the same fingerprint pattern, no two zebras will have the same stripe pattern.

How many different zebra species are there in the Park?

Basing their opinion on the fact that no two animals have the same stripe pattern, some taxonomists have considered the possibility that there could be two subspecies. However, it is now accepted that there is just one subspecies (*Equus quagga*) in the Park.

How does the mountain zebra differ from the Burchell's zebra?

The stripes on the mountain zebra are narrower and do not meet under the belly. Shadow stripes are absent and the stripes on the rump of the mountain zebra form a 'gridiron' pattern. A dewlap is present in the mountain zebra and their ears are larger than those of the Burchell's zebra.

What are the habits and behaviour of the Burchell's zebra?

They are diurnal and nocturnal, with grazing peaks in the early morning and late afternoon.

They form harem herds usually comprising a stallion with between two and seven mares and their foals but, through temporary aggregations, herds of more than 50 individuals have regularly been recorded in the Park.

Home-range sizes are determined by habitat and distribution. Zebras utilise well-used paths within the home range. Mares remain with the stallion that sired their offspring.

Stallions that do not hold breeding herds join bachelor groups of up to 15, with dominance rank depending on age. Groups are bonded by mutual grooming. On meeting, herd stallions sniff nose to nose, rub their cheeks together, sniff each other's genitals, stamp their forefeet and toss their heads. Submission is signalled by lowering of the head, pinning the ears back and making chewing motions. Dominance and threat displays include holding the head high, with ears cocked forward or turned inwards and back, baring the teeth and chasing. Lowering the head with an open-mouthed gape indicates a very serious threat.

Zebras are gregarious and always stay in groups as a protective measure. It is thought that the mass of stripes may confuse predators, as it is difficult for them to distinguish an individual member in the herd. At dawn and at night, the stripe pattern also distorts distance, making it difficult for predators to determine distance for attack.

How stable are the family units?

Family groups are quite stable but it is not uncommon for another stallion to take over a whole group if the lead stallion dies.

Where do the stallions without a family group fit in?

Stallions without their own family group join up to form bachelor groups residing on the fringes of harem groups, but are kept at bay by the aggression of the resident herd stallion.

Do stallions fight for mares?

They do fight, but fatalities are very rare. A sex ratio of about 1.5 mares per stallion has been determined for adult zebras.

How do they fight?

They chop, kick and bite each other. They often concentrate on attempts to bite each other's genitals, and these fights are often accompanied by a lot of neighing and the kicking up of dust.

Is the stallion the leader of the group?

As is the case with many other herbivores, the dominance of the stallion is more or less restricted to the mating privileges and to keeping the mares together. The actual leadership rests with the dominant mare.

Does a mare sometimes leave her family group?

When young mares reach sexual maturity, they are often abducted from their families by other stallions to form the nucleus of a new family group.

What happens to the young stallions?

They leave the family groups of their own accord to join up with bachelor groups, or they are forcefully evicted by the dominant stallion.

What sounds do they make?

Contact calls include a distinctive, high-pitched 'kwa-ha', from which the original name 'quagga' was derived. Short whinnying calls serve as an initial warning. The alarm signal is a snort. If threatened by predators, herds flee in close noisy bunches, with speeds reaching 55 km/h.

Do zebras move about?

In the Park zebras, especially those from the central areas, undertake seasonal movements determined by the availability of food and water.

What are the reasons behind these movements?

Their seasonal and local movements are closely correlated with the distribution and palatability of grasses and the availability of surface water. Predator pressure, density of the bush, and interspecific competition also affect their movements. Before moving off, they congregate in large numbers and then move in long files to their new grazing grounds.

Do they often associate with other animals?

The fact that zebras are highly gregarious leads to their frequent association with other species, particularly wildebeest. Some stallions and small herds of zebra frequently associate with species such as impala, waterbuck, kudu, giraffe and wildebeest.

Do they derive any benefit from this association with other animals?

In these mixed groups the additional sensory receptors of the different species augment each other, especially in the detection of predators.

Zebras and wildebeest are very often found together. Is there any specific reason for this?

Many people believe that one of the two species can hear or see better than the other. The one with the poorer sense will therefore benefit from this association.

Their association is probably more fortuitous than anything else due to their similar habitat preference, gregarious habits and especially their grazing preference.

What are their breeding habits?

They breed all year round, but about 80% of foals are born during the rainy summer season. Stallions check the mares' reproductive condition by sniffing and *flehmen* of their urine. Receptive mares stand with their legs apart, their tails to one side, the mouth open and the lips drawn back. The vulva swells and discharges mucus. Copulation is brief and is repeated every one to three hours for about a day. Oestrus lasts for up to five days. After a gestation period of about

360 days, a single foal, with a mass of about 30 to 35 kg, is born. It can stand within minutes of being born and can run with its mother after about an hour. The foal is kept from the herd for two or three days until maternal imprinting has been established. It starts grazing within a few days and is weaned at 11 months.

At what age do mares produce their offspring?

Mares produce their first foal at about 3.5 years and can continue to breed until old age, considered to be about 18 years.

Can a mare produce twins?

It is possible but, in a study conducted over a number of years, no indication of twins was found.

How can one determine a zebra's age?

Rings, resembling the year rings of a tree, can be counted when teeth taken from skulls are ground down. This method has established that zebras can live to about 20 years.

Which predators are their major enemies?

In the Park, zebras are primarily preyed upon by lions, providing 16% of lion kills. Leopards, hyaenas, cheetahs and African wild dogs make up the rest of the major predator element. Foals fall prey to African wild dogs and cheetahs. Hyaenas usually try to dodge the stallion and concentrate on the rest of the group. Lions kill more stallions than mares, while, in the few cases where hyaenas kill adult zebras, they kill more mares than stallions.

Are zebras very susceptible to diseases?

Zebras are free of many of the diseases common to wild bovids, particularly foot-and-mouth disease.

Have they been hunted heavily?

Because of their excellent senses of smell, hearing and sight, zebras are very difficult animals to approach. It therefore requires skill and cunning to approach them on foot.

The adult stallion of a family group is more susceptible to being hunted than a mare. This is largely due to the investigatory and protective role assumed by the stallion when danger threatens. The mares and the young will be the first to flee from any danger, whereas the stallion takes up his position behind them, often stopping to face the suspected danger. Because of this, he is exposed to danger more often than the mares and young ones.

The mortality rate for stallions is about twice that of mares. Generally, however, zebras are better adapted to escape from danger than most of the other herbivores.

Their meat is not very palatable, but in the pioneer days their hides were tanned and used for thongs, straps, in furniture and for whips.

Do they defend themselves against predators?

Usually not where lions are concerned, but they will often attack smaller adversaries. Stallions sometimes chase hyaenas for 100 m or more when they threaten members of the stallion's herd.

Is foal mortality high?

Mortality due to predation and, to a lesser extent, disease could be as high as 60 to 80% in the first year of life.

Does the zebra have any relatives in the Park?

Zebras belong to the order Perissodactyla, or odd-toed mammals, which includes three recent families: the Equidae (horses), the Tapiridae (tapirs), and the Rhinocerotidae (rhinoceroses). As the latter, represented by the white and black rhinoceroses, are found in the Park, they must be considered the closest relatives to the zebras in the Park.

WHITE RHINOCEROS   *Ceratotherium simum* (Burchell 1817)

Where can the white rhino be found in South Africa?

It has been claimed that by 1920 there were only 20 left in southern Africa, all of them confined to the area between the Hluhluwe and iMfolozi rivers in KwaZulu-Natal. This was probably a deliberate underestimate to raise awareness of the plight of the white rhino.

About 50 years later there were more than a thousand as a result of intensive conservation practices by the then Natal Parks Board.

White rhinos are now found in many conservation areas, national and provincial parks, private reserves and game farms.

When did the white rhino become extinct in the Kruger National Park?

According to the hunter Frederick Vaughan Kirby, the last white rhino was seen near the Sabie River in 1896, some two years before the proclamation of the Sabi Game Reserve.

Why did the white rhino disappear before the black rhino?

The normally non-aggressive white rhino frequented the more open areas because of its grazing preference and was easier to hunt than the more aggressive, bush-living, browsing black rhinos.

Historically, white rhinos also had a much more restricted distribution than black rhinos.

When were white rhinos reintroduced to the Kruger National Park?

This historic event occurred on 14 October 1961, when two bulls and two cows were released near Pretoriuskop in the southwestern section of the Kruger National Park. Between 1961 and 1972, a total of 345 white rhinos were translocated to the Park, and their numbers have increased to the extent that rhinos have been relocated from the Park to other conservation areas and also sold to game farmers.

Were all the translocated white rhinos kept in a camp for some time before they were released?

The first few groups were kept in an enclosure near Pretoriuskop Rest Camp, but later arrivals were released directly into the wild.

Are they widely distributed in the Park?

The highest concentrations of white rhinos are found in the southern section of the Park but, as a result of recent releases and territorial movements, they have spread over an extensive area and are seen in a wide range of ecozones.

They occur in ecozones A, B, C, D, E, F, G, K and P of the Park. Populations also occur in the Tshokwane, Kingfisherspruit, Satara and N'wanetsi areas, with scattered populations between the Tsendze and Shingwedzi rivers. The highest densities of white rhinos are to be found between the Biyamiti and Mlambane rivers in the Pretoriuskop, Stolsnek and Berg-en-Dal/Malelane areas.

What type of habitat do white rhinos prefer?

In the southern part of the Park, they prefer the flat and undulating granitic plains with *Combretum* woodlands and the Malelane Mountain Bushveld. Other preferred habitats include grassland savanna, Delagoa thorn thickets, knobthorn/marula savanna, stunted knobthorn savanna and sourveld areas.

Open woodland areas, with mud wallows and water nearby, are an important habitat requirement.

What do they eat?

They are grazers, with grass forming 99% of their diet. They prefer short, fresh growth, eating both leaves and stems, and preferring perennials. They are water dependent and sometimes drink twice a day, but can apparently go without water for up to four days.

How much do they eat per day?

They eat about 50 kg of (mainly) grass.

When do they visit water holes?

They usually drink in the late afternoon and into the night, every day if water is freely available. They also wallow in water and mud to cool down and to remove ectoparasites.

What are their main physical features?

The white rhino is the second-largest land mammal. Its skin is rough and appears to be naked, but is sparsely covered with coarse bristles. The colour is grey to dark grey, depending on its last mud bath. The soles of the feet have elastic pads that expand when weight is applied and contract when the feet are lifted off the ground.

The head is long in proportion to the neck and is carried low, even when the white rhino is not grazing. The neck is massive, with a distinct hump at its base and at the shoulders. The ears, set high up on the head, are somewhat trumpet-shaped and fringed with hair. The tail is about 1 m long, with tufts of dark hair at the tip. The huge, barrel-shaped body is low-slung on short, stocky legs, with three toes on each foot. The spoor shows a characteristic cleft at the rear of the foot, which forms a 'W'.

The muzzle is broad, the lips up to 20 cm wide and square, hence the alternative name of 'square-lipped rhino'.

Males have a thick fold of skin running down between the back of the hind legs.

The anterior horn grows to an average of 60 to 90 cm, but one has been measured at 1.58 m. The posterior horn is usually not much more than a pronounced hump resembling an upturned cone with flattened sides. The strong anterior horn curves slightly backwards from a sound, flat-fronted base. Horns are used in fights and to uproot small bushes or trees. The horns of cows are more slender and sometimes longer than those of bulls.

The horns are made up of bundles of dermal papillae in the skin, i.e. keratinised hair and skin. The anterior horn is smooth in texture, mainly because it is rubbed against anthills, stones or trees. Horns grow at a rate of 2.5 to 6.5 cm a year.

Bulls stand about 1.8 to 1.9 m at the shoulder and cows around 1.7 m. Bulls have a mass of up to 2 300 kg and cows about 1 600 kg.

Can broken horns regrow?

Yes, a new horn can replace one that has been broken off, but this will take some time. If it breaks, the fracture usually occurs at the base where it is attached to the skin that covers the nasal bones of the skull.

What speed can the white rhino reach?

Unsubstantiated claims indicate that this animal can reach a speed of about 40 km/h, which can be maintained for a considerable distance. Whether or not it can really attain this speed, this huge animal is nevertheless very agile and nimble on its feet.

Why is it called the white rhino when it is not white in colour?

There are various explanations for the origin of the name, but the most acceptable is that it is a corruption of the Dutch word *wijd* describing the wide mouth. Over the years this turned into white rhino; since the opposite of white is black, this serves to distinguish the two rhino species from each other.

As is the case with the black rhino, the name has nothing to do with the colour of the animal's hide.

What are the differences between the white and the black rhino?

The white rhino is a grazer with a broad, square muzzle, while the black rhino is a browser with a pointed muzzle and a prehensile upper lip that is used to strip leaves from branches and twigs.

The latter can lift its head above the horizontal in order to browse on higher vegetation. The white rhino, with its longer head carried low most of the time because of its grazing preference, has a different profile from that of the black rhino. It is said that, over the many thousands of years of its evolution, the muscles in the neck of the white rhino adapted to its bent grazing posture and shortened to the extent that it cannot lift its head above the horizontal.

Apart from the pronounced hump on the back of its neck – which is absent in the black rhino – the middle of the back is slightly arched, in contrast to the more-or-less concave back-line of the black rhino.

There is little or no difference in colour of the hide. The black rhino also tends to be more aggressive than the white rhino.

What are the habits and behaviour of white rhino?

They are diurnal and nocturnal, but avoid the hotter parts of the day by lying up in the shade or resting on the watersheds where there is normally a breeze. About half their time is spent grazing. The grass is cropped short between the 20-cm-wide lips. The rhino takes a few steps, swinging its head in an arc, stepping forward and repeating the process to crop the grass with the head low.

Cows and their young live in overlapping home ranges where food is abundant. Small amicable groups can form on patches of good grazing. The current author counted 18 white rhinos together on the gabbro plains at Afsaal picnic site during November 2009. Home ranges of cows may overlap the territories of several bulls.

Mature bulls are territorial and solitary. They will tolerate other bulls in their territory provided they show submission and keep away from the cows. Only territorial bulls spray urine backwards onto vegetation. Territorial borders are marked with well-used paths, spray-urinating as well as depositing faeces in middens. After defecating, the territorial bull kicks the dung around and gouges the midden with its hind feet. As he walks through his territory, the pheromone identifying the bull is rubbed off on grass and vegetation, advertising the presence of a dominant bull in the territory.

If confronted when passing through another bull's territory on their way to water, rhinos will squeal and shriek, hold their ears back and show their flank, which is the rhino's most vulnerable area, to demonstrate submissiveness. This action will usually allow them to proceed.

Fights are usually over territory or cows and can be fatal. The skin is about 2 cm thick on the back and 5 cm thick on the forehead, which provides some protection during fights. Bulls supplanted by challengers may be allowed to remain in their old territory provided they are submissive.

Their eyesight is not particularly good, but hearing and smell are very acute.

Do they have a social hierarchy?

A hierarchy, such as is found with true herd-forming animals, is absent, but there is a definite order of dominance. Bulls often fight fiercely for the favour of a cow, and in a family or social group the dominant bull will drive away any young mature bulls if he is able to do so.

Are they aggressive?

They are placid, even-tempered animals.

What sounds do they make and how do they communicate?

They communicate by sound and visual signals. Contact calls include grunts and bellows. Snorting and snarling with ears turned back is a signal to back off, while panting is an invitation to move closer.

Squealing and shrieking are submissive signals and also occur during fights or when a bull herds cows in his territory. Calves squeal and make whining sounds.

Are they accompanied by tick-eating birds, as is the case with black rhino?
Yes, but, although these birds are called *Renoster Voëls* (rhino birds) in Afrikaans, they are Red-Billed Oxpecker (*Buphagus erythrorhynchus*) and are by no means restricted to rhinos; they are found on many other herbivores such as giraffes, African buffaloes and some antelope.

What are their breeding habits?
Bulls test the reproductive condition of cows passing through their territory by sniffing urine and *flehmen*, and they try to stop cows in oestrus from leaving their territory. Herding and courtship may go on for two weeks and copulation may last for 30 minutes. They mate only once, with multiple ejaculations.

They breed all year round, with birth peaks during the summer. After a gestation period of 16 months, a single calf, with a mass of 45 to 60 kg, is born in dense cover. Calves are not fully mobile for about three days and stay hidden while the mother grazes nearby. Although they start taking solid food after two months, they are not weaned until 12 to 18 months and remain with the mother for two or three years. Although males are sexually mature at five years, they will only mate successfully after establishing own territories at about 12 years. The average birth interval is 22 to 40 months. Females are sexually mature at four or five years and will have their first calf at six or seven years. Bulls become solitary when they are about 10 years old.

Calves run ahead or alongside the mother.

What is their potential life span?
White rhinos live for 40 to 50 years.

Is the relationship between mother and calf strong?
The bond is very strong and the mother will fiercely defend and protect her calf.

Do they have natural enemies?
Young rhinos may fall prey to lions, spotted hyaenas and African wild dogs. Man is the main enemy through poaching for their horn, which is prized as a fever-reducing drug and an aphrodisiac in the Far East, and as handles for ceremonial daggers in the Arab countries.

BLACK RHINOCEROS   *Diceros bicornis* (Linnaeus 1758)

What is the distribution of the black rhino in the Park?

They occur in ecozones A, D, E, F, G and K of the Park. Populations have been established in the Lubyelubye area near Lower Sabie and along the N'waswitsontso and Sweni rivers near Tshokwane and Satara.

What type of habitat do black rhinos prefer?

They have a wider habitat range than the white rhino and are found in many different types of terrain. In the Park they are found in mixed bushwillow woodlands, thorn thickets, thornveld, Delagoa thorn thickets, knobthorn/marula savanna, stunted knobthorn savanna habitats and wooded mountain regions. They are dependent on water holes for mud wallows and are not found far away from water.

What do they eat?

Black rhinos are selective browsers, utilising a wide variety of trees and shrubs. The prehensile upper lip is used to grasp leaves and twigs from small trees and shrubs up to a browsing height of 0.5 to 1.2 m. The twigs are snapped off and cut at a 45-degree angle by the cheek teeth.

Their food plants include the euphorbias such as the candelabra tree (*Euphorbia ingens*) and the tamboti (*Spirostachys africana*), of which the milky latex is poisonous to humans.

They are water dependent and may drink twice a day. They can go without water for about four days if their diet contains sufficient moisture.

When did black rhinos disappear from the Kruger National Park?

A black rhino cow was seen between Skukuza and Lower Sabie in the N'watimhiri bush in 1936 by ranger Harry Kirkman. He followed her spoor for days and eventually saw her for a few minutes. She then disappeared into the bush, never to be seen again.

Have black rhinos always been in the Kruger National Park?

At the time of the proclamation of the old Sabi Game Reserve there was still a small number of black rhinos in the area between the Sabie and Crocodile rivers. At times the black rhinos moved to and fro between the Park and Mozambique, but by 1946 the last black rhino had definitely disappeared.

How did they become extinct in the Park?

There were very few black rhinos and they were dispersed over a wide area, therefore making breeding opportunities very unfavourable. They also roamed extensively over large areas and probably often found themselves outside the borders of the Park, where they fell prey to hunters.

When and from where were they reintroduced?

Twenty animals were brought in from the present KwaZulu-Natal in 1971 and 10 animals from what is now Zimbabwe the following year. An additional translocation programme comprising 36 animals from KwaZulu-Natal was started in 1977 and undertaken again in 1980 to 1982.

The last translocation of 10 animals from KwaZulu-Natal took place in 1989.

Have the reintroduced animals settled down well?

Yes. Breeding populations now occur over most of the southern Kruger Park and also between Tshokwane and Satara. After initial mortalities due to fights, botulism and poaching, the black rhino population settled down well and they bred successfully. The present population exceeds 450 animals.

Were they released immediately after translocation?
After arrival in the Park they were first kept in bomas to allow them to get used to their new environment, before being released. The latest arrivals were released directly into the Park.

What are their main physical features?
The black rhino is a large and robust animal. The skin colour is slightly darker than that of the white rhino, depending on the colour of the soil in which it had its last mud wallow or dust bath. The naked-looking skin is sparsely covered with coarse bristles.

It has a prehensile, muscular upper lip that is used to grasp twigs and branches while feeding. It has a thick neck and a relatively short head, which is carried high, compared with that of the white rhino. The ears are rounded, with hair on the edges.

Males have a thick fold of skin running down between the backs of the hind legs.

Two horns are found on the top of the nose. The anterior horn is heavy and positioned on a rounded base, while the posterior horn is short and resembles a cone. The cow's horns are longer and more slender than those of the bull. The strong anterior horn has a slight backwards curve and is used for fighting, digging and uprooting bushes. As is the case with the white rhino, the horns consist of outgrowths of dermal papillae of the hide, and are composed of keratinised hair fibres. Horns grow at a rate of about 4 to 6 cm per year.

The anterior horn can reach a length of up to about 1.3 m, and the posterior horn 0.52 m.

There is no distinct hump on the shoulders and, in the Lowveld and the Park, the flanks of the black rhino are usually marked by dark, sometimes bloody patches, caused by parasitic worms carried by biting flies.

The legs are short and sturdy, with three toes on each foot. As with the white rhino, the soles of the feet have elastic pads that expand when weight is applied and contract when the feet are lifted off the ground. Black rhino spoor is smaller than that of the white rhino and appears rounded at the back. The tail has a tuft of short hair at the tip.

Bulls and cows have almost the same shoulder height of about 1.4 to 1.6 m. Bulls can attain a mass of about 1 400 kg and females about 1 200 kg.

Can a broken horn grow again?
Yes, a new horn can replace a broken one. Horns usually break at the base.

Why do some rhinos seem to be lighter in colour than others?
Their normal colour is light to dark grey. The difference in skin colour relates to the colour of the soil in which it had its last wallow or dust bath.

Where does the name black rhino come from?
Apart from the fact that black is the opposite to white to distinguish between the two rhino species, the origin of the name is not clear. Black rhinos were first seen on Table Mountain. It is possible that these animals seemed darker than the white rhino, which were first seen on lighter-coloured soil in the Kuruman area.

How fast can they run?
Claims of up to 50 km/h have appeared in literature, but no proof of this speed has been found.

Is it true that they are short-sighted?
They are very short-sighted and must therefore rely on their excellent sense of smell and well-developed hearing.

What are their habits and behaviour?

Black rhinos are diurnal and nocturnal, being active for 90% of the night. They avoid the heat of the day by resting in the shade or on watersheds where there is usually a breeze. They are generally solitary, but cows with calves or males courting females are often seen. They may form small aggregations at suitable browsing areas or water holes.

Female home ranges may overlap, while males have exclusive territories. Both sexes defecate in middens and kick the dung around. Males spray urine on vegetation, use well-used paths, dung middens, ground scuffing and vegetation horning to demarcate home ranges or territories.

Cows are non-territorial, and home-range sizes depend on population density and availability of food. Female home ranges may cross several bull territories.

Do bulls fight frequently?

Fights for the favours of a female occur fairly often and are sometimes fatal. When a bull and a cow encounter another adult male, a fight may ensue. The cow takes little or no interest in the fight and will accept the winner without any fuss.

What are their breeding habits?

Bulls investigate the reproductive condition of a cow by smelling and *flehmen* of her urine. Advances are initially rebuffed by the female and the bull will follow her for up to six days. Copulation can last up to 40 minutes. They breed all year round, with a peak in births recorded during the summer rainy season.

After a gestation period of 15 months a single calf, weighing about 40 kg, is born in dense cover. The calf is mobile within three hours but will stay hidden for the first week. After about a month it starts browsing, and it is weaned at 12 to 19 months, but stays with its mother for two to four years. Calving intervals are about two to four years.

What is the black rhino's probable life span?

About 30 to 40 years.

Does the black rhino calf follow its mother?

The black rhino calf follows its mother, as opposed to the white rhino calf that runs ahead of its mother. This adaptation might be as a result of the denser habitat of the black rhino, where the cow creates a path through the bush when she runs.

How strong is the relationship between mother and calf?

A very strong bond exists between them. The mother will fiercely defend her calf and the calf will protect its mother should she be injured or wounded. A calf has been recorded staying with a mother's carcass for a few days after she died and chasing away any animals that approached it. Calves usually stay with their mothers until they reach sexual maturity, even after the mother has given birth to another calf in the meantime.

Is the black rhino as aggressive as people believe?

The black rhino has been singled out by hunters as being the most unpredictable and short-tempered beast of the African bush. This suited hunters as an excuse to kill the animals and to appear heroic in killing such a 'dangerous' animal.

Its huge horns are certainly not designed for playing, but on the other hand it is not as dangerous as believed. It is nevertheless temperamental and aggressive to some extent, and should be treated with respect.

Why are rhinos so fond of mud baths?

In addition to the cooling effect on a hot day, the mud also affords protection against stinging insects and ectoparasites. Many of these parasites become dislodged when the mud dries and is rubbed off against trees, rocks and termite mounds.

Are rhinos responsible for leaving big dung heaps alongside the road?

One often sees big dung heaps along the sides of the roads, especially in the southern part of the Park. Rhinos regularly defecate in the same spot and then kick open the dung as a means of demarcating their home ranges or territories.

What is the difference between rhino and elephant dung?

The dung balls of rhino dung are smaller and darker and not as coarse as elephant dung.

Is there a noticeable difference between the dung of white and black rhino?

Although the heaps of dung are about the same size, the dung of white rhinos is finer (because they eat grass) and darker than the dung of black rhinos. The dung of black rhinos is conspicuous because of the remains of leaves and twigs visible in it. Because of the latex in their diet from browsing on tamboti (*Spirostachys africana*) and the candelabra tree (*Euphorbia ingens*), black rhino dung tends to turn a rusty brown colour when it dries out.

When do black rhinos drink water?

They prefer to drink daily if water is available and usually drink at night, but are also often seen at water holes in the early morning or late afternoon.

Do they move around a lot?

They wander around a lot and when food or water is scarce they will move to better areas.

What are their major enemies?

Man is the main enemy. Rhinos are poached for their horns, which are said to have fever-reducing and aphrodisiacal properties and are used as handles for ceremonial daggers in Arabian countries. Small calves fall prey to lions, hyaenas and African wild dogs.

Why are they hunted so heavily?
Because of the high prices fetched by intact or powdered rhino horn in Asia and Africa, the survival of the rhino is under serious threat.

Is disease an important mortality factor?
Mortality due to disease, starvation and parasites seems to be fairly low.

Which birds are associated with the rhino?
The Red-Billed Oxpecker (*Buphagus erythrorhynchus*), which rids the animals of ectoparasites, especially ticks, and serves as a sentinel, is usually seen in the company of rhinos and other big game.

To which other animals is the black rhino related?
It is related to the horse and the tapir.

They look prehistoric. Did they evolve a long time ago?
They do have a long prehistory and have probably existed in their current form for many thousands of years.

AFRICAN ELEPHANT *Loxodonta africana* (Blumenbach 1797)

Are they evenly distributed throughout the Park?
Elephants occur in all the ecozones of the Kruger National Park. The main densities were traditionally found north of Letaba, but increases in numbers have been recorded in the Satara, Lower Sabie and Crocodile Bridge areas. Nowadays, they are relatively evenly distributed throughout the Park.

How many were there in the old Sabi Game Reserve when it was proclaimed in 1898?
There were none left. Not even in the Shingwedzi Game Reserve, which was proclaimed shortly after the Sabi Reserve, were there any resident elephants.
    Small numbers of elephants migrated between Mozambique and the Shingwedzi area. In 1905 only four elephants were recorded in the Shingwedzi River and six in the Olifants River, all near the Mozambican border.

Did the present population come from this small herd?
This herd did contribute to the population, but large numbers of elephants entered the Park from Mozambique and present-day Zimbabwe before the completion of the elephant-proof fence in 1976.

What is the status of elephants in the rest of Africa?
Their range is more restricted than before, but they occur throughout central, West and East Africa. They are considered endangered; although a substantial population, estimated to be in excess of 600 000, remains, illegal hunting and poaching for ivory, as well as the increased demand for agricultural land and competition with domestic stock – which is allowed in many African parks – still pose a great threat to their survival.

Are elephant populations found elsewhere in South Africa?
Since the western border fence between the Kruger National Park and adjoining private nature reserves was removed in 1994, elephants have migrated into the private game reserves.
    The Addo Elephant National Park in the Eastern Cape has a present population in excess of 400, and the

last elephant of the Knysna Forest was sighted late in 2008. Considerable numbers of elephants were relocated from the Kruger National Park to the Hluhluwe-iMfolozi Park and the Ndumo Game Reserve in KwaZulu-Natal. Tembe Elephant Park and Ithala Game Reserve in northern KwaZulu-Natal also have elephant populations.

Many of the inland national parks have been populated with elephants from the Kruger National Park, as were the Pilanesberg National Park in the North West province and many smaller private conservation areas and game farms.

What type of habitat do they prefer?

They occur in all the habitats of the Park, provided there is sufficient water, dense vegetation, woodland and grass-land savanna.

Historically, elephants had a very wide habitat range; their present habitats are constrained by human encroachment.

What is their favourite food?

Because of their adaptability to a wide range of habitats, they utilise many different plant species. Depending on circumstances, they either browse or graze, and there are pronounced seasonal variations in the composition of their diet. It is said that, if sufficient palatable grass is available, they will graze more than browse. They also show preference for the bark of trees, especially that of the knobthorn (*Acacia nigrescens*), as well as fruit, roots and herbs.

Grasses are preferred during the rainy season, with a shift to browsing on woody vegetation in the dry season.

How much does a fully grown elephant eat per day?

Claims by different authors vary between 150 and 300 kg consumed in 24 hours. Since about 18 out of 24 hours are spent feeding, an estimated 200 kg of vegetation

consumed per day seems realistic. Elephants are very extravagant and also destructive in their feeding habits, often destroying more than they actually consume.

How much water can an elephant drink?

Research in the Park indicates a figure of about 90 litres per day. Large bulls can drink up to 300 litres at a time, averaging about 200 litres per day. While drinking, they squirt copious amounts of water over their bodies to cool themselves.

Do elephants prefer natural water holes to artificial reservoirs and drinking troughs?

They prefer natural water holes where they can wallow in the mud or, if they are deep enough, swim and play. However, they prefer to drink clean water and will readily drink at reservoirs, dipping their trunks to the bottom of the reservoir to obtain the cooler water.

Cows have been seen to suck water from the reservoir and then squirt it into a hollow in the ground for their calves to drink and wallow in the mud.

At what time of the day do elephants drink?

In summer they tend to drink in the morning and late afternoon, though they will drink at any time of the day or night. They tend to spend a lot of time in the water to cool down in the heat of the day in summer. During winter they usually drink around midday.

Do elephants dig for water in dry river beds?

They have been seen to dig holes of up to 1.8 m deep in dry river beds. They regularly dig these holes, even when a river is flowing only a few metres away. This is to obtain clean, cool, filtered water. After they have had their fill, other animals drink from the holes.

How long can they go without water?

In arid areas they can probably go without water for many days, depending on the climatic conditions and the moisture content of their food.

In the Park, where water is readily available, they drink more in the summer months than in the cooler winter.

Can an elephant withdraw water from its stomach?

Elephants are able to store several litres of water in a pharyngeal pouch located at the base of the tongue, from where it can be extracted. The water is then squirted over the body, or over a calf to cool it down. This may be a physiological reaction to extreme stress. This structure is unique to the elephant and is thought to be an adaption evolved as elephants ventured into more arid lands in the Miocene Era.

Do elephants follow specific routes to water?

Elephant footpaths are well known. These huge beasts are very adept at finding the easiest and shortest route to water, and this route is used over and over and is eventually passed on to the calves. They remember this route and, when they are mature, they will pass this information on to their young. Many an old transport route has been built on an original elephant path.

What are the differences between African and Asian elephants?

The African elephant (*Loxodonta africana*) has a more-or-less concave and saddle-shaped back, enormous ears that cover the shoulders, a rounded or sloping forehead, a trunk with two pointed projections at the upper and lower parts of the tip, and large and developed tusks in both sexes. It is bulkier and higher at the shoulder than the Indian species.

The Asian or Indian elephant (*Elephas maximus*) has a convex, steeply sloping back, small triangular ears that do not cover the shoulders, prominent bulges on the forehead above the eyes, a trunk with only one projection at the upper part of

the tip, and small tusks that are usually visible in the male only. It is noticeably smaller than its African counterpart.

What are their behavioural patterns and habits?

They are considered both diurnal and nocturnal, readily alternating activities such as feeding, relocation, resting and drinking between night and day. Feeding occupies about 18 hours of the day. Food is picked up or plucked with the trunk, passed to the mouth and then roughly chewed.

The trunk consists of more than 100 000 muscles, which makes it a very dexterous appendage. To feed, trees are pushed over, bark is chiselled off trees with the tusks and ripped off with the trunk, and roots and tubers are dug up with the tusks or feet.

In its lifetime an elephant has six sets of molars. As a set is worn away, it is replaced from the back by the following set. As they move forward to make room for the next set, fragments of the old set break off. By the time the new tooth is in position, the last fragment of the previous one has disappeared. Each tooth that comes into wear is longer and wider than the previous one, and this progression aids in establishing the age of the animal.

Sets are replaced at about 1, 2, 6, 15, 28 and 47 years of age. Once the last set is worn away, the elephant can no longer chew its food properly and it slowly starves to death.

Elephants drink by sucking water into the trunk and emptying it into the mouth. Although the trunk has a capacity of about 18 litres, only four to six litres of water is sucked up at a time.

Are elephants social animals?

Elephants are highly social animals. The social unit usually consists of a cow with her calves. Female offspring remain with their mother in coherent family groups. Family units are therefore composed of the old female – the matriarch – and all of her daughters and their offspring. The matriarch leads the herd to water and grazing. Family groups may join others temporarily in herds, or, more correctly, aggregations of 100 animals or more.

Males are tolerated in the natal herd until they reach puberty at about 14 years, after which they leave the herd to live in unstable, loosely bonded bachelor groups of between two and seven individuals, moving back into the female herds in search of cows in oestrus.

Elephants show an unexplained fascination with their dead and even old elephant bones are investigated and carried around with reverence.

I have heard of an elephant being 'in musth'. What is this?

Bachelor bulls have a dominance hierarchy. From the age of 25, bulls annually come into musth (or must), when their testosterone levels rise to about six times the normal level. During musth, the temporal glands in the bulls, situated about halfway between the eye and the ear, swell and discharge a sticky, dark, oily secretion. They dribble green urine continuously with the penis sheathed, staining the sheath and the inside of the hind legs, and producing a strong, pungent odour. They walk with their heads held high and become very aggressive towards other males, which avoid them. Musth bulls wander widely in search of females in oestrus, joining female herds, checking the females and consorting with cows that are close to oestrus. Oestrus cows are more likely to mate with bulls in musth than with bulls that are not.

By the age of 30 years the majority of bulls have experienced their first musth. This is a period of heightened sexual and aggressive activity, characterised by a distinct posture, the 'musth walk', swollen and secreting temporal glands, dribbling pungent-smelling, green urine and a very low-frequency vocalisation, the 'musth rumble'.

During musth, bulls experience dramatic surges of circulating testosterone. They interact aggressively with other bulls, particularly those also in musth, and spend much of their time attempting to get access to, or guarding, oestrus cows. The duration of musth is age-related, and these periods are asynchronous and each male is on his own cycle. Musth has a dramatic effect on the relative dominance ranks of bulls. With few exceptions, a musth bull, irrespective of size, ranks above all non-musth bulls.

Bulls in musth interact aggressively whenever they encounter one another, and the presence of an oestrus female is not a prerequisite for a fight.

Why do elephants flap their ears?

Elephants do not have sweat glands. They lower their body temperature by flapping their ears, by splashing themselves with water and by taking mud- and sand baths.

An elephant's ears make up about 20% of its total skin surface area, and up to 12 litres of blood per minute flows through the network of large blood vessels just under the thin skin on the back of the ears.

By flapping its ears an elephant can cool the blood flowing through them by 3 or 4°C.

What is the normal height of an elephant?

Bulls can attain a shoulder height of about 3.4 m and females 2.7 m. It is said that the shoulder height of an elephant can be established by measuring the length of the hind footprint. Shoulder height of a bull is approximately 5.8 times the length of the hind footprint and that of a female about 5.5 times. The tallest bull ever measured was 4.42 m at the shoulder.

What is the mass of an elephant?

Bulls can attain a mass of up to 6 550 kg and cows around 3 500 kg.

What is the all-time mass record?

A hunter by the name of Fenykovi shot an exceptionally large elephant bull in Angola on 13 November 1955. Its shoulder height was 4 m and its mass estimated at 10 900 kg. J. M. Oosterveen shot an elephant with a shoulder height of 4.42 m in Namibia in 1977. Unfortunately the mass was not determined.

What is the record length of a tusk?

According to Rowland Ward, the longest tusk measured was 3.384 m, from an elephant shot in East Africa. The Kruger Park record is 3.17 m (Nshawu, also known as Groot Haaktand).

What is the record mass of a tusk?

It stands at 102.3 kg for a bull and 25.46 kg for a cow. The Park record is 73.5 kg for a bull (Mandleve). Nowadays tusks weighing more than 40 kg each are rare.

How long is it before the tusks develop?

Permanent tusks erupt at about 18 months in males and at about 27 months in females. In both sexes tusk growth is continuous throughout life. The growth rates vary considerably in bulls. The tusks of cows usually grow fairly long and slender, while those of bulls continue to thicken as they lengthen.

How is it possible for an elephant to walk so quietly through the bush?

Thick elastic pads in the feet enable the animal to move about without much sound. The feet expand when weight is applied and contract when the feet are lifted.

Are there features to distinguish between bulls and cows?

The absence of a visible scrotum in the bull is due to the testes being situated internally, and the fact that the cow's genitals are quite often not visible makes it difficult to tell the sexes apart.

Bulls are bulkier and taller than cows. Bulls typically have thicker tusks and heavier heads. In profile, bulls have a more rounded forehead, with cows having a more angled, straight forehead, and bulls' backs have a more curved outline.

What is the purpose of the tusks?
The tusks are used in fighting, for defence, digging up roots and stripping bark from trees.

Is it true that African elephants are left- or right-'handed' in the use of their tusks?
An elephant tends to make use of one tusk only, or use one more regularly than the other. This is commonly referred to as the 'slave tusk'. It is usually this tusk that is broken or damaged. It appears to be mostly the right tusk. The tusk less used, being larger, is known as the 'master tusk'.

Are the tusks modified canine teeth?
No. They are modified, elongated upper incisors. They consist of a unique combination of dentine, cartilaginous material and calcium salts, which make them highly prized ivory. They project from the upper jaw. Instead of the four incisors found in many mammals, the elephant has two tusks, no canines and only three functional molars on each side of the jaw at a time.

What is the trunk's capacity and size?
The trunk can be up to 2 m long, with a mass of 100 kg or more and a capacity of about 18 litres.

Are elephants really short-sighted?
They cannot see very well, but it would be dangerous to underestimate their visual capability.

Are their other senses well developed?
Their senses of hearing and smell are very well developed.

How do elephants sleep?
Adults usually rest standing up during the day, but at night they frequently sleep lying down for several hours. Calves often flop down in the grass to sleep for an hour or so while the adults feed nearby. Adults lie down to sleep less frequently than younger animals, but all do it, lying flat on their sides, accompanied by considerable and very loud snoring!

More often, adults doze on their feet in the shade, often resting their heads or tusks against the trunk of a tree for support.

How do they communicate?
Communication is by touch, smell and sound. Elephants are also very vocal, with a repertoire limited to four different sounds, with gradations in pitch, duration and volume. Sounds include rumbling, trumpeting, squealing and screaming. About three-quarters of their vocal communication uses frequencies too low for humans to hear. Hunters of yesteryear called the upper harmonics of these calls 'tummy rumbles'. Some infrasonic calls are very loud, up to 103 decibels, and can be detected by other elephants at distances of over 10 km.

Trumpeting is a sound produced by blowing through the nostrils, making the trunk resonate. Trumpeting could be a sound of alarm or a cry for help, but is also voiced during intense greetings.

Calves squeal as a distress call, usually eliciting immediate response from the mother and other females.

Screaming is the adult equivalent of the squealing by the calf.

Is it true that elephants are clever?
Intelligence is actually a human virtue, but, if we could ascribe this characteristic to animals, the elephant would have a high rating. It is generally perceived to be one of the most intelligent of animals, after the large primates.

How big is an elephant's brain?

It is about four times the size of a human brain. Taking the size of the animal into consideration, it means that a human has proportionately 15 times more brain matter than an elephant.

Does the elephant have a good memory?

The relatively large brain and long life span probably imply a good memory. Recent translocations of captive elephants indicated that they instantly recognised other elephants with which they had had no contact for 23 years.

What is the size of the elephant's heart?

The heart of an elephant, with a body mass of 5 000 kg, weighs about 25 kg, or about 0.5% of its body mass. If this seems small for such a huge beast, one has to remember that an elephant seldom has to run or exert itself.

How fast does its heart beat?

Under normal circumstances it beats at about 25 beats per minute, but under stress this can go up to 90 to 100 beats a minute.

Does an elephant have a tongue?

Yes, and it can weigh up to 12 kg. Unlike that of the giraffe, it does not protrude.

What is the average herd size?

Family groups of up to 13 individuals are common. Family groups may at times aggregate to form the large herds that are sometimes reported. In the Park herds usually consist of between 10 and 30 animals.

What type of hierarchy exists in an elephant herd?

The social life of elephants is essentially matriarchal, and a basic family unit is organised around an adult cow and her offspring or other closely related cows and their offspring. At puberty, males leave the family groups and join or form bachelor groups.

Is there a dominant bull in a herd?

Adult bulls looking for a cow or cows in oestrus join family units or herds consisting of a number of family units. The bull in the herd that is in musth is considered the dominant bull at that time.

Who leads the family unit or the herd?

The oldest and biggest cow in the herd usually takes the lead in ordinary herd movements and activities such as flight or attack. When a family unit is disturbed, there is an immediate tendency for members of the unit to bunch around the lead cow. If she stands, charges or takes flight, the rest will follow her example.

Members of a bachelor group tend to react individually when danger threatens. If they take flight they often run in different directions, with complete disregard for other group members.

Are elephants territorial in habit?

There is no convincing evidence of territorial behaviour, although solitary bulls, bachelor groups and herds have fairly distinct home ranges.

How stable is the herd composition?

Cow families form nursery herds of about 12 individuals, comprising a dominant cow as the matriarch and related cows and calves. They tend to stay together, but the composition of the rest of the herd may vary considerably from time to time. Larger herds sometimes break up into smaller herds, and could subsequently reform.

Are old bulls evicted from the herd?

No, they leave the herd voluntarily but may return at a later stage. When bulls born within the herd reach sexual maturity they may be evicted by the matriarch in order to prevent the possibility of inbreeding.

Bulls are never permanent members of any herd. They leave their natal herd at around 14 years of age. They enter herds from time to time, but as they are not members of a herd, they cannot be 'evicted'.

Do bulls often fight?

Mock fights or playful sparring sessions are common, but serious fighting is not common. The dominance hierarchy is established and maintained through play fighting. Serious fights, in which one or both combatants may be killed, are rare and usually occur only between bulls in musth, when rights to an oestrus female are contested.

Can elephants be killed in a fight?

It does happen but recorded mortalities due to fighting are rare.

Are solitary bulls rogue animals?

Usually not. The few that do become rogue animals are eventually destroyed when they leave the sanctuary of the Park. Elephant bulls are often seen on their own. They may join other elephants. However, associations with other elephants are always temporary.

Why do some elephants become rogue animals?

All the reasons will probably never be known, but animals wounded by hunters or injured in some or other way could well turn rogue. Elephants sometimes leave the Park to raid crops in adjoining areas, where they come into contact with man and may be shot at and wounded.

This leaves them in pain and with bad memories, which could cause them to become rogue animals.

Are the elephants in the Park dangerous to man?

Any elephant is potentially dangerous. When you stop to observe elephants it is advisable to keep a distance of at least 50 m, and be prepared to drive forward in the case of an unexpected charge.

How will one know when it is safe to pass elephants?

Elephants are unpredictable and when you see them standing close to the road, rather wait for them to move away before driving on.

Have elephants actually attacked any vehicles in the Park?

Since 1927, when the first three cars with visitors were allowed into the Park, a few vehicles have been damaged by elephants. In almost all the cases the drivers were either negligent, approaching too close to the animals, or intimidated the animal by hooting or shouting to get some response or action for photographs.

Do they often charge cars?

No, not often. Even when an elephant does charge, it is more often than not a mock charge. As it is difficult to distinguish between a real and a mock charge, it is advisable not to wait around to find out which of the two it is, by moving on when the animal shows signs of agitation.

Have people been killed by elephants in the Park?

No visitors have been killed by elephants in the Park. During the time of the civil war in Mozambique some of the people crossing the Park to and from South Africa encountered elephants, some fatally. Some ranger staff in the Park have been killed, but the incidence is extremely low.

What are the signs of agitation in an elephant?

The first sign is when the animal approaches with the head held high and staring down at the vehicle. The next important sign is when it shakes its head while standing in an almost side-on position. At the same time they tend to kick up dust with their forefeet and perform a mock charge. By the time the ears are flat against the head and the trunk curled under the chin, your vehicle should already be moving away. Trumpeting is another indication of agitation.

What does one do when surrounded by elephants?

It can happen that, while watching elephants, they may cross the road in front as well as behind a vehicle. Do not panic and try to drive through the herd. Rather switch off the engine of the vehicle and remain silent and stationary until the herd has passed and it is safe to drive on.

Is ear-flapping a sign of danger?

Elephants usually flap their ears to help regulate their body temperature on a hot day. The blood in the large blood vessels of the ears is cooled by about 3 or 4°C through this action. The cooled blood plays an important role in the regulation of the body temperature.

The flapping of ears associated with head shaking could, however, also be a sign of annoyance.

Are elephants aggressive towards other animals?

They are usually tolerant of other animals at water holes. However, they can sometimes be aggressive towards other animals, and a number of different species have been killed by elephants. They lash the unfortunate animal with the trunk, breaking its back, which leads to its eventual death. A kudu was once found with its back broken in eight places. This is a rare occurrence, however, as animals usually give way when elephants approach a water hole.

Elephants specifically do not like lions and it is quite hilarious to see the kings of the beasts fleeing with their tails tucked between their legs when elephants approach them at a water hole.

Have any cases been reported of elephants attacking larger game, such as rhinos?

Although this rarely occurs, confrontations between elephants and rhinos have been recorded. Rhinos put up a fierce fight but elephants are usually victorious in these encounters.

Do elephants migrate?

In the past elephants seasonally moved between the Park in the dry season and Mozambique during the rains. These migrations came to an end with the erecting of the elephant-proof fence between the two countries. They do move from one area to another within the boundaries of the Park, depending on the availability of water and food. With the anticipated removal of the mentioned fence, such movements may resume.

How far can they walk in a day?

Daily movements of elephants are determined by the availability and localities of food and water. During winter, when food is scarce, they can cover up to 50 km per day. During summer, when food and water are more readily available, they move around a lot less and cover about 4 to 7 km a day. Their walking speed is about 4 to 8 km/h.

How fast can an elephant run?

Elephants can reach a speed of 50 km/h over short distances.

What are their breeding habits?

An oestrus female is usually followed around by a high-ranking bull, generally one in musth. When she becomes receptive, the bull puts his trunk on her back, levers himself upright against her while supporting himself on his back legs and she backs towards him. Copulation lasts about 45 seconds. Mating can be repeated three or four times over a 24-hour period and a cow may mate with more than one bull during this time, but this is usually prevented by the musth bull.

They breed throughout the year, with more births in early summer. Cows are in oestrus for between three and six days.

After a gestation period of 22 months a single calf, with a shoulder height of 85 to 90 cm and a mass of 100 to 140 kg, is born. The calf can stand within an hour of birth, being continually encouraged and assisted by the mother to stand. Calves are weaned at two to four years, just before the birth of the next calf. Calving intervals range between three and a half and six years, but reproduction could be slowed down and calving intervals extended by factors such as prolonged droughts and times of stress due to famine, as has occurred in other parts of Africa.

What is the life expectancy of an elephant?

In the wild an elephant can reach an age of 60 years.

Does the cow dig a hole to facilitate mating?

No, their anatomy is adapted for normal copulation.

Do they mate in water?

They are very fond of playing in water and some of the play movements often resemble the mating act. Mating normally takes place on land.

Can a cow produce twins?

Births of twins have been recorded in the Park, but this is a very rare occurrence.

Does the cow make a bed of grass and leaves for the calf to fall on when it is born?

No, the cow gives birth standing upright and the calf does not fall far, due to the low position of the cow's birth canal.

How many teats does the mother have?

The cow has two teats situated between the front legs.

How does the calf suckle?

The calf suckles with its mouth, while the trunk is bent over backwards or to the side. It gradually learns to use the trunk to drink water, which it does by sucking up water and squirting it into its mouth.

Is calf mortality high?

Usually not. Calves are very well protected against predators and they seem not to be very susceptible to disease. Droughts, however, can take a high toll, and calf mortality can be as high as 30% under such conditions.

What are their major enemies?

For all practical purposes, elephants have no natural enemies except man, who hunt them for their tusks, which are prized in the illegal ivory trade.

Calves are vulnerable to lions and spotted hyaenas, but are well protected by their mothers and relatives. In exceptional cases adult elephants may fall victim to predators, but these are almost always old, sick or injured animals, or animals weakened by drought and malnutrition.

Are elephants prone to diseases?

No epizootics have in recent history been recorded in the Kruger Park, and the effect of parasites and diseases in general appears to be negligible. Foot-and-mouth disease has been induced artificially in elephants, but in the wild they seem to be immune to this disease.

Although death due to arteriosclerosis appears to be limited, postmortems have revealed that arteriosclerotic lesions occur more frequently with age, particularly in cows. This is particularly interesting because in humans it is usually the males who show the first signs of arteriosclerosis.

Sporadic outbreaks of anthrax, *Bacillus anthracis*, have caused some mortalities. The *Picoma* virus, which causes encephalomyocarditis (EMC) and is transmitted by rodents, has also caused some deaths. No cases of foot-and-mouth disease or bovine tuberculosis have ever been recorded in free-living elephants. Other recorded conditions affecting elephants include heart diseases, twisted gut, septicaemia and abnormal cancerous growths on the soles of the feet.

A condition known as 'floppy or flaccid trunk syndrome' (FTS), caused by a deterioration of the nerves of the trunk, has been recorded in the Park. This progressive condition, leading to total paralysis of the trunk, can be fatal as feeding becomes severely impaired. It is suspected that plant toxins and/or pollutants may be the cause of this condition.

Occasionally the cartilage of an ear collapses and results in a 'floppy' ear. This is not a serious condition and does not affect the wellbeing of the animal.

Do other mortality factors affect elephants?

Accidents, droughts, starvation, fighting, stress due to scarcity of food, hunting and especially poaching are all factors contributing to elephant mortality.

There is talk of elephant cemeteries. Are there reported cases of elephants dying in large numbers?

There is no evidence of elephant cemeteries.

The Tsavo disaster in Kenya is the most spectacular documented case of mass deaths in recent times. During the drought years of 1970 and 1971, an estimated 5 900 elephants died of starvation. Juveniles and lactating cows suffered most. Even during these conditions there was no evidence of cemeteries. This disaster and suffering could have been minimised to a great

extent if a sound management policy, including the policy of controlling their numbers, had been in place during the preceding years when water and food were still available in sufficient quantities.

What is the annual increase in numbers?

The annual recruitment in the Park varies between 4% and 7.5%.

Do elephants destroy and damage many trees in the Park?

Elephants are the main cause of decline in mature trees in the Kruger Park. Solitary bulls and small bull groups are often considered to be the main culprits, pushing over trees, tearing down branches and debarking trees. Cows, however, also cause considerable damage through ring-barking, particularly during the dry season.

With the dramatic increase in the numbers of elephants over the past 17 years, the damage done to woody vegetation is giving rise to concern, especially during the winter when the availability of food is under pressure.

Why do they push trees over?

One is often left with the impression that they do this for little reason. A big tree is often pushed over for the sake of a few leaves at the top. This action probably assisted in the formation of savanna veld types, which in turn created favourable conditions for grazing for several other species of herbivores. Under conditions of elephant overpopulation, however, trees can disappear at an alarming rate and with them the habitats and food of a variety of mammalian browsers, as well as birds and reptiles.

Elephants strip bark off trees as a food source during the dry season. A ring-barked tree always dies as its physiology is disrupted. This is probably the major cause of tree mortality in the Park.

What size of tree can be pushed over?
This depends on the root system of the tree and the nature of the soil in which it grows. One often see trees with a trunk diameter of about 0.5 m that have been pushed over.

Does an elephant have a special technique to push over a tree?
The elephant usually places its fore-head against the tree and rocks forwards and backwards. If this is not successful the elephant will try pushing from a different position.

Is it true that elephants sometimes eat soil due to a deficiency in their diet?
Elephants have been known to dig up termite mounds and eat the soil, probably for the sodium content. It has also been established that they show a marked preference for water with high sodium content.

The eating of mud and soil can be regarded as a form of pica. Pica, or the eating of strange objects, is a well-known phenomenon among herbivores and is caused by deficiencies in their diet. Such behaviour is occasionally recorded in the Kruger Park.

At times it is difficult to find elephants. Why would that be?
The large herds usually keep clear of the roads during the wet season. After rain the elephants, like many other game species, disperse to utilise the temporary water holes that are often some distance from the roads. They do this to avoid the disturbances associated with busy tourist roads. In winter, when water is scarce, they concentrate along the rivers and at permanent water holes where there are more tourist roads and it is easier for visitors to see them.

It is often heard that visitors blame the culling programme of the Park when they don't see elephants. Is there any truth in this statement?
This statement does not hold water any more. In 1994 a moratorium was placed on the culling of elephants in the Park. Elephant numbers have increased to the extent that, at the time of publication, there are more than 15 000 elephants in the Park.

There was never any evidence to suggest that the culling programme had any effect on the behaviour of elephants towards tourists. Culling was conducted from a helicopter and any negative associations would be directed towards helicopters, not tourists. Elephants affected were culled and did not survive to harbour any ill feeling towards visitors or their vehicles.

An elephant population has the ability to double its number every 15 years and this is exactly what has happened in the Kruger Park. In 1994 the number of elephants in the Park was about 7 500 and now, some 20 years later, the number of elephants has doubled.

With the destruction of vegetation that accompanies the increase in the numbers of elephants, the possibility of the Park eventually becoming an elephant reserve cannot be excluded. If it is accepted that the Park cannot accommodate unlimited numbers of elephants, then it must also be accepted that culling in the future should be seen as a management option.

AARDVARK

Orycteropus afer (Pallas 1766)

How widely is the aardvark distributed in the Park?

They are patchily distributed throughout the Park but fairly common in savanna areas with termitaria. Termitaria are seen in all the ecozones, with the exception of ecozone M. Aardvarks prefer sandy soils and are therefore seldom found in montane areas.

What type of habitat do they prefer?

The main habitat requirement must include termites and ants. They favour sandy and clayish soils in open woodland, scrubland and savanna, particularly where there is an abundance of termite mounds. In the Park they are absent on the alluvial plains of the north.

What do they eat?

Their main dietary components are ants and termites. More ants are eaten in winter and more termites in summer. They also eat small rodents, insects and their larvae, and fungi.

The 45-cm-long, sticky tongue is used to lap up termites and ants. Gravel and soil are ingested with the prey and aid digestion in the gizzard-like stomach.

They also eat the fruit of the aardvark cucumber (*Cucumis humifructus*) for its water content. The pips pass through the aardvark's digestive system and germinate in its droppings.

Aardvarks are water independent, obtaining enough moisture from their diet, but will drink water whenever it is readily available.

What are the main physical features?

A unique and unmistakable animal, covered in a sparse coat of coarse white or buff-coloured hair. The skin is pinkish, but usually takes on the colour of the surrounding soil, and is thick for protection against biting and stinging insects.

The hair on the limbs and base of the tail is darker, while the tail is white, thick at the base and tapers to a point. The hindquarters are heavier than the forequarters, with the back sloping upwards towards the rump. The snout is long and pig-like, with slit-shaped nostrils that can close when digging. The ears are long with pointed tips. The legs are sturdy and exceptionally strong. There are four toes on the front feet with long claws that are concave underneath with sharp edges, and five toes on the hind feet with shorter, more curved claws. They have no incisors or canines, and the molar teeth are reduced and columnar and are replaced from the back to the front.

Males and females have a shoulder height of about 65 cm, with a mass of up to 70 kg and a total body length of about 2 m.

Are their senses well developed?

Their sense of smell is acute and their hearing is also well developed. Their sight appears to be poor, particularly in daylight.

Do they make a sound?

They are usually silent animals, but contact sounds include loud sniffs and grunts while foraging. Distress calls include bleating cries and squeals like a pig.

What are their habits?

They are predominantly nocturnal and seldom seen during the day. Aardvarks are solitary, except for mating pairs or mothers with young. Territoriality is uncertain. Home ranges are marked with thick perineal-gland secretions and the size depends on food availability.

They are very strong diggers and a metre-long tunnel can be dug in about five minutes. Once inside the tunnel, the aardvark blocks it off with soil. Two sorts of burrows are dug for shelter. Tunnels about a metre deep with one or two entrances are used for a few days at a time and possibly returned to at a later stage. Large tunnel systems with several entrances, extending up to 6 m down into the soil and up to 25 m long, are used regularly. These tunnels are also where females give birth to their young. Aardvarks enter and exit burrows head first.

Underground ant and termite nests are detected by smell and scraped open with the strong front claws, to a depth of 20 to 40 cm. The long, sticky tongue is inserted into the nest up to 25 to 30 cm and then withdrawn with the insects sticking to it. Termite nests on the surface are torn open to such a degree that the aardvark can disappear into the termite mound.

How do they prevent dust from entering their lungs?
Dense bristles around the nostrils prevent dust from entering the nose.

Are aardvarks clumsy?
Their normal slow gait may create the impression that they are clumsy, but in fact they can run deceptively fast if necessary.

Are they useful animals?
These strange animals play an important, two-fold ecological role. Firstly, they keep termites in check, and secondly, their disused burrows provide shelter and breeding sites for at least 17 other mammalian species.

Can they defend themselves?
Although their teeth are useless for defence, their huge claws are lethal weapons and they defend themselves ferociously when cornered.

What are their breeding habits?
After a gestation period of seven months, usually a single cub is born during the winter, from May to August. The cub, with a mass of up to 2 kg, is born in the nesting chamber of the burrow, with its eyes open at birth. Cubs leave the burrow after two weeks, take solid food after three months, are weaned at four months and independent after six months. They are fully grown after a year and sexually mature at two years.

What is their potential life span?
They can live up to about 20 years.

What are their major enemies?
Their main threat is man. Their flesh is considered a delicacy among indigenous people, and the snout and claws are used in traditional medicines and as charms. Aardvarks are killed by farmers because it is said that their burrows cause damage to stocks, crops, dams and roads.

Natural predators include lions, hyaenas, leopards and pythons.

CAPE PANGOLIN (SCALY ANTEATER)

Manis temminckii (Smuts, 1832)

What is their distribution in the Kruger Park?

They are widely and irregularly distributed throughout the Park, occurring only in areas where termitaria are found. They are abundant in the area between the Phalaborwa entrance gate and Letaba, as well as in the western part of the Park between Skukuza and the Orpen area.

What are the Cape pangolin's main physical features?

This unmistakable animal is not related to the armadillo found in South and Central America, to which it has some external resemblance. Large brown to rust-coloured heavy overlapping scales cover the head, sides and back of the body. The tail scales are sharply edged and become a very effective defence mechanism, with which serious injuries may be inflicted using sideswipes. The scales are derived from the dermis and are composed of agglutinated hairs.

The softer underparts of the body and inner limbs are sparsely covered with hair and lack any scales. The small eyes are found in soft, bulbous tissue and situated forward on a small, pointed head. The ears are covered in fine hairs, and both the ears and nostrils can close to prevent sand, ants and termites from entering these organs during foraging expeditions.

Pangolins are good swimmers and diggers. Although the long, bent and sharp claws are formidable weapons, their main function is to break open the compressed soil of termitaria.

The tongue, part of which folds into a throat pouch, is longer than the animal's full body length.

The males and females are equal in size and mass. Length ranges from 35 to 60 cm,

with the tail an additional 30 to 45 cm. Their mass is between 15 and 18 kg.

What is their general behaviour?

They are almost exclusively nocturnal and are seldom seen during the day. Solitary animals have territories of about 1.5 to 8 km². Male territories may overlap with adjoining female territories but same-sex territories do not.

These creatures inhabit the abandoned burrows of animals such as the aardvark, jackals, hyaenas and springhare, and they will also use caves and piles of debris. They move their sleeping areas within their territory every few weeks, to allow the ants and termites to rebuild their nests. They can move up to 6 km at night during foraging expeditions.

Pangolins walk on their well-developed hind feet, tucking their front feet under the chin, the tail off the ground and a distinctly arched back.

When the female perceives any danger she will wrap herself around her infant for protection. Pangolins are timid animals and have a tendency to freeze at the slightest sign of possible danger. This makes them difficult to observe. When threatened or attacked, they roll themselves into a ball and raise their scales, protecting their soft underparts and head. It is not advisable to touch or to attempt to pick them up when they are rolled up. Their very sharp, raised scales and the sideswipe of the tail can inflict serious and painful injuries.

Do Cape pangolins demarcate their territory?

Pangolins demarcate their territories with odorous anal-gland secretions, urine and dung. Due to their secretive natures, little is known about their territorial habits.

What are their breeding habits?

They breed during the dry winter months. A single young, very seldom twins, is born after a gestation period of about four months. The precocious infant is born with soft scales that harden after a few days. After about five months the infant is independent. It is believed that females will adopt orphaned young of other females. The baby is usually carried on the mother's tail.

How well are their senses developed and how do they communicate?

They have poor eyesight but excellent senses of smell and hearing.

Contact calls consist of grunts, puffs, hisses and snorts.

What do they eat?

They are insectivorous, consuming a diet of ants, termites, eggs, larvae, pupae and sand. Once the termitarium has been broken open, the pangolin sticks its long, sticky tongue into the tunnels. As the tongue is withdrawn it ingests the ants and termites as well as soil and gravel.

Pangolins do not have teeth. The sand and gravel ingested with their food aids digestion in the gizzard-like stomach.

They drink water regularly.

What are their major enemies?

The main predator is man. The flesh of the pangolin is considered a delicacy among indigenous people and the organs and scales are favoured for medicinal purposes by indigenous healers. Human encroachment and loss of habitat, and therefore availability of food, is also a major factor in their survival.

Their armour and their habit of rolling into a tight protective ball afford excellent protection, and few predators could harm this creature. The effect of disease is not clear.

Leopards, lions, hyaenas and pythons count among their enemies.

SMALLER MAMMALS

SOUTHERN AFRICAN HEDGEHOG
Atelerix frontalis (A. Smith 1831)

What is the distribution of the Southern African hedgehog in the Kruger Park?

The Southern African hedgehog is rarely seen in the Kruger Park, as this area is the furthest east of its normal distribution. In the Park, it occurs only in ecozone B and is largely confined to the higher-lying grassland around the Pretoriuskop Rest Camp area.

Two hedgehogs were recently found in close proximity to one another on the same day at the Shangoni rangers' quarters, on the western boundary of the Park, south of Punda Maria Rest Camp. No further sightings in this area have been recorded.

What type of habitat do hedgehogs prefer?

Hedgehogs have a wide habitat tolerance, occurring in open thornveld, grassland, bush, scrubland, savanna and rocky outcrops. They tend to prefer dry, overgrazed areas with patchy grass cover and an annual rainfall of 300 to 800 mm.

What do they eat?

They are insectivorous, tending towards omnivory. Their diet consists mainly of insects, beetles, termites, grasshoppers and moths. Centipedes, millipedes, earthworms, small reptiles, small rodents, frogs, birds' eggs, carrion, vegetable matter, fungi and wild fruits are also included in their diet. They are water independent, obtaining sufficient moisture from their diet, but will readily drink water when it is available.

What are their main physical features?

The hedgehog is unmistakable, being the only African mammal with short spines covering the whole of the back and flanks. The spines are in fact thick, stiff hairs, white at the base, dark brown to black in the middle and white or buff at the tip. White spines are interspersed in a broad band along the back. The face, legs and tail are covered in dark brownish hair, with the underside slightly lighter. A conspicuous white band across the forehead, a pointed snout, small ears and a short tail are features of this small animal. Each foot has five toes.

Both sexes are up to 30 cm in length; males have a mass of about 450 g and females about 420 g. Albinism often occurs.

What are their habits?

Hedgehogs are predominantly nocturnal and are seldom seen by day. However, in cool weather they may be spotted during the day. They are usually solitary but pairs or family groups are sometimes seen foraging together. They have small home ranges and territoriality has not been observed. Meetings are noisy, with much sniffing, snorting and head-butting.

They shelter under thick vegetable debris and logs, in bushes, termite mounds, holes in the ground and rock crevices. As they move around their home range, the shelter changes daily.

Hedgehogs move slowly when foraging but can run at 6 to 7 km/h when they need to. Their very keen sense of smell is used to detect prey, which is rooted out from litter and under rocks and logs.

Hedgehogs rely on their spines rather than concealment for protection against predators. When disturbed, they roll up and pull the spiny skin on their back over their head and legs, producing a uniform ball of intertwined and springy spines in a defensive move that is effective even against predators as large as lions. They are very active during spring and summer months and during the rainy season. During winter, when there is a shortage of food, they become torpid and inactive, slowing down their metabolism. True hibernation, however, has not been confirmed.

Are hedgehogs related to porcupines?

Although both have spines or quills, these two animals are not related. The hedgehog is an insectivore, while the porcupine is a rodent.

What are their breeding habits?

Hedgehog courtship is noisy and prolonged. The male and female circle each other with much sniffing and snorting. During copulation the female flattens the spines on her rump, and the male, who has a particularly long penis, holds himself in position by biting the spines on her shoulders.

After a gestation period of five weeks, up to nine pups, but on average four, are born during the summer rainy season. The pups, with a mass of between 7.5 and 10 g each, are born naked and blind in debris or leaf-lined nests in crevices, under logs or in holes. The spines, visible under the skin, start appearing within 24 hours. Infant spines are replaced after four to six weeks when the young begin to forage with their mother. Young are weaned at five weeks and are independent at about seven weeks.

What is their life expectancy?

They live for about five years.

What are their main enemies?

The hedgehog's main enemy is man. The spines and meat are sought after by traditional healers for use in traditional medicines. Eagle-Owls (*Bubo* spp.) and other large raptors also take their toll.

CAPE PORCUPINE *Hystrix africaeaustralis* (Peters 1852)

What is the porcupine's distribution?

It occurs commonly and is widespread in suitable habitat in all the ecozones of the Park.

What type of habitat do they prefer?

Porcupines can tolerate a wide range of habitats, preferring broken country with rocky terrain in dry areas, grasslands and adjoining forest margins, boulder areas and rock crevices and piles of loose rock.

What do they eat?

They are omnivorous, taking bulbs, tubers, roots, bark, seeds, wild fruits and carrion. Cape porcupines ring-bark trees like the wild mango (*Cordyla africana*), *Ficus* spp. and tamboti (*Spirostachys africana*). They chew on bones for their calcium and phosphorus content.

Porcupines are water independent, obtaining sufficient moisture from their diet, but will drink water when it is available.

Is porcupine meat edible?

It is apparently quite tasty and is regarded as a delicacy by some rural South Africans.

What are their main physical features?

Porcupines are unmistakable among southern African mammals. From the shoulders to the tail, the upper body and flanks are covered in long, pliable black-and-white banded spines that are up to 50 cm long, and shorter stiff quills, up to 25 cm long. There is a crest of long, coarse, black-and-white hair from the top of the head to the shoulders. The rest of the body and the limbs are covered in short, coarse, flattened black hair, with patches of white hair on each side of the base of the neck. The end of the short tail carries a rattle of hollow, open-ended quills with narrow stalk-like bases. Quills are composed of fused hairs.

The muzzle is heavy and blunt and the eyes and ears are small. The legs are short and heavily built, with large feet and sturdy nails. Females are heavier than males, having a mass of up to 25 kg, and males about 22 kg. Males measure about 90 cm and females about 95 cm in total length, standing about 30 cm high at the shoulder.

Can porcupines eject their quills?
No, but it is a common belief that they can 'shoot' their quills at enemies. The quills are easily dislodged and may become embedded in the bodies of attackers. It is also normal for them to shed quills from time to time. Quills lying around indicate the presence of porcupiness.

What are their habits?
Porcupines are predominantly nocturnal but are sometimes seen in the early morning or late afternoon, especially during winter. They shelter during the day in rock crevices or burrows and holes in the ground.

Porcupines are either solitary or occur in family clans comprising a monogamous dominant breeding pair and their offspring. Pairs are bonded through daily mating.

Clans have a home range of up to 400 ha, part of which is defended as a territory. Home ranges are scent-marked with urine.

When a porcupine is threatened it erects its crest, spines and quills, especially on the side facing the threat. It growls, rattles its quills, stamps its feet and shakes its tail to rattle the hollow quills at its tip. When approached, it rushes backwards or sideways at the attacker, trying to drive quills into it. The quills are not barbed, and the porcupine cannot shoot them, but they are only loosely rooted in the skin, so they pull loose and stay embedded in the target. Scenes of confrontation are usually littered with quills.

What sounds do they make?
Contact calls include grunts, sniffles and piping calls. Alarm calls include growls and snarls.

To which animal group do porcupines belong?
Porcupines are the largest of the African rodents.

What are their breeding habits?

Only the dominant pair in a clan breeds; subordinate females mate but do not conceive. The female oestrus cycle lasts between 17 and 42 days. Physical contact with a male is necessary for the female's cycle. Mating takes place from May to December and the gestation period is about three months. Usually one pup, seldom more than three, is born between August and January, with a peak in January. Pups with a mass of 300 to 440 g are born in leaf-lined nursery chambers in burrows.

Pups are born with hair and soft spines that are about 3 cm long. Their eyes open within hours of being born. Pups leave the den at about two weeks, take solid food at two to three weeks and are weaned at 10 to 14 weeks. They are fully grown at one year.

What is their potential life span?

Porcupines can live up to about 12 years.

What are their major enemies?

Lions, leopards and hyaenas are their major enemies.

It takes a skilled and experienced predator to attack a porcupine and emerge unscathed. In the Park there was a pride of lions that specialised in hunting and killing porcupines.

Is it difficult for a predator to kill a porcupine?

It is no easy task and the predator has to exercise caution. To be successful it has to surprise the porcupine, strike it on the head or muzzle where there are no quills, and upend it quickly in order to get to the unprotected soft belly.

Can a porcupine actively defend itself?

With an arched back, the head tucked away and peeping backwards beneath its belly, the porcupine turns its back on the attacker and charges backwards or sideways, in an effort to drive its quills into the attacker. When an assailant is struck by these sharp quills, they are usually embedded deeply into its flesh, causing serious wounds, which rapidly become septic. When quills are lodged in the throat or mouth of the attacker, the affected area becomes swollen, the animal cannot eat and starvation is the result.

A miscalculated blow from a predator to the body of the porcupine, and not the head, can result in a paw full of quills. Apart from being very painful, this also prevents the predator from moving around and hunting. This usually ends in the predator eventually dying of starvation.

Are the quills poisonous?

Many people believe they are, but this is not true. Sepsis in the wound is simply caused by the dirt on the quills.

Do porcupines issue a warning to potential attackers?

The vibrating of the hollow quills produces a warning sound to potential attackers. When annoyed, porcupines thump their feet and rattle their quills.

ROCK DASSIE
Procavia capensis (Pallas 1766)

Are dassies widely distributed in the Park?

They are found in suitable habitat in ecozones E, J, L and P of the Park, between the Lepelle and Bububu rivers, and in the northern parts of ecozone I, in the Lebombo Mountain Bushveld north of the Lepelle River.

What habitat do they prefer?

As the common name suggests, they prefer rocky hills, koppies or stony outcrops, generally in the drier areas of the Park. The presence of dassies in an area is betrayed by the urine stains on the rocks and the piles of droppings in specific places. They are not found in forested areas.

What do they eat?

They are vegetarians, preferring grass, forbs, shrubs, berries and fruit. They are water independent, but will drink when it is readily available.

What are their main physical features?

Resembling a rabbit in size and shape, the dassie has a light to dark brown or greyish-brown coat of short thick hairs, with long tactile hairs scattered throughout the coat. The ears are small and round and it has no tail. Behind the ears is a buffy patch, and the dorsal patch is usually black. There is a pale spot above the eyes, and underparts are pale.

The soles of the feet are naked, with soft, elastic pads that are moistened with glandular secretions. The moist soles function as suction pads that enable the dassie to climb steep rock faces and trees. The front feet have four toes without nails and the hind feet have three toes with flattened nails.

The shoulder height is about 25 cm. The males have a mass of about 5 kg and the females slightly less. Both male and female can attain lengths of about 45 to 55 cm. The tips of the incisor teeth in the male show below the upper lip. There is a pronounced gap between the incisors and the molars, which is known as the diastema.

What are their habits?

Predominantly diurnal, dassies feed mostly in the morning and afternoon, resting in shelter to avoid the midday heat. On occasion they feed on moonlit nights.

They are gregarious animals, sometimes found in clans of up to 25 individuals, comprising a dominant male and several females and their young. Several clans may share the same area, but core areas are defended as territories. Home ranges are marked with communal dung and urine middens. The dung is white and the urine crystallises into white streaks on the rocks, accumulating into substantial amber-coloured deposits that are used in folk remedies.

Dassies have a very low tolerance for low temperatures, and conserve energy by basking in the sun or huddling together.

Are their senses well developed?

Their senses of sight and hearing are very keen and it is difficult to surprise them. They have a good sense of smell.

What sounds do they make?

Contact calls include whistles, twitters, growls, grunts and screams. Alarm calls include shrieks, squeaks and sharp barks.

What are their breeding habits?

Reproduction is triggered by the length of the day. Mating usually takes place from May to July, and births between December and February. After a gestation period of seven months, considered very long for such a small animal, two to five pups are born. They have a mass of about 200 to 300 g each, and are born fully furred, with their eyes open and active.

Each pup is allocated a specific teat and does not suckle from another teat. Solid food is taken after a week and they are weaned at between three and five months. They continue growing for the next three years, with females reaching sexual maturity at about 17 months and males at about 29 months.

What is their potential life span?

Their life span rarely exceeds 10 years in the wild.

Do they damage crops?
Where their enemies have been eliminated they can become so numerous that they are forced to supplement their natural diet with cultivated crops.

What are their main enemies?
The rock dassie's main predators include leopards, cheetahs, jackals, caracal and servals. Other predators include Verreaux's (Black) Eagle (*Aquila verreauxii*) and Southern African python.

Are they really related to the elephant?
The teeth and structure of the feet are similar, but otherwise the two animals are as far apart as their respective sizes.

YELLOW-SPOTTED ROCK DASSIE
Heterohyrax brucei (Gray 1868)

What is the distribution?
A number of subspecies of *H. brucei* are distributed throughout most of the African savanna areas. *H. b. ruddi* (Wroughton 1910) is the subspecies found furthest south and its range extends from the northeastern parts of South Africa through northeastern Botswana and Zimbabwe to Mozambique. In the Park it is confined to the extreme northern parts of ecozones M and N, north of the Punda Maria-Pafuri Road and along the northeastern boundary as far south as the Malonga Spring. Although the rock dassie and the yellow-spotted rock dassie live in the same habitats in many parts of their range, they are usually not found together in the Kruger National Park.

What type of habitat do these dassies prefer?
Like the common rock dassie, they are also confined to rocky outcrops, broken veld and koppies.

What is the difference between the Yellow-Spotted rock dassie and the rock dassie?
The yellow-spotted rock dassie looks very much like the ordinary rock dassie but is more brownish in colour, with lighter flanks, and has a conspicuous white patch above each eye and a large white to yellowish patch on the back. The body mass is about 4 kg, the shoulder height up to 30 cm and the length 45 cm.

What do they eat?
They are vegetarians and their diet includes fruit, berries, grass, bark and roots.

Do they differ in habits?
Their habits are more or less the same, except that the yellow-spotted rock dassie is an even better climber than its relative and is partly arboreal.

Aren't they sometimes called tree dassies?
No. The tree dassie, *Dendrohyrax arboreus* (A. Smith 1827) is a different species. It is more arboreal, more nocturnal and less gregarious than the two species described in this book.

What are the breeding habits of the yellow-spotted rock dassie?
One or two pups are born in late summer or autumn, after a gestation period of about seven months.

What are their major enemies?
They are preyed upon by caracals, leopards, raptorial birds and pythons.

TREE SQUIRREL *Paraxerus cepapi* (A. Smith 1836)

Are tree squirrels widely distributed throughout the Park?
They occur commonly and widely in all the ecozones of the Park.

What habitat do they prefer?
Tree squirrels commonly occur in savanna woodlands, especially in the Mopane woodland of the northern section of the Park. Also in *Acacia/Terminalia* and mixed *Acacia/Combretum* woodlands. They avoid forest and open grassland.

What do they eat?
Being omnivorous, they feed on a variety of seeds, nuts, fruits, kernels of various kinds, roots, grass, bark of a wide range of plants, acacia gum, lichens, insects and even nesting birds and their eggs. They cache nuts, seeds and kernels by burying them in the soil.

They are water independent, obtaining enough moisture from their diet, but will drink readily when water is available.

What are their main physical features?
The grizzled, greyish-yellow to dark brown colour and the bushy tail are the most characteristic features. The underparts are lighter. There are no stripes or bands on the body, but the tail has indistinct blackish bars. There are prominent black whiskers. Strong nails on forefeet and hind feet assist in tree-climbing. They have small eyes and small, rounded ears. The nose-to-tail length in both males and females can be up to 40 cm. Females are slightly heavier than males, about 265 g, and males about 250 g.

Does albinism occur among tree squirrels?
A number of albino squirrels have been reported, especially from the northern part of the Park.

What are their habits?
They are exclusively diurnal, being less active during the hotter parts of the day.

Tree squirrels are generally solitary, but are found in groups comprising a male, a few females and their offspring. Territory is marked by anal-gland secretions, urine and secretions deposited through mouth-wiping. A drawn-out 'chuck-chuck-chuck' call given while sitting in a prominent position is probably a territorial advertisement.

Members of the same group anal-mark each other and recognise one another by their shared odour. Social bonds between group members are maintained through mutual grooming.

Tree squirrels are predominantly arboreal but spend a considerable time foraging on the ground.

They shelter in nests lined with leaves and grass in natural holes in trees and in holes made by other species, such as woodpeckers.

Predators are mobbed with loud clicking calls and tail flicking. When threatened, tree squirrels flee to their nest directly or via other trees, or they hide in dense foliage or lie along the top of a branch. They climb around the trunks of trees keeping the trunk between them and danger.

What sounds do they make?

Contact calls include a long 'chuck-chuck-chuck', rattles and croaks. Alarm calls include loud clicks for ground predators and rattles and high-pitched whistles for avian predators.

Do they hibernate?

No, they are active throughout the year, but will store seeds, nuts and kernels, like other squirrels.

What are their breeding habits?

They breed at any time of the year, but births peak during the summer rainy season. After a gestation period of 53 to 57 days, usually two cubs, with a mass of about 10 g each, are born in grass- and leaf-lined nests in tree hollows. They are born blind, their eyes opening at about 10 days. Cubs leave the nest at about three weeks, remaining on branches near the nest entrance until they are about five weeks old. They are weaned at about five weeks and are sexually mature at 10 months.

What is the average life expectancy?

The potential life span is about 10 years.

What are their major enemies?

Enemies include all predators their size or larger, such as genets, as well as predatory birds and snakes.

REPTILES

SNAKES

Why are so few snakes seen in the Park?

Most snakes are elusive and tend to keep away from human activities. They also dislike traffic and vehicles. Unlike farms, where cultivated crops attract large numbers of rodents that in turn support the snakes, the Park accommodates a greater diversity of habitats and consequently a more evenly spread snake population. Furthermore, the natural enemies of snakes, such as hawks, eagles, mongooses and other predators, abound in the Park.

What is the most dangerous snake in the Park?

The Park harbours Africa's most feared snake, the black mamba (*Dendroaspis polylepis*). Its potent neurotoxic venom and the large amount it is capable of injecting makes it a very dangerous snake. There are, however, a number of other dangerous snakes in the Park.

What are the chances of being bitten by a snake in the Park?

The chances are remote. If you are reasonably careful and treat them with respect, there is no reason why you should fear a snakebite.

Do snakes come into rest camps?

Because of the high level of human activity, snakes very seldom enter rest camps. However, as a precaution one should not venture out at night without footwear and a good flashlight. Stumbling over an obstacle in the dark could be more dangerous than merely encountering a snake in the camp.

How does one know if a snake is dangerous?

The layman should treat all snakes as potentially dangerous. Snakes that rear and spread a hood, hiss or adopt a flattened defensive attitude prior to striking should be given a wide berth.

Where on the body do most snakebites occur?

Studies have indicated that 67% of bites are below the ankle, 20% below the knee and 8% on the hand or wrist. This indicates that the majority of bites are from low-striking snakes such as the adder species.

How many snake species are there in the Park?

Fifty-one species have been recorded, of which only a few are dangerous. The southern African subcontinent harbours about 156 different species, of which 83 are technically venomous. Only 14 are regarded as dangerously venomous. No more than a dozen of the snake species in the Park can be regarded as dangerous.

Is it true that a snake can suck milk from a cow?

No. Snakes are physically unable to suck.

Do snakes have well-developed senses?

Their sense of sight is acute at short range but poor at long distances. They cannot hear airborne sounds due to the absence of external ear holes but are very sensitive to vibrations. Their sense of smell is well developed. The snake pushes its tongue out through a groove in the front of the mouth and flicks it, picking up particles in the air. As the tongue is withdrawn into the mouth, it passes over the Jacobson's organ in the roof of the mouth. This organ analyses the air particles and informs the brain.

Where are the venom glands located?
Snake venom is produced and stored in modified salivary glands that are situated roughly on either side of the head, behind the eyes. The venom not only assists the snake in killing its prey, but also aids with digestion. The majority of snakes cannot chew their food but swallow it whole, relying on the saliva and venom to aid in the digestive processes. Egg-eaters crush eggs in their neck region, swallow the contents and then regurgitate the crushed shell.

Can a snake die from its own venom?
Snakes generally exhibit a very high resistance to their own venom and, to a certain degree, to that of other snakes.

Can a snake hypnotise its prey?
Not in the way we understand hypnotism, but it appears that a snake's intended victim is sometimes paralysed with fear.

Do snakes have vocal cords?
No. The hissing sound they make is produced by the expulsion of air through the throat.

When are snakes most active?
Warm, humid weather, especially during summer, is ideal for snakes to move around. Cool weather tends to inhibit their activities.

How often do they kill prey?
Active hunters like the sand snakes (*Psammophis* spp.) may feed several times a month. Even mambas may eat more than once a week in summer, depending on the size of the prey.

Are Secretarybirds and other enemies of snakes immune to snake venom?
It is said that Secretarybirds, mongooses and jackals apparently have some resistance to snake venom, but they are not completely immune to snakebite.

Birds of prey attacking snakes usually deal out blows with their wings to stun the snake, before finishing it off with their talons. It is difficult for the snake to get hold of the feathers on the flailing wings and, unless the venom is injected into the shafts of primary feathers, there is not much chance of inflicting damage on the bird.

Do snakes move around in pairs?
Snakes are solitary animals and are found in pairs only during the courting and mating season.

Do snakes shed their teeth?
Fangs are continually being shed and replaced. The shedding and replacing are synchronised in such a manner that a snake is never without functional fangs. Even if it loses its fangs for some abnormal reason, they are quickly replaced.

PUFF ADDER   *Bitis arietans* (Merrem 1820)

Do puff adders often bite humans?
Puff adders are responsible for more bites than all other snakes combined in the whole of Africa. It is now known that bites that were attributed to puff adders in the past were bites from the Mozambique spitting cobra (*Naja mossambica).*

Why are so many people bitten by puff adders?
The puff adder is a slow-moving, sluggish snake and reluctant to move away from its basking place, which quite often happens to be a footpath. They rely on their cryptic coloration as camouflage and therefore do

not move out of people's way. As a result, people often step on or very close to the puff adder, and are bitten before they are even aware of the snake's presence.

Is the puff adder diurnal or nocturnal?
Like most adder species, it is more active during the night than the day.

Is the puff adder widely distributed?
It is the most widely distributed snake species in the whole of Africa, occurring in most environments except the Sahara and rainforest areas. It is very common and widespread in the Park, with its range of distribution covering the entire area.

What are the physical features of the puff adder?
It is a very thickset snake, on average about 90 cm in length, although specimens of up to 1.2 m have been reported. A 90-cm specimen may have a body circumference of more than 20 cm or a diameter of 7 cm or more. The body colour is yellowish or light brown to olive brown, with roughly regular, backward-pointing chevron-shaped dark brown to black bars or bands over the back and the tail. The body could also be dark brown to black, with yellow to orange markings. The tail is much longer in males than in females.

What is the origin of the name?
When disturbed, it inflates itself with air, which is let out in loud hisses or puffs as a warning that it is ready to strike.

Can puff adders strike backwards?
It is commonly believed that they can strike backwards, but this is not true. Although generally very sluggish, they strike very quickly, either forwards or sideways. They can very quickly turn around and strike in the opposite direction.

Where are the fangs situated?
The long, curved, hollow fangs are hinged and situated in the front of the upper jaw.

Do they hold onto their prey after biting?
Unlike the back-fanged snakes and some of the elapids, puff adders seldom hold on after biting.

What is the nature of their venom?
The venom is predominantly cytotoxic, which leads to tissue destruction around the site of the bite, with localised bleeding and sometimes severe swelling.

Is the venom fast acting?
The venom is usually fairly slow acting and a life-endangering effect, such as

pronounced shock, is usually not observed until 12 hours or longer after the bite. It is therefore imperative to get medical treatment as soon as possible to minimise complications such as the loss of a limb or serious infection.

Although not common, cases have been reported of death resulting between 30 minutes and two hours after being bitten. This depends on the site of the bite.

How much venom is needed to kill a healthy adult person?

Probably as little as four drops, but the size and fitness of the victim is also very important. The bigger the person and the fitter they are, the more venom will be needed to result in a fatality. Here, too, it also depends on the site of the bite.

How much venom is discharged?

A large puff adder could possibly discharge as much as 15 drops at a time. The amount injected would vary according to the state of excitement of the snake.

Between 100 and 350 mg of venom could be injected, and as little as 100 mg is considered enough to be fatal to humans. The majority of snakes, with the exception of those like the boomslang (*Dispholidus typus*) that have primitive venom glands, have good control over the amount of venom injected. So-called 'dry bites', where no venom is injected, are quite common, especially among snake handlers.

How potent is puff adder venom?

The venom of the puff adder is very potent. The Gaboon adder (*Bitis gabonica gabonica*) also has very potent venom but, because of its size, the Gaboon adder injects a lot more venom: between 450 and 650 mg at a time, of which 100 mg is fatal to humans.

Will a puff adder deliberately attack humans?

It will attack only when disturbed or when under pressure.

What are their breeding habits?

Puff adders are oviparous, which means that the eggs develop completely within the body of the female. When laid they contain the fully developed young, which wriggle free of the egg capsule within minutes. Newborn young measure between 15 and 20 cm. An average of 20 to 40 are produced at a time, usually in late summer or early autumn.

It is said that young puff adders eat their way out of their mother's body. Is this true?

On occasion some of the young may hatch inside the mother and are born alive, but they never eat their way out.

Are newly born puff adders venomous?

Young puff adders are active almost immediately after hatching and certainly venomous.

What are their major enemies?

Man is their major enemy, but they also fall prey to Secretarybirds, eagles and other birds of prey, mongooses and small carnivores.

Which other adder species are found in the Park?

The horned adder (*Bitis caudalis*), the snouted night adder (*Causus defilippii*) and the common night adder (*Causus rhombeatus*) have been recorded in the Kruger Park.

Do the different adder species differ a lot from each other?

They differ in size and colouring. Night adders (*Causus* spp.) do not have characteristic adder features – triangular heads, thin necks and stout bodies.

The smaller adders, including the horned adders, have very mild venom compared with that of the puff adder. The venom of the night adders is also not considered lethal.

BOOMSLANG

Dispholidus typus (A. Smith 1829)

What is their distribution?

Boomslang are widely distributed throughout Africa south of the Sahara and well represented throughout the Park.

What type of habitat do they prefer?

As they are arboreal, they tend to confine themselves to wooded areas.

What do they eat?

Their favourite diet seems to be chameleons and tree-living lizards, although small birds, mice and frogs are also taken.

What are their main physical features?

Because of its different colour phases the boomslang is often confused with either the black or green mamba, or even some harmless green snakes. It is important to note that there are no green mambas in the Kruger Park.

The boomslang can vary in colour from light brown to dark brown in one phase to green in another. Most adult males are green and adult females brown in colour. Body lengths of up to 1.85 m have been recorded, but the average length is between 1.35 and 1.5 m.

Is their venom very potent?

Their venom is highly toxic, containing predominantly haemotoxic, or blood-destroying, elements. Boomslang venom is very slow acting, allowing sufficient time to treat victims. There are very few deaths nowadays.

What are the effects of the venom?

Severe headache and drowsiness, confusion, nausea and vomiting are the first symptoms. This is followed by bleeding from the nose and mouth, subcutaneous bleeding and finally internal haemorrhaging, which will be fatal if not treated promptly. Further complications include necrosis of the liver and kidneys.

Do many people die after being bitten by a boomslang?

Very few, and there are very good reasons for this. The boomslang is not an aggressive snake. When cornered, it will inflate its neck but attack only as a last resort. The boomslang is capable of biting onto the arm or leg of a human. It is important to note that they very seldom bite unless physically handled. The venom, in serious bites, could take several days to kill a human if it is not treated.

Is boomslang antivenom available?

It is obtainable on request from the antivenom unit at the National Health Laboratory Service (NHLS) in Johannesburg. However, it is very seldom needed.

What are the boomslang's breeding habits?

Mating takes place in trees, after which 10 to 15 eggs are deposited in holes in tree trunks, and even in the ground where suitable conditions of moisture and warmth exist. The eggs hatch after four months, usually in late spring or early summer. The newly hatched young average about 33 cm in length.

What are the boomslang's major enemies?

Their main enemies are birds of prey.

SOUTHERN VINE SNAKE

Thelotornis capensis
(A. Smith 1849)

What is their distribution?

The subspecies *T.c. capensis* is confined to northern KwaZulu-Natal, northern Limpopo and the eastern Lowveld regions of Limpopo and Mpumalanga.

In the Park it is apparently absent from open grassland regions such as the Tsendze and Babalala flats, but otherwise it is widely distributed throughout the Park.

What habitat does it prefer?

It is very well adapted to an arboreal way of life and is therefore mostly found in trees or shrubs, usually close to the ground where it can move about with astonishing speed.

What does it eat?

It feeds mainly on reptiles and frogs and, to a lesser degree, birds and their eggs.

What are its main physical features?

The southern vine snake has cryptic coloration consisting of a mixture of green, grey, brown and even pink, providing excellent camouflage. It is a slender snake, with a body length of about 1.2 m. The pupil of the eye is horizontally oval, but dumbbell shaped in strong light. The tongue is a conspicuous orange with a black tip.

When the snake is at rest, the anterior third of its body is often projected into the air and held motionless for long periods. It can also inflate its throat like the boomslang.

Is the venom potent?

The snake's venom is similar to that of the boomslang, and therefore very potent.

Is the vine snake aggressive?

It is docile and will seldom attempt to bite humans, but when molested it will strike out and will even follow up unsuccessful strikes. Like the boomslang, it has a small mouth with the fangs situated far back. Very few human fatalities have been recorded.

How does it catch its prey?

More often than not the southern vine snake remains motionless on low branches, less than 1.5 m from the ground, looking for potential prey on the ground. When it spots something, the snake rapidly moves to the ground to catch the prey.

What are its breeding habits?

Between six and 10 eggs are laid in mid-summer. The newly hatched young are about 24 cm long.

SNOUTED COBRA

Naja annulifera (Peters 1854)

What is the distribution in the Park?

Snouted cobras are widely distributed throughout the Park.

What type of habitat does the snouted cobra prefer?

It is a terrestrial and savanna species found in drier regions.

What does it eat?

It feeds mainly on birds, eggs, frogs, other snakes and small mammals. These snakes hunt mainly at night.

What are their main physical features?

The snouted cobra, previously known as the Egyptian cobra, is the largest of

the cobra species in the Park, attaining average lengths of 1.2 to 1.8 m, with a maximum recorded length of 2.24 m. The body colour varies from yellowish or greyish-brown to very dark brown, with broad black bands encircling the body. Contrary to the usual situation among snakes, the males appear to grow to a greater length than females.

When disturbed it can rear up some 45 to 60 cm and at the same time spread a broad hood, which can be more than 12 cm across. It is a very fast-moving snake.

Does the snouted cobra spit like the spitting cobra?
No.

Are snouted cobras very aggressive?
They are very docile, but will strike out when cornered.

Is their venom very potent?
The venom, which contains very powerful neurotoxins, is very potent indeed. The bite of an adult specimen takes rapid effect and can be fatal if not treated promptly.

Are they nocturnal?
They are nocturnal but are often seen during the day.

What are their enemies?
Their main enemies are birds of prey, mongooses and small predators.

MOZAMBIQUE SPITTING COBRA
Naja mossambica (Peters 1854)

What is its distribution?
The Mozambique spitting cobra is probably the most common cobra of the savanna regions of Africa and occurs throughout the Park.

What type of habitat does the Mozambique spitting cobra prefer?
It is usually found near water and likes to shelter in hollow tree stumps or in old termitaria.

What do spitting cobras eat?

They take a wide variety of food including birds, eggs, small mammals, rodents, frogs and reptiles, including other snakes. The wide range of food may explain this snake's abundance and extensive distribution.

What are the main physical features?

The top of the body is olive-brown to dark brown, while the under surface is pinkish-brown with a few irregular and conspicuous black bands or blotches across the throat. The snake usually attains a length of about 1 m, but specimens of more than 1.5 m have been recorded.

How far and how accurately can they 'spit'?

This nervous and highly strung snake is not the only snake that can 'spit' venom. Other 'spitting' snakes include the rinkhals (*Hemachatus haemachatus*) and other cobras such as *Naja nigricincta nigricincta*, *Naja nigricincta woodi* and *Naja nigricollis*. This species is far more active, though; it is also faster moving than the last mentioned. It usually rears up before spitting, but can also spit very accurately from ground level without raising its head. Two different streams of venom are ejected from recurved canals opening at right angles to the surface of the fangs near the tips. The venom is directed as a spray and can reach the target over a distance of 2 to 3 m.

Can they spit more than once in quick succession?

They can spit several times in quick succession. The poison glands appear to replenish the venom rapidly for further use.

Can a victim be blinded by the venom?

Permanent blindness as a result of venom entering the eyes has not been recorded in more than 30 years. If venom enters the eye, the effect is instantaneous and it can be very painful if not washed out with copious amounts of water and the eye treated immediately. The victim should refrain from rubbing the eyes, as this will increase the possibility of the poison entering the system.

How potent is the venom?

It consists of very potent neurotoxins and cytotoxins and can be fatal if not treated. The bite may cause severe local tissue destruction.

Are spitting cobras very aggressive?

These are very dangerous snakes; although they will not attack unless provoked, they will attack without hesitation when cornered. They can rear up more than a third of their length, spreading the hood at the same time.

Are they nocturnal?

They are nocturnal to a great extent but are often seen during the day. They like to bask in the sun.

What are their major enemies?

Birds of prey and lesser predators.

BLACK MAMBA   *Dendroaspis polylepis* (Günther 1864)

What is their distribution?
In South Africa this snake occurs in KwaZulu-Natal and the Lowveld and bushveld of Limpopo and Mpumalanga, including the whole of the Kruger National Park.

What type of habitat does the black mamba prefer?
Unlike the arboreal green mamba (*Dendroaspis angusticeps*), which is absent from the Kruger Park area and confined to the more densely forested coastal areas, the black mamba shows a greater preference for the low-lying, drier and more open bush country, at altitudes not exceeding 1 200 m. This snake is commonly found in old termitaria and in aardvark and other animal holes, among rocks and boulders or under old tree stumps. Although primarily a ground-living snake, it is also at home in trees or shrubs and moves gracefully and effortlessly over rough terrain.

What do these snakes eat?
Their diet consists mainly of warm-blooded prey such as birds, rodents and small mammals.

What are the black mamba's main physical features?
Despite its name, the black mamba is seldom really black. The newly hatched snake is greyish-green to greyish-olive, but with age it gradually darkens, becoming dark olive, olive brown, greyish-brown or a gunmetal colour on top. The underparts are greyish-white and frequently have irregular darker spots or blotches over the posterior half of the belly and under the tail. The inside of the mouth is black, a characteristic that distinguishes it from most other snakes and to which it owes its name. The body can reach a length of

1.8 to 2.4 m, and even as much as 3.6 m. The black mamba's length, slenderness, speed and elongated head are its main distinguishing features.

Do black mambas spread a hood?
When really angered they inflate the throat to a half hood, which is not as pronounced as that of a cobra but still clearly visible.

How swiftly can they move?
It is popularly claimed that a man cannot outrun a mamba, but this is exaggerated as their maximum speed is probably not more than about 15 km/h. They strike very fast and can reach a distance of 1.5 to 1.8 m in the striking process. When they are on the move, the head and forepart of the body are well off the ground.

Are they very dangerous?
Their size, speed of movement and ability to strike swiftly and in just about any direction, even when on the move, make black mambas extremely dangerous. These snakes are very fond of basking in the sun; when disturbed, they usually make for their lair and, if a person happens to be in their way, they will not hesitate to attack.

Are they aggressive?
Although they will not seek out a human to attack, they are extremely unpredictable and can strike suddenly and with little or no warning. Fortunately they are usually very quick to go into hiding and don't permit humans to approach closely.

Do they hold on after biting?
Mambas do not usually hold on after a bite but release immediately to be ready for another swift strike.

How potent is their venom?
Mamba venom per unit is as potent as that of the Cape cobra (*Naja nivea*), both needing about 15 to 20 mg to kill a human, but it is more potent than that of either the spitting or the snouted cobra. However, the amount injected at a single bite and the large reserve of venom, as well as the rapid onset of symptoms, make them by far the most dangerous of the African snakes and certainly one of the most dangerous snakes in the world.

What is the nature of their venom?
It is essentially neurotoxic and is rapidly absorbed, causing paralysis of the nerves controlling the cardio-respiratory functions.

Is it true that a victim can die within minutes of being bitten?
If the venom is delivered intravenously it could take about 30 minutes, but collapse and death may occur in seven to 15 hours in serious cases where the venom enters the body through muscle tissue.

Are black mambas territorial?
Mambas can wander far afield in search of food or to mate, but they often frequent the same lair for extensive periods of time.

Are their senses well developed?
Mambas have very keen eyesight and their general alertness makes it very difficult to approach these snakes unnoticed.

What are their breeding habits?
After mating, which takes place in the early spring or early summer, up to 14 eggs are laid. The newly hatched young may measure anything up to 50 cm, and are capable of killing prey and possibly humans soon after hatching.

What are their main enemies?
Birds of prey and, when small, they often fall prey to mongooses.

SOUTHERN AFRICAN PYTHON
Python natalensis (Smith 1840)

What is the distribution of the Southern African python?
The Southern African python occurs in many parts of Africa as far north as Burundi. It is found in suitable habitats throughout the Park.

What type of habitat do they prefer?
They do not venture far from water, even lying submerged in ambush for prey coming to drink, with only their eyes and nostrils exposed. They are excellent climbers, often found on overhanging branches.

What do they eat?

Pythons eat mostly dassies, hares, cane rats, other rodents, antelope up to the size of impala, the young of warthogs and bushpig, monkeys and birds.

What are their main physical features?

The body colour is variable but the base colour on the dorsal side is usually light brown to greyish-brown, with dark brown, black-edged and somewhat sinuous crossbars or transverse blotches. By far the largest snake in Africa, it attains a length of 3.6 to 4.5 m. Exceptional individuals measure up to 5.5 m or more and the mass can be as much as 60 kg.

How do they compare in size with the anaconda and the reticulated python?

There is still some controversy about the size of these large snakes, but it would appear that the Southern African python is exceeded in length and mass by both the South American giant anaconda (*Eunectes murinus*) and the reticulated python (*Python reticulatus*) of India and Asia.

Are pythons nocturnal?

Although more nocturnal than diurnal, they are very often seen during the day.

How do they kill their prey?

After gripping their prey with their teeth, they coil around the victim's body and constrict it before swallowing it. Once the coils are wrapped around the victim, the coils are tightened every time the victim exhales. They do not really suffocate their prey, but through the constriction prevent the heart from functioning properly, virtually inducing heart attacks.

Do they wet their victims by licking them before swallowing them?

This is a common belief, but false. Saliva is excreted during the swallowing process, but the movement of the tongue has no salivating function.

Can they disgorge a swallowed victim?

When a python is disturbed while swallowing its prey, it invariably disgorges the prey in order to escape more easily.

Is the python venomous?

No, but the two rows of needle-sharp teeth can cause a very painful wound.

What is their potential life span?

They have lived for more than 27 years in captivity, but their life span in the wild is uncertain.

Do they kill human beings?

Substantiated claims of attacks on humans by pythons are very rare.

Are pythons a protected species?

Pythons are protected by law. Latest surveys indicate that they are not rare and will soon be listed as 'Least Concern' by the IUCN. Pythons perform a very important function in controlling rodents.

What are their breeding habits?

Up to 50 eggs are laid. Unlike most other snakes, the female guards the eggs until they hatch.

What are their major enemies?

Honey badgers rank high on their list of natural enemies. They are sometimes killed by larger predators, including lions, leopards, hyaenas and Nile crocodiles.

LIZARDS

Are snakes and lizards the only reptiles represented in the Park?

No, the Park harbours a large variety of reptiles. In addition to the 50 snake and 50 lizard species, including two leguaan species, there are three terrapin species, two tortoise species, six amphisbaenids and the Nile crocodile represented in the Park.

Are there any venomous lizards in the Park?

There are no venomous lizards in Africa, although latest research indicates that varanids, agamids and the chameleons are in fact part of the venom clade and are technically venomous.

Which are the more extraordinary lizards?

Most of the lizard species are relatively small, but the giant plated rock lizard (*Gerrhosaurus validus validus*) is quite conspicuous. These very dark, blackish-brown lizards are heavily plated and attain a length of up to 70 cm, including the tail. Mostly confined to granitic or other boulder-strewn hills and outcrops, they are very wary and will scramble back to their rocky retreats at the slightest sign of danger.

There are four different species of *Gerrhosaurus* in the Park. A number of smaller types of lizards, many with striking coloration, are also well represented.

To what extent can the chameleon change colour?

Although it can change its colour considerably, depending on the background, it cannot change into a wide variety of colours. The normal colour is green, ranging from pale, yellowish-green to dark green. However, it can also change from a light brown or light grey to a very dark, nearly blackish-grey.

Do some lizards resemble snakes?

Legless lizards and skinks occur in the Park, and the giant legless skink (*Acontias plumbeus*), with a body length of about 55 cm, is very conspicuous. It usually emerges from its underground retreat after heavy rains. Some of the legless lizards resemble snakes to such an extent that only an expert can identify them. There are also a number of worm lizards, amphisbaenids, which live a subterranean life and look more like earthworms than lizards.

LEGUAAN   *Varanus* spp.

Are they well represented in the Park?

Two leguaan, or monitor lizard, species are represented in the Park, and are well distributed throughout the area. They are the common rock, or white-throated leguaan (*Varanus albigularis*) and the Nile monitor, or water leguaan (*Varanus niloticus*).

What type of habitat do they prefer?

Rock leguaans commonly inhabit savanna and open bush or forest country, and are often found far from water. Although

terrestrial, they are excellent climbers. Rock crevices and fissures, as well as hollow trees and holes in the ground, are used as dens.

Nile monitors or water leguaans live in or near permanent water and are never far away from water.

What size can they attain?

The water leguaan can reach lengths of up to 2.1 m, of which about two thirds comprise the tail, while rock leguaans can reach lengths of up to 1.5 m.

What do they eat?

As can be expected, the diets of the two species differ to some extent. The water leguaan feeds mainly on fish, crabs, mussels, small mammals and birds' eggs. They are also persistent robbers of crocodile and terrapin nests.

Rock leguaans are not as active, and prey mainly on small mammals, birds, eggs, other reptiles, invertebrates such as the large *Achatina* snails and insects.

What are their main physical features?

These monitors are typical lizards, with short, powerful limbs and long, muscular tails. The rock leguaan is dark greyish-brown, while the water leguaan is greenish to greyish-brown. The water leguaan has a dark reticulation with scattered yellow spots, or interrupted greenish-yellow transverse bands on the head, back and limbs. The lower surfaces of the body are yellowish, with more-or-less grey to dark grey or even black cross bands. Bands are also visible on the tail.

The tongue, which is up to 23 cm long, has sensory functions.

Can a leguaan suck milk from a cow?

There is no truth in the claim that they can suck milk from the udder of a cow.

Are they solitary?

They are usually solitary and occur in pairs only during periods of courtship and mating.

Are they nocturnal?

Both species are predominantly diurnal and they are regularly seen during the day.

Are they territorial in habit?

The water leguaan is probably more territorial than the rock leguaan, which is a great wanderer and can therefore not be considered territorial.

Do they hibernate?

There are indications that leguaans go into a state of torpor during severe winters and periods of extreme cold. Cases have been recorded of their having been dug up and eaten by honey badgers. It is evident that, if they go into a state of torpor, it is very sporadic and not a regular annual occurrence.

What are their breeding habits?

Up to 40 eggs are laid in termite mounds or in holes that the female digs up to 20 cm deep in soft soil. After covering the hole neatly, she leaves the eggs to hatch.

What are their major enemies?

Birds of prey, especially the Martial Eagle (*Polemaetus bellicosus*), prey on the leguaan and honey badger and some of the medium to larger predators also attack these reptiles.

How do they defend themselves?

When cornered, leguaans adopt a very menacing attitude by arching their necks and hissing loudly. They lash out with their powerful tails and will bite viciously at any object within reach, holding onto it for some time.

As a last resort they will feign death and will even allow themselves to be savaged, in the hope of getting away when left for dead. Not only do they have amazing recuperative powers, they are such formidable fighters that their attackers often come off second best.

Can they shed their tails like other lizards?
No, their long tails cannot be shed.

Can leguaans run well?
They are strong, fast runners, usually running in short spurts.

Are they dangerous to humans?
They will not attack humans without provocation, but when cornered will not hesitate to defend themselves. They can inflict severe injuries when biting with their razor-sharp teeth.

CROCODILE
NILE CROCODILE
Crocodylus niloticus (Laurenti 1768)

What is the distribution of the Nile crocodile?
The order Crocodylia has one family, the Crocodylidae, which includes 23 living species distributed throughout the tropical and subtropical regions of the world, including Africa, Asia, northern Australia and tropical America. The Nile crocodile occurs widely throughout Africa south of the Sahara and is well represented throughout the Park, especially in the major rivers.

What type of habitat do crocodiles prefer?
They occur near rivers, streams, lakes and dams spreading from the subtropical to the tropical zones. Moving from rivers to man-made enclosures is common.

How many crocodiles are there in the Kruger National Park?
It is almost impossible to determine an exact number, but there are several hundred.

When dams and rivers dry up, what happens to the crocodiles?
They move to more permanent water or adopt a resting phase until the next rains come.

What do they eat?
The diet of a crocodile varies according to age and size. A baby crocodile feeds on insects, snails, small crabs and frogs. At about a metre in length they will progress to include fish as the staple item in their diet, particularly catfish or barbel (*Clarias gariepinus*). Crocodiles over 2.6 m in length are considered mature, and they feed on fish, birds, terrapins, snakes, otters, antelope and even other crocodiles. Depending on where they occur, a crocodile's staple diet seems to be fish.

They are opportunistic feeders, taking live prey and sometimes carrion.

Is it true that crocodiles do not kill waterbuck?
No, crocodiles will kill waterbuck should the opportunity arise.

Are crocodiles cannibalistic?
Yes.

What is the biggest animal a Nile Crocodile can kill?
Animals as large as giraffes, African buffalo bulls and male lions have fallen prey to very large crocodiles, but these

cases are rare. Their mammalian prey usually consists of average-sized antelope.

How often does an average-sized crocodile kill?

In hot weather a large crocodile of about 4 m can make do with a full meal every two to three weeks. Crocodiles of about 1.5 m need a full meal every week, while baby crocodiles need to eat every day. Crocodiles are ectotherms and they need very little energy to maintain their metabolism and body temperature and, as they are fairly inactive, they do not need much food either. During cold or rainy weather they will eat less food than usual.

Do crocodiles show a predilection for domestic dogs?

It is easy for a Nile crocodile to catch a dog, as dogs have, through many years of domestication, lost much of the natural instinct that helps other animals to survive.

There is no evidence that crocodiles have any special preference for dog meat.

Do crocodiles store their food for some time before eating it?

The prey is drowned and usually consumed immediately. Crocodiles never store food, and half-eaten carcasses that are sometimes found under river banks are usually the leftovers from a crocodile meal. These remains may be eaten by other crocodiles.

Do crocodiles feed in a specific manner?

The more than 60 teeth, which are designed for gripping and not for chewing, interlock when the jaws close, exposing the fourth mandibular tooth. As crocodiles cannot chew their food, they swallow it whole. In the case of large prey, a crocodile flicks it back and forth with sideways movements or grips a portion of flesh and spins on its long axis to tear off a chunk small enough to be swallowed whole.

Do they stash food and eat carrion?

There is a belief that crocodiles will deliberately leave a carcass to decay before consuming it. This is not true. They do not stash food as is often believed. Crocodiles prefer fresh meat and will eat carrion only if nothing else is available. By feeding on carrion, crocodiles ensure that rotten material is removed from an aquatic environment.

Can food be swallowed underwater?

No. When catching a fish, or drowning its prey, a crocodile can open its mouth underwater to catch the fish without drowning. This is because the nostrils close and the valve at the back of the mouth, the gular flap, closes, preventing water from entering the lungs or alimentary canal. A crocodile therefore has to come to the surface for the gular flap to open, which permits the crocodile to swallow. Fish are swallowed headfirst.

How do crocodiles kill their prey?

Mammalian prey are usually seized by the muzzle or any part of the body, pulled into and under the water and drowned. It has long been believed that the tail was used to bowl the prey over, but this has now been proven not to be true. Prey may also be captured on dry land.

When do crocodiles kill their prey?

They kill at any time when the opportunity presents itself, but they are more active at dusk and during the night.

Do they have stronger digestive juices than other predators?

Yes. As crocodiles cannot chew, they have strong digestive juices that soon dissolve the food, even the bones and hooves. Horns and hair are passed in the faeces.

Do crocodiles attack hippos?

Hippo calves are occasionally killed. A fully grown hippo is more than a match for a crocodile but old, injured or weak individuals have been killed by very large crocodiles.

How big can a crocodile grow?
In nature a large crocodile will probably be about 5.5 m in length and attain a mass of up to 1 000 kg. The tail makes up about 40% of the total length of the crocodile's body. A crocodile of this length and mass could be anything between 50 and 100 years old.

When is a crocodile mature?
A Nile crocodile grows throughout its lifetime, but the growth curve flattens out in later life. Sexual maturity is reached at 12 to 15 years, when the crocodile is about 2.6 to 3 m in length, with a mass of 80 to 160 kg.

How many toes do they have?
They have five toes on the forefeet and four on the hind feet. The toes on the hind feet are partially webbed.

What is the Nile crocodile's body temperature?
Like other ectothermic animals, its body temperature varies with the ambient temperature. The maximum body temperature in summer could be over 40°C and on a very cold winter's day the temperature could be as low as 5°C. The crocodile then goes into a state of torpor until the temperatures rise.

What is the potential life span of a crocodile?
They live for a very long time, probably up to 100 years or more, but the exact life span has not yet been determined.

Why does a crocodile lie with its mouth open?
The crocodile does this to regulate the body temperature and it can either cool down or warm up the body, but it is probably a relaxed way to lie.

Do crocodiles have tongues?
Yes. The entire length of the broad, flat tongue is fixed to the bottom of the buccal cavity, giving the impression that the crocodile has no tongue.

What function does the tongue serve?
The tongue plays an important part in swallowing food.

Is the blood circulation the same as in other reptiles?
Instead of the three-chambered heart of other reptiles, a crocodile has a four-chambered heart and therefore a more efficient circulatory system.

Are crocodiles intelligent animals?
Crocodiles have the best-developed brain of all reptiles, even though it is only the size of a man's thumb. Although they lack brain size, crocodiles have very keenly developed senses and strong instincts. They can see, hear and smell well and their hunting, maternal and survival instincts are exceptionally good. Experiments in captivity have also shown that crocodiles are quick to adapt to new conditions and to develop new 'skills' to make the best of their environment, so we can indeed credit them with a fair amount of 'intelligence'.

Are crocodiles well adapted to survive?
They are well adapted and have survived in their present form for more than 60 million years. Proof of their adaptability is their inexhaustible patience when hunting, and the ability to move in water with a high degree of concealment, the eyes and nostrils placed in such a position that they can still breathe and see while practically submerged.

It is said that crocodiles have stones in their stomachs. What is the purpose of these stones?
The stones sometimes found in the stomachs of crocodiles play no part whatsoever in

digestion or balance. Stones are sometimes accidentally swallowed when crocodiles eat their prey. In areas without stones, crocodiles do not have stones in their stomachs.

What is their general body colour?
The colour varies from yellow, with black irregular markings on the back and sides, to dark grey with black markings. The underparts are cream-coloured.

What is the colour of their eyes?
The eyes are yellow-green with a vertical pupil, resembling cats' eyes in the daytime.

Are their senses well developed?
Their senses of smell, hearing and sight are well developed.

What is the difference between a crocodile and an alligator?
The most obvious difference is the head. The alligator's snout is broad and rounded, while that of the crocodile is pointed. The crocodile's teeth are very prominent, whereas those of the alligator are smaller and less visible. The fourth tooth on either side of the lower jaw of crocodiles protrudes prominently, whereas alligator teeth on the lower jaw fit into the upper jaw.

Do crocodiles shed their teeth?
The teeth are constantly shed. Young crocodiles shed their teeth every few months, but older crocodiles probably shed them every year or so. The more than 60 teeth are not all shed at once, but in stages, to leave the crocodile with functional teeth at all times.

Can they smell under water?
No, the nostrils are kept closed under water to prevent them from drowning.

How long can a crocodile stay submerged?
The time they can remain submerged depends on the temperature of the water and how active they are. In warm water, during summer, at crocodile farms, they have been recorded as remaining submerged for almost an hour. In cold water their heart beat is much slower and their metabolism low, requiring very little oxygen, which means that they can stay submerged for longer periods, apparently for up to an hour. In the wild it is difficult to determine the time they are submerged, as they may move away from the observer's position.

Can crocodiles see underwater?
Yes, they can see underwater in order to catch fish. The eyes are protected by well-developed eyelids and behind them lie the ears, seen as two slits that flap closed when underwater.

Are crocodiles gregarious?
Crocodiles are gregarious and they like being in groups where they have a very definite form of communication with each other. Large aggregations of crocodiles are found where there is a good supply of food. If there is not enough food, the big groups break up into smaller units, or the crocodiles may even become solitary to ensure survival. The current author counted 99 crocodiles on a 0.5-km stretch of sandbanks in the Luvuvhu River in the late 1980s.

Are crocodiles territorial?
Males usually have a small territory in which they live and feed, while females are migratory, moving to the males for mating and then on to their traditional breeding areas for nesting.

Do crocodiles hibernate?
In tropical areas such as central Africa, crocodiles do not hibernate. During severe droughts crocodiles bury themselves in sandbanks or river beds to shield themselves from dehydration and high temperatures. While buried, they live on

body fat and are capable in doing so for many months until the rains come again. True hibernation does not occur.

Do crocodiles move about?
Females move to the males for mating and then back to the nesting areas. Males usually stay in one place. When rivers and dams dry up, crocodiles will move to the next available water source.

Can they move overland?
Crocodiles have been known to travel several kilometres overland to new habitats. Some of the Park's man-made dams are occupied by crocodiles that have moved overland.

Are they diurnal?
Although they are seen basking in the sun during the day, they are more active at night.

Do crocodiles make any sound?
They utter a kind of roar during mating and fighting.

Do crocodiles prefer quiet water?
They do not like rough water or swiftly flowing streams that force them to lift their heads high to breathe. During floods they move to the shore.

Can crocodiles run fast?
No one has timed a running crocodile accurately, but they are deceptively fast for their long bodies and short limbs. They can only run a short distance at a time, however.

How do they swim?
They use the tail to propel themselves in water and also for directional changes. The feet are used for stopping and floating.

Where do crocodiles mate?
Mating takes place in shallow water.

How do they mate?
With the female suspended in a horizontal position in the water, the male approaches her from behind, holding onto her body with his feet while bending his pelvic area underneath hers, to accomplish fertilisation.

Do crocodiles mate any time of the year?
The crocodile's reproductive cycle starts in May, when the males develop a dominance hierarchy and an elaborate courtship ensues. A physical, but non-sexual, contact now stimulates the development of the eggs. During July and August mating, which is always initiated by the female, takes place in the water.

The eggs are laid in suitable soil with good drainage and a sunny position above the flood level of the river, in October to December. The female will usually use the same nest site for the rest of her life.

How many eggs are laid?
The size of the clutch can be up to 80 hard-shelled eggs, of 80 to 120 g each.

Where are the eggs laid?
Usually at night, the female digs a boot-shaped hole 30 to 40 cm deep in the sand with her hind legs, well above the flood line of the river. Having dug the hole, she forms a chute with her hind legs and deposits the eggs in two layers. She then covers the nest with about 12 cm of sand and presses it down with her hind legs.

Does the female guard the nest?
During the incubation period the female protects the nest, especially at night, and she will remain in the immediate vicinity. Despite the female's attention, the nest is often robbed by water leguaans, otters, water mongooses, hyaenas, baboons and even Marabou Stork.

How long is the incubation period?
Crocodile eggs are incubated by the heat of the sun on the sand of the nest and can take about 90 days to hatch.

It is said that the temperature in the nest determines the sex of the unborn hatchling. Is this true?

The sex of the hatchlings is indeed dependent on the temperature incubating the eggs in the nest hole. Female crocodiles develop at temperatures of 26 to 30°C and form the bottom layer of the eggs in the nest. Males develop from the upper layer of eggs, at a higher temperature of 31 to 34°C.

How do the baby crocodiles get out of the nest after hatching?

When the young crocodiles are about to hatch, they utter a high-pitched cheeping noise while still in the egg, which can be heard up to 20 m away. This is a sign for the mother to dig them out with her forelegs. At this stage some of the hatchlings have already come out of the eggs by piercing or slashing the eggshell with the 'egg tooth', a small hard projection on the tip of the snout. This projection, called a caruncle, is shed after a few weeks.

The mother now picks up the hatchlings and the unhatched eggs in her mouth and carries them to the water, where they are washed and released. She gently breaks the unhatched eggs between her jaws to release the young crocodiles that have not yet hatched.

The hatchlings stay together in a 'crèche' area for six to eight weeks.

How big is a newly hatched crocodile?

They are 25 to 30 cm long and have a mass of 80 to 100 g.

What happens to the baby crocodiles when they reach the water?

The hatchlings stay with their mother for about two weeks while they become stronger. She usually chooses a small stream or shallow pool surrounded by dense vegetation as a first home, for both safety and food supply. Here she protects them against enemies such as other crocodiles, storks and herons, and they live on insects, frogs, dragonfly larvae and small fish.

What are the crocodile's major enemies?

After they have reached a length of 1.5 m crocodiles have almost no enemies. Hippos and elephants are capable of killing large crocodiles but this is an extremely rare occurrence. Baby crocodiles, however, have many enemies, including other crocodiles,

leguaans, eagles, herons, storks, ground hornbills, water mongoose, genets, otters, tiger fish, catfish, terrapins and owls. Eggs are eaten by leguaans, mongooses, otters, hyaenas, baboons, warthogs and bushpigs.

Probably no more than one crocodile out of a nest of 50 eggs will eventually reach maturity.

Do crocodiles kill many people?

Crocodiles are extremely dangerous and crafty reptiles and many people are killed every year by them when they go into, or even too close to rivers, dams and pools where crocodiles are present.

Have any humans been killed by crocodiles in the Park?

Yes, but fortunately only a few. These unfortunate victims, none of them visitors, were mostly Park employees who met their fate through negligence. During the civil war in Mozambique, some so-called refugees, entering the Park via the rivers flowing through the Park to Mozambique, were killed by crocodiles, but the number will never be known.

Are crocodiles of any benefit to man?

Crocodiles are an integral, and important, link in the web of interrelated species comprising natural ecosystems. Their main diet consists of catfish. In rivers where crocodiles have been exterminated, catfish numbers increase so dramatically that they overutilise their food source, most of the smaller indigenous fish species, such as kurper, and in the process create an unbalanced food chain. This in turn affects many species of fish-eating birds by adversely influencing their food source.

This shift in the ecology may result in an increase in other organisms, such as mosquitoes and black flies, thus increasing health hazards such as malaria.

As well as maintaining a natural balance, crocodiles play a very important part in clearing the waterways of carcass pollution. They are often seen feeding on dead hippos or other dead animals in the water.

By laying numerous eggs every year, of which only a few ever survive to maturity, crocodiles are a very important source of food to a number of predators that live off their eggs or young ones.

Do birds really clean crocodiles' teeth?

No. A crocodile emerging from the water onto a sandbank often has blood-sucking leeches attached to its body, and birds sometimes peck these leeches from the crocodile's body and head. This has probably led to the belief that birds clean the crocodile's teeth.

Since about 2005, many crocodiles have died in the Lepelle River in the Park. What is the reason?

The reason for the deaths was a condition called *Pansteatitis*. In this condition the fat in the body of the crocodile, especially the tail, hardens to a yellow, rubber-like consistency, which makes it painful and almost impossible for the crocodile to move about in the water. As a result the crocodile is not able to catch fish or prey. It also cannot utilise the stored fat. Eventually this leads to starvation and death.

LARGER BIRDS

The birds discussed are ones
that are often seen and attract
the most attention and interest.

SECRETARYBIRD *Sagittarius serpentarius* (Miller 1779)

How widely is the Secretarybird distributed?

It occurs widely, but is sparsely distributed throughout Africa south of the Sahara, except for forested areas. It is distributed throughout South Africa and can be seen all over the Park.

What is its preferred habitat?

In the Park it can be seen in the grassland, savanna and open woodland areas.

Does this bird belong to the eagle family?

The Secretarybird is generally regarded as the world's only terrestrial eagle, because it is more at home on the ground than in the air or in trees. It has the hooked bill that is characteristic of eagles, and its display flight and breeding behaviour are also similar to those of eagles.

Are Secretarybirds solitary?

Secretarybirds are almost always seen in pairs and occupy and defend territories that can be up to 50 km². The focal point of the territories is the nesting or roosting tree to which the birds return in the evening. A solitary bird is usually a male foraging for food while the female is on the nest.

What are their habits?

They walk across the veld in measured strides of about 100 paces a minute at about 3 km/h. They are mostly seen on the ground walking with their long, steady stride, nodding the head to and fro.

Secretarybirds seldom fly, but they fly well and undertake daily territorial flights during which they may soar to great heights. They usually take off with a run, and on landing run for several paces with open wings.

How can one recognise this bird?

An unmistakable bird, the Secretarybird is long-legged, standing about 1.3 m tall, with a long tail, a wingspan of about 1.4 m and a mass of around 4.2 kg. It has a long tail with grey-and-black feathers and a conspicuous drooping crest of black feathers at the nape.

The body is mainly grey, with black belly, tibial feathers, rump, remiges and sub-terminal tail bands. The bare facial skin of the adults is deep orange, and yellow in juveniles.

Where do they build their nest?

They build a nest of about 2 m in diameter out of sticks and line it with grass. The nest is built in the crest of a flat-crowned tree, especially *Acacia* species, about 4 to 6 m above the ground.

Does the Secretarybird use the same nest year after year?

Nests are seldom reused; this may be due to their habit of building the nest in the top

of a tree, where branches are likely to grow through and up around the nest, eventually making it less accessible to the birds.

When is the breeding season?
Unlike most birds of prey, Secretarybirds do not breed at a regular time of the year, although there seems to be a peak from August to December when there is an abundance of food.

Depending on the availability of food, these birds will sometimes vacate their long-occupied territory for many months.

What are their breeding habits?
Usually two eggs are laid up to eight days apart. They are mainly or entirely incubated by the female, who is fed by the male during this period, and hatch after 42 to 46 days. The chick/s fledge after about 75 to 85 days.

What does their diet consist of and how do they hunt?
Although renowned as snake-catchers, they feed far less on snakes than on insects and other prey. Among the most important components of their diet are lizards, rodents, young hares, young birds and eggs, and insects, especially grasshoppers; in fact any food item they can catch and overpower.

Agile prey animals, including snakes, are dealt with and stunned or killed with a flurry of very swift kicks or warded off with swipes of the wings. They sometimes stamp grass tufts to flush out prey, which is then killed by stamping or kicking.

The bird's large gape allows it to swallow prey whole, but, if it is too large for this, it is torn up into manageable portions with the bill, while held by the feet.

How did this bird get its interesting name?
The name Secretarybird is widely thought to be derived from the crest's resemblance to quill pens behind the ears of a secretary, but it actually seems to be a corruption of the Arabic *saqr-et-tair*, which means hunter-bird.

MARTIAL EAGLE *Polemaetus bellicosus* (Daudin 1800)

How widely is the Martial Eagle species distributed?

The Martial Eagle is widely distributed throughout southern Africa, but is declining in numbers, especially in the more developed parts of the subcontinent. It is one of the more common large raptors in the Park and is seen throughout the area.

Is it true that the Martial Eagle is the largest eagle species in Africa?

It is true. It is Africa's largest and one of its most powerful eagles.

How large is this eagle?

It is interesting to note that the female is larger and heavier than the male. The wingspan of the female can reach up to 2.6 m and she can have a mass of more than 6 kg. The male has a wingspan of less than 2 m and a mass of about 5.1 kg.

Why is the female larger than the male?

The probable reason is that the female is the protector of the nest and the chick, while the smaller male is more streamlined and acrobatic, and better suited to hunting to provide food for the female on the nest. He brings the food to the nest but the female does the actual feeding of the chick.

Where can one look for a nest of this bird?

These eagles build a nest in the shape of a large basin, about 2 m in diameter, with thick sticks in the fork of a large tree. Nests are usually 10 to 20 m above ground and found in their typical habitat of woodland, savanna or grassland with clumps of large trees.

Do they build a new nest every breeding season?

No, nests seem to be used for many successive breeding seasons.

When is the breeding season?

They breed from February to August, but mainly between April and June.

Do they breed every year?

Records show that they usually breed twice every three years.

How many eggs are laid?

Usually one but sometimes two eggs are laid.

What is the incubation time of the eggs?

The female primarily does the incubation, which takes about 48 to 50 days.

When does the chick reach fledgling status?

The chick fledges about 109 days after hatching but is cared for by the parents for up to eight months after its first flight.

What are the main distinguishing features of this eagle?

This large bird has a distinctive broad, dark brown head, crop area and upper parts. The underparts are white with dark brown spots, and the legs are long. The eyes are yellow, and the cere and feet are greenish-grey.

When seen in flight it is dark brown under the wing, with faint bars.

Immature birds have an overall white appearance with grey upper parts and white underparts.

Martial Eagles appear to have a crest when the wind ruffles the feathers.

How does it hunt?

The Martial Eagle soars to amazing heights, sometimes so high that it is not visible with the naked eye. Its power of vision is phenomenal. This powerful and rapacious eagle does most of its hunting from the air, soaring to great heights until prey is sighted, then diving down and catching it with the talons.

What is their preferred prey?
They seem to have a wide variety of prey preferences, with different prey species in different localities. Among birds, guineafowl, spurfowl and francolins are taken, as well as Common Ostrich chicks. In the Park there seems to be a preference for monitor lizards (leguaans) and among

mammalian species hares, squirrels, mongooses and even small antelope such as duikers and baby impalas are favoured.

What are its habits?
It is a shy bird, avoiding humans. When seen alone, it is usually the male out hunting while the female is on the nest or tending to the chick. They are sometimes seen in pairs. They soar to great heights and like perching on top of tall trees, scanning the surroundings for prey.

AFRICAN FISH EAGLE *Haliaeetus vocifer* (Daudin 1800)

Is the African Fish Eagle seen throughout the Kruger Park?
The African Fish Eagle occurs over most of Africa south of the Sahara, and its characteristic call is one of the most haunting sounds heard in Africa. In the Park it is widely distributed but is absent from areas where there is no aquatic habitat.

Where should one look for this eagle?
Fish Eagles need to be close to water because of their diet. Look for them at larger dams and along perennial rivers where they usually hunt from perches overlooking water.

How large is the African Fish Eagle?
The female is larger than the male and has a wingspan of up to 2.3 m, compared with the 1.9 m of the male. The female has a mass of up to 3.6 kg and the male up to 2.5 kg.

What size prey can African Fish Eagles catch?
African Fish Eagles have been recorded taking fish of up to 3.5 kg but this is a rare occurrence. Fish of up to 2.5 kg can be carried, but heavier fish are usually dragged across the water, accompanied by flapping wings, and then eaten on the shore.

Do mishaps often occur with heavy fish?
Yes, but the eagle usually lets go of the catch when it finds that it has 'bitten off more than it can chew'.

Do African Fish Eagles dive deep for their prey?
When hunting, the African Fish Eagle makes a shallow, swooping dive from its perch near the water. They normally catch fish swimming near the surface, such as tilapia and catfish (*Clarias gariepinus*), snatching them up with their talons, usually within 15 cm of the surface.

What are the distinguishing features of the African Fish Eagle?
This bird is unmistakable, with its white head, chest and mantle. The wings and back are black in colour, with chestnut underparts. The tail is short, square and white in colour. Sexes are alike, but the female is larger.

The immature bird is a dull, mottled brown above, with heavy blackish blotching on the belly and streaking on the chest. The square, white tail has a dark terminal bar.

At what age does the bird attain adult plumage?
At five years or more.

Do they only eat fish?
No. Although they eat mainly fish, they will take nestlings of water birds and even adult water birds and occasionally also carrion.

When do they breed?
In the Park they breed between March and September, with a peak from June to August.

How regularly do they breed?
They breed every year.

How many eggs are laid at a time?
A clutch can consist of one to three eggs, but normally two.

What is the incubation time of the eggs?
Both male and female incubate the eggs, which hatch after 42 to 45 days. Chicks fledge 70 to 75 days after hatching and are dependent on the parents for about 60 days after fledging.

Do they nest on cliffs?
They build a nest up to 1.8 m in diameter out of sticks, and lined with grass and leaves, about 15 to 20 m high in the fork of a large tree, usually close to water. Very seldom do they nest on cliff ledges unless the cliff is very close to the river.

What are their habits?
They often perch together on tall trees near water for 85 to 95% of daylight time. They often call in flight and are most vocal at dawn.

With the pollution of the rivers, is the African Fish Eagle endangered?
Although there is serious concern about the quality of water in our river systems, the entire South African population of the African Fish Eagle is about 400 pairs. In the Kruger Park there are possibly about 100 breeding pairs.

Compared with other *Haliaeetus* eagles in the world, notably the Bald Eagle of North America, the status of the African Fish Eagle seems to be quite healthy.

BATELEUR
Terathopius ecaudatus (Daudin 1800)

What is the distribution of the Bateleur?
In South Africa this eagle occurs from the Kgalagadi Transfrontier Park, along the Limpopo Valley and into the Kruger Park, and further south to the northern parts of KwaZulu-Natal. The presence of the Bateleur is now almost exclusively restricted to conservation areas. This bird can be seen throughout the Kruger Park, preferring woodland and open plain savanna.

What are the characteristics of the Bateleur?
Probably the most colourful eagle in Africa, this bird has a deep brown iris, a yellowish bill with a dark tip, and bright red bare facial skin, cere, legs and feet. It has a mass of about 2.7 kg and a wingspan of up to 1.7 m

This large bird is predominantly black with a chestnut mantle, back and tail with grey wing coverts. When perched, the female shows greyish secondary feathers, which are black in the male. The wing tips extend beyond the very short tail.

In flight the underwings show mainly white, and there is a black trailing edge, which is broader in the male than the female. The wing tips are upswept and the feet extend slightly beyond the very short tail.

Immature birds are mainly brown, flecked with white, the bill is black and the bare facial skin and cere a pale greenish-blue. The legs and feet are whitish and the tail longer than the feet in flight.

They attain adult plumage after about seven years.

Is it true that the Bateleur has keen eyesight?
The fact that the Bateleur has very keen eyesight could be the reason why their numbers have declined so rapidly from their former range in the recent past.

The Bateleur has evolved to find and feed on carrion. If a piece of meat is lying in the veld, the Bateleur is sure to find it and eat it. Unfortunately, since the meat is sometimes laced with poison to control scavengers, the Bateleur will die after feeding off this poisoned meat.

It is said that vultures keep Bateleurs in sight. When the Bateleur descends, the vultures follow it to the carrion.

What are its habits?
Bateleurs are usually solitary but have been seen in a loose aggregation of 40 birds. They are often in the company of Tawny Eagles (*Aquila rapax*). They spend much of the day soaring and gliding in circling flight at 60 to 80 km/h, seldom flapping their wings. They glide on rigidly held wings, at times rocking to and fro. Prey is hunted in stooped flight and they may rob other eagles of their prey. They seldom fly in wet weather.

Immature birds sometimes scavenge and are often seen roosting in trees along roads waiting for road kills.

They roost in trees by day, sunbathing with spread wings. They bathe frequently.

Do they eat only carrion?
They have a wide dietary range. Apart from eating carrion, they prey on game and other smaller birds, smaller mammals, reptiles, eggs of ground-roosting birds, insects and even fish. They patrol roads for road kills and feed on carcasses of larger animals.

What is their breeding biology?
In the Park they breed from December to June, with a peak from January to March. They breed annually on a platform nest made of sticks. The leaf-lined nest is about 60 cm in diameter, anything up to 16 m above the ground, usually under the tree's canopy where it is shaded and

well concealed. The nest is usually placed on a horizontal fork of a large tree. They sometimes use the abandoned nests of other raptors.

Only one egg is laid, which is incubated mainly by the female with some assistance from the male. The chick hatches after 52 to 59 days and fledges after about 111 days but stays dependent on the parents for a further 90 to 120 days after its first flight.

The name Bateleur sounds French. What does it mean?

The biological name *Terathopius ecaudatus*, given by naturalist Le Vaillant, loosely translates as 'marvellous face, short tail'.

The canting flight of the Bateleur, a street performer or tightrope walker in French, brings to mind the image of a circus acrobat using his balancing pole.

LAPPET-FACED VULTURE

Torgos tracheliotus
(J. R. Forster 1796 or 1791)

What is the distribution of this vulture?

In South Africa the range of the Lappet-faced Vulture has decreased and it is now absent south of the Orange, Vaal and uThukela rivers, and found mainly in conservation areas. It is found in areas south of the Limpopo River through to the Kgalagadi Transfrontier Park. This vulture is found throughout the Kruger Park, preferring the woodland savanna areas.

Is it a very large bird?

This is one of Africa's largest flying birds, with a mass of about 7 kg and a wingspan close to 3 m.

What are its main characteristics?

The largest African bird of prey, the Lappet-faced Vulture is about 1.2 m in length and has a wingspan of 2.8 m. It has an overall black appearance, with black-and-white streaked underparts. It has a conspicuous, vivid red, naked head with a heavy yellow-grey bill. The thighs are white. In flight it is black under the wings, with a white strip along the leading edge of the wing. The cere and legs are greyish. The sexes are similar, but the female is larger than the male.

Is this an aggressive vulture?

Not really. Because of its size, it dominates other vultures at a carcass, and when it is seen in action it is obvious why it is sometimes called the King Vulture. An energetic Lappet-faced Vulture is capable of keeping up to 30 smaller vultures of different species at bay at a carcass by means of fierce sallies.

Its outstretched foot is about the size of a man's opened hand and is used well with the large bill when the need arises.

It rarely steals carrion from smaller vultures, but because of its size exerts dominance over all other species at a carcass. It will feed until satisfied and then usually retires to the periphery of the group and will stay near the carcass.

Does it feed on specific parts of the carcass?

It will obviously take softer flesh when available, and it can rip and tear at skin and sinews with which other vultures cannot cope.

Do they fight at a carcass?

There are always squabbles among vultures at a carcass. In an aggressive mood, it will stalk forward with a lowered head and wings held half open, the tail sticking upwards, and will attack the lowered head of its opponent with its feet.

What are their habits?
They mostly fly around in pairs and sit together at bathing spots. They are not gregarious but are seen in groups at a carcass. It is possible they that pair for life. They maintain relatively small breeding territories, but they forage for food over extended areas.

They roost in trees at night and fly with difficulty in the absence of thermals. On cold, overcast days they are seen roosting, sometimes all day, as it is difficult for them to fly, gain height and soar without the help of thermals.

Do they eat only carrion?
It has been reported that the Lappet-faced Vulture is also a predator of smaller animals such as hares, mongooses, guineafowl and leguaans. It is not certain to what extent these animals make up the bird's diet.

What are their breeding habits?
There is no obvious courtship display other than flying together. In the Park breeding seems to take place mainly during the winter months.

The nest is about 2.5 m in diameter, larger than that of any vulture, and is built out of sticks, about 10 to 15 m up in a tree. The nest is lined with grass, hair and skin, and may be used for many years in succession.

A single egg is laid, very rarely two. Both parents incubate the egg, which hatches after about 56 days. The chick fledges after about 125 days but is still cared for by both parents for up to six months after its first flight.

How often do they breed?
Pairs observed seem to breed every second year, but this can differ from one region to another.

Vultures soar to great heights from where they look for food. Do they really have keen eyesight?
Vultures have excellent eyesight and do indeed detect food from great heights. It is said that their sight is so acute that they are able to see a matchbox at 800 m.

Does the smell at a rotten carcass not bother vultures?
There is no evidence that vultures, in common with most birds, have any sense of smell. Because they cannot smell, the bad smells at carcasses do not have any affect on scavenger birds such as the vultures. However, this is a rather anthropomorphic point of view: to scavengers, mammals and birds, the smell of the most putrid carcass would be an immediate attraction.

SADDLE-BILLED STORK
Ephippiorhynchus senegalensis (Shaw 1800)

Is this stork widely distributed?
This mainly tropical bird is found in the northeastern parts of South Africa, in the Lowveld, through Swaziland into northern KwaZulu-Natal. It is seen throughout the Park in suitable habitat.

Where should one look for Saddle-billed Storks?
Saddle-billed Storks are waterside birds. They are found on banks of rivers, pans, dams and flood plain pools, usually in open or lightly wooded areas.

What are its distinguishing features?

There certainly are few more distinctive birds in Africa than this stately stork.

This rather tall bird has a wingspan of up to 2.7 m. The female is smaller than the male. The sexes look alike but the female has a yellow iris and the male's is dark brown; the male has a yellow wattle that hangs below the gape of the bill.

It has sharply contrasting black-and-white plumage, with the head and neck all black, as are the wing coverts above and below, scapulars and tail. The rest of the plumage is white.

The heavy bill curves slightly upward, is red and black with a bright yellow saddle-shaped frontal shield on top of the bill. The long legs are black with red tarsal joints and feet. There is a naked red brood patch on the breast.

What are their habits?

These storks are not gregarious and are seen alone or in pairs. They apparently mate for life and use the same nest year after year. They do not breed in colonies. Pairs roost together in trees. They are very territorial and intruders are seen off smartly.

They forage in shallow water, walking slowly while stabbing at prey with their heavy bills. Sometimes they stand still and wait for prey, or they may stir the mud up, while feeling for prey.

Males sometimes run through shallow water with their wings flapping, stop, turn and race back to their mate, where they show off the distinctive plumage of their outstretched wings for a few seconds. These storks fly with outstretched neck and trailing legs, and soar well.

When do they breed?

Saddle-Billed Storks perform a very striking mating display.

In the Park they normally breed every year from March to July, building a nest of sticks lined with grass, reeds and sedges. Both sexes build the nest, which is about 2 m in diameter and can be as high as 30 m above the ground in a sturdy tree near water.

What are their breeding habits?

Usually two eggs, sometimes up to five, are laid and are then incubated by both parents. Chicks hatch after about 32 days and fledge at 70 to 100 days.

What do they eat?

The diet consists mainly of fish of up to about 500 g. Frogs, crustaceans, small mammals, reptiles, molluscs and small birds are also included in their diet. They nip off the spines of larger fish to make swallowing easier, and always swallow fish headfirst. They may toss prey into the air before catching and swallowing it.

Is this stork endangered?

The Red Data List of South Africa lists the Saddle-Billed Stork as Endangered, with a population estimated at less than 150 individuals. It is common only in the Kruger National Park. Because of habitat encroachment and water pollution there is a reduction of its numbers outside of conservation areas.

KORI BUSTARD
Ardeotis kori (Burchell 1822)

What is the distribution of this bird?

The Kori Bustard prefers open short-grass areas, and is found in South Africa's drier and semi-arid regions and absent from well-wooded or forested areas. This bird is seen throughout the Kruger National Park, especially in the open grassland savanna regions.

Why would such a big bird prefer open areas?

This bustard is said to be the world's heaviest flying bird. To carry its weight, it has a very big wingspan and therefore it requires open, unobstructed areas in order to get airborne and land without difficulty.

What are the distinguishing features of the Kori Bustard?

It is a very large bird, about 1.2 m tall, with a mass of up to 19 kg and a wingspan of up to 2.8 m. The female is about half the size of the male. The male has black feathers on the forehead, which form the slight crest. There is a definite white stripe above the yellow eye. The neck and throat are grey and have fine black barring. The chest and belly are very light and the back is brown. The upper-wing coverts are mottled, giving a striped effect when folded. The large bill is horn-coloured and the legs greyish-yellow.

What are their habits?

They normally occur in pairs but tend to forage up to 100 m apart. Kori Bustards are wary and nervous birds, walking hesitantly when foraging. They avoid intruders by moving off quietly with the neck held at an angle.

They fly reluctantly, but with powerful wing beats. Kori Bustards have to run to take off and land with outstretched wings, which are folded only when walking speed is reached. In flight the neck is extended and the legs folded under the body.

The male displays with the neck inflated, the neck feathers turned upwards, the crest erect, the wings slightly drooped, the tail raised over the back and the under-tail coverts fanned out. These displays usually take place in the mornings and evenings. They feed during the morning and evening, resting in shade in the heat of the day.

What do they eat?

Kori Bustards have a wide dietary range, which includes locusts, grasshoppers, caterpillars, small mammals, reptiles, seeds, sometimes carrion and the gum of *Acacia* trees, hence the Afrikaans name 'Gompou'.

What are their breeding habits?

Kori Bustards breed from October to February every year and usually lay two eggs, sometimes only one, in a slight hollow scraped in the ground. The nest on the ground is normally near tufts of grass, which the bird uses for camouflage or to hide behind. Incubation lasts about 30 days, but there is no information about the nestling or fledging of the chick. The chick is able to feed itself soon after hatching.

Is this bird considered endangered?

The Kori Bustard is a strictly protected species, and is still found in acceptable numbers throughout its range and especially in conservation areas. They are very vulnerable to power lines, so markers have been attached to power lines in the Park to reduce collisions.

VERREAUX'S (GIANT/MILKY) EAGLE-OWL

Bubo lacteus (Temminck 1820)

How widely is this owl species distributed?

In South Africa it is found from the Orange River and from KwaZulu-Natal northwards. This owl species is found throughout the Park in suitable habitat.

What is its habitat preference?

It is seen in woodland and savanna areas and favours tall riverine trees, particularly *Acacia* and *Ficus* species.

Is this the largest owl?

It is one of the largest owl species in Africa, but slightly smaller than a few of its Eurasian counterparts. Pel's Fishing Owl (*Scotopelia peli*) is also larger than this owl.

Owls are nocturnal birds. Can one observe them during the day?

These owls are regularly seen on night drives from the various rest camps in the Park. They are often seen along rivers, roosting in large, shady trees during the day. Look for large trees with thick, horizontal-growing branches on which this big bird often perches.

What size are their territories?

As would be expected with a bird of this size, it maintains large territories, which can be up to 7 000 ha and include their regular roosting trees.

Do they share territories with other predatory birds?

These owls are intolerant towards other large owls but readily share the same hunting grounds with eagles and falcons of various sizes. The reason why they can peacefully coexist with these other raptors is that owls are nocturnal hunters, while eagles and other raptors hunt during the day. Although they operate in the same area, the difference in their hunting times cuts out competition.

What does their diet consist of?

This owl has an amazingly diverse diet. It is an opportunistic hunter and has been seen to overpower mammals the size of a vervet monkey and even an adult Secretarybird, a springhare and a warthog piglet, and can carry a mongoose with a mass of up to 1.8 kg in flight.

At the other end of the spectrum, it will eat insects, rodents, hares, birds of varying sizes as well as bats. It regularly also takes ground birds such as guineafowl. Records also show that even other avian predators, including different species of owls, eagles, hawks, falcons and even vultures, are not safe from this bird.

Between these extremes, it will eat any living creature of manageable size that comes within its range. It has also been recorded feeding on carrion.

How does it hunt?

The varied diet indicates flexible hunting behaviour. Most kills are made from a perch, from where the owl swoops down to snatch its prey. The construction of the owl's wing feathers is such that its flight is virtually silent. The kill is made by slamming the heavy feet and sharp talons into the prey, killing smaller prey instantly.

At night these owls can be seen flying silently and with their broad wings dexterously manoeuvring in pursuit of flying insects, bats and even birds. At other times they will move about on their long legs picking insects up in their big bills. They frequently hunt before dusk and after dawn when sight is important for locating prey.

What are their habits?

During the day they are often seen roosting in the shade, on a stout horizontal branch of a large tree. When scared or injured, they sometimes feign death, and in extreme situations hang upside-down and inert from their perch. They are usually seen singly, but also in pairs or family groups of three birds. They regularly prey at night on roosting birds and even smaller arboreal mammals.

What are their prominent identification features?

This is a large bird, the male at about 2.6 kg, approximately 35% lighter than the female, which is about 3.1 kg.

Notable features include a pale facial disc, boldly outlined with black. It has short, rounded 'ear tufts', conspicuous pink eyelids and dark brown eyes. The overall colour is grey, finely barred above and below, with white feathers down the length of the legs. Along the side of the horn-coloured bill are very prominent rictal bristles. Immature birds are paler than adults.

Do they build new nests every year?

They build their nests in big forks of large trees or in a hole in the tree. They very often use the abandoned nest of other predatory birds such as eagles, and use the top of other larger nests, especially those of the Red-Billed Buffalo-Weaver (*Bubalornis niger*) and the Hamerkop (*Scopus umbretta*), to build their own.

They may use the nest year after year until it collapses.

What are their breeding habits?

Breeding occurs from March to September, with a peak during the winter months of June to August. Usually two eggs are laid, seldom one. The eggs are incubated for about 39 days, with the female on the nest most of the time. After about three months the chicks can fly but remain with the parents until the next breeding season.

The two eggs are laid about a week apart, the second egg being smaller. By the time the second egg hatches, the first chick weighs almost three to four times more than the second chick. The younger chick will gain weight much more slowly than the first because the first dominates the feeding ritual. The second chick invariably dies of starvation. As remains are rarely found, it is probably fed to the surviving chick.

These owls do not necessarily breed every year. They may raise a chick in each of four successive years or breed only every two to three years.

SOUTHERN GROUND HORNBILL
Bucorvus leadbeateri (Vigors 1825)

Is the Southern Ground Hornbill widely distributed?

In South Africa the distribution of these birds is restricted to the eastern parts of the country: from the Eastern Cape north of Port Elizabeth, through KwaZulu-Natal, the eastern Lowveld and along the Limpopo Valley of Limpopo province. It is represented in suitable habitat throughout the entire Kruger Park.

What is considered as suitable habitat?

They prefer woodland savanna and open grasslands.

How would one identify this bird?

It is a very large bird, about the size of a turkey, with the male having a mass of up to 3.9 kg. The plumage appears entirely black when on the ground but the white primary feathers are conspicuous in flight.

The bare facial and orbital skin as well as the throat, which resembles a resonance sac, are bright red. The female sometimes shows a purplish-blue tinge to this red. The bill is very large and black, not joined in the middle section, and surmounted by a casque.

The legs are long, stout and dark grey to black. The immature bird has dark brown plumage with yellowish-grey facial skin and wattle.

What are their habits?

They are sociable birds, mostly seen in pairs or in family groups, sometimes as many as eight walking and foraging together. It is interesting to note that in more than 75% of sightings the group consisted of uneven numbers. This possibly has something to do with their breeding habits.

They are almost completely terrestrial, roosting in trees only at night, with their head tucked into the shoulders with the bill pointing upwards; they also perch in trees when alarmed or disturbed.

Neighbouring groups chase each other in aerial pursuits. They are vocal mostly at dawn, their deep, booming territorial calls repeated and answered several times.

Flight is powerful with deep wing beats and some gliding. It is possibly the only bird in the southern African region that walks on the tips of its toes, its stiff rolling gait resembling a woman walking in high-heeled shoes. The large bill is used to dig for food.

What do they eat?

They are considered carnivorous, because their varied diet includes insects, reptiles, frogs, tortoises, rodents, snails, small mammals up to the size of a hare, birds and the nestlings of ground-roosting birds. They forage through the veld, grabbing any prey they come across. Often seen foraging on recently burnt veld for food items killed by the fire.

They are reputed to be good hunters of snakes, normally attacking the snake as a group, each darting in to peck at the victim. Prey is usually swallowed whole.

What are the breeding habits of the Southern Ground Hornbill?

It breeds mainly in October and November. The nest is usually in a hole in a tree or in a cleft or hole in a rock face. The nest, which may be up to 7 m above the ground, is lined with grass and leaves. Unlike other hornbills, the Southern Ground Hornbill female is not sealed into the nest. Two eggs are laid and incubated almost exclusively by the female. During incubation, the breeding bird seldom leaves the nest and is fed by her mate and others of the group.

After about 40 days the chicks hatch, and fledge after a further 85 to 87 days. The young stay dependent on the adults for food for six to 12 months. Only one chick is raised, which may be why most of the group sightings of these birds are in uneven numbers.

What is the Southern Ground Hornbill's status?

In conservation areas throughout its distribution range, they are common residents, but scarce in settled areas. In the Park they are well represented in their choice of habitat.

APPENDIX

GENERAL CODE OF CONDUCT

To ensure a pleasant and successful trip through the Park, it is essential that you adhere strictly to the regulations that are intended for your protection and enjoyment. Speeding, the feeding of animals and alighting from your vehicle other than at recognised areas, and littering are especially considered as serious offences.

The National Environmental Management: Protected Areas Act (Act 57, 2003 Amended 2004) as amended provides *inter alia* that:

> *It shall be an offence to alight from a motor vehicle at an unauthorised place other than in a rest camp, at a picnic spot or an authorized view site, even if you are only partly out of your vehicle.*

In some national parks in other countries visitors are permitted to alight from their vehicles, so why is this regulation applied in the Kruger National Park?

Wild animals are naturally afraid of man. Animals have come to accept the outline of your vehicle, but when you are inside your vehicle they do not recognise you as a human being, which allows you to observe them even at close quarters. Should you leave your vehicle, even partly, they will immediately recognise you as a human being, which will make them move or even run away. This would deprive you and other visitors of the pleasure of observing them and you might even be attacked.

Is there proof that it could be dangerous to alight from your vehicle?

On occasions visitors who left their vehicles have been charged by lions, narrowly escaping serious injury or death. Cases are known of people being killed by wild animals in reserves where visitors were allowed to leave their vehicles. Long grass can conceal dangerous animals, and it could also harbour dangerous snakes and insects such as scorpions.

What do I do in an emergency?

You may leave your vehicle to repair a breakdown, but you do so entirely at your own risk. It is important to make sure that there are no dangerous animals around. Alternatively, a passing visitor could be requested to report your predicament to the nearest rest camp, or you could call the nearest rest camp that offers a breakdown service for assistance.

Should your car break down towards the end of the day and there are no longer visitors on the road or you do not have cellphone reception where you are stranded, stay in your vehicle at all times; even sleep in your vehicle. Someone is bound to drive in your direction the next day. Under no circumstances should you attempt to walk in search of help. The Park has a 24-hour Control Centre that can be contacted on 013 735 4325 or 076 801 9679.

It is an offence to drive anywhere that is not a recognised tourist road.

Why are we not allowed to drive off the road?

Driving off the road to follow animals disturbs them. Additionally, stones, stumps, thorns and holes that are concealed by grass, or just unobserved, have caused many a tourist serious problems. Roads with 'no entry' signs are constructed as firebreaks and are used by rangers on patrol, as well as by research staff concerned with nature management activities. These roads often cannot be negotiated by vehicles and are not patrolled regularly. Should you have a mishap on a firebreak road, it could take days to locate you. These firebreak roads are not signposted and you could get lost.

Such incidents have occurred, and in one instance an elderly couple were stranded on a firebreak and located by helicopter after a three-day search. They suffered severe shock and almost died of thirst.

It is an offence to exceed the indicated speed limit.

Why is the speed limit so low?

Speed limits are there to protect the animals. High speeds could be dangerous because wild animals frequently run across the roads. Drivers exceeding the speed limit have often been involved in serious accidents with game or with other vehicles. The practice of following too closely behind another vehicle also leads to accidents from time to time.

To enjoy your game viewing, it is better to drive slowly and observe carefully, which enhances the chances of spotting game. A game-spotting speed of 20 to 30 km/h is recommended.

Some SANParks officials seem to exceed the speed limits at times. Why?

Park officials on official duty are allowed to travel at speeds not exceeding 65 km/h. If Park officials were bound to the same speed limits as the public, many man-

hours of labour would be lost. In an emergency they may exceed the 65 km/h speed limit, but, should they do so without a valid reason, they will be prosecuted.

It is said that high speed is dangerous with wild animals around. Does this not apply to employees?

A visitor's main objective is to see as much game as possible and he/she does not devote all his/her attention to the road. The official on the other hand has a job to do, has seen the animals many times before and has to get from point A to point B to discharge his responsibility, and he therefore concentrates on the road with better-trained eyes than those of the visitor.

Large Park vehicles seem to travel too fast. Is this necessary?

The size of the vehicles and the noise they make create the impression that they are travelling faster than they actually do. These vehicles are timed from time to time and it was found that they mostly kept within the speed limit. Drivers have strict orders not to exceed the speed limit and those caught in a speed trap could be heavily fined. All large vehicles are fitted with tachographs as an additional measure.

It is an offence to injure, feed or disturb any form of wildlife

Why may I not feed the animals?

Feeding animals, especially baboons, monkeys and even hyaenas, causes them to lose their natural fear of humans and they could become aggressive towards the feeder. A number of people have been bitten as a result of feeding. Injuries sustained in this manner can be serious and the wounds tend to turn septic, often resulting in septicaemia. Once an animal becomes a danger or a nuisance to human beings, it unfortunately has to be destroyed. This can be avoided by not feeding animals.

Is it true that monkeys and baboons become so dependent on feeding that they can starve if the practice is discontinued?

No, they do not become domesticated. When hungry, they will forage for items in their natural diet. Feeding can, however, lead to deficiency diseases.

Are the high fines for feeding animals justifiable?

When one considers that innocent people can be seriously injured and bitten or mauled as a result of feeding, one is inclined to regard the fines as too lenient. Furthermore, a primary consideration in the management of the Park is to keep it as natural and unspoilt as possible.

It is understood that one should not injure an animal, but is one prohibited from helping an injured animal?

Yes. Firstly, alighting from your vehicle is against regulations; secondly, very few injured animals recover; and, lastly, it could be dangerous. Seriously injured animals may be reported to veterinary officers or the ranger and through any of the reception offices at rest camps.

The current author once came across an injured lion cub. While he was watching the cub, a visitor stopped his car at the side of the road, put his head out of the window and asked whether he should take the cub to the veterinary surgeon at Skukuza. Although no other animals were visible, he was advised that such an act could be dangerous. The author then drove a little closer to the cub, only to be confronted by a growling, tail-swishing, aggressive lioness that appeared from the long grass. The visitor got the message!

Am I allowed to make tape recordings of lion roaring and replay them to entice lion to come closer to the vehicle?

Nothing stops you from making the recordings. Playing a recording back to elicit a response from lion could disturb the animals and that is against regulations. It could also be dangerous as the lion can become aggressive in trying to determine the source of the roars. It is therefore advisable to enjoy your recordings at home.

It is an offence to uproot, pick or damage any plant or be in possession of any part of a plant that is indigenous to the Park.

May I collect seeds of plants in rest camps?

According to regulations, this is not permitted. Plants indigenous to the Park are sold at rest camps and at some entrance gates. It is therefore not necessary to collect seeds. There is also a well-run nursery at Skukuza where indigenous plants can be bought.

It is an offence to place any name, letter or figure, symbol, mark, sticker or picture on any object in the Park.

Is graffiti allowed in the Park?

Defacing items in the Park is certainly not allowed, so please no graffiti!

You may not discard a burning object in such a manner or place where a fire could develop.

Have any fires been caused through the negligence of visitors?

Several serious veld fires have been traced back to visitors. In most cases the negligent discarding of cigarette butts or use of matches was the cause. Throwing anything away, other than in a proper receptacle or dustbin, even an extinguished cigarette butt, is against regulations and is seen as a form of pollution.

> *It is an offence to be in possession of any explosives or an unsealed firearm.*

Have there been any incidents regarding the above regulation?

Cases of poaching and injury to animals have been recorded and, where the offenders have been apprehended and found guilty, they were imprisoned for lengthy periods or had to pay heavy fines. Their firearms and vehicles were also confiscated.

What do I do with my firearm?

On entering the Park you have to declare your firearm to the official at the entrance gate. The firearm will then be sealed. On leaving the Park your firearm will be unsealed and returned to you.

> *It is an offence to introduce into the Park any pets, whether domestic or otherwise.*

What is the purpose of this regulation?

Diseases that are alien to the indigenous fauna of the Park can be brought in and spread by pets. On leaving the Park, these same pets could also transmit wildlife diseases to animals outside the Park. Pets also tend to get lost. Even if the pets were tame wild animals, rather than domestic animals, they could still be alien to the Park's fauna and therefore unwanted.

What would happen if you should be caught smuggling in a pet?

An admission of guilt fine can be paid or you could be summonsed to appear in court. You could also be requested to leave the Park immediately with your pet. The animal concerned may also be destroyed.

Why then do rangers keep dogs?

Rangers are allowed to keep dogs to assist them during their patrols in the veld. They are an early warning system for the rangers when they move through difficult terrain. The dogs are kept in very good condition and are visited by the State Veterinarian on a regular basis. The dogs are prevented from inter-breeding with any canids in the Park. Should a ranger terminate his service and leave the Park, his dogs may not leave the Park unless veterinary regulations have been complied with.

Are staff members allowed to keep pets?

Apart from caged birds, staff are not allowed to keep pets. Domestic cats can interbreed with the wild cats, especially the African wild cat (*Felis sylvestris lybica*) and kill birds. Dogs tend to chase animals and their barking would disturb the atmosphere in rest camps. Pets also attract predators, especially leopards, to the staff villages.

What about stray or orphaned animals found and reared by rangers?

Some attempts have been successful, but there have also been many failures. A wild animal is seldom reared successfully and one wonders whether the animal concerned really gains anything from this process. The best approach is to discourage this activity. Very few of these semi-tame animals are successfully rehabilitated and released in the wild. Not only do they battle to find their place in the social hierarchy of their species, but they most probably have not learned to fend for themselves and can seldom manage to do so. These animals are likely to be beyond the point at which they could adapt to living in the wild.

It is an offence to discard any article or refuse other than placing it in a receptacle or place intended therefore.

Does SANParks experience problems in this regard?

Yes indeed. Many man-hours are spent cleaning up along the roads and in the rest camps, as well as at the picnic spots. One should not litter anywhere. Park authorities consider littering a serious offence.

Apart from the aesthetic point of view, are there recorded cases where littering actually harmed wildlife?

A number of incidents have been recorded in which tins with sharp edges have become wedged over the muzzle of animals, opener rings of cans have become wedged between the hooves of animals, and snakes and lizards have got their heads stuck in the narrow openings of beer or cold-drink cans, causing severe injuries and in some cases fatalities.

A plastic bag swallowed by an animal can cause fatal blockage of the alimentary canal. Broken glass can cause obvious external injuries.

It is an offence to drive or park in a manner that is a nuisance, disturbance or inconvenience to other persons.

Are the usual traffic laws also applicable in the Park?

Yes.

Have any problems been encountered in this respect?

Often traffic jams occur at sightings of lions, leopard or other interesting animals, causing prolonged delays. Small children, elderly or sick passengers may suffer great discomfort while stuck in such a jam. Always be considerate towards fellow visitors.

What precautions should one take?

Travel on the left-hand side of the road and do not park on a bend or any other place on the road that could be dangerous to yourself or other road users.

If it is necessary to park on the right-hand side of the road, pull slightly off the road but do not park in the veld. Adhere to normal traffic rules for safety's sake, adhere to the speed limits and be considerate and courteous to fellow visitors.

It is an offence to make a noise after 21h30 and before 06h00 that may disturb fellow visitors.

Why must visitors be quiet during this period?

Some visitors simply want to enjoy an early night to rise early the next morning for game-viewing, others may just want to rest and still others would like to listen to the sounds made by nocturnal animals and birds.

These days radios and even television sets are being taken to the Park, and it is imperative that the volume be at a level that does not cause any disturbance.

What does one do in the case of continuous noise disturbance?

Should people not heed requests to turn down the noise levels, do not get involved in altercations. Go to the gate where there is always a gate guard on duty. Request him to inform the duty manager of the disturbance and the duty manager will handle the situation.

> *It is an offence to advertise or offer any goods for sale.*

Why may goods not be offered for sale in the Park?

In the late 1990s the Board of SANParks entered into contracts with concessionaires to run the various shops, delicatessens and restaurants in the Park. Trading in any way in the Park will constitute breach of contract and could cause the Park authorities lots of problems. The various concessionaires have the sole rights to trade in the Park. Should there be any complaints about the quality of merchandise or service, the complaint should be taken up with the concessionaire as well as with the Park authorities.

> *It is an offence to collect any money from the public or give public entertainment for reward.*

May visitors supply free entertainment in the Park?

If the programme fits in with nature conservation, permission may be granted. Prior permission should be obtained from the Park's Management Executive at Skukuza or his designated official or from the rest camp manager. Educational programmes on nature conservation such as slide shows or talks and videos would be considered. On the other hand, permission may be refused, with explanation.

Young people would sometimes like to have some form of entertainment. Is this possible?

The Kruger National Park was never intended to be a pleasure resort. The atmosphere experienced in this sanctuary is unique and should be kept that way. One could imagine what the effect would be if dancing and discotheques were allowed. The peace and quiet that is among the main attractions of the Park would be destroyed.

Is it possible for young people to get together and have some fun without disturbing other visitors?

A request like this should be made to the rest camp manager. It depends on what they have in mind. If it is merely to chat around a camp fire, it might be perfectly in order. However, there is always the possibility that a large group of people could tend to become noisy.

Considering that it is possible to have an active social life all year round, one can surely forego the socialising for a short period while in the Park. People who complain about the Park being too quiet amount to a fraction of 1%, the overwhelming majority preferring it as quiet as it is.

> *It is an offence to spend the night in any rest camp without the knowledge of the camp manager.*

If you sleep in your vehicle, is it really necessary to report to the camp manager?

Any person staying overnight must at least pay camping fees, whether he sleeps in his vehicle or a tent, because he uses the ablution facilities and other amenities. Should a visitor fail to comply with this regulation, camping fees for every night not paid for will be collected at the next rest camp or at the exit gate, where documents are checked. A fine may also be imposed.

Kruger National Park travelling hours

Month	Camps open	Entrance gates open	Camps and gates close
January	04h30	05h30	18h30
February	05h30	05h30	18h30
March	05h30	05h30	18h00
April	06h00	06h00	18h00
May	06h00	06h00	17h30
June	06h00	06h00	17h30
July	06h00	06h00	17h30
August	06h00	06h00	18h00
September	06h00	06h00	18h00
October	05h30	05h30	18h00
November	04h30	05h30	18h30
December	04h30	05h30	18h30

It is an offence to travel in the Kruger National Park during times other than those approved.

Why are visitors not allowed to drive around the Kruger National Park at night?

One's view at night is restricted to the beams of the vehicle's headlights and very few animals can be seen. Animals blinded by the lights may dash across the road and cause accidents; others, such as nightjars, may be blinded and killed. Near rivers hippos are especially dangerous as they feed mainly at night and are very difficult to see.

How can I get to see the nocturnal activities?

Since the mid-1990s organised night drives have been available at all rest camps and from most entrance gates. Bookings may be made for these drives at the rest camp reception offices and at the receptions of the entrance gates. The drives leave at about 17h00 and return at about 20h00. The drives are done by qualified staff, who offer relevant interpretation of the nightlife encountered. Unfortunately, children under the age of six years are not allowed on night drives.

What are the normal travelling hours in the Park?

The times during which visitors may travel in the Park are subject to change without notice, and it is recommended that visitors check the times as they appear on the entrance permit. At the time of writing, travelling hours were as reflected in the table above.

Can visitors be prosecuted if they turn up late at a camp or exit gate?

Gate times must be strictly adhered to, and travelling in the Park outside these hours is not allowed. Visitors must be inside their allocated overnight rest camp by gate closing time. Day visitors should also leave the Park before entrance/exit gate closing times. Entrance gates may, at their discretion, refuse entry to visitors who arrive too late to reach their overnight camps by gate closing time. Avoidable travelling after the gates have closed is subject to a fine or, in serious cases, prosecution.

What happens if you are late due to unavoidable circumstances?

Some visitors offer the most unusual excuses when they could in fact have been on time. Officials know most of these excuses and can therefore usually determine whether they are genuine. The 'flat tyre' excuse is wearing thin by now! It is better to play open cards with officials. They have been through most of the genuine experiences offered for arriving late at gates and will judge each situation on merit.

Being late after being held up by large animals on the road would usually result in more than just you being late at the gate, which corroborates your reason. Having said this, it is better to play it safe and obey the speed limit, rather than endanger yourself and your passengers.

It is an offence to spend the night in a place other than a rest camp.

Is it dangerous to sleep in your vehicle in the bush?

Not necessarily. If you stayed inside your vehicle you should be safe but, if you had to get out of your vehicle for some reason, it could be dangerous. If visitors were allowed to sleep in the bush, it would be difficult to control the whereabouts and movements of people. In this way it would be difficult to control law-breakers such as

organised poachers. It is a serious offence to spend the night outside a rest camp.

It is an offence to drive a vehicle in the Park without a legitimate driver's licence.

Is it a serious offence to drive a vehicle in the Park without a driver's licence?

Yes, it is regarded as a serious offence. The driver of a vehicle must have a licence valid for the type of vehicle he/she is driving.

With relatively light traffic in the Park, it is considered by many visitors as an opportune time and place to allow their children to gain experience in driving their vehicles. There is a heavy fine for both the child driving and the registered owner of the vehicle for allowing the child to drive the vehicle without a licence. It is also deemed a serious offence to allow a child to sit on your lap while you are driving. Not only can the child be seriously or even fatally injured in the case of an accident, but also the driver does not have full control of the vehicle, especially in the event of having to take emergency evasive action.

What is the maximum fine imposed in the Park?

This depends on the type of infringement of the regulations. Obviously poaching in the Park would carry the heaviest fines. It is at the discretion of the magistrate hearing the case what the fine should be, as laid down within certain parameters. Poaching of endangered species or for ivory or rhino horn would carry a heavier fine than poaching an impala. The seriousness of the offence would dictate the fine or imprisonment term.

At present the illegal shooting of large game such as elephants and rhinos carries very heavy fines and/or long terms of imprisonment. Recent court cases have produced prison terms of 29 and 40 years for poachers of rhino horn. Feeding of animals and speeding are also seen in a serious light and are subject to stiff fines!

Why are there such heavy fines?

Heavy fines are there to deter the offence. A lenient fine could result in the offender's paying the fine and then going on to contravene the regulations again. Teasing or disturbing potentially dangerous animals, such as lions, African elephants, rhinos or African buffaloes, to mention but a few, can be dangerous not only to the culprit, but also, and more importantly, to innocent fellow visitors to the Park.

Arson is another grave offence that could have serious consequences, and a heavy fine may be expected for this offence. In 2007 a visitor suffering from depression set fire to the veld at seven different locations along the Doispane road (S1), causing serious unplanned burning in the southwestern area of the Park. He was sentenced to two years' imprisonment.

Is it necessary to have to have one's entrance and accommodation documents in the car?

It is important to have your entrance documents and all relevant receipts readily accessible for inspection on request by any official while you are in the Park.

Last, but not least, all the above regulations are there for the protection of the visiting public and to enable visitors to enjoy their stay in this wonderful wildlife sanctuary.

ECOLOGY OF THE KRUGER NATIONAL PARK

Topography

The Park is generally gently undulating, more or less flat, primarily with occasional rocky outcrops, hills and limited mountains, and the vegetation consists of bush and parkland savanna. Altitudes vary from 442 m above sea level at Punda Maria in the north to 839 m at Khandizwe near Malelane in the south. The central part is about 260 m above sea level. The lowest point in the Park is the Sabie River gorge, which is 122 m above sea level. Other river gorges are in the Shingwedzi (244 m), the Lepelle (152 m), the Nwanetsi (152 m) and the N'waswitsontso (183 m).

Geologically, the Park is divided from north to south in almost equal halves, roughly along the tar road to the north. A narrow belt of shale and sandstone divides the predominantly granitic formations in the west and basalts in the east. The granites to the west give rise to large-grained, sandy, light-coloured soils, which permit good root penetration and thus more woody vegetation and stands of trees. The basalts are more finely grained, darker soils with a high clay content, which give rise to more superficial root structures; hence the more open grasslands of the east. Two sandveld communities occur in the far northern section of the Park. The Punda Maria sandveld and the Nwambiya/Nyandu sandveld areas on the eastern border to the east of Punda Maria have a vegetation community that is very different from the rest of the Park.

Rivers

Of the major rivers the Crocodile River forms the southern boundary of the Park and the Limpopo River the northern boundary. Other major rivers flowing through the Park in a west-to-east direction, eventually draining into the Indian Ocean, include the Luvuvhu, Shingwedzi, Letaba, Lepelle and Sabie. Due to extensive utilisation by outside agencies of rivers flowing through the Park, except for the Sabie, these rivers can no longer be considered perennial.

Other rivers of importance include the Shisa, Tsendze, Mphongolo, Timbavati, N'waswitsontso, N'watindlopfu and the Biyamiti.

Rainfall

The rainy season starts in September or October and lasts until March or April, and is followed by a period of very low or no rainfall. About 80% of the precipitation occurs in the form of quick, very erratic thunder showers. Around the Pretoriuskop area in the south the annual rainfall can be as high as 760 mm. Rainfall decreases noticeably further north, and in the central area the rainfall is about 540 mm per year. It rises to about 640 mm per annum in the Punda Maria area in the northwest, while at Pafuri, not too far from there to the north, it can be as low as 210 mm.

Temperatures

The average daily temperature during January is about 30°C and in July about 23°C. Extreme maximums for January can reach 47°C and in July about 35°C. Average night temperatures in January are roughly 18°C and as low as –4°C in July. Light frost occurs occasionally in winter, mostly in low-lying areas.

Vegetation

The plant life varies from tropical to subtropical as about one third of the Park lies within the tropic belt to the north of the Tropic of Capricorn. The vegetation can be divided into 16 vegetation types or ecozones as shown on the map on the inside cover. On a finer scale a total of 35 landscape types have been identified.

A total of 1 986 plant species, including 457 tree and shrub species, as well as 235 species of grass, have been recorded in the Park. Succulents, xerophytes and epiphytes, including orchids, are also fairly well represented.

Animals

Rainforests and our Fynbos biomes have a high biodiversity but few, if any, of the national parks in the world can boast a diversity of animal and plant life comparable to that of the Kruger National Park. Of the true cat species alone, six of the seven found in Africa occur in the Park.

Annually, during winter, an aerial census used to be conducted of the animal component of the Park. This action became prohibitively expensive and at the time of writing a census sample is done. Methods of determining numbers include block counts (aerial), transects using distance sampling (aerial), total counts (aerial), guestimates usually from ranger experience, photographic mark-recapture, call-up surveys and sample surveys using fixed width transects (aerial).

It must be emphasised that the following numbers are the latest **approximate** numbers of the more obvious animal species, but are as accurate as possible:

Predators

Lion	1 700
Leopard	1 000
Cheetah	120
Spotted hyaena	> 4 000
Wild dog	> 120
Nile crocodile	4 400

Herbivores

Impala	> 150 000
African buffalo	40 000
Burchell's zebra	> 26 000
Blue wildebeest	> 12 000
Kudu	> 15 300
African elephant	> 13 000
Giraffe	7 500
Waterbuck	> 4 900
Warthog	> 3 800
Hippopotamus	3 100
Sable antelope	290
Bushbuck	> 500
Reedbuck	300
White rhino	> 10 500
Black rhino	600
Nyala	> 300
Eland	> 450
Tsessebe	> 200
Roan antelope	90
Mountain reedbuck	150

The mammals of the Kruger National Park are fairly well known, with 148 recorded species, including the lesser-seen rodent and bat species; the bird life has been well documented at about 507 species; reptiles at 119 species and amphibians at 35 species. A new species for the Park, the forest cobra (*Naja melanoleuca*), was recorded in the far northern section of the Park in 2007.

The gently flowing waters of the rivers and streams are sanctuary to 53 species of fish (including four vagrant marine species and unfortunately also three alien species), which are not often seen by visitors. A bull shark (*Carcharhinus leucas*) was found at the confluence of the Limpopo and Luvuvhu rivers in 1950, but these cartilaginous fish are not normally represented in the rivers of the Park.

Two species of the rare and unusual seasonal killifish, *Nothobranchius rachovii* and *Nothobranchius orthonotus*, were restricted to a few seasonal pans on the eastern boundary of the Park, but have since been reintroduced into other suitable pans. The most extraordinary feature of this approximately 50-mm fish is that it lives for only one season. Eggs are laid in the mud of the pans, where they lie dormant. After the pans have dried up, they are often covered with grass-like vegetation that becomes dry at the end of winter and is sometimes destroyed by fire. The eggs survive this harsh treatment because of the protective mud cover. Only after sufficient rain has accumulated water in the pan to ensure the correct osmotic pressure do the eggs hatch. This mechanism of nature ensures that hatching occurs only when there is sufficient water for survival and for propagation by the adults. The male *Nothobranchius* displays a splendid array of colours.

One of the most sought-after sporting fish, the tigerfish (*Hydrocynus vittatus*), is also found in some of the rivers of the Park.

RIVERS AND RIVER ECOLOGY

Water is a biological necessity for all life on Earth; that is why rivers are so important in a natural system. While they are a vital source of drinking water for terrestrial animals, there are still more animals that live in river water. Without rivers, the Kruger Park would be immeasurably poorer with regard to a large variety of organisms.

River fish

Fifty fish species are found in the Kruger National Park, and three exotic species have been recorded in the waters of the Park.

Fish prefer certain habitats and water conditions in which they choose to live and to which they are physically adapted for survival.

Certain species prefer water that flows over rocks, forming rapids, where the water is rich in food and oxygen, but they have to adapt to the faster-flowing water during periods of flooding.

Many species prefer rivers where the water flow is more limited and allows the formation of pools. Smaller fish move to the shallower parts of pools, finding shelter from predatory fish under overhanging branches, reeds and leaves.

Not all species are found in all the rivers. Some species are restricted to certain rivers or even certain parts of rivers. For instance, certain cichlid (kurper) species are restricted to particular rivers. The Lowveld largemouth (*Serranochromis meridianus*) is found only in the Sabie River, and the orange-finned river bream (*Chetia brevis*) is found only in the Crocodile and Komati rivers.

Although found in many rivers in the Park, the butter catfish (*Schilbe intermedius*) is commonly found where trees overhang a pool.

The ordinary barbel, or sharptooth catfish (*Clarias gariepinus*), not being a strong swimmer, prefers pools with slow-flowing water. In contrast, the fast-flowing water in the main stream of a river accommodates, among others, stronger swimmers such as mudfish (*Labeo* spp.), yellowfish (*Barbus marequensis*) and, in certain rivers, the tigerfish (*Hydrocynus vittatus*).

Fish migration

Fish migrate to spawn, as in European and American rivers. Seasonal rivers that flow during the rainy season have a definite attraction for certain fish species. As soon as these rivers are in flood, the fish swim upstream where they find a mate and reproduce in a suitable pool. After the eggs are laid, the fish move back to the main stream.

The majority of fish species move upstream and can be seen jumping up rapids or congregating under obstructions. Some species have developed to such an extent that they wriggle up rocks using their fins and their lips, while others jump over obstructions at high speed.

In contrast, tigerfish migrate downstream in order to breed in shallow flood plains, especially in Mozambique.

Fish sometimes need to migrate past large obstructions, such as dams built in rivers. Certain dams in the Park have a system of fish ladders built on the downstream side of the dam wall. The fish ladders consist of several compartments that are filled with water from the natural downstream flow of the river. From the bottom level of the dam wall the fish ladder leads at a flat angle to the overflow of the dam wall. By jumping from one compartment to the other, as they would over rocks to migrate upstream, the fish eventually reach the higher water from where they progress to their spawning grounds.

Other aquatic life

It is not always possible to see aquatic life in the Park, but many tourist roads are found next to rivers because this is where most animals are usually seen. Rivers give life and are important as a source of drinking water for terrestrial organisms. It is therefore not a coincidence that many kilometres of tourist roads wind beside the rivers.

Many rest camps are also built near rivers from which water is extracted for human consumption.

A number of animals that form an integral part of the river ecology live in the rivers or are found on the banks of the rivers.

One of the best known of these animals is the Nile crocodile, a dreaded predator at the top of the river's food chain.

Also well known and very dependent on the rivers are the hippos. These giants are often seen basking on the sandbanks, especially during the winter when the sun is not as harsh, or seen with only their ears, eyes and nostrils above the water level.

Other animals, although not often seen, include the Cape clawless otter (*Aonyx capensis*), rodents such as the greater cane rat (*Thryonomys swinderianus*), and the rare (for the Park) water mongoose (*Atilax paludinosus*).

A large variety of birds, reptiles and amphibians, although not strictly aquatic organisms, cannot survive without surface water.

River pollution

The rivers flowing through the Park are under severe ecological pressure. Over the past decades parts of the Mpumalanga and Limpopo Lowveld have developed very rapidly into highly sought-after agricultural, mining and industrial areas. In 1896 the tsetse fly was eradicated from the Lowveld, and effective anti-malarial remedies led to the influx to and settlement of large numbers of people in the area.

This rapid progress of human settlement caught the authorities unawares. The Lowveld is relatively poor as regards water, and planning for the effective utilisation of water sources was ineffective.

At the end of the east-flowing rivers lies the Kruger Park, in the midst of this dilemma. The Crocodile, Sabie, Lepelle, Letaba, Luvuvhu and Limpopo rivers are essential arteries of life, sustaining the survival of this wonderful and world-renowned conservation area.

However, these rivers also act as channels along which pollution, invader plants and silt flow into the Park.

The increased activities of afforestation, agriculture, irrigation, industries and settlements outside the Park's boundaries withdrew large amounts of water, which has now put a lot of pressure on all the river systems.

Apart from the decreased flow, the quality of water in the river systems shows a dramatic turn for the worse. The upstream catchment areas are the root of the problem.

The shorter rivers rising in the mountains are faster flowing and are not subject to as much pollution as the slower-flowing rivers rising on the flatter area of the Highveld. During the droughts of 1984/5 and 1992/3, the spotlight once again focused on the problems of the rivers flowing through the Park and especially on the catchment areas of the respective rivers. Thanks to the efforts of the Kruger National Park's Rivers Research

Programme, which ran from 1987 to about 2000, the general public has come to realise that these rivers need protection for the survival of the ecology and of all the inhabitants of the Lowveld.

The rivers considered to be perennial in the Park rise mainly on the slopes of the Drakensberg Escarpment, while the Lepelle River rises on the Highveld. With their higher rainfall and many springs, the mountain areas are the feeder sources of the perennial rivers.

Rivers mean life and the Kruger National Park has a number of these life-giving arteries essential to its continuous existence.

Considering the enormous catchment area and the distance it flows through the Highveld and the Lowveld before reaching the Kruger Park, the Lepelle River is seen as the river under most pressure.

The Lepelle River has a catchment area in excess of 54 000 km² that includes towns as distant as Witbank (eMalahleni). Well-known rivers, such as the Bronkhorstspruit, Steelpoort and Motlatse (Blyde) rivers, form the larger tributaries of this long river. A number of dams, including Loskop, Witbank, Arabie and Blyderivierspoort, have been constructed in the Lepelle River and its tributaries to regulate water in the catchment area.

Both past and present mining activities in the Witbank area, almost exclusively coal mining, have led to the leaching of acid water into the tributaries of the Lepelle River, leaving large sections of the river sterile. On its way to the Kruger Park, the river flows through industrial areas of towns and villages, human settlements, agricultural activities and badly eroded areas caused by overgrazing. A last setback before reaching the Park is at Phalaborwa where the backflow of waste water from industrial and mining activities results in the complete deterioration of the quality of water in the river. Leaching from the slime dams increases the salt and heavy-metal levels in the river.

Large quantities of sediment are borne along the Lepelle River from the overgrazed areas in the catchment area, resulting in the silting up of the river and eventual fish mortalities, due to either smothering or a shortage of oxygen.

Owing to circumstances outside the boundaries of the Kruger National Park, this once-mighty river has been transformed into the river with the poorest water quality flowing through the Park. The poor quality of water now regularly forces rest camps such as Satara and Olifants, which are dependent on water from the Lepelle River, to get their drinking water from boreholes.

Crocodile deaths

In 2010 it was established that the pollution of the Lepelle River seemed to be responsible for the reported spate of deaths of Nile crocodiles. The condition of the river and pansteatitis found in the crocodile population in the river seem to point to the level of pollution of the Lepelle River.

Dead Nile crocodiles found in the lower reaches of the Sabie River also appear to have died as a result of pansteatitis, which, if proven to be the case, opens new areas of concern.

The water of the Lepelle River flows at a reasonable rate until it reaches the Olifants Gorge. The water from the Massingir Dam in Mozambique has now pushed into the gorge within the Kruger Park. This causes the flow of the Lepelle River to diminish drastically, resulting in the polluting elements sinking to the silt at the bottom of the now very slow-flowing river and the upper reaches of the Massingir Dam.

The slow flow of the river causes the sediment and silt to accumulate along the bottom of the river and the dam, which causes the river to become stagnant.

Bottom feeders, especially the ordinary barbel, the sharptooth catfish (*Clarias gariepinus*), act as indicator species for pansteatitis, showing the relevant lesions in its liver and fat, in appearance similar to rancid fat. These Catfish feeds on the bottom of the river or dam and take in the polluting elements, which eventually manifest in the liver and fat of the fish.

These fish are then taken by crocodiles and subsequently the pansteatitis is transferred to the crocodile.

The effect of pansteatitis is obvious in the fatty tissue of the animal, especially in the tail. The pansteatitis appears as a yellowish, almost margarine-like substance in the tail, which is very painful and restricts the movement of the animal. This in turn leads to a situation where the animal cannot hunt, resulting in its death.

With the construction of the Corumana Dam on the Sabie River, near where it flows into Mozambique, similar river conditions to those in the Lepelle River apply. Dead crocodiles, showing the same symptoms as those in the Lepelle River, have been found.

River degradation

There are seven major rivers flowing through the Kruger National Park: the Limpopo, Luvuvhu, Shingwedzi, Letaba, Lepelle, Sabie and Crocodile rivers – all still regarded as perennial.

However, with the pressures from outside the Park on the rivers flowing through it, both the flow and quality of water encountered in the Park have decreased alarmingly. As a result of the afforestation in the major catchments of the Park's rivers and the increase in water usage by communities, industries and agriculture, all the rivers, with the exception of the Sabie, stop flowing for short periods during extreme droughts. However, although they lose their perenniality for these short periods, downgrading them will add to their demise and therefore they should still be treated as perennial rivers.

Even though the catchment areas may be far away, problems can stem from these areas. With the influx of development into the Lowveld area, especially bordering on the Park, associated environmental problems arose, which will have a lasting detrimental effect on the Park.

All the rivers flowing through the Park originate on the Highveld or near the Drakensberg Escarpment. Extensive areas, especially along the Escarpment, have been afforested with exotic, rapidly growing trees that withdraw huge quantities of water. Together with irrigation, millions of litres of water are withdrawn every day, causing many streams to dry up.

Agricultural, industrial, municipal and settlement areas cause problems when many tons of chemical fertilisers, pesticides and untreated sewage are drained directly into the river systems, or over the years leach into the rivers through underground seepage.

Apart from organisms ingesting these pesticides, they also accumulate in the organisms that feed upon them.

Mining activities are also responsible for discharging large quantities of salts and dangerous substances such as acid water and heavy metals into the river systems that eventually drain into the rivers flowing into the Park; this has an adverse affect on aquatic and terrestrial life downstream.

Exotic plants originating from outside the borders of the Park are borne through the river systems, infesting the rivers and river banks and causing severe problems for terrestrial and aquatic life. Lantana (*Lantana camara*) is a notorious example of a riparian invader. Water lettuce (*Pistia stratiotes*) and water hyacinth (*Eichhornia crassipes*) have become serious problems, especially in the southern watercourses in the Park.

Many of the larger dams seem to be silting up. Poor farming methods in areas surrounding the Park are leading to serious erosion problems. This can be seen in the brown water during floods, when tons of topsoil is borne away through the river systems, ending up in the dams of the Park.

When the silt load is very high it causes fish and other organisms to suffocate. The slower flow of the rivers after the summer rains causes the hippo pools and dams to silt up altogether and rapids and bedrock, with their wide variety of habitats, are transformed into sandy rivers. Bottom feeders find it difficult as the silt covers the natural fauna and flora upon which they feed, and nesting fish have to find nesting place elsewhere because of the layer of mud.

Dams are important in an ecosystem as they provide water in times of reduced flow, but they also have disadvantages.

Water quality in dams changes because of evaporation, which raises salt concentrations. The increase in algae due to the higher salt levels cuts off sunlight to the deeper parts of the dam. This causes cold layers deeper down and warmer water towards the surface. Decomposition in the bottom layers consumes oxygen, creating an oxygen-depleted zone.

Water released from the bottom of dams results in cold, oxygen-depleted water, and water flowing over the dam wall is warmer and rich in oxygen. These differing water releases also differ from water flowing into the dam and may cause changes in the downstream ecology of the river.

Fairly regular water releases stop the system from having natural floods. As a result the large number of organisms depending on the stimulation by floods experience problems with natural breeding migrations.

The dam wall also acts as a barrier to migration, separating fish communities from each other. The reduction in or the absence of floods proves to be advantageous to the exotic invader plant communities, as the plants and seeds are no longer washed away; because reeds are not regularly washed open, they overgrow the river bed.

Exotic plants and animals associated with rivers create problems as they deprive the river of its natural character and have a detrimental effect on the system.

NATURE CONSERVATION

How many species of vertebrate animals are there in the Park?

Mammalia (mammals)	148
Aves (birds)	507
Reptilia (reptiles)	119
Amphibia (amphibians)	35
Pisces (fish – including 3 exotics)	53

How many of the animal species represented in the Park are normally seen by visitors?

Some animals are nocturnal in habit, some are very small, others are burrowers and some others are very rare. In general about

50 of the more conspicuous animal species are seen regularly. On any one day, viewing can result in seeing anything between 15 and 20 or more of the mammal species.

Are any animals in the Kruger Park threatened with extinction?

Not at this stage. However, it would be gratifying to see an increase in the numbers of cheetahs, African wild dogs, sable antelope, roan antelope and black rhino.

What does SANParks do to ensure the survival of rare species?

A team of highly specialised scientists, comprising zoologists, botanists and veterinarians, is employed by SANParks. These people are constantly engaged in research to ascertain the best methods of conserving the different species in general and rare species in particular.

Breeding camps for rare species such as roan antelope and tsessebe have been established in areas in the vicinity of Pretoriuskop, Mopani and Shingwedzi rest camps.

Has any species of game become extinct in the Park?

Yes. The white rhino became extinct shortly before the Sabi Game Reserve was proclaimed in 1898, and the black rhino disappeared from the Park around the late 1930s. Oribi also disappeared from the Park. Oribi were reintroduced, but once again they seem not to have established themselves. Some Lichtenstein's hartebeest were reintroduced from Malawi during the late 1980s but have not adapted to their new environs. Since their reintroduction, it has been established that they apparently did not naturally occur in the Kruger National Park and most of these animals have been translocated to the Limpopo National Park in Mozambique. The few loners that could not be captured have been left to die off naturally.

Is there an animal hospital in the Park?

No, but the Ministry of Agriculture has a research station at Skukuza, which consists of veterinarians and qualified wildlife staff. SANParks also have veterinarians whose responsibilities are to see to the wellbeing of all animals and birds in the Park.

Occasionally animals are treated at this station, but it is not an animal hospital in the true sense of the word. It is not open to the public because of quarantine restrictions.

Seriously injured animals are euthanised, especially where their injuries were the result of human action, such as being hit by a vehicle. If they are injured in a natural incident, it is the policy to let nature take its course.

In exceptional cases, rare animals are treated, provided the prognosis is good.

In cooperation with SANParks, the Ministry also takes the necessary precautions to curb the spread of diseases such as anthrax and foot-and-mouth disease within the Park.

Are there many diseases that pose a threat to wildlife?

Wild animals are susceptible to a wide range of diseases, but only three of them – anthrax, foot-and-mouth disease and, recently, bovine tuberculosis – have posed a danger in recent years.

Are some animals more susceptible to these diseases than others?

All mammals are susceptible to anthrax, with kudu and roan antelope top of the list. During the last extensive outbreak in 1990, many fatalities were reported among kudu, and many other animals were affected in the outbreak. Fortunately sable antelope do not appear to be affected.

Foot-and-mouth disease is more prevalent among African buffaloes and impalas, although most cloven-hoofed animals are susceptible to it. Other than domestic stock, wild herbivores seldom succumb to this disease.

Bovine tuberculosis was initially diagnosed in the Park's buffalo population. Most of the buffalo herds in the Park show infection. It manifests itself in gregarious populations of animals and is now found in animals where large herds occur. Even predators feeding on infected animals are showing the spread of bovine tuberculosis to be more widespread than was thought.

Recent studies have shown that wild animals are capable of adapting to these diseases, and bovine tuberculosis is showing signs of a decrease.

Are these diseases highly contagious?
Yes, they are indeed.

What measures are taken to combat these diseases?
It is impossible to control foot-and-mouth disease within the boundaries of the Park and there is no effective measure to treat it. A fence was erected on the western and southern boundaries in 1961 to prevent animals from leaving the Park and so spreading the disease.

During an outbreak of foot-and-mouth disease or anthrax, wildlife inspections are intensified to keep track of the direction in which the disease spreads, so that the necessary steps can be taken in areas adjoining the Park.

To prevent accidental spreading of the disease, no animal or animal product may be removed from the Park without the written permission of the State Veterinarian

at Skukuza. This arrangement is effective even when there is no active outbreak of the disease. The exceptions to this rule are elephants, rhinos and zebras, which are immune to foot-and-mouth disease.

Additional precautions in the case of anthrax near the boundaries of the Park are the burning of all infected carcasses found and the disinfecting of water holes in the area. This also includes providing alternative food sources that will draw vultures, the main spreaders of the disease, away from the infected carcasses.

What is being done regarding the bovine tuberculosis problem?
Nothing is done due to the extent of the problem. Continuous monitoring of the disease is done. Latest studies show that there are signs of a decrease in the occurrence of this disease.

How do these diseases affect the animals involved?
Mortality from foot-and-mouth disease in wild animals is very low, and most of the affected animals recover within about 24 days. Secondary infection of the hoof and mouth may have a more serious effect if sepsis sets in and the animal becomes crippled, and thus easy prey for predators.

Anthrax is a particularly unpleasant and usually fatal disease that leads to death within a very short period.

Are there any prophylactic measures taken for these diseases?
The relatively mild nature of foot-and-mouth disease renders special measures unnecessary and uneconomical. It is an entirely different matter as far as domestic stock is concerned; contaminated meat is unfit for human consumption and many domestic animals die of the disease.

Have there been any outbreaks of rinderpest recently?

The only known rinderpest epizootic occurred in 1896 when large numbers of African buffaloes, and other animals, were decimated.

Is the Park completely fenced in?

Since the mid-1970s the Park has been completely fenced in. In 1993 the western fence, where it borders on private game reserves and conservation areas, was removed. Theoretically this made the private game reserves bordering on the western side of the Park part of the greater Kruger National Park.

The eastern boundary of the Park is also an international border between South Africa and Mozambique. This fence is maintained as far as possible as an international boundary. The far northern section, however, now forms part of the newly established Great Limpopo Transfrontier Park (GLTP), and the fence was partially removed in order for game to migrate into this new conservation area in Mozambique.

Why is the whole of the Park not enclosed with an elephant-proof fence?

The cost of such a project would be prohibitive, as the length of fencing would involve 668 km of fencing at a cost of about R150 000 to R230 000 per kilometre at the time of writing.

Do larger animals damage the fence?

Elephants, and to a lesser extent giraffes and African buffaloes, occasionally damage the portion of the fence still demarcating the western boundary. The fence on the eastern boundary, which under normal conditions could be considered elephant-resistant, is sometimes damaged by these huge animals.

Do the fences interfere with animal migrations or movements?

Before the erection of the fence between the Park and Mozambique, some animal species, particularly African elephants and eland, migrated to Mozambique after good rains fell there. They usually returned during winter because of more permanent water in the Park.

Species like Burchell's zebra and blue wildebeest migrated westward towards late autumn and winter, returning with the onset of spring. The development of farming areas and the fences ended these migrations.

In its fenced-in state the Park can no longer be considered a natural ecological unit, a fact that is recognised in its management programme.

Do animals move around in the Park?

The main reason animals move around in the Park is their need for food and water. When this becomes scarce they will move around to more optimal grazing areas where there is also sufficient water.

Some animals show a tendency for seasonal movement. Large herds of zebra and wildebeest, for example, find their summer grazing in the Satara area and their winter food supplies in the Tshokwane and Lower Sabie areas.

Do certain species frequent specific areas or habitats?

Predators are usually found near water holes, where it is easier to surprise their prey, especially during times of drought and during winter. Lion can remain in one area for a considerable length of time, but, if the herbivores move away in search of better grazing and water, the lion will follow.

Waterbuck are dependent on water and will very seldom wander far away from it.

Impalas, to a lesser extent, also frequent the vicinity of water holes and rivers. Bushbuck and nyalas are restricted to riverine thickets, and klipspringers are regularly found on koppies or nearby rocks.

Wildebeest and zebras prefer open areas with short grass, while kudu keep to denser growth. Eland, African wild dogs, African buffaloes and African elephants are nomadic and move around constantly.

Most animals, however, are territorial and males will defend an area against a member of its own species. Some, like giraffe, will stay in an area for years without marking or defending it. In this case the area is known as a home range, as opposed to a territory, which is marked and defended.

Is it worthwhile stopping at a water hole and waiting for the animals to come to drink?

There are usually some animals to be seen at a water hole, and, even when it appears to be deserted, it could be worthwhile to stop for a while and wait for game to come and drink. During winter or periods of drought, large concentrations of game can be found at the more permanent watering points or rivers and pools.

After good rains many temporary water holes appear all over the veld and the animals are therefore scattered over large areas. A slow drive along the roads could be more rewarding than waiting at the water holes.

What time of the day is best for watching game?

During the summer heat it is advisable to go on early-morning and late-afternoon drives and to spend the hottest part of the day in camp resting, or doing bird-watching or identifying and learning about the trees.

In the winter months more game can be seen throughout the day and early drives are not really necessary. Under cool conditions animals tend to drink during the morning. In summer, during the heat of the day, elephants frequent water holes and rivers to cool down.

Which roads are the best for game watching?

Some visitors believe that there is more game on the firebreak roads not open to tourists. However, in contrast to the firebreaks, which often cut across relatively waterless areas, tourist roads either follow watercourses for some distance or have a number of dams or water holes near them.

Some visitors also believe that there is more game to be seen along gravel roads than the tarred roads, while others prefer a smooth, dustless ride on the tarred roads.

Both types of road have their advantages: vegetation along tarred roads is relatively free of dust all year round, whereas the more natural-looking, quiet gravel roads are more appealing to some visitors, especially keen photographers. There is no proof that more game can generally be seen from gravel roads.

Where am I most likely to see a kill?

Most kills take place near a water hole, especially during winter.

Is game evenly distributed throughout the Park?

The topography, geology, climate and biotic factors have been instrumental in creating many clearly defined plant communities. It is important to note that there is a very close correlation between soil type and the distribution of plant species.

Animal distribution is affected by a number of ecological factors, such as the vegetation and the particular habits of the species – some prefer dense bush, some more open spaces, while others have very specialised habitat requirements.

More information on this aspect can be found in the discussions on the different species.

The Pretoriuskop area was once known as the haunt of large herds of wildebeest and zebra. Why are these species now so rare in that area?

Until 1924 farmers still had grazing rights in this area, and, to ensure good grazing for the winter, they burned the veld every year. This policy kept the grass short. Very little burning was carried out after 1924, and in 1943 Colonel Stevenson-Hamilton reported that a serious problem was being created by the encroachment of bush and by tall, unpalatable grasses replacing the short grass. He stated in his report: 'The result is seen in the immense increase of the browsers – impalas and kudu – and the decrease by emigration to more open country in the west, of the grazing species – wildebeest, zebras, sable, roan and waterbuck.'

Can previous conditions be restored?

Burning the veld was reimplemented in the 1950s to establish more suitable conditions for the grazers, and there is now good reason to believe that the pendulum is swinging back.

Will more water holes be established?

By 1990 there were more than 450 functional boreholes with windmills and/ or pumps to provide water to reservoirs and troughs. There were also more than 86 dams of various sizes and capacities.

Some boreholes dry up during prolonged spells of drought. However, the sinking of boreholes could not continue indefinitely.

Artificial water holes are not the complete answer; even when the stage has been reached where there is enough water from a sufficient number of water holes and dams, rain for plant growth will still be necessary.

When was the water-provisioning scheme initiated?

Since the 1930s boreholes have been sunk and dams built on a small scale. As the number of animals increased, progressively more water had to be supplied and the programme was speeded up, especially during the 1960s and 1970s.

Is the Park becoming drier?

In his early reports, Colonel Stevenson-Hamilton expressed the opinion that a process of increasing desiccation was taking place. However, it has subsequently been shown that the summer rainfall areas of southern Africa are subject to a 20-year climatic cycle, with periods of approximately 10 years of generally above and below average rainfall.

Increased farming, industrial, mining and forestry activities, and the increase in human settlement in the catchments of the rivers flowing through the Park, have resulted in an increased demand for water. This has dramatically impaired the flow of the major rivers of the Park, and only the Sabie River may still be considered a perennial river.

The periodic drying up of springs could be attributed to the cyclic nature of the rainfall.

Is intensive research being done in the Park?

The SANParks research team consists of highly qualified and experienced individuals, most of them specialists in their respective fields. Research is not confined to the survival of rare species, but also involves the more prolific species and the control of their numbers. Zoological and veterinary research is supplemented by intensive study of plants and plant communities, with special reference to pastures. Soil types and their influence on vegetation are also studied, as are the river systems and the associated fresh-water ecology.

What is the purpose of this research?

To conserve successfully, one must have a thorough and intimate knowledge and understanding of the processes and functions of natural ecosystems. The Kruger National Park and most other conservation areas are no longer entirely natural ecological units and man, by way of sound nature management techniques, must therefore aid nature.

The more prolific species in the Park pose a threat to the rare species by virtue of their numbers and the resulting over-utilisation of the available habitat.

Apart from the fact that there is still so much that we do not know, new problems still arise all the time and have to be addressed.

How are the numbers of animals in the Park ascertained?

For years the annual aerial census of game used to take place during the winter months, between May and September, when most of the trees are bare, the grass short and the game concentrated near permanent water. The Park was divided into flying grids with counts done by six observers in a low-flying, fixed-wing aircraft and from a helicopter. The results were then correlated with censuses on the ground.

Because of the escalating costs of conducting a full annual aerial census, this has now been replaced by a sample count.

Counts by helicopter are still done, mainly to establish more accurate numbers for African elephants, hippopotamus and African buffaloes, as they form the group of animals of which numbers can have major influences on the environment, including associated animal populations.

What procedure is followed for counting a herd of elephants or buffaloes on the run?

With the helicopter flying directly above the herd, elephants are directly counted, while colour slides are taken of the buffalo herds and afterwards projected onto a screen for counting. Figures for African elephants and African buffaloes are therefore very accurate and the herd dynamics can also be established.

It is obviously impossible to cover the whole of the Park in flying grids in a single day. How are double counts avoided?

During the time of the year that the census is undertaken, animals tend to remain in the vicinity of permanent water holes and do not move around significantly.

Have any rangers or other members of staff been attacked or killed by animals?

In the entire existence of the Park, animals have killed about 35 people. Most of them were killed by leopards, African elephants and Nile crocodiles, and, strangely, relatively few by lions. Some were killed while not busy with their normal duties. However, others were attacked while carrying out their duties, which highlights the fact that one must always be on full alert when entering the realm of the wild animals.

Have there been exceptional encounters between humans and animals in the Park?

One or two encounters from the earlier years of the Park's existence are very well documented. Certainly the best-known is that of ranger Harry Wolhuter and his horse that were attacked by two lions late one afternoon in August 1903. Keeping his presence of mind, Wolhuter killed one of the lions with his sheath knife and climbed in a tree. As he feared, the other lions, that had unsuccessfully attacked the horse, soon returned and reared up against the tree trunk in an endeavour to reach the badly injured man. Fortunately Wolhuter's dog, Bull, returned and started barking, which distracted the lions. Meanwhile his field assistants, who had lagged behind owing to the slow-moving pack donkeys, arrived and managed to frighten off the lions.

The skin of the lion and the knife used to kill it are on display in the Stevenson-Hamilton Memorial Library in Skukuza.

There is also the incident in 1926 when Glen Leary, father-in-law of ranger Harold Trollope, was fatally injured by a wounded leopard.

In the 1970s student ranger Tom Yssel was attacked in shallow water of the Sabie River by a Nile crocodile. After hours of tug-of-war between the huge crocodile and Tom's rescuers, his colleagues Louis Olivier and Hans Kolver eventually freed him from the vice-like jaws. The latter two were both awarded the Wolraad Woltemade medal, at the time the highest South African award for civil bravery.

Many other incidents have been recorded of fatal encounters and numerous close encounters with animals in the Park, but this would be material for a publication of its own.

Taking into account the number of cases in which humans were killed by wild animals since the proclamation of the Park in 1898, it amounts to a mere fraction of the encounters between staff and potentially dangerous animals in the normal course of their duties. If one views it in perspective, it has been proved through the experience of people living in the bush that wild animals, if left undisturbed, very seldom deliberately try to harm human beings.

How many rangers are there in the ranger corps in the Kruger National Park?

There are 220 staff members involved in ranger services in the Park.

What are the qualifications required to become a ranger?

In order to become a ranger, one must meet the following requirements:

- South African citizenship.
- Efficiency in speaking, reading and writing in English and another language.
- A diploma in Wildlife Management, but preference may be given to applicants with higher academic qualifications.
- In addition, applicants are recommended to have the following:
  - Knowledge of one or more of the following: Tsonga, Siswati and Zulu.
  - Proficiency in the use of firearms.
  - Practical knowledge of nature conservation and the Kruger Park.
  - Experience in law enforcement.

A ranger is also required to be able to adapt to a quiet life, which is often devoid of normal social life and amenities such as shops, schools, medical services and service stations for vehicles. This is because rangers' quarters are often situated in remote parts of the Park.

Ranger positions are frequently filled from a list of suitable internal candidates, which include guides and wilderness trails rangers.

It is important to note that rangers' children would have to attend boarding school from an early age. Family life is restricted and rangers must be prepared to accept this.

What are the general duties of a ranger?

A ranger is responsible for the implementation of all management activities in the area under his/her control. These include all security issues and patrolling his section regularly and reporting on the condition of grazing and game, water resources, weather conditions, roads, firebreaks and fences.

A ranger must execute a programme of controlled, rotational veld burning, control accidental fires, combat poaching and assist in research programmes. He is also responsible for law enforcement on the roads and within rest camps, and, if necessary, must undertake other police duties as well. A ranger is expected to assist the research staff during game censuses and epizootics as well as with scientific observations. Administrative duties include correspondence and keeping a diary, and the extermination of exotic plants and animals are also his responsibility.

Will any more national parks be created?

SANParks is continually negotiating for new parks. There are quite a number of biomes in South Africa that are still not sufficiently protected.

THE ROLE OF FIRE

Parts of the Park have obviously been burned. Is this done deliberately?

Yes, a programme of controlled veld burning has been followed since 1954, whereby some of the burns in the Park are prescribed and therefore deliberate. Veld burning is one of the emotive wildlife management issues and the current fire policy implemented in the Park has changed significantly over time. This was to ensure that veld fires fulfil their role as an integral part of natural ecosystems. All forms of ignition (controlled burns, lightning, accidental fires and cross-border fires) are taken into account. A primary concern is to allow lightning to serve as the major source of ignition.

Other areas that are burnt are due to the many firebreaks established to protect Park infrastructures. Various experimental burning plots have been established in various landscapes in the Park over many years, in an attempt to establish the best fire regime for the respective landscapes. Certain of these experimental plots are burnt at various times of the year and at varying intervals.

Would it not be better for the vegetation in a nature reserve to be protected against fire?

Fire is a natural and very necessary phenomenon. Just as rain is required and is important to rejuvenate the landscape, fire is essential for successful ecosystem functioning. The Kruger National Park biome is classified as savanna. Savannas are a mixture of trees and grassland. Fire is an important ecological process required to maintain this tree-grassland ecosystem balance and its associated biodiversity.

This system has evolved over millennia, with fire as part of it, and has been shaped by various fire regimes. The Kruger Park has the climate and vegetation to support fires, and suppressing fires would be unnatural and unrealistic, and could be more harmful to the environment.

What would happen if fires were curbed in the Park?

Research has shown that areas to be burnt are controlled by rainfall. Rainfall during the previous two seasons usually determines how much of the Park is to be burnt. Areas that are not burnt and where herbivores are unable to consume the grass become moribund and unpalatable and accumulate in high densities of combustible material. This accumulation of biomass increases the risk of uncontrollable fires. Biomass accumulation also reduces plant growth and the establishment of fresh growth due to the shading out of key resources.

How is the burning programme carried out?

Two considerations are used to calculate the percentage to be burnt per ranger section.

The first is the rainfall during the past two rainy seasons. In addition, at the end of the growing season, the rangers conduct a veld-condition analysis, where the biomass of grass is measured. After the rainfall and biomass of grass have been taken into account, a final percentage per ranger section to be burnt is calculated.

The section ranger then burns the majority of this allocated area early in the fire season (April–July), depending on climatic and environmental factors. Burning is ceased in the peak fire season, in anticipation of lightning strikes. Unplanned fires are monitored and are included in the section ranger's target, as are lightning fires. All fires are set as point ignitions and are allowed to burn in a natural way, resulting in a mosaic pattern of burns. Fires are monitored by the ranger and mapped with satellite images.

Suppression of fires will be considered only if life or infrastructure is threatened, or when the threshold of the area to be burnt in a ranger section is reached.

Is a rigid pattern of burning followed?

The burning programme is not rigid and is driven by lightning, rainfall and accumulated biomass. Natural, lightning-induced fires create a mosaic of unburnt, poorly burnt and intensively burnt areas, i.e. natural diversity to be exploited by the range of different animal populations. The current fire policy is attempting to achieve a range of fire patterns and intensities.

Are some areas of the Park protected against fire?

There are no areas in the Park that are specifically protected from fires, other than the experimental fire blocks. Fire frequency and intensity may be reduced in particular areas, such as river catchments, riverine areas, vleis, wetlands and other areas due to their location and site characteristics. Other areas may be inadvertently protected from fires due to the extensive road network in the Kruger Park, as roads often form man-made barriers to fires.

Why are these areas exempted?

One reason why riverine areas have reduced fire frequency is the fact that, through a high grazing regime near the watercourses, there is a reduction of fuel load. The vegetation along rivers, such as tall trees and patches of forest vegetation, does not allow for grasses to grow under the canopy, with the result that fires are very infrequent within these systems.

Are some plants fire-tolerant?

The majority of flora within savanna ecosystems has developed and evolved in this fire-prone environment. These plants are usually burnt back to the ground on a regular basis, but are not dead and are able to regrow and coppice from root stores after a fire.

How much of the vegetation can be destroyed by a fire?

Flora is not destroyed by fire. The impact of fire on vegetation varies, depending on the intensity and frequency of the fire and the height of the vegetation. The firetrap for plants in the Kruger Park has been calculated at 2.5 to 3 m.

Is it true that fire inhibits the growth of certain plants and stimulates the growth of others?

Although fires generally stunt growth, especially in young trees and shrubs, there are some plant species that require fire to stimulate their growth. This may be through heat from the fires, which scarifies or breaks the seed husks. The heat can stimulate seed embryos, while the high temperatures desiccate the seed coats.

Smoke from fires can act as a cue for germination through the release of either ethylene or ammonia.

This interaction between fire and plants is more common in the fynbos systems and is not usually found in the savanna vegetation.

What is the effect of burning at different times of the year?

Burning at different times of the year has the greatest influence on the intensity of a fire. The moisture content of the biomass significantly influences the fire intensity. During the growing season, the moisture content of the biomass is high (vegetation is green), resulting in the fires' being cooler and of lower intensity. During the dry, dormant season the moisture content of the biomass is low (vegetation is brown), causing the fire intensity to be higher. Therefore, burning at different times of the year significantly influences fire intensity.

Has the burning programme in the Park been a success?

The Park has gone through four different fire policies since 1926. The current fire policy at the time of writing has been implemented since 2002. Analysis indicates that the desired fire patterns are being achieved, but the reduction of high-intensity fires has not been significant.

What about small animals that succumb in these fires?

Investigations after a fire show that very few small animals die. When the flames approach, many escape by moving away in good time, while many of them take refuge underground in holes and crevices. These fires usually progress very fast and, although the temperatures at ground level can be very high, subterranean levels are shielded by even a few centimetres of soil.

It must also be kept in mind that small animals such as mice and small reptiles have a very high reproduction rate, which ensures that their recruitment rate is also very high.

What about big animals?

Animals are able to sense fire from a long way off and usually move away before the flames reach them. However, it is possible that under extreme environmental conditions, such as strong winds, high ambient temperatures, low relative humidity and fuel moisture content, situations may arise where fires can trap animals.

It can happen that the veld is set alight by a number of lightning strikes, creating conditions in which animals could be trapped. Instances have been recorded where elephants and rhinos were severely burnt in accidental fires and were humanely destroyed, as they could not be saved.

During a very extensive fire, started by various lightning strikes over a wide area from Satara southwards to the Crocodile River in 1996, which destroyed about 10% of the Park, not a single fire-related mortality among animals was reported.

Averaged over the years, fire mortalities are negligible and constitute only a minute percentage of the larger animals.

What are the main causes of accidental fires?

Ignition sources other than management fires (controlled burns) or lightning strikes are considered to be fires started deliberately. These fires include fires started by poachers, illegal transmigrants, across-border fires and fires started by tourists, whether accidental or deliberate. In 2007 an overseas tourist set fire to the veld along the Doispane road at seven different locations. This caused damage as far south as Berg-en-Dal Rest Camp.

Poachers also set fire to the veld at the Park's borders to lure animals to the young palatable growth of grass that follows.

To sum up, what are the benefits of burning the veld?

After good summer rainfalls it is certain that fires will occur during the following dry season of August/September. In order to prevent large and uncontrollable fires in

the dry season, management of the Park took the decision to do as many patch burns as possible during the early dry season of May/June.

The reasoning behind this decision was:

● To break up the combustible load in the veld with cool, low-intensity fires early in the dry season of May/June, thereby creating a mosaic of burnt and unburnt areas throughout the Park. This template will assist in preventing hot, high-intensity fires from becoming unmanageable in the dry season.

● Results from fire research indicates that the present fire policy could reduce bush encroachment by certain woody vegetation, such as sicklebush (*Dichrostachys cinerea*), and possibly promote the growth of larger species, such as knobthorn acacia (*Acacia nigrescens*) and marula (*Sclerocarya birrea*), through early-season fires. The positive spin-off from this is improved game-viewing.

● The areas of the early burns will resprout and the resulting green flush during the early dry season benefits a variety of antelope species.

● Taking into account the size of the Park, the implementation of the patch mosaic-burning programme is an effort to carry out feasible, timeous interventions producing the various ecosystem effects required. It is believed that this approach will emulate or reinstate the natural burning patterns that took place over centuries before man moved into this area and that are believed to have shaped this savanna.

POACHING

Is poaching a problem in the Park?

Poaching has always been a factor in the Park and, as long as there are human populations along the borders of the Park, it can be accepted that there will be poaching incidents. Subsistence poaching is the most common occurrence, but poaching for ivory and rhino horn has become more frequent over the years; rhino poaching in particular has recently taken on alarming proportions. Regular patrols by rangers, with support provided by a specialised proactive, focused intelligence and investigations unit, as well as assistance from the South African Defence Force and the South African Police, attempt to keep this activity within a manageable level.

How do poachers manage to enter the Park?

No fence has ever been able to deter a determined poacher from entering a conservation area. Poachers either climb the fence or cut the fence where entry is required. Breaches in the fence caused by animals leaving or entering the Park are also used on occasion. Unfortunately it is almost impossible, due to extensive fence lines and remoteness of some areas, to seal the Park off completely by way of fences alone. Rhino poachers are now brazenly entering the Park as bona fide visitors and poaching from the quieter tourist roads.

In which areas do these poaching activities mostly take place?

Most of the poaching occurs within areas that are close to the borders of the Park, where it is easiest to enter and leave the Park quickly, especially when poachers are pursued by rangers. This also makes it easier for the poachers to remove their haul.

How do these poachers kill the animals?

In the past animals were mostly killed with snares, spears, hunting with dogs or a variety of trap devices. Although snares are still a common method, it is alarming to note the escalation in the use of firearms, especially semiautomatic rifles, in poaching.

Which animals are mostly trapped in snares?

Animals ranging from the size of a hare to an elephant fall prey to poachers' snares, but antelope make up the bulk of the victims.

Quite a number of elephants have lost part of their trunks, or have sustained serious injuries to their trunks, through snares. When an elephant gets a foot caught in a snare it is generally strong enough to break the thin cable used to snare larger game. However, it usually sustains serious injuries when the cable cuts into the flesh, causing severe wounds that may lead to sepsis and even gangrene.

Animals trapped in snares always die a lingering and painful death.

Many animals are saved when they are found in time; they are immobilised, and the snare is removed and the wound treated before they are released.

Do poachers kill animals mainly for food?

Some poachers are what is known as subsistence poachers. This means that they kill for food. However, few really need to kill to eat, but they apparently regard poaching as a cheap and fairly easy means of earning an income from the sale of the meat and other body parts. In a small percentage of cases, animals are poached for trophies.

Animals are also poached for certain body parts, which are used in traditional medicine and in witchcraft.

Crocodile fat and some of the organs are regarded as potent medicine for different ailments. There is, however, a growing trend to poach animals, particularly rhinos, purely for financial gain. This activity is generally highly syndicated and well organised, with local hunters who live within the communities being exploited by well-financed poaching syndicates, which operate far from the area, to do the poaching of the animals.

Are poachers considered dangerous?

Poaching has progressed to the point where a large percentage of incidents involve the use of firearms. This obviously places field staff at risk of being shot at and subsequently in danger of being wounded or even killed.

A special anti-poaching unit has been established to support the ongoing ranger anti-poaching operations to combat this type of poaching.

Poaching is no longer done using only snares and the 'quieter' methods of killing animals, but has escalated into activities run by syndicates and involving the targeting of larger animals, such as rhinos for their horns and elephants for their tusks.

The increased use of, and easy availability of, firearms by poachers aggravates the threat and therefore increases the element of danger.

Are many of these poachers brought to justice?

Many convictions are recorded every year and sentences can be either a heavy fine or a jail term, or both. Efforts are continually being made to increase the penalties in order to act as a definite deterrent.

Vehicles, firearms and any other equipment used by poachers are confiscated in the event of their being found guilty and convicted.

Do Kruger Park employees and poachers often clash?

As described above, a very professional and highly trained anti-poaching unit has been established in the Park to support ongoing ranger anti-poaching operations. Ranger staff have on occasion clashed with poachers. In any armed poaching activity, both ranger staff and the poachers themselves are at high risk of serious injury or even death.

Have poachers been killed by their animal victims?

It is not uncommon for a wild animal to break loose from a snare or a trap. The animal then takes flight or may attack its human enemy.

Only very recently the remains of a poacher were found near a snare. He apparently went to inspect his snares when he was surprised and almost totally devoured by lions.

Recently rhino poaching has regularly been in the news. Has the Kruger Park lost many rhino?

The threat to rhino populations, both in the Park as well as on privately owned land throughout South Africa, has increased dramatically since 2008. The Kruger Park, due to its well-managed high populations of rhino, remains a preferred target for poaching syndicates and therefore experiences rhino poaching on an increasing basis. This sustained effort of the rhino poaching syndicates, both within the Park and elsewhere in the country, remains a very high priority for all conservation and law-enforcement agencies.

How successful has the Kruger National Park been in arresting these rhino poachers?

At the time of writing SANParks is focusing its counter-poaching operations at all levels of the syndicated and organised rhino-poaching activities. These operations include support both to and from all of the relevant government and provincial law-enforcement agencies. Current investigations and ongoing joint law-enforcement operations have been very successful in the arrest and prosecution of both poachers and the higher-ranking members of the syndicates in operation.

Are syndicates involved in these poaching activities?

The current rhino poaching activities, which are plaguing both the Park and the country as a whole, are generally driven by well-organised syndicates operating within the country. These syndicates are, more often than not, being driven by international groups.

How many rhinos in the Kruger National Park have been killed for their horns?

Unfortunately the Kruger National Park has suffered unacceptably high mortalities of the rhino population, mainly due to the fact that the Park has the highest population of these magnificent animals in Africa.

The numbers during the last few years reflect a sad picture. Since 2005 reported rhino killings were as follows, with the number of animals killed in Kruger, and the total poached in the country in brackets:

2005	10
2006	17
2007	10
2008	36
2009	50 (122)
2010	146 (333)
2011	25 (448)
2012	362 (633)

MALARIA

What is malaria and how serious is this disease?

Malaria is a serious and life-threatening disease caused by parasites that are transmitted to people through the bites of mosquitoes.

- One child in the world dies of malaria every 30 seconds.
- In 2010 there were 256 million cases of malaria, resulting in the deaths of more than a million people, mostly in Africa.
- Almost half of the world's population is at risk of contracting malaria.
- Malaria takes a very high economic toll by decreasing economic growth by as much as 1.5% in countries with a high disease rate.
- Malaria is curable and preventable.

Does the Kruger National Park fall within a malaria area?

Yes, the Park falls within the endemic malaria area, which in South Africa includes the Limpopo Valley, along the Lowveld of Mpumalanga and Limpopo and into northern KwaZulu-Natal.

Is Kruger considered to be a high-risk area?

The Park is considered to be a medium-risk area for most of the year, although precautions should still be taken. During the summer months of October to April, the Park is considered a high-risk area.

What precautions should be taken?

The period between dusk and dawn is considered the high-risk time during the day and the following precautions are recommended:

- Before travelling to the Park, it is advisable to consult your doctor for advice on oral anti-malarial prophylactics.

- Take the prescribed anti-malarial prophylactics before leaving for the Park. Medicine to be taken weekly should be taken on the same day of the week as when the first dosage is taken and at the same time every day if prescribed on a daily basis.
- It is imperative that you continue the prophylaxis for at least three to four weeks after leaving the malaria area.
- There are various mosquito repellents on the market. Apply copiously to the exposed skin area, especially at dusk and in the early morning.
- It is recommended that you wear long-sleeved clothing, long trousers and socks when outdoors during the dusk to dawn period.
- Wherever possible, sleep under a mosquito net. If this is not available, keep the ceiling or standing fan running to create movement of air, which mosquitoes do not like.
- If the windows and door are not screened, close them before dusk.
- Shortly before going to bed, spray an aerosol insecticide in the room and apply an insect repellent to the exposed parts of the skin.

Are there special precautions for children?

Discuss your child's anti-malarial precautions with your doctor or pharmacist. There are children's versions of anti-malarial drugs on the market.

Children should wear appropriate clothing, as described above, especially early morning and evening, and apply insect repellent to exposed areas of the body.

Are certain people more at risk of contracting malaria than others?

Persons particularly at risk could include the following:
- Adults over 65.
- Children under five.
- Pregnant women.
- AIDS patients.

- Persons who have had their spleens removed.
- Persons receiving chemotherapy.
- Persons with porphyria or epilepsy and chronically ill patients.

What are the symptoms of malaria?

Symptoms of malaria are very flu-like. They include feverishness, chills, muscle aches, sweating, abdominal pain, headache and general tiredness. Sometimes the symptoms can also include diarrhoea, nausea and vomiting. At times malaria can cause the skin colouring to be yellowish due to the breakdown of the red blood cells.

Symptoms of malaria need not always be dramatic, and can easily be dismissed as flu and as unimportant.

How long does it take for the symptoms to appear?

Malaria symptoms normally appear seven to 28 days after infection.

Is malaria curable?

Malaria is completely curable when treated as soon as possible after infection.

What treatment can be expected?

Treatment depends on the type of strain of malaria, the area where infection occurred, the age and condition of the patient and the type of prescription medicine and duration of the treatment.

Should infection not be treated immediately, deterioration in the infected person is normally very sudden and drastic due to the rapid increase of the parasites in the blood stream and liver.

What is the most common type of malaria infection in the Kruger Park?

In the Kruger National Park the most common malaria infection is that of

Plasmodium falciparum and *Plasmodium vivax*, but the former is the more deadly.

How is the parasite transmitted?

Transmission to the human host takes place when an infected *Anopheles* mosquito bites a human to feed off the blood.

Does the parasite have a specific lifecycle?

The *Plasmodium* parasite has an extremely complex life cycle. Upon entering the human host, it goes through a series of changes until it reaches the sexual stage.

In this sexual maturity stage, the parasite can be transmitted from one person to another through the vector agency of the mosquito when the mosquito feeds on an infected human host and then feeds again within 10 to 14 days on a different person.

During the various stages in the life cycle of the *Plasmodium* parasite, it manages to confuse the body's immune system, which allows the parasite to multiply, invade and infect the liver and destroy the red blood cells.

When the infection reaches an advanced state, the capillaries carrying blood to the brain and other organs of the body start to clog, which can lead to delirium and coma.

Is the taking of anti-malarial prophylactics a guarantee against contracting malaria?

Even when you take oral anti-malarial prophylactics, there is no guarantee that you will not contract malaria if bitten by an infected *Anopheles* mosquito. The cheapest, easiest and most effective prevention and precaution against contracting malaria is to use a good insect repellent and to wear suitable clothing.

I forgot to take malaria prophylactics prior to entering the Park. Is it too late to start taking the oral prophylactics now that I am in the Park?

It is never too late to take the necessary preventative measures. All the shops in the Park stock oral anti-malarial medication. Also apply the insect repellent as discussed and you should be sufficiently protected.

It is important to continue with the oral medication for at least three to four weeks after leaving the Park, and to watch out for the symptoms of malaria during this time. Consult your doctor as soon as flu-like symptoms appear and tell him/her that you have visited a malaria area.

Where can I get more information about malaria in this region?

There is a resident medical practitioner in Skukuza. You may also get more information about malaria in the Kruger National Park, its treatment and effects by dialling 082 234 1800.

PLACE NAMES OF THE KRUGER NATIONAL PARK

Over the years many names have been given to various places of historic, geological, ethnical and personal importance in the Kruger National Park. In this way visitors and staff were able to orientate themselves as to where in the Park they were.

Nowadays a number of good road maps, with all kinds of additional features, are available in the shops of the Park, on which visitors can orientate themselves accurately, and it is almost impossible to get lost or not calculate the distance and time to reach one's destination before gate closure times.

Many of the names recorded on the maps of the Park have been derived from six main languages: Afrikaans, English, Xitsonga, Siswati, Sepedi and Tshivenda. Add to this a sprinkling of Dutch, Portuguese, French, Isizulu, Setswana and even Hindi, and a rich treasure-trove of the history of the Kruger National Park is opened.

Many of the names, especially those of boreholes, were given by the rangers on whose section they were drilled and a good many by the boreman responsible for the drilling. However, by far the most names were given by Dr U. de V. Pienaar, former Chief Director of the National Parks of South Africa and for many years the Park Warden of the Kruger National Park. Also responsible for many of the names was Mr J. J. Kloppers, General Manager, Nature Conservation: KNP.

A great deal of research went into establishing the historical and ethnic aspects of the names of the Park, and it is with sincere appreciation that the author of this book acknowledges the work of Mr J. J. Kloppers and the specialists who helped him with the publication (in 1992) of *Place Names in the Kruger National Park*, from which the following explanations are taken.

Entrance gates

Crocodile Bridge

Entrance gate and rest camp on the northern bank of the Crocodile River.
English: Crocodile Bridge – named after the river flowing past the entrance gate as well as past the rest camp and the train bridge of the erstwhile Selati Line (c. 1935).

Malelane

Entrance gate and ranger post on the northern bank of the Crocodile River.
Siswati: Malelane – a subunit of the Malalane Regiment, which had to do duty along the Crocodile River, 'out of sight' of the main base of the royal village, Hhohho.

The name was originally given in 1891 to the railway station outside the Kruger Park, after which it was taken over for the ranger post in 1924 and later also for the entrance gate.

Numbi

Entrance gate, opened in about 1927, and named after the granite outcrop just outside the Park and northwest of the entrance gate.
Siswati: iNumbi – the fruits of the um-numbela shrub (*Bequaertiodendron magalismontanum*). Historical name.

Phabeni

A new entrance gate into the southwestern part of the Kruger Park, opened in 2005.
Sesotho: Phabeni – a shelter or a cave. Historical name.

Kruger Gate

The busiest, main entrance gate to the Park, especially to Skukuza. Situated at the bridge over the Sabie River.
Afrikaans: Named after the President of the Zuid-Afrikaansche Republiek (Transvaal Republic), S. J. P. Kruger. An impressive bust of the old president, hewn out of granite, is situated at this entrance gate.

Orpen

Entrance gate serving the central region of the Park, also with accommodation facilities, and closest gate to Satara Rest Camp.
Afrikaans: Named after Mr and Mrs J. H. Orpen, benefactors of the Kruger National Park. The entrance gate and rest camp are situated on one of the eight farms donated by this couple to the Kruger National Park. This entrance gate, opened in 1954,

replaced the Rabelais entrance gate that served in this capacity from 1932 to 1954.

Phalaborwa

Entrance gate between the Lepelle and Letaba rivers, opened in 1960, and bordering on Phalaborwa town. Replaced the Malopeni entrance gate.

Sesotho: Phalaborwa – 'better than the south', because it was warmer here than the area where the BaPhalaborwa came from. Named after the adjacent town.

Punda Maria

Entrance gate serving the northern section of the Park. Opened in 1976.

Kiswahili/Afrikaans: Named after the nearby rest camp. It is a combination of Punda, from *punda milia*, 'striped donkey' in Swahili, because of the first animals seen by ranger J. J. Coetser when he arrived there from East Africa in 1919, and Maria, his wife's name. See also additional explanations under rest camp names.

Pafuri

Entrance gate serving the far northern area of the Kruger National Park. Opened in 1978.

Tshivenda: A corruption of the name Mphaphuli, the dynastic name of a previous Venda chief from the area.

Rest camps

Crocodile Bridge

Small rest camp situated on the northern bank of the Crocodile River. Established in 1935.

English: Named after the Crocodile River that flows past this small rest camp and the bridge over the river, which formed part of the Selati Line between the then Lourenço Marques and the Selati gold fields.

Lower Sabie

One of the older rest camps in the Park, being established in 1930. The camp is situated on the southern bank of the Sabie River.

English: The name is derived from its position downstream from Skukuza, on the lower reaches of the Sabie River.

Berg-en-Dal

One of the newer and more modern rest camps in the Park. Opened in February 1984. Situated about 11 km from Malelane Entrance Gate on the bank of the Matjulu River, a tributary of the Crocodile River.

Afrikaans: Named because of the mountainous area in which the camp is situated and where many valleys also form part of the landscape.

Pretoriuskop

One of the first rest camps in the Kruger Park. Built in 1928.

Afrikaans: Derives its name from the granite outcrop nearby, named after Willem Pretorius, a member of Carl Trichardt's 1848 expedition to Delagoa Bay (Maputo). Pretorius was buried nearby by João Albasini.

Skukuza

This is the largest rest camp and administrative headquarters of the Kruger Park. Situated on the southern bank of the Sabie River.

Isizulu: A corruption of the original Isizulu word, *sikhukhuza*, 'he who sweeps clean' (as in a new broom) or 'he who changes everything'. Skukuza was the nickname given to Colonel James Stevenson-Hamilton, first warden of the Kruger Park, who made Skukuza his headquarters. Dr H. P. Junod, expert of the Tsonga nation, their history and emotions, interpreted the name and the inclination with which it was given as follows:

As the Tsonga were the earliest inhabitants of this part of the Lowveld, the name Skukuza ('the broom') indicates the resentment they felt that Stevenson-Hamilton had deprived them of their place of habitation after the proclamation of the Kruger National Park.

It is only recently that a kinder disposition became apparent as the Park is now acknowledged as the largest single supplier of work opportunities nearer to their homes.

Skukuza was formerly also known as Reserve, Sabi Bridge and Sikhukhuza.

Satara

A rest camp in the central area of the Park. Opened in 1928.

Hindi: Misspelling of the word *satrah*, meaning fourteenth. The name was given by the surveyor (who, according to Stevenson-Hamilton, had an Indian servant) to the farm Satara 305 when the area south of the Lepelle River was subdivided during the 19th century.

Olifants

A large rest camp, situated on the northern bank of the Olifants (now Lepelle) River. Opened in 1959.

Afrikaans: Named after the river that flows past and below the rest camp. The outcrop on which the rest camp was built is Mangwanduna (Xitsonga), which means 'zebra stallion'.

Letaba

A large rest camp, situated on the western bank of the Letaba River.

Sesotho: Derived from the Sesotho word *lehlaba* and the dialect form *lethaba* for 'sand river'. The Xitsonga name is Ritavi.

Mopani

The newest and last of the large rest camps to be constructed in the Park. Completed in 1991. Situated on the banks of the Pionier Dam.

English: The mopani tree (*Colophospermum mopane*), the most abundant tree and shrub species in this area, gave its name to the new camp.

Shingwedzi

Rest camp in the northern section of the Park. Situated on the southern bank of the river after which it was named. Opened in 1933.

Xitsonga: From *ngwetse*, 'the sound of two metal objects grating against each other'.

Punda Maria

The northernmost rest camp in the Kruger National Park. Situated at the foot of Dimbo Kop.

Kiswahili/Afrikaans: Named by ranger J. J. Coetser when he arrived here from East Africa in 1919. The name is a combination of Punda, from *punda milia*, Kiswahili for 'striped donkey' (zebra), because this was the first animal he saw there, and Maria, his wife's name.

In 1959 the name was changed to Punda Milia as it was thought that this was what Coetser had meant it to be. These facts were brought to the attention of the Board by Dr U. de V. Pienaar, and the original name was reinstated by the Board in 1981.

The original Xitsonga name was Dimbyeni a Shikokololo, 'water or fountain of Shikokololo', named for an important earlier inhabitant of this area.

The Punda Maria surroundings are also called Phande Mariha by the older generation of Venda people. It means 'boundary of the winter(s)' as they noticed that the area from here towards the west was greener during the winter and the climate more moderate than the plains further east, where frost, cold and brown winter vegetation were prevalent during the winter months. Thus, *phande* (stop, up to here or border of) and *mariha* (the plural of *vuriha*, winters). They claim that Punda Maria is a corruption of Phande Mariha.

Smaller camps and bushveld camps

Biyamiti

One of the smaller bushveld camps, situated on the southern bank of the dry river after which it was named. Opened in 1990.

Xitsonga: Biyamiti – 'where ramparts had to be constructed around dwellings,' from *ku biya*, 'to build a rampart', and *miti*, 'huts or dwellings'.

The best explanation for this is that the first Tsonga that moved into this area were forced to build ramparts in the form of a stockade, probably since the Biyamiti area was sought after because of plentiful water, and that there was opposition from the occupants of the area against the new inhabitants.

Maroela Caravan Park

Satellite accommodation situated east of Orpen Entrance Gate and Rest Camp and administered from there.

Afrikaans: From the original Sesotho *morula*, a well-known tree of the Lowveld (*Sclerocarya birrea*).

Tamboti Tented Camp

Satellite accommodation situated east of Orpen Entrance Gate and Rest Camp and administered from there.

Afrikaans: Named after the many tamboti trees (*Spirostachys africana*) found in the vicinity of this tented camp.

Talamati

A small bushveld camp situated on the southern bank of the N'waswitsontso River.

Xitsonga: Named after the borehole nearby. Given the name *Talamati* ('an abundance of water') by ranger Gus Adendorff for the strong flow of water found when the borehole was drilled in 1962.

Roodewal

A small private camp on the S39 on the banks of the Timbavati River, opposite the confluence with the Shisakashangondzo River. Opened in 1983.

Dutch: Named after the original farm, it owes its name Roodewal to the high red banks at the confluence of the Timbavati and Shisakashangondzo rivers. In the new Xitsonga spelling the 'Sh' may also be substituted with 'X', thus it may also be spelled Xisakaxangondzo.

Balule

A small rest camp with limited accommodation and caravan stands, situated on the southern bank of the Lepelle River and administered from Olifants Rest Camp.

Xitsonga: The name is an abridgment of Rimbelule, the Xitsonga name for the Lepelle River. This small camp was originally known as Olifants Rest Camp but was officially changed to Balule in 1961 as 'Olifants' was deemed a more appropriate name for the new and larger rest camp.

Shimuwini

A small bushveld camp on the northern bank of the Letaba River, overlooking the Shimuwini Dam. Opened in 1990.

Xitsonga: Named after the dam at the rest camp and after a large baobab tree (*Adansonia digitata*) in the vicinity; Shimuwini means 'at the baobab tree'.

Boulders

A private camp situated on the S136, west of the Ngodzi Kop, southwest of Mopani Rest Camp.
English: The name refers to the granite boulders among which this little camp was built. Named by Dr U. de V. Pienaar in 1985.

Tsendze Rustic Camp Site

A rustic caravan and camping site situated on the bank of the Tsendze River and administered from Mopani Rest Camp.
Xitsonga: The name, derived from *tsendzeleka*, 'to wander about like someone lost in the bush', probably refers to the winding course of the river on which the camp is situated.

Bateleur

The first bushveld camp of its kind, situated west of Shingwedzi Rest Camp, on the S52 and on the northern bank of the Mashokwe Spruit.
French: Named after the beautiful eagle (*Terathopius ecaudatus*) often seen in the Park.

Sirheni

A bushveld camp northwest of Shingwedzi Rest Camp on the S56; situated on the northern bank of the Sirheni Dam built in the Mphongolo River. Opened in 1990.
Tsonga: Sirheni, 'at the grave', is an abridged version of *Sira ra ndlopfu*, 'grave of the elephant', the name of the water hole submerged by the waters of the dam.

This water hole got its name when an elephant that died from anthrax during the outbreak of 1959/60 was buried near the water hole.

Picnic sites

Afsaal

A picnic spot situated along the H3 main tar road between Skukuza and Malelane Entrance Gate. Named by Dr U. de V. Pienaar and completed in 1985.
Afrikaans: 'A place to rest'.

Mlondozi

A picnic spot north of Lower Sabie Rest Camp and overlooking the Mlondozi Dam. Opened in 1951. The picnic spot is situated on the N'wagovila Koppie, a granophyre koppie named after an earlier inhabitant of this area.
Siswati: 'A strong-flowing river', meaning that there is enough water for man, animal and irrigation.

There is a second explanation for the Siswati name as found in the historical research done by Mr H. Bornman. The Balondolozi, a section of the Inyatsi regiment of Mswati II, at some stage during their skirmishes with the Tsonga (1856–1860), were stationed alongside the Mlondozi River and so the place got the name Mlondozi, 'the place of the Balondolozi'.

Nkuhlu

A picnic spot on the western bank of the Sabie River along the H4-1 about halfway between Skukuza and Lower Sabie rest camps. Opened in 1957.
Xitsonga: 'Natal mahogany' (*Trichilia emetica*). Several of these beautiful evergreen trees are found along the river banks in this area.

Tshokwane

This is a well-known picnic spot on the H1-2/H1-3 between Skukuza and Satara rest camps.

Sesotho: Named after an old Shangaan chief who lived there until his death in 1915. He knew all about the local tribal history and about early Swazi and Zulu raids into the area.

Orpen Dam

Picnic spot and viewpoint east of Tshokwane Picnic Spot. Situated on the southern foothills of N'wamuriwa Kop and overlooking the small Orpen Dam in the N'waswitsontso River. Opened in 1944.
Family name: Orpen – Named after Mr and Mrs J. H. Orpen, benefactors of the Park.

Nhlanguleni

Picnic spot along the S36 near the western border of the Park. Opened in 1956 and named after the spruit along which it is situated.
Xitsonga: 'At the guarri bush' (*Euclea divinorum*).

Muzandzeni

A picnic spot on the S36, south of the H7 tar road between Orpen Entrance Gate and Satara Rest Camp. Situated on the northern bank of the Sweni River.
Xitsonga: 'At the tsessebe' (*Damaliscus lunatus*). Named by ranger J. J. Kloppers in 1958 while measuring out the firebreak road, the present tourist road, when he found a small herd of tsessebe in the area.

N'wanetsi

A picnic spot on the eastern border, east of Satara Rest Camp and situated on the northern bank of the Sweni Spruit.
Xitsonga: From *n'wetsi-n'wetsi*, 'to flicker or shine', and means 'the river with shiny or crystal-clear water'.

Before the present facilities existed, this was a recruiting post for mineworkers. They called this place Isweni (c. 1945).

Timbavati

A picnic spot northwest of Satara Rest Camp, on the banks of the river after which it was named. Opened in 1964.
Xitsonga: From *ku bava*, 'bitter or brackish water' and not from *mbavala*, 'bushbuck', as many people believe.

Makhadzi

This is a new picnic spot northeast of Letaba on the H15 and on the banks of the Makhadzi Spruit.
Tshivenda: 'Father's or chief's sister'. It is uncertain how a Tshivenda name appears this far south and east.

During the 1970s and 1980s this was a military base; in the 1980s it was taken over by the South African Police. The base was used to apprehend those who crossed from Mozambique to South Africa during the Mozambican civil war.

Mooiplaas

This picnic spot is on the H1-6 just south of Mopani Rest Camp and on the northern bank of the Tsendze River. Opened in 1980.
Afrikaans: 'Beautiful place'. This picnic spot replaced the Nshawu picnic spot on the old main road to the north.

Babalala

A picnic spot on the H1-7 on the Dungile Spruit between Shingwedzi and Punda Maria rest camps.
Xitsonga: Named after an earlier inhabitant. Also means 'sleep, my father' in Siswati.

Pafuri

The northernmost picnic spot in the Kruger Park and situated on the southern bank of the Luvuvhu River, on the S63.
Tshivenda: A corruption of Mphaphuli,

the dynastic name of a Venda chief through whose area the river flowed.

This used to be the name of the present Luvuvhu River and is the name of the area in which the picnic spot is situated.

The picnic spot was previously situated further downstream, near the confluence of the Luvuvhu and Limpopo rivers. It was later abandoned due to the potential threat that worsening international relations held for the visitors to the area. The picnic spot was then moved to the eastern bank of the nearby Thambwe Spruit and in 1985 to its present position. It is now situated on the same spot where the tent camp was in 1939.

Rivers

Only the major rivers and a few of the more obvious rivers crossed by visitors are discussed.

Crocodile River

A tributary of the Komati River. This river forms the largest part of the southern border of the Kruger National Park.
English: 'River of crocodiles' because of the high density of crocodiles found in the river. A translation of the original Sesotho, Siswazi, Xitsonga and Afrikaans names – all with the same meaning.

Sabie River

A beautiful, perennial river that flows past Skukuza and Lower Sabie rest camps. A tributary of the Komati River.
Siswati: From *sabisa*, 'to be careful'. The river used to be called Sabana and Lusaba by locals.

The word for 'scared', 'fear' or 'to be careful' is closely related in the various local African languages: *tshaba* (Sesotho), *chava* (Xitsonga), *esaba* (Seswati) and *sabayo* (Isizulu), and various authors refer to the fact that fear could have given rise to the name Sabie. Explanations why the river instilled fear among the locals are, however, divergent.

Nwaswitsontso River

Seasonal river, mostly dry. A tributary of the Komati River. Flows through the central part of the Park for more than 60 km before eventually reaching the Komati River inside Mozambique.
Xitsonga: From *ntonto*, 'intermittent drip', for example when a fountain produces its water through a pulsing action, or 'a river flowing under the sand and is only seen here and there'.

Timbavati River

Seasonal river, mostly dry. A tributary of the Lepelle River. Enters the Park near Orpen Entrance Gate and flows in a northeasterly direction through the Park, eventually flowing into the Lepelle River.
Xitsonga: From *ku bava*, 'bitter or brackish water', and **not** from *mbavala*, 'bushbuck', as believed by many people.

Lepelle (Olifants) River

The largest mostly perennial river flowing through the Park. It separates the central and northern regions of the Park.
Afrikaans: 'River of elephants'.

Letaba River

Main tributary of the Lepelle River.
Sesotho: 'Sand river'. The standard Sesotho form is *lehlaba* and the dialect form, from which Letaba is derived, is *lethaba*.

Tsendze River

Seasonal river, mostly dry. The largest tributary of the Letaba River that rises in its entirety within the Kruger Park.

Xitsonga: From *tsendzeleka*, 'to wander around like someone in the bush', most probably referring to the winding course of the river.

Shingwedzi River

Seasonal river, mostly dry. Flows through the Kruger National Park to become a tributary of the Rio dos Elefantes after entering Mozambique.

Xitsonga: From *ngwetse*, 'the sound of two metal objects rubbing together'. West of the rest camp, the Shingwedzi River is fed by two main tributaries, the Phugwane and the Mphongolo rivers.

Luvuvhu River

Seasonal river, a tributary of the Limpopo River. Forms the extreme northwestern boundary of the Park.

Tshivenda: From *muvuvhu*, the river bushwillow tree (*Combretum erythrophyllum*), and **not** from *mvuvhu* (Tshivenda) or *mpfuvu* (Xitsonga), both names for the hippopotamus. The Xitsonga pronunciation of the name is 'rivubye'. For many years the river was erroneously called the Pafuri River.

Limpopo River

Large river, predominantly perennial, forming the northern boundary of the Kruger National Park with Zimbabwe.

Sesotho: English corruption of the Sesotho name Lebepe, of which the meaning is not known. The Venda call the river Vhembe and the Tsonga call it Minti, 'many channels'.

Dams

Matjulu

A small concrete dam built in 1982 in the Matjulu Spruit, a tributary of the Crocodile River. At the same time Berg-en-Dal Rest Camp was built on the banks of the dam.

Sepedi: Matjulu, also Matsulu – 'places of the Zulus'; from the original Sesotho, as the Bapedi of this region called the people from Swaziland who arrived here during the reign of Sobhuza I (1815–1836). The Swazis occupied the area north of the Crocodile River and south of the Sabie River during the reign of Mswati II (1840–1868); the Bapedi called all the places where the Swazis lived Matjulu and Matsulu.

Mpondo

A large earthen dam built on the S102 in 1972, in the Mpondo Spruit, a tributary of the Bume River.

Xitsonga: From the original Afrikaans *pond* (pound sterling). The origin of this name is uncertain.

Shitlhave

A small earthen dam on the H1-1 tar road near Pretoriuskop Rest Camp. Built in 1964 in the spruit after which it was named. Also the name of the nearby gabbro outcrop.

Xitsonga: Named after Colonel Stevenson-Hamilton's first ranger, Sergeant Jafuta Shitlhave.

Transport

A small earthen dam on the S66, off the H1-1 tar road between Skukuza and Pretoriuskop rest camps. Completed in 1971.

English: Named for the Department of Transport, which donated the funds for its construction.

Sunset

Built at Lower Sabie as an emergency water supply facility for the rest camp.

English: Named by a regular visitor, Mr H. Hutchinson, in 1992, as the dam is immediately west of Lower Sabie Rest Camp and is very popular with visitors for its spectacular sunsets.

Mlondozi

An average-sized concrete dam built in 1951 in the spruit after which it is named. **Siswati:** 'A strong stream of water', referring to the spruit and indicating that there was enough water for human and animal consumption as well as for irrigation.

According to historical research, a second explanation of the name is that the Balondolozi, a section of the Inyatsi regiment of Mswati II, was stationed in this area during their skirmishes with the Tsongas (1856–1860) and that this area got the name of Mlondozi, 'the place of the Balondolozi regiment'.

Mantimahle

A small earthen dam next to the H1-2 tar road near Skukuza. The dam was built in the spruit with the same name, to supply water for the construction of the tar road in 1969.
Siswati: 'Clean or clear water'.

Jones's Dam

A small earthen dam built on the S36, west of Tshokwane Picnic Spot in 1957.
English: Named by Mr J. J. Kloppers after Colonel Rowland-Jones, a former senior ranger, who was involved in the construction of the dam.

Silolweni

A medium-sized earthen dam on the H1-2, near Tshokwane Picnic Spot, built in 1969 to supply water for the building of the tar road to the north. This dam is no longer accessible to the public.
Siswati: 'Marshy during rainy seasons'.

Orpen

A small concrete dam in the N'waswitsontso River, at the southern foothills of N'wamuriwa Kop east of Tshokwane Picnic Spot. Completed in 1944.
Family name: Named after Mr and Mrs J. H. Orpen, benefactors of the Kruger National Park.

Lugmag

A medium-sized earthen dam on the S36, built in the Ripape Spruit near the western border of the Park, west of Tshokwane. This dam wall was breached in the January 2012 floods and will not be rebuilt.
Afrikaans: Named after the South African Air Force, which donated the dam to the Kruger Park on completion of the runway at the Skukuza airport in 1957.

Refer also to Lugmag Dam near Punda Maria, which was built under the same circumstances after the completion of the airstrip near Punda Maria Rest Camp.

Mazithi

A small earthen dam next to the H1-3 tar road north of Tshokwane Picnic Spot. Completed in 1935.
Xitsonga: The name of an early inhabitant of the area.

Kumana

A small earthen dam next to the H1-3 tar road, north of Tshokwane Picnic Spot.
Xitsonga: The name of an early inhabitant of the area. This historical name was given to the dam when it was built in 1933.

Nwanetsi

A small concrete dam built below the picnic spot with the same name, just downstream of the confluence of the Nwanetsi and Sweni rivers. Completed in 1952.

Xitsonga: From *n'wetsi-n'wetsi* meaning 'to shimmer or flicker'. This refers to the crystal-clear water of the river.

Gudzani

A medium-sized concrete dam on the S41, east of Satara Rest Camp and built in the spruit with the same name. Completed in 1950.

Xitsonga: The name of an early inhabitant of the area.

Rabelais

A small earthen dam on the S106, east of the Orpen Entrance Gate. Built in the Makukutswana Spruit, it was completed in 1941.

French: Named after the original farm on which the dam is built.

Nsemani

A medium-sized earthen dam built north of the H7 tar road west of Satara Rest Camp. Built in the spruit with the same name, it was completed in 1979.

Xitsonga: No meaning, possibly the name of an earlier inhabitant.

Piet Grobler

A large concrete dam in the Timbavati River on the S39, north of the Timbavati Picnic Spot.

Afrikaans: Named Groblershoop in 1988 by Dr U. de V. Pienaar in honour of Minister Piet Grobler, who was instrumental in the establishment of the then National Parks Board. At the request of the Grobler family, the name was changed to Piet Grobler Dam.

Ngotso

A medium-sized earthen dam along the H1-4 tar road north of Satara Rest Camp. Built in the Ngotso Spruit and completed in 1964.

Xitsonga: The name of an early inhabitant, possibly one of ranger Harry Wolhuter's guides. Literal meaning: 'a small calabash for the storage of fat or for the collection of water'.

Nhlanganini

A medium-sized concrete dam on the H9 tar road west of Letaba Rest Camp. Built in the spruit after which it was named, it was completed in 1968.

Xitsonga: Historical name, 'at the reeds'. The dam was previously known as the Winkelhaak Dam, because, when viewed from the air, it is shaped like a carpenter's square or set square.

Sable

A medium-sized earthen dam east of the Phalaborwa Entrance Gate on the S51, near the Masorini Archaeological Site. Built in the Mashangani spruit and completed in 1973.

English: Named after the sable antelope (*Hippotragus niger*) by ranger Dirk Swart because this dam was one of the known preferred habitats of this graceful antelope.

Engelhard

A large concrete dam built in 1971 in the Letaba River downstream from the Letaba Rest Camp.

Family name: Named after Mr Charles Engelhard, American millionaire businessman and philanthropist who donated the funds for the construction of this dam. The extent of this beautiful dam is best viewed from the Longwe lookout point on the S62, north of the Letaba River.

Mingerhout

A small concrete dam built in the Letaba River upstream from Letaba Rest Camp and on the S47.

Afrikaans: Named after the mingerhout (matumi) tree (*Breonadia salicina*), by Dr U. de V. Pienaar when the dam was completed in 1974.

According to ranger Mike English, the name Mingerhout is derived from the Dutch for mixer wood, *mengerhout*. The offshoots of this tree grow at a slight angle in rosettes from the primary branches. When bark is stripped off a small branch and the rosette shoots are cut a few centimetres long, a very effective little mixer (or whisk) is produced, which can be used by rubbing it back and forth between the palms of the hands.

Shimuwini

A concrete dam built in the Letaba River opposite the Shimuwini Bushveld Camp on the S141.

Xitsonga: Given the name Shimuwini, 'at the baobab tree' (*Adansonia digitata*), by Dr U. de V. Pienaar on completion of the dam in 1973 because of the large baobab tree nearby.

Stapelkop

A large earthen dam on the S146 and built in the Shipikane Spruit west of Mopani Rest Camp.

Afrikaans: Named in 1977 by Dr U. de V. Pienaar after the distinctive granite formations nearby that appear to be stacked one upon the other.

Pionier

A large concrete dam built in the Tsendze River on the banks of which the last large rest camp, Mopani, was built.

Afrikaans: 'The first person to explore or discover an area or place'. Named by Dr U. de V. Pienaar in 1977 when the dam was under construction, after the pioneer hunters that utilised this area in earlier years.

Grootvlei (Hlamvu)

A small earthen dam on the S50 along the eastern border between Mopani and Shingwedzi rest camps. Built in the Hlamvu Spruit and completed in 1967.

Afrikaans: The name given by the park engineer to the Hlamvu Dam, a name that is more commonly used.

Rooibosrant

A large earthen dam built in the Mashokwe Spruit on the S52 west of Bateleur Bushveld Camp.

Afrikaans: Named by Dr U. de V. Pienaar after the abundance of red bushwillow trees and shrubs (*Combretum apiculatum*) found in this area.

Silwervis

A large concrete dam built in the Shingwedzi River at the Tshanga lookout point on the S52, west of Shingwedzi Rest Camp.

Afrikaans: Named after the rare fish species, bushveld papermouth (*Barbus mattozi*), found in the Shingwedzi River. It was given this name by Dr U. de V. Pienaar when the dam was constructed in 1982.

Kanniedood

A large concrete dam built in the Shingwedzi River immediately downstream from the Shingwedzi Rest Camp and on the S50 road.

Afrikaans: The collective name for a number of species of the genus *Commiphora*, which is plentiful in this area. Named by Dr U. de V. Pienaar when the dam was under construction in 1975.

Matukwale

A small earthen dam on the S99 west of Punda Maria. Built in the spruit after which it was named and completed in 1941.

Tshivenda: The name of an early inhabitant.

Klopperfontein

A small concrete dam on the S61 northeast of Punda Maria.

Afrikaans: The dam is fed by a fountain of the same name and was named after Hans Klopper, a well-known hunter from the Makhado (Louis Trichardt) area, who regularly camped here at the beginning of the 1900s.

TRANSFRONTIER NATIONAL PARKS

What is a transfrontier park?

The IUCN defines a Transboundary Protected Area as 'an area of land and/or sea that straddles one or more boundaries between states, sub-national units such as provinces and regions, autonomous areas and/or areas beyond the limits of national sovereignty or jurisdiction, whose constituent parts are especially dedicated to the protection and maintenance of biological diversity, and of natural and associated cultural resources, and managed cooperatively through legal or other means'.

Why did this concept become necessary?

This concept aims to establish large conservation and wildlife areas, not only through the integration of vast landscapes and reconnecting ecological systems, but also through development of cross-border tourism linkages, ensuring sustainable benefits to local communities through socio-economic upliftment, and the promotion of peace and stability in the region.

How many of these transfrontier parks exist in South Africa?

Currently there are six transfrontier conservation areas that involve South Africa. These are the Great Limpopo Transfrontier Park, the |Ai-|Ais/ Richtersveld Transfrontier Park, the Kgalagadi Transfrontier Park, the Greater Mapungubwe Transfrontier Conservation Area, the Maloti-Drakensberg Transfrontier Conservation and Development Area and the Lubombo Transfrontier Conservation and Resource Area.

What is the size of the transfrontier park involving the Kruger National Park and the adjoining areas in Mozambique and Zimbabwe?

The Great Limpopo Transfrontier Park (GLTP) will link the Limpopo National Park in Mozambique; the Kruger National Park in South Africa; Gonarezhou National Park, Majinji Pan Sanctuary and Malipati Safari Area in Zimbabwe, as well as two areas between Kruger and Gonarezhou, namely the Sengwe communal land in Zimbabwe and the Makuleke region in South Africa into one huge conservation area of 35 000 km².

Is there a possibility of increasing the size of this conservation area?

The establishment of the GLTP is the first phase in the establishment of a bigger transfrontier conservation area (GLTFCA), which will encompass almost 100 000 km² and include Banhine and Zinave national parks, the Massingir and Corumana areas and interlinking regions in Mozambique, as well as various privately and state-owned conservation and communal areas in South Africa and Zimbabwe bordering on the transfrontier park. The final delineation of the area will be determined by way of broadly consultative processes, which are currently under way.

When was this specific transfrontier park proclaimed?

The GLTP was established in 2002.

What role does SANParks play in this transfrontier park?

SANParks is the implementing agent of the South African side of the GLTP. Two of SANParks' members serve on the Joint Management Board of the GLTP, giving full input into joint conservation issues.

Given the fact that Mozambique and Zimbabwe are very poor countries and conservation is a very low priority for their governments, is it not throwing good money after bad for SANParks to get involved in this venture?

The South African government has decided that transfrontier parks are an important mechanism to promote conservation at a regional scale and to enhance socioeconomic benefits to poor rural neighbours. The individual parks will also benefit from being part of a larger conservation area. In addition, it is beneficial to the Kruger National Park to have a conservation buffer along its border with Mozambique and Zimbabwe, with law enforcement in the adjacent areas to deal with illegal activities.

What conservation and/or tourism infrastructure has been or is being developed in these areas?

A number of tourist products have been developed recently in the Limpopo National Park in Mozambique and some are in the process of being developed in Gonarezhou National Park. Please visit the following website for more up-to-date information and contact details for bookings: www.greatlimpopopark.com.

How many animals and of which species have been translocated to these adjoining areas?

Between 2002 and 2008 a total of 4 725 animals of various species were translocated from the Kruger National Park to the Limpopo National Park. The animals were first placed in an enclosure of about 35 000 ha for a few years to settle and the fence was then dropped to allow the animals to colonise the rest of the area.

Have these animals settled successfully in their new areas?

Yes. All animal numbers in the Limpopo National Park seem to be on the increase.

What species of fauna and flora, not readily found in the Kruger National Park, can one expect to see in these areas?

The areas in the Limpopo National Park and the Gonarhezhou National Park are underlain by different geological formations from those found in the Kruger National Park. This gave rise to different landscapes, vegetation types and animal communities. Large parts of Limpopo National Park are underlain by deep sand as a result of a receding Indian Ocean and one finds a number of pans of all sizes here. Some of these pans harbour the rare killifish (*Nothobranchius* spp.) and also lungfish (*Protopterus annectens brieni*), which are very rare in the Kruger National Park.

Although full bird lists have not yet been compiled for the whole area, one would expect to see a number of bird species not readily found in the Kruger National Park.

Are there still human populations in the adjoining conservation areas?

Yes. There are people still living along the Shingwedzi River in the Limpopo National Park as well as along the banks of the Limpopo River.

Will they remain in these areas, and, if so, will this not have a negative impact on conservation management of the natural resources so intensively protected on the South African side?

The Mozambican government has reached an agreement with the communities along the Shingwedzi River to resettle them in areas outside the park. The resettlement process has started, but will take some time as significant funding is required to build houses and establish the necessary infrastructure for the resettlement of these people in the new areas.

There are too many people living along the Limpopo River to resettle and in this instance, game corridors down to the river will need to be created. It must be remembered that most parks in Africa, with the exception of South Africa, are unfenced; fences sometimes have more of a negative impact on animal populations, by disrupting their movements, than on people.

The area around the Limpopo National Park has been zoned as a resource use area, with neighbouring communities to benefit from the resources of the park in a controlled and sustainable manner.

As these are poor countries where poaching is the order of the day, will the translocated animals not be in danger of being killed for food?

Poaching is an issue that most large conservation areas have to deal with on a continuous basis. There are management structures and rangers employed in all three parks to manage and protect wildlife.

Are there any passport control points on the Park's borders with Mozambique and Zimbabwe?

Currently there are border control points between the Kruger National Park and

Limpopo National Park at Giriyondo, northeast of Letaba Rest Camp, and at Pafuri in the far north. A crossing point over the Limpopo River, linking South Africa and Zimbabwe, is currently in the planning process. Sites upstream from the Park's western boundary are being investigated for this purpose.

Are there any overnight facilities available for visitors to these areas?

Yes. Visit www.greatlimpopopark.com for up-to-date information and contact details regarding bookings for accommodation.

Can one visit the area with ordinary vehicles or is it accessible to 4x4 vehicles only?

Certain areas are accessible to ordinary vehicles, but this depends on such factors as the condition of the dirt roads and if the area has recently had rain. It is advisable to ascertain from the specific parks ahead of the intended visit where one can drive in an ordinary vehicle.

Will updates on the areas be communicated with the interested public on a regular basis?

Updates can be obtained by visiting www.greatlimpopopark.com.

CONCESSIONS AND OUTSOURCING

Concessions

How many concessions for lodges have been granted in the Park?

There are seven concession lodges in the Kruger National Park:

- Jock Safari Lodge
- Lukimbi Safari Lodge

- Shishangeni Lodge
- Tinga Private Game Lodges
- Rhino Walking Safaris
- Imbali Safari Lodge
- Singita Lebombo

In some of the concession areas there is more than one accommodation facility: a satellite- or fly-camp.

What is the total area under concession?

At the time of writing it is 73 439 ha.

Will there be more concessions awarded in the future?

It is not anticipated that any additional lodge concessions with exclusive traversing rights will be awarded in the near future.

What is the concession term?

Twenty years.

What was the rationale behind the awarding of these concession areas?

In September 1998, the Department of Environmental Affairs and Tourism articulated the need for SANParks to prepare for reduced dependence on state funding, which would increasingly be aimed at funding essential conservation requirements.

These are among the commercialisation objectives for SANParks, which include revenue generation, loss minimisation or savings on existing operations, job creation, poverty alleviation, infrastructure upgrades, upgrading/developing of historical and/or cultural sites, tourism promotion and further biodiversity protection and conservation.

What happens at the termination of the concession?

On termination of the concession term, the asset reverts to SANParks, whereafter

SANParks will review and possibly re-tender the concession lodge.

Is SANParks still in control of the concession area as far as conservation management is concerned, e.g. controlled-burning programmes, anti-poaching action and patrols and, should it again become part of future management, culling?

Yes. SANParks, in terms of its conservation mandate, was responsible for conservation in all conservation areas within the Park prior to the concession process, and remains responsible for conservation in these areas.

In line with the environmental guidelines underwritten in the agreement, concessionaires have to undertake the monitoring of their concession area and provide a monthly written monitoring report to the Park's Section Ranger of the area in which the concession falls.

Are the guides from the concessionaires who take visitors on drives and walks into the bush allowed to carry rifles? How is this controlled?

Concession guides are allowed to carry firearms, and the system is controlled by contractual agreements to which the concessionaires have to adhere.

Guides have to be in possession of a THETA Nature Site Guides qualification, which allows them to operate under various competency requirements. These guides must also undergo a Kruger National Park Firearm Proficiency Assessment, to evaluate their firearm-handling skills. Guides are also expected to undergo regular evaluations of their firearm-handling skills.

Once SANParks is satisfied of their ability, a special permit to carry and use a licensed firearm may be issued to a person who is not an employee of SANParks, subject to the provisions of Section 46 of the Protected Areas Act; Act 57 of 2003 and in accordance with Regulations 46 and 56 of this Act.

Do any normal tourist roads enter a concession area and, if so, are visitors to the Kruger Park allowed to drive onto the concession area?
No. Concession areas were tracts of land where there was no public access prior to the concession process. Roads that existed in these areas for the purpose of conservation management are still being used by SANParks for these purposes.

If visitors to concession areas are allowed to drive on Park roads and areas, should Park visitors not be allowed to visit concession areas?
No, as described above, concession areas were identified as tracts of land to which the general public had no access prior to the concession's being established, as there were no public roads in these areas.

Are visitors to concession areas also bound to gate opening and closing times as visitors to the Park are?
Staff and guests to the concession areas must adhere to all normal gate hours, speed limits and other general regulations of the Park.

All guests, deliveries and other vehicles entering concession areas must do so through Kruger's designated entrance gates.

Extended gate times will be permitted under controlled conditions and approval by the Park's Regional Manager under whose jurisdiction the concession area falls.

Does the overall legal and disciplinary jurisdiction of SANParks in Kruger apply to the concession areas?
Yes, it does.

Outsourcing

Why were most of the services and facilities in the Park outsourced?
The rationale to commercialise was to reduce the dependence on state funding and to improve operational efficiency.

What did SANParks gain by this decision, monetarily and/or otherwise?
Monetarily, the gain in March 2009 was R252 million net and, infrastructurally, R340 million in 2006 terms.

Socioeconomically it created 620 new jobs, BEE equity exceeded the requirements of the tourism charter and it substantially transferred risk to the private sector.

Was the outsourcing done by tender?
Yes.

What is the length of the contract?
Most lodges have a 20-year term, and the restaurant and retail opportunities are 10 years each.

Some staff from the period prior to outsourcing are still working in the shops and restaurants. Are they SANParks staff or are they now in the employ of the concessionaires?
They are employed by the concessionaires.

Since outsourcing, shop items and meals in the restaurants have become exorbitantly expensive. South African visitors cannot afford these prices. Why was it necessary for the concessionaires to increase prices so drastically?
The prices in the shops compare favourably with convenience stores, and continuous efforts are made to ensure that the restaurants offer options for both the overseas and local market.

GLOSSARY OF TERMS

Alpha A prefix denoting that a specific individual animal is the highest ranking in a group, i.e. alpha male.

Amphisbaenid Worm-like lizard.

Antelope Common name for a large group of ruminants of the Bovidae family; possess hollow, unbranched horns that are never shed.

Aquatic Living in water, also readily move about on land.

Arboreal Living principally in trees.

Boss Heavy mass of horns at the base of the horn structure, as found in buffaloes.

Brood patch A patch of featherless skin that is visible on the underside of birds during the nesting season. It is well supplied with blood and the warmth helps incubate their eggs.

Browser Animal feeding primarily on leaves, twigs, shoots and stems of bushes, shrubs and trees.

Buccal cavity The portion of the oral cavity bounded by the lips, cheeks and gums.

Callosity Patch of hardened, thickened skin.

Carnivore Animal of the order Carnivora, feeding primarily on meat.

Carrion Dead and usually rotting flesh.

Caruncle A small, fleshy mass on the body.

Casque The helmet, ridge-like horny structure on top of the upper mandible of some hornbills.

Cere A distinct area of bare skin at the base of the upper mandible of certain birds, surrounding the nostrils.

Clan A social grouping of two or more individuals of carnivores; refer to hyaenas.

Coverts Small feathers on the wings and tail of a bird that surround the bases of larger feathers and help to smoothe air flow.

Crepuscular Active at dawn and dusk.

Cytotoxic A toxin or antibody having a toxic effect on tissue and cells. Dominant in adder venom.

Dermis Inner layer of skin of vertebrates, containing sweat and sebaceous glands, nerve endings, blood and lymph vessels.

Dew claw Innermost digit in carnivores; a digit that does not touch the ground.

Diastema A space or gap between two teeth.

Digit Finger or toe in vertebrates.

Diurnal Active primarily during daylight.

Dominance Social status that allows privileged access because subordinate animals defer to dominant ones.

Dorsal On or pertaining to the back.

Dung midden Site where faeces is regularly deposited, accumulating into piles; refer to rhino.

Ecology Study of organisms; refer plants and animals, in relation to their environment.

Ecozone Area of specific ecology.

Ectotherm Cold-blooded reptile, regulating its body temperature according to the ambient temperature.

Egg tooth A projection of the beak used for piercing the egg shell.

Endemic Occurring only within a certain area.

Exotic Originating from a different country or area.

Flehmen An act performed by some animals in which the upper lip is drawn back, the nostrils wrinkled, the head sometimes raised and the tongue moved rhythmically. This act is used by males to determine the female's reproductive condition by detecting chemicals from her vulva or urine.

Forbs Herbs and other grasses found abundantly in grasslands.

Gape The width of a widely opened mouth.

Gestation period Time between conception and birth.

Grazer An animal feeding on grass and herbs.

Gregarious Living together in colonies or groups.

Ground horning Tossing up or digging into soil with the horns. A display of aggression and/ or dominance.

Haemotoxic Toxin having the effect of destroying red blood cells; has a negative effect on blood circulation.

Herbivorous Feeding on plants.

Herd Term used to describe two or more animals of the same species, usually ungulates.

Holt Den or lair, usually of otters.

Home range Area in which an animal goes about its daily routine activities such as searching for food, shelter and mates.

Indigenous Originating in and native to a particular region or country.

Inguinal Pertaining to the groin.

Insectivorous Feeding primarily on insects.

Interdigital Between the digits (toes or hooves).

Intraspecific Of the same species.

Invertebrates Organisms lacking a backbone, i.e. spiders and insects.

Jacobson's organ *See* Vomeronasal organ.

Laufschlag Courtship behaviour whereby a bull courts a cow on heat by following her closely and tapping between her hind legs with his foreleg.

Maternal imprinting The process whereby offspring is isolated from the rest of the group members in order to establish the maternal bond between the mother and offspring.

Monogamous Having only one sexual partner, forming permanent pair bonds.

Montane Pertaining to mountain habitats.

Muzzle The part of the face lying in front of the eyes.

Neurotoxic (of venom) Affecting the nerve system. This type of toxin is dominant in the venom of cobras and mambas.

New World monkey A monkey from the five families of primates that are found in Central and South America and portions of Mexico.

Nocturnal Active during the night.

Nomad Moving from place to place without having a defined or fixed place of residence.

Oestrus Associated with ovulation, occuring in most female mammals (excluding humans), the only time the female is sexually receptive; also 'in heat'.

Olfactory Pertaining to the sense of smell.

Omnivorous Feeding on both plant and animal material.

Ossify To harden into bone.

Pan Hollow area or basin in the ground where rainwater accumulates during the rainy season; a natural water hole.

Parietal bone Either of the two bones forming part of the roof and sides of the skull.

Parturition The process of giving birth.

Pasting The habit of demarcating territories by anal-gland secretions deposited on grass stalks.

Perianal The area around the anus.

Perineal The area between the anus and the genitals.

Pharyngeal pouch A bulging pocket at the top of the oesophagus.

Plantigrade Walking on the whole underside of the foot; flatfooted.

Posterior Towards the back; behind.

Pheromones Substance secreted and released by an animal for detection and response by another of the same species.

Polyoestrous Coming into oestrus many times in a year at irregular intervals.

Preorbital In front of the eyes.

Prehensile Capable of grasping.

Preputial Loose skin (foreskin) over the penis.

Preputial glands Glands next to the penis or vaginal opening.

Remiges Flight feathers of the wing.

Rictal bristles Short, bare feather shafts at the base of the bill.

Rugose Corrugated or ridged in appearance.

Rut Mating season; period of concentrated sexual activity.

Savanna Areas of natural grasslands interspersed with scattered trees; characteristic of areas with defined wet and dry seasons.

Scent gland Specialised area of skin, packed with complex chemical compounds that, when secreted, communicate information regarding identity or reproductive status of the individual animal.

Sebaceous gland Most common type of skin gland. Secretes sebum, an oily substance composed of fat and outer skin debris.

Sounder Collective name for a group of pigs.

Species Interbreeding populations of animals, derived from a common ancestor, with common characteristics and qualities.

Spoor Footprint.

Spruit Small river, watercourse or creek.

Stotting action Jumping into the air with all four legs held stiff and straight. Performed by several antelope species when alarmed.

Termitary Termite mound.

Terrestrial Living principally on the ground.

Territory Area occupied by an individual or group and effectively defended against members of the same species.

Tibial Relating to the shinbone.

Torpor State of reduced metabolic activity, lowered body temperature and reduced oxygen consumption.

Ungulate An animal that has hooves.

Vegetation horning A dominance or aggression display when the horns are used to thrash or damage vegetation.

Veld Afrikaans for an open area dominated by grassland.

Vertebrate An organism with a backbone.

Vlei Wet, marshy area, especially during rainy, wet season.

Vomeronasal organ An auxiliary olfactory sense organ found at the base of the nasal cavity. It is mainly used to detect pheromones.

Voortrekkers Early pioneers who moved inland from the east coast of the then Cape Province during the mid-1800s.

REFERENCES AND FURTHER READING

Alexander, G. & Marais, J. 2007. *A Guide to the Reptiles of Southern Africa*. Struik Nature, Cape Town.

Apps, P. (ed). 2012. *Smithers' Mammals of Southern Africa – A Field Guide*. Struik Nature, Cape Town.

Deacon, A. R. 1994. 'Kruger's Rivers'. *Custos*, March. National Parks Board, Pretoria.

De Graaff, G. 1974. 'A familiar pattern deviation of the cheetah'. *Custos* 3(12): 2–28.

De Vos, V., Van Rooyen, G. L. & Kloppers, J. J. 1973. 'Anthrax immunisation of free-ranging roan antelope, *Hippotragus equinus*, in the Kruger National Park'. *Koedoe* 16: 11–25.

Eaton, R. I. 1974. *The Cheetah*. Van Nostrand, Reinhold, New York.

Fourie, P. F. 1992. *Kruger National Park. Questions and Answers*. Struik Publishers, Cape Town.

Ginn, P. J., McIlleron, W. G. & Milstein, P. le S. 1989. *The Complete Book of South African Birds*. Struik Winchester, Cape Town.

Jacana Education. 2000. *Kruger National Park Ecozone Map*. Jacana Education, Houghton.

Kemp, A. 1987. *The Owls of Southern Africa*. Struik Winchester, Cape Town.

Maclean, G. 1993. *Roberts' Birds of Southern Africa*. The Trustees of the John Voelcker Bird Book Fund, Cape Town.

Marais, J. 2004. *'n Volledige Gids tot die Slange van Suider-Afrika*. Struik Publishers, Cape Town.

Meester, J. A. J., Rautenbach, I. L., Dippenaar, N. J. & Baker, C. M. 1986. 'Classification of Southern African Mammals'. *Transvaal Museum Monograph* 5: 1–359.

Pienaar, U. de V. 1969. 'Predator–prey relationships amongst the larger mammals of the Kruger National Park'. *Koedoe* 12: 108–176.

Pienaar, U. de V. 1990. *Neem uit die Verlede*. National Parks Board, Pretoria.

Pienaar, U. de V., Joubert, S. C. J., Hall-Martin, A. J., De Graaff, G. & Rautenbach, I. L. 1987. *Field Guide to the Mammals of the Kruger National Park*. Struik Publishers, Cape Town.

Schaller, G. B. 1972. *The Serengeti Lion*. University of Chicago Press, Chicago.

Schütze, H. 2002. *Field Guide to the Mammals of the Kruger National Park*. Struik Publishers, Cape Town.

Sinclair, I., Hockey, P., Tarboton, W. & Ryan, P. 2011. *Sasol Birds of Southern Africa*. Struik Nature, Cape Town.

Skinner, J. D. & Smithers, R. H. N. 1990. *The Mammals of the Southern African Subregion*. University of Pretoria, Pretoria.

Smuts, G. L. 1975. 'Predator–prey relationships in the Central District of the Kruger National Park with emphasis on wildebeest and zebra populations'. Unpublished Report, National Parks Board, Skukuza.

Turnbull-Kemp, P. 1967. *The Leopard*. Howard Timmins, Cape Town.

Visser, J. & Chapman, D. S. 1978. *Snakes and Snakebite. Venomous Snakes and Management of Snakebite in Southern Africa*. Purnell, Cape Town.

INDEX

NOTES